SQL Quer
for
Mere Mortals

A Hands-On Guide to Data Manipulation in SQL

Michael J. Hernandez
John L. Viescas

Addison-Wesley

Boston • San Francisco • New York • Toronto • Montreal
London • Munich • Paris • Madrid
Capetown • Sydney • Tokyo • Singapore • Mexico City

The publisher offers discounts on this book when ordered in quantity for special sales. For more information, please contact:

Pearson Education Corporate Sales Division
One Lake Street
Upper Saddle River, NJ 07458
(800) 382-3419
corpsales@pearsontechgroup.com

Visit us on the Web at *www.awl.com/cseng/*

Library of Congress Cataloging-in-Publication Data

Hernandez, Michael J. (Michael James)
SQL queries for mere mortals : a hands-on guide to data manipulation in SQL / Michael J. Hernandez, John L. Viescas.
p. cm.
Includes bibliographical references and index.
ISBN 0-201-43336-2 (alk. paper)
1. SQL (Computer program language) 2. Database searching. I. Viescas, John II. Title.

QA76.73.S67 H48 2000
005.75'6--dc21

00-044749

ISBN 0-201-43336-2

Text printed on recycled paper.

1 2 3 4 5 6 7 8 9 10 - CRS - 04 03 02 01 00
First printing, August 2000

For Alastair M. Black, who took me under his wing, patiently taught me about the craft of writing, and imbued me with an appreciation for the written word. —MJH

For Suzanne, who still loves me even when I take forever to grind through a chapter that she has to fix for me later. —JLV

Dedicated to anyone who has unsuccessfully attempted to retrieve seemingly simple information from a database. —MJH & JLV

Contents

PART II SQL Basics 65

CHAPTER 4 Creating a Simple Query 67

CHAPTER 5 Getting More Than Simple Columns 99

Foreword

SQL Queries for Mere Mortals is an excellent introduction to queries in SQL and fits in well with the earlier title, *Database Design for Mere Mortals* from Addison-Wesley. This is an even better introductory book than the first for many of us. A real (Mere Mortal) programmer spends his time writing SQL queries and seldom gets to design the database itself. Highly paid DBAs with corner offices and sports cars do schemas. Most programmers get stuck trying to make their SQL work on a frozen design.

I earn my living tuning databases and teaching advanced SQL, so I can attest to the fact that a lot of SQL code out there is about as appealing to read as Egyptian hieroglyphics. Once the code runs, the original programmer moves on to the next task, never looking back at what he did. And when that code goes bad, the next guy posts desperate messages on the Internet discussion groups, where John and Mike save his tail with a few words of wisdom and a rewrite. They have been helping people with their SQL problems for years. It's about time they put this stuff in a book that everyone can grab!

Good code does not have to be hard to write or slow to write. If you understand what you are doing, most problems are pretty straightforward. First, you have to get the basics down. Here is your chance to learn those basics in an easy-to-understand and very readable book. Next, the trick is to understand when and how to tune that straightforward solution to fit your particular database and SQL engine. When you have the basics down, come back to me and I will teach you the really tricky stuff.

Joe Celko
Atlanta, GA

Preface and Acknowledgments

"Language is by its very nature a communal thing; that is, it expresses never the exact thing but a compromise—that which is common to you, me, and everybody."
—Thomas Earnest Hulme, *Speculations*

Learning how to retrieve information from a database is commonly a perplexing exercise. However, it can be a relatively easy task—as long as you understand the question you're posing to the database. Once you understand the question, you can translate it into the language used by any database system, which in most cases is Structured Query Language (SQL). You have to translate your request into an SQL statement so that your database system knows what information you want to retrieve. SQL provides the means for you and your database system to communicate with each other.

Throughout our many years as database consultants, we've found that the number of people who merely need to retrieve information from a database far outnumber those who are charged with the task of creating programs and applications for a database. Unfortunately, no books focus solely on the subject of retrieving information, particularly from a "mere mortals" viewpoint. There are numerous good books on SQL, to be sure, but most are targeted toward database programming and development.

With this in mind, we decided it was time to write a book that would help people learn how to query a database properly and effectively. The result of our decision is in your hands. This book is unique among SQL books in that *it focuses only on the querying portion of SQL*. When you finish reading this book, you'll have the skills you need to retrieve any information you require.

Writing a book such as this is always a cooperative effort. There are always editors, colleagues, friends, and relatives willing to lend their support and provide valuable advice when we need it the most. These folks continually provide us with encouragement, help us to remain focused, and motivate us to see this project through to the end.

First and foremost, we want to thank our editor, Mary O'Brien, for the opportunity to write this book. She saw the potential of an idea we had and pursued it with great dedication. We'd also like to thank Mary and her assistant, Mariann Kourafas, for their great patience and unwavering support throughout the many months we were writing this book. And we can't forget Marilyn Rash and the production staff—great job, guys!

Next, we'd like to acknowledge our technical editors Malcom C. Rubel, Michael Blaha, Alexander Tarasul, and Keith W. Hare. Malcom, as always, it's great to have you on the team! Michael and Alexander, thanks for all your thoughtful comments and suggestions. And a special thanks to Keith—he corrected a few minor errors we had in the SQL history timeline and provided much of the information for the What the Future Holds section of Chapter 3. Thanks once again to all of you for your time and input and for helping us to make this a solid treatise on SQL queries.

Finally, a very special thanks to Joe Celko for providing the Foreword. Joe is an SQL expert, a colleague, and a good friend. We have a lot of respect for Joe's knowledge and expertise on the subject, and we're pleased to have his thoughts and comments at the beginning of our book.

I want to give my most sincere thanks to my dear friend and colleague, John L. Viescas, for the opportunity of co-authoring this book with him. It was John who had the initial idea for this book, and over dinner one evening he talked me into writing it with him. John has been in the business a long time and is an established, respected author. It is my honor to share authorship with him on this work.

Finally, I want to thank my wife Kendra. Once again, she has exhibited extreme patience while I toiled away at my writing. Her help has been invaluable, and yet again, I owe her a great debt. I would tell you that she is the love of my life, my closest confidant, and my best friend, but she abhors any sort of public displays of affection. (She refers to this as PDA.) So I'll just end with this:

Well, Ked, we can resume a normal life again—until the next book!

Michael J. Hernandez
Bellevue, Washington

Gee, Mike! Are you trying to give me a big head or something? You're not such a slouch yourself. I may have talked you into doing the "next" *Mere Mortals* book on SQL, but you're the one who invented the now well-proven format and "voice" for this audience. It has been a fun and interesting task bringing the complex world of SQL (one of my favorite subjects) to such a wide audience. Thanks for letting me in on the project.

Unlike yours, my wife, Suzanne, does not abhor PDAs. We both owe her a big hug—not just for putting up with me while I was "offline" doing this book but also for providing excellent behind-the-scenes editing and critical commentary of our material. She's no stranger when it comes to computers, but she's definitely a "mere mortal" when it comes to databases. She provided a perfect audience to test the draft chapters. I only had to make her one promise: I'm leaving my laptop home this spring on our next trip to Hawaii!

John L. Viescas
Austin, Texas

About the Authors

John L. Viescas and Michael J. Hernandez

Michael J. Hernandez is a veteran database developer with more than 13 years of experience developing applications for a wide variety of clients in diverse industries. Mike specializes in relational database design and is the author of the best-selling database design book *Database Design for Mere Mortals* (Addison-Wesley, 1997). He has worked with SQL throughout his career, developing applications using SQL-based databases such as Microrim's R:BASE, Microsoft Access, and now Microsoft SQL Server. Mike has also been a contributing author and technical editor to various Access books and periodicals.

Aside from his continuing work on various database development projects and writing projects, Mike travels around the country teaching Microsoft Access for AppDev (formerly known as Application Developers Training Company) and is consistently one of their most top-rated instructors. He also conducts a four-day course on relational database design based on the design methodology presented in his book. Mike speaks at various conferences, such as the Microsoft Office and VBA Solutions Conference and Expo and the Microsoft Office Deployment & Development Conference, which were held in 1999 and 2000, respectively.

In a previous life, Mike had a career as a musician and performed for audiences far and wide. He attributes both his easy-going style of instruction and ability to connect with an audience to his days as a performer. To this day, he can be found tinkering on his guitar, playing the latest Steely Dan tune. Mike enjoys the little things in life, such as spending long hours at Barnes & Noble, sipping a tall Americano at Starbucks, puffing on a fine cigar, and riding his mountain bike along with his wife Kendra.

You can visit Mike's Web site at *www.datatexcg.com* or contact him via e-mail at *mjhernandez@msn.com*.

John Viescas is an independent consultant with more than 35 years of experience. He began his career as a systems analyst, designing large database applications for IBM mainframe systems. He spent six years at Applied Data Research in Dallas, Texas, where he directed a staff of more than 30 people and was responsible for research, product development, and customer support of database products for IBM mainframe computers. While working at Applied Data Research, John completed a degree in business finance at the University of Texas at Dallas, graduating *cum laude.*

John joined Tandem Computers, Inc., in 1988, where he was responsible for the development and implementation of database marketing programs in Tandem's U.S. Western Sales region. He developed and delivered technical seminars on Tandem's relational database management system, NonStop SQL, in a geographic area spanning Hawaii to Colorado and Alaska to Arizona. John wrote his first book, *A Quick Reference Guide to SQL* (Microsoft Press), as a research project to document the similarities in the syntax among the ANSI-86 SQL standard, IBM's DB2, Microsoft's SQL Server, Oracle Corporation's Oracle, and Tandem's NonStop SQL. He wrote the first edition of *Running*

Microsoft Access (Microsoft Press) while on sabbatical from Tandem and has written four other editions since then.

John formed his own company in 1993. He provides information systems management consulting for a variety of small to large businesses in the Puget Sound area, with a specialty in the Microsoft Access and SQL Server database management products. He also maintains an office in Austin, Texas. He has written numerous articles for technical publications such as *Smart Access* and *Access Advisor.* John has lectured at conferences and user group meetings around the world, including highly rated sessions at the Microsoft Tech*Ed conferences and the European WinSummit conference. He has been recognized as a "Most Valuable Professional" every year since 1993 by Microsoft Product Support Services for his assistance with technical questions on public support forums.

You can visit John's Web site at *www.viescas.com* or contact him by e-mail at *johnv@viescas.com*.

Introduction

"I presume you're mortal, and may err."
—James Shirley, *The Lady of Pleasure*

If you've used a computer more than casually, you have probably used Structured Query Language, or SQL—perhaps without even knowing it. SQL is *the* standard language for communicating with most database systems. Any time you import data into a spreadsheet or perform a merge into a word processing program, you're most likely using SQL in some form or another. Every time you go online to an "e-commerce" site on the Web and place an order for a book, a recording, a movie, or any of the dozens of other products you can order, there's a very high probability that the code behind the Web page you're using is accessing its databases with SQL. If you need to get information from a database system that uses SQL, you can enhance your understanding of the language by reading this book.

Are You a "Mere Mortal"?

You might ask, "Who is a 'Mere Mortal'? Me?" The answer is not simple. When we started to write this book, we thought we were "experts" in the database language called SQL. Along the way, we discovered we were "mere mortals" too, in several areas. We understood a few specific implementations of SQL very well, but we unraveled many of the complex intricacies of the language as we studied how the language is used in many commercial products. So if you fit any of the following descriptions, you're a mere mortal too!

- If you use computer applications that let you access information from a database system, you're probably a "mere mortal." The first time you don't get the information you expected using the query tools built in to your application, you'll need to explore the underlying SQL statements to find out why.

- If you have recently discovered one of the many available desktop database applications but are struggling with defining and querying the data you need, you're a "mere mortal."
- If you're a database programmer who needs to "think out of the box" to solve some complex problems, you're a "mere mortal."
- If you're a database "guru" in one product but are now faced with integrating the data from your existing system into another system that supports SQL, you're a "mere mortal."

In short, *anyone* who has to use a database system that supports SQL can use this book: For a beginning database user who has just discovered that the data he needs is fetched using SQL, this book will teach all the basics and more. For an "expert" user who is suddenly faced with solving complex problems or integrating multiple systems that support SQL, this book will provide insights into leveraging the complex abilities of the SQL database language.

About This Book

Everything you read in this book is based on the current American Standards Institute (ANSI) Standard for the SQL database language (document ANSI X3.135-1992), as currently implemented in most of the popular commercial database systems. The ANSI document was also adopted by ISO/IEC (International Organization for Standardization/International Electrotechnical Commission) and published as document ISO/IEC 9075: 1992, so this is truly an international standard. The SQL you'll learn here *is not* specific to any particular software product.

As you'll learn in more detail in Chapter 3, the SQL Standard defines both more and less than you'll find implemented in most commercial database products. Most database vendors have yet to implement many of the more advanced features, but most do support the core of the standard.

We researched a wide range of popular products to make sure that you can use what we're teaching in this book. When we found parts of the core of the language not supported by some major products, we warned you and showed you alternative ways to state your database requests in standard SQL. When we found significant parts of the Standard supported by only a few vendors, we introduced you to the syntax and then suggested alternatives.

We have organized this book into four major sections.

- Part I, Relational Databases and SQL, explains how modern database systems are based on a rigorous mathematical model and provides a concise history of the database query language that has evolved into what we know as "SQL." We also discuss some simple rules that you can use to make sure your database design is sound.
- Part II, SQL Basics, introduces you to the SELECT Statement, creating expressions, and sorting information with an ORDER BY clause. You'll also learn how to filter data by using a WHERE clause.
- Part III, Working with Multiple Tables, shows you how to formulate queries that draw data from more than one table. We also show you how to link tables in a query using the INNER JOIN, OUTER JOIN, and UNION operators and how to work with Subqueries.
- Part IV, Summarizing and Grouping Data, discusses how to obtain summary information and group and filter summarized data. You'll also learn about the GROUP BY and HAVING clauses.

At the end of the book in the Appendices, you'll find syntax diagrams for all the SQL elements you've learned, layouts of the sample databases, and book recommendations to further your study of SQL. There is also a CD containing all the sample databases used throughout the book.

How to Use This Book

We have designed the chapters in this book to be read in sequence, and each succeeding chapter builds on concepts taught in earlier chapters. However, you can jump into the middle of the book without getting lost. For example, if you are already familiar with the basic clauses in a SELECT Statement and want to learn more about JOINs, you can jump right in to Chapters 7, 8, and 9.

At the end of many of the chapters you'll find an extensive set of sample problems, their solutions, and sample Result Sets. We recommend that you study several of the samples to gain a better understanding of the techniques involved, then try solving some of the later samples yourself without looking at the solutions we propose.

Note that where a particular query returns dozens of rows in the Result Set, we show you only the first few rows in this book to give you an idea of how the answer should look. You may not see the exact same result on your system, however, because each database system that supports SQL has its own optimizer that figures out the fastest way to solve the query. Additionally, the first few rows you see returned by your database system may not exactly match the first few we show you unless the query contains an ORDER BY clause that requires the rows to be returned in a specific sequence.

We've also included a complete set of problems for you to solve on your own, which you'll find just after the chapters' Summary section. This gives you the opportunity to really practice what you've just learned in the chapter. Don't worry—the solutions are included in the sample databases on the CD. We've also included hints for those problems that might be a little tricky.

After you have worked your way through the entire book, you'll find the complete SQL diagrams in Appendix A to be an invaluable reference for all the SQL techniques we showed you. You will also be able to use the sample database layouts in Appendix B to help you design your own databases.

Reading the Diagrams Used in This Book

The numerous diagrams throughout the book illustrate the proper syntax for the statements, terms, and phrases you'll use when you work with SQL. Each diagram provides a clear picture of the overall construction of the SQL element currently being discussed. You can also use any of these diagrams as a template to create your own SQL statement or to help you acquire a clearer understanding of a specific example.

All the diagrams are built from a set of core elements and can be divided into two categories: *statements* and *defined terms*. A statement is always a major SQL operation, such as the SELECT Statement we discuss in this book, while a defined term is always a component used to build part of a statement, such as *Value Expression*, *Search Condition*, or *Conditional Expression*. (Don't worry—we'll explain all of these terms later in the book.) The only difference between a syntax diagram for a statement and a syntax diagram for a defined term is the manner in which the main syntax line begins and ends. Figure 1 shows the beginning and end points for both diagram categories. Aside from this difference, the diagrams are built from the same elements. Figure 2 shows an example of each type of syntax diagram and is followed by a brief explanation of each diagram element.

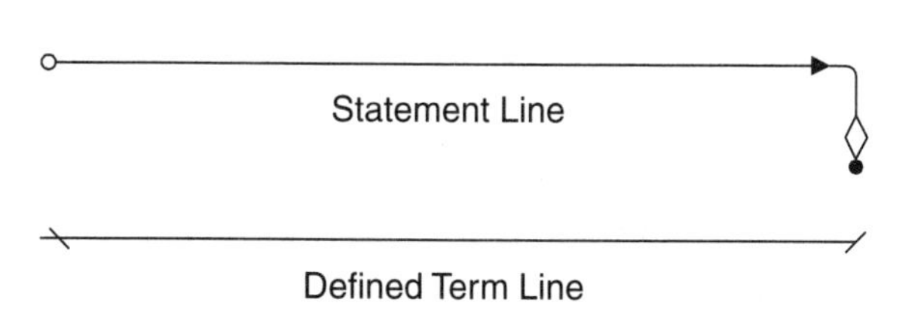

Figure 1 *Syntax line endpoints for statements and defined terms.*

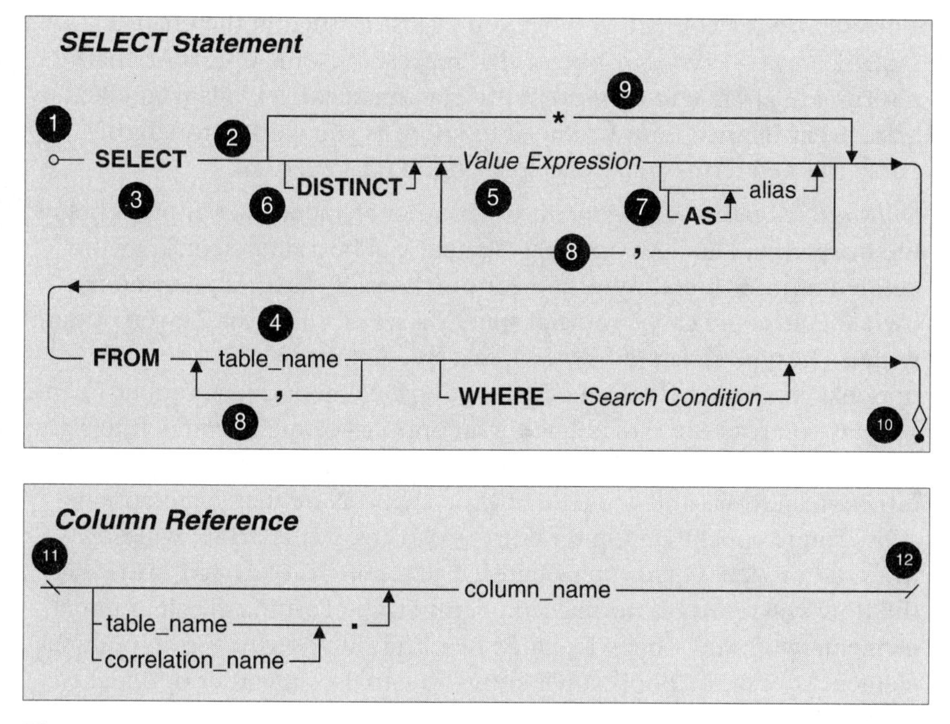

Figure 2 *Sample statement and defined term diagrams.*

1 *Statement start point*—denotes the beginning of the main syntax line for a statement. Any element that appears *directly on* the main syntax line is a *required element* and any element that appears *below* it is considered an *optional element*.

2 *Main syntax line*—determines the order of all required and optional elements for the statement or defined term. Follow this line from left to right (or in the direction of the arrows) to build the syntax for the statement or defined term.

3 *Keyword(s)*—a major word in SQL grammar that is a required part of the syntax for a statement or defined term. In a diagram, keywords are formatted in capital letters and bold font. (You don't have to worry about typing a keyword in capital letters when you actually write the statement in your database program, but it does make the statement easier to read.)

4 *Literal entry*—the name of a value you explicitly supply to the statement. A literal entry is represented by a word or phrase that indicates the type of value you need to supply. Literal entries in a diagram are formatted in all lowercase letters.

5 *Defined term*—a word or phrase that represents some operation that returns a final value to be used in this statement. We'll explain and diagram every defined term you need to know as you work through the book. Defined terms are always formatted in italic letters.

6 *Optional element*—any element or group of elements that appears below the main syntax line. An optional element can be a statement, keyword, defined term, or literal value and, for purposes of clarity, is placed on its own line. In some cases, you can specify a set of values for a given option, with each value separated by a comma (see number 8). Also, several optional elements have a set of sub-optional elements (see number 7). In general, you read the syntax line for an optional element from left to right, in the same manner that you read the main syntax line. Always follow the directional arrows and you'll be in good shape. Note that some options allow you to specify multiple values or choices, so the arrow will flow from right to left. Once you've entered all the items you need, however, the flow will return to normal from left to right. Fortunately, all optional elements work the same way. Once we show you how to use an optional element later in the book, you'll know how to use any other optional element you encounter in a syntax diagram.

7 *Sub-optional element*—any element or group of elements that appears below an option element. Sub-optional elements allow you to fine-tune your statements so that you can work with more complex problems.

8 *Option list separator*—denotes that you can specify more than one value for this option and that each value must be separated with a comma.

9 *Alternate option*—denotes a keyword or defined term that can be used as an alternative to one or more optional elements. The syntax line for an alternate option will bypass the syntax lines of the optional elements it is meant to replace.

10 *Statement end point*—denotes the end of the main syntax line for a statement.

11 *Defined term start point*—denotes the beginning of the main syntax line for a defined term.

12 *Defined term end point*—denotes the end of the main syntax line for a defined term.

Now that you're familiar with these elements, you'll be able to read all of the syntax diagrams in the book. And on those occasions when a diagram requires further explanation, we provide you with the information you need to read the diagram clearly and easily. To help you better understand how the diagrams work, here's a sample SELECT Statement that we built using the diagram above.

```
SELECT FirstName, LastName, City, DOB AS DateOfBirth
FROM Students
WHERE City = 'El Paso'
```

This SELECT Statement retrieves four columns from the Students table, as we've indicated in the SELECT and FROM clauses. As you follow the main syntax line from left to right, you see that you have to indicate at least one *Value Expression*. A Value Expression can represent a column name, and you can indicate as many columns as you need with the Value Expression's *option list separator*. This is how we were able to use four column names from the Students table. We were concerned that some people viewing the information returned by this SELECT Statement might not know what DOB means, so we assigned an *alias* to the DOB column with the Value Expression's AS suboption. Finally, we used the WHERE clause to make certain the SELECT Statement shows only those students who live in El Paso. (If this doesn't quite make sense to you just now, there's no cause for alarm. You'll learn all this in great detail throughout the remainder of the book.)

You'll find a full set of syntax diagrams in Appendix A. They show the complete and proper syntax for all the statements and defined terms we discuss in the book. If you happen to refer to these diagrams as you work through each chapter, you'll notice a slight disparity between some of the diagrams in a given chapter and the corresponding diagrams in the appendix. The diagrams in the chapters are just simplified versions of the diagrams in the appendix. These simplified versions allow us to explain complex statements and defined terms more easily and give us the ability to focus on particular elements as needed. But don't worry—all of the diagrams in the appendix will make perfect sense once you work through the material in the book.

Sample Databases Used in This Book

Bound into the back of the book, you'll find a CD-ROM containing five sample databases that we use for the example queries throughout the book. We've also included diagrams of the database structures in Appendix B: Schema for the Sample Databases.

1. **Sales Order.** This is a typical order entry database for a store that sells bicycles and accessories. (Every database book needs at least *one* order entry example, right?)
2. **Entertainment Agency.** We structured this database to manage entertainers, agents, customers, and bookings. You would use a similar design to handle event bookings or hotel reservations.
3. **School Scheduling.** You might use this database design to register students at a high school or community college. This database tracks not only class registrations but also which instructors are assigned to each class and what grades the students received.
4. **Bowling League.** This database tracks bowling teams, team members, the matches they played, and the results.
5. **Recipes.** You can use this database to save and manage all your favorite recipes. We even added a few that you might want to try out.

In the root folder of the CD, you'll find all five sample databases in three versions. Because of the great popularity of the Microsoft Access desktop database, we created one set of databases (.mdb file extension) using Microsoft Access 2000 (Version 9.0). We chose Version 9 of this product because it more closely supports the current ANSI SQL Standard than any previous version. The second version consists of database files (.mdf file extension) for Microsoft SQL Server Version 7. We have also included SQL command files (.sql file extension) that you can use to attach the samples to a Microsoft SQL Server catalog. As an added bonus, we have included a trial version of Microsoft SQL Server Version 7 that you can install on any computer running Microsoft Windows 95, 98, 2000, or NT desktop. If you do not have database software, you can use this trial version to work through all the examples in the book. There is a README.TXT file in the root directory and in each of the chapter directories on the CD that contains complete instructions on how to load the sample databases. It is very important that you read these files so that you can load the sample databases properly and successfully.

You can find the third version in text files containing SQL commands to build the databases and load the data into your favorite database system. Although we were very careful to use the most common and simplest syntax for the CREATE TABLE and INSERT commands, you (or your database administrator) may need to modify these files slightly to work with your database system. We did not include any commands to create indexes for any of the tables because the syntax for CREATE INDEX varies widely from one database system to another. You may find that many of the sample statements run very slowly because of the lack of indexes. Consult your database documentation for information about how to create indexes to improve performance. If you're working with a database system on a remote server, you may need to gain permission from your database administrator to build the samples from the SQL commands we supplied.

You will also find one subfolder on the CD for each chapter that contains a Sample Statements section. We arranged the sample data this way to make it easy for you to find the samples for each chapter. In addition, we modified the sample data in some cases so that all the sample statements return at least one row in the Result Set. You can use the Microsoft Access 2000 databases directly in these subfolders or attach the Microsoft SQL Server versions you find there. If you are working with another database, you'll find one set of text files containing the SQL to load the sample data and another set of text files with the SQL for the sample statements.

"Follow the Yellow Brick Road"

—Munchkin to Dorothy in "The Wizard of OZ"

Now that you've read through the Introduction, you're ready to start learning SQL, right? Well, maybe. At this point, you're still in the house, it's still being tossed about by the tornado, and you haven't left Kansas.

Before you make that jump to Chapter 4, take our advice and read through the first three chapters. Chapter 1 will give you an idea of how the relational database was conceived and how it has grown to be the most widely used type of database in the industry today. We hope this will give you some amount of insight into the database system you're currently using. In Chapter 2, you'll learn how to fine-tune your data structures so that your data is reliable and, above all, accurate. You're going to have a tough time working with some of the SQL statements if you have poorly designed data structures,so we suggest you read this chapter carefully.

Chapter 3 is literally the beginning of the Yellow Brick Road. Here you'll learn the origins of SQL and how it evolved into its current form. You'll also learn about some of the people and companies who helped pioneer the language, and why there are so many flavors of SQL. Finally, you'll learn how SQL came to be a national and international standard and what the outlook for SQL will be in the years to come.

Once you've read these chapters, consider yourself well on your way to OZ. Just follow the road we've laid out through each of the remaining chapters. When you've finished the book, you'll find that you've found the Wizard—and he is you.

Part I

Relational Databases and SQL

1

What Is Relational?

"Knowledge is the small part of ignorance that we arrange and classify."
—Ambrose Bierce

Topics Covered in This Chapter

Types of Databases

A Brief History of the Relational Model

Anatomy of a Relational Database

What's in It for Me?

Summary

Before delving into the subject of SQL, we need to cover some general background information on the Relational database. You'll learn why the Relational database was invented, how it is constructed, and why you should use it. This information provides the foundation you need to really understand what SQL is all about and will eventually help to clarify how you can leverage SQL to your best advantage.

Types of Databases

What is a database? As you probably know, a database is an organized collection of data used to model some type of organization or organizational process. It really doesn't matter whether you're using paper or a computer program to collect and store the data. As long as you're collecting and storing data in some organized manner for a specific purpose, you've got a database. Throughout the remainder of this discussion, we'll assume that you're using a computer program to collect and maintain your data.

In general, two types of databases are used in database management: *Operational* databases and *Analytical* databases.

Operational databases are the backbone of many companies, organizations, and institutions throughout the world today. This type of database is primarily used to collect, modify, and maintain data on a day-to-day basis. The type of data stored is *dynamic*, meaning that it changes constantly and always reflects up-to-the-minute information. Organizations such as retail stores, manufacturing companies, hospitals and clinics, and publishing houses use Operational databases because their data is in a constant state of flux.

In contrast, an Analytical database stores and tracks historical and time-dependent data. An Analytical database is a valuable asset for tracking trends, viewing statistical data over a long period of time, or making tactical or strategic business projections. The type of data stored is *static*, meaning that the data is never (or very rarely) modified. The information gleaned from an Analytical database reflects a point-in-time snapshot of the data and is usually not up-to-date. Chemical labs, geological companies, and marketing analysis firms are examples of organizations that use Analytical databases.

A Brief History of the Relational Model

Several types of database models exist; some, such as Hierarchical and Network, are waning in use, while others, such as Relational, are gaining wide acceptance. You may also encounter discussions in other books about "Object" or "Object-Relational" models. While these newer models are currently undergoing further research and development, we believe that they will most likely be implemented as extensions to the Relational Model. In fact, much of the work of the ANSI committee on the next version of the SQL standard involves enhancements to SQL to embrace object-oriented concepts. For our purposes, however, we will focus strictly on the Relational Model.

In the Beginning . . .

The Relational database was first conceived in 1969 and has arguably become the most widely used database model in database management today. The father of the Relational Model, Dr. Edgar F. Codd, was an IBM research scientist in the late 1960s and was at that time looking into new ways to handle large amounts of data. His dissatisfaction with database models and database products of the time led him to begin thinking of ways to apply the disciplines and structures of mathematics to solve the myriad problems he had been encountering. A mathematician by profession, he strongly believed that he could apply specific branches of mathematics to solve problems such as data redundancy, weak data integrity, and a database structure's overdependence to its physical implementation.

Dr. Codd formally presented his new Relational Model in a landmark work titled "A Relational Model of Data for Large Shared Databanks" in June 1970.[1] He based his new model on two branches of mathematics—Set Theory and First Order Predicate Logic. Indeed, the name of the model itself is derived from the term "relation," which is part of Set Theory. (A widely held misconception is that the Relational Model derives its name from the fact that tables within a Relational database can be related to one another. Now that you know the truth, you'll have a peaceful, restful sleep tonight!) Fortunately, you need not know anything about Set Theory or First Order Predicate Logic to design and use a Relational database. If you use a good database design methodology—such as the one presented in Mike Hernandez's *Database Design for Mere Mortals*—you can develop a sound and effective database structure that you can confidently use to collect and maintain any data. (Well, OK, you *do* need to understand a little bit about Set Theory to solve more complex problems. We cover the bits you need to know in Chapter 7.)

Relational Database Software

Since its introduction, the Relational Model has been the basis for database products known as Relational Database Management Systems (RDBMS). Produced by a variety of vendors, they have gained acceptance over the years by diverse industries and organizations and are used within many types of environments. In the 1970s, mainframe computers used programs such as *System R*, developed by IBM, and *INGRES*, developed at the University of California at Berkeley. The development of RDBMSs for the mainframe continued in the 1980s with programs such as Oracle Corporation's *Oracle* and IBM's *DB2*. The PC (Personal Computer) boom of the mid-1980s gave rise to such programs as Ashton Tate's *dBase*, Ansa Software's *Paradox*, and Microrim's *R:BASE*. When the need to share data among PCs became apparent in the late 1980s and early 1990s, the concept of client/server computing was born along with the idea of centrally located, common data that would be both easy to manage

[1] *Communications of the ACM*, June 1970, 377–87.

and make secure. This concept gave rise to products such as Oracle's *Oracle 8i* and Microsoft's *SQL Server 7*. Since approximately 1996, there have been more concerted efforts to move database accessibility to the Internet. Software vendors are taking these efforts seriously and are now rising to the occasion by providing products that are more "Web-centric," such as Allaire's *Cold Fusion*, Sybase's *Sybase Enterprise Application Studio*, and Microsoft's *Visual InterDev*.

Anatomy of a Relational Database

According to the Relational Model, data in a Relational database is stored in *relations*, which are perceived by the user as tables. Each relation is composed of *tuples* (records) and *attributes* (fields). A Relational database has several other characteristics, which are discussed below.

An example of a table is shown in Figure 1-1.

Tables

Tables are the chief structures in the database; each table always represents a single, specific subject. The logical order of records and fields within a table is of absolutely no importance. Every table contains at least one field—known as a *Primary Key*—that uniquely identifies each of its records. (In Figure 1-1, for example, CustomerID is the Primary Key of the Customers table.) In fact, data in a Relational database can exist independent of the way it is physically

Customers

CustomerID	FirstName	LastName	StreetAddress	City	State	ZipCode
1010	Michael	Davolio	672 Lamont Ave	Houston	TX	77201
1011	Margaret	Peacock	667 Red River Road	Austin	TX	78710
1012	Estella	Pundt	2500 Rosales Lane	Dallas	TX	75260
1013	Mark	Rosales	323 Advocate Lane	El Paso	TX	79915
1014	Consuelo	Maynez	3445 Cheyenne Road	El Paso	TX	79915
1015	Ryan	Ehrlich	455 West Palm Ave	San Antonio	TX	78284

RECORDS

FIELDS

Figure 1-1 *A sample table.*

stored in the computer because of these last two table characteristics. This is great news for users because they aren't required to know the physical location of a record in order to retrieve its data.

The subject that a given table represents can be either an *object* or *event*. When the subject is an object, the table represents something that is tangible, such as a person, place, or thing. Regardless of its type, every object has characteristics that can be stored as data. This data can then be processed in an almost infinite number of ways. Pilots, products, machines, students, buildings, and equipment are all examples of objects that can be represented by a table. Figure 1-1 illustrates one of the most common examples of this type of table.

When the subject of a table is an event, the table represents something that occurs at a given point in time and has characteristics you wish to record. These characteristics can be stored as data and then processed as information in exactly the same manner as a table that represents some specific object. Examples of events you may need to record include judicial hearings, distributions of funds, lab test results, and geological surveys. Figure 1-2 shows an example of a table representing an event that we all have experienced at one time or another—a doctor's appointment.

Patient Visit

Patient ID	Visit Date	Visit Time	Physician	Blood Pressure	Temperature
92001	1998-05-01	10:30	Hernandez	120 / 80	98.8
97002	1998-05-01	13:00	Piercy	112 / 74	97.5
99014	1998-05-02	09:30	Rolson	120 / 80	98.8
96105	1998-05-02	11:00	Hernandez	160 / 90	99.1
96203	1998-05-02	14:00	Hernandez	110 / 75	99.3
98003	1998-05-02	09:30	Rolson	120 / 80	98.8

Figure 1-2 *A table representing an "event."*

Fields

A field is the smallest structure in the database, and it represents a characteristic of the subject of the table to which it belongs. Fields are the structures that are actually used to store data. The data in these fields can then be retrieved and presented as information in almost any configuration imaginable. Remember that the quality of the information you get from your data is in direct proportion to the amount of time you've dedicated to ensuring the structural integrity and data integrity of the fields themselves. There is just no way to underestimate the importance of fields.

Every field in a properly designed database contains one and only one value and its name identifies the type of value it holds. This makes entering data into a field very intuitive. If you see fields with names such as FirstName, LastName, City, State, and ZipCode, you know exactly what type of value goes into each field. You'll also find it very easy to sort the data by state or to look for everyone whose last name is Hernandez.

Records

A record represents a unique instance of the subject of a table. It is composed of the entire set of fields in a table, regardless of whether or not the fields contain any values. Because of the manner in which a table is defined, each record is identified throughout the database by a unique value in the Primary Key field of that record.

In Figure 1-1, for example, each record represents a unique customer within the table and the CustomerID field identifies a given customer throughout the database. In turn, each record includes all of the fields within the table, and each field describes some aspect of the customer represented by the record. Records are a key factor in understanding table relationships because you need to know how a record in one table relates to other records in another table.

Keys

Keys are special fields that play very specific roles within a table; the type of key determines its purpose within the table. Although a table may contain several types of keys, we will limit our discussion to the two most important ones: the *Primary Key* and the *Foreign Key*.

A Primary Key is a field or group of fields that uniquely identifies each record within a table. (When a Primary Key is composed of two or more fields, it is known as a Composite Primary Key.) The Primary Key is the most important of all for two reasons: Its *value* identifies *a specific record* throughout the entire database, and its *field* identifies *a given table* throughout the entire database. Primary Keys also enforce table-level integrity and help establish relationships with other tables. Every table in your database should have a Primary Key.

The AgentID field in Figure 1-3 is a good example of a Primary Key because it uniquely identifies each agent within the Agents table and helps to guarantee table-level integrity by ensuring non-duplicate records. It is also used to establish relationships between the Agents table and other tables in the database, such as the Entertainers table shown in the example.

Agents

PRIMARY KEY → AgentID

AgentID	AgentFirstName	AgentLastName	DateofHire	AgentHomePhone	<<*otherfields*>>
1001	Stella	Rosales	1994-07-11	299-5764	...
1002	Steve	Pundt	1994-05-01	515-5762	...
1003	Randi	Nathanson	1994-09-11	998-3882	...

Entertainers

PRIMARY KEY → EntertainerID; FOREIGN KEY → AgentID

EntertainerID	AgentID	EntertainerName	EntertainerPhone	<<*otherfields*>>
98100	1002	The Mike Hernandez Trio	959-8837	...
98101	1002	Jazz Times	555-9928	...
98102	1003	The Country Squires	709-3542	...

Figure 1-3 *Primary and Foreign Keys.*

When you determine that a pair of tables bear a relationship to each other, you typically establish the relationship by taking a copy of the Primary Key from the first table and inserting it into the second table, where it becomes a Foreign Key. (The term "Foreign Key" is derived from the fact that the second table already has a Primary Key of its own, and the Primary Key you are introducing from the first table is "foreign" to the second table.)

Figure 1-3 shows a good example of a Foreign Key. In this example, AgentID is the Primary Key of the Agents table, and it is a Foreign Key in the Entertainers table. As you can see, the Entertainers table already has a Primary Key—EntertainerID. In this relationship, AgentID is the field that establishes the connection between Agents and Entertainers.

Foreign Keys are important not only for the obvious reason that they help establish relationships between pairs of tables, but also because they help ensure relationship-level integrity. This means that the records in both tables will always be properly related because the values of a Foreign Key *must* be drawn from the values of the Primary Key to which it refers. Foreign Keys also help to avoid the dreaded "orphaned records," a classic example of which is an order record without an associated customer. If you don't know who made the order, you can't process it and you obviously can't invoice it. That'll throw your quarterly sales off!

Views

A *View* is a virtual table composed of fields from one or more tables in the database; the tables that comprise the View are known as *base tables*. The Relational Model refers to a View as virtual because it draws data from base tables rather than storing any data on its own. In fact, the only information about a View that is stored in the database is its structure.

Views enable you to see the information in your database from many different perspectives, thus providing great flexibility for working with data. You can create Views in a variety of ways; they are especially useful when based on multiple related tables. For example, you can create a View that summarizes information such as the total number of hours worked by every carpenter within the downtown El Paso area. Or you can create a View that groups data by specific fields. An example of this type of View is displaying the total number of employees in each city within every state of a specified set of regions.

An example of a typical View is shown in Figure 1-4.

In many RDBMS programs, a View is commonly implemented and referred to as a *saved query*; or, more simply, a *Query*. In most cases, a Query has all the characteristics of a View, so the only difference is that it is referred to by a different name. (We often wonder if someone in some marketing department had something to do with this.) It's important to note that some vendors are now beginning to call a Query by its real name. Regardless of what it's called in your RDBMS program, you'll certainly use Views in your database.

Relationships

If records in a given table can be associated in some way with records in another table, the tables are said to have a *relationship* between them. The manner in which the relationship is established depends on the type of relationship, and there are three types of relationships that can exist between a pair of tables: One-to-One, One-to-Many, or Many-to-Many. Understanding relationships is crucial to understanding how Views work and, by definition, how multitable SQL queries are designed and used. (You'll learn more about this in Part III: Working with Multiple Tables.)

Customers

CustomerID	CustFirstName	CustLastName	CustPhone	*<<other fields>>*
10001	Sally	Callahan	555-2671	...
10002	Ann	Fuller	555-2496	...
10003	James	Leverling	555-2501	...
<<~More Rows Here ~~~~~~>>				

Engagements

EngagementNumber	CustomerID	StartDate	End Date	StartTime	*<<other fields>>*
1	52113	1999-07-01	1199-07-04	13:00	...
2	54223	1999-07-01	1999-07-05	13:00	...
3	52233	1999-07-10	1999-07-15	13:00	...
<<~More Rows Here ~~~~~~>>					

Customer_Engagements *(View)*

EngagementNumber	CustFirstName	CustLastName	StartDate	EndDate
1	Mark	Rosales	1999-07-01	1999-07-04
2	Thomas	Fuller	1999-07-01	1999-07-05
3	Sally	Callahan	1999-07-10	1999-07-15
<<~More Rows Here ~~~~~~>>				

Figure 1-4 *A sample View.*

One-to-One

A pair of tables bears a One-to-One relationship when a single record in the first table is related to *only one* record in the second table, and a single record in the second table is related to *only one* record in the first table. In this type of relationship, one table is referred to as the *primary table* and the other is referred to as the *secondary table*. The relationship is established by taking the Primary Key of the primary table and inserting it into the secondary table, where it becomes a Foreign Key. This is a special type of relationship because in many cases the Foreign Key also acts as the Primary Key of the secondary table.

An example of a typical One-to-One relationship is shown in Figure 1-5, where Agents is the primary table and Compensation is the secondary table. The relationship between these tables is such that a single record in the Agents table can be related to only one record in the Compensation table, and a single record in the Compensation table can be related to only one record in the Agents table. Note that AgentID is indeed the Primary Key in both tables but also serves as a Foreign Key in the secondary table.

Agents

AgentID	AgentFirstName	AgentLastName	DateofHire	AgentHomePhone	*<<other fields>>*
1001	Stella	Rosales	1994-07-11	299-5764	...
1002	Steve	Pundt	1994-05-01	515-5762	...
1003	Randi	Nathanson	1994-09-11	998-3882	...

Compensation

AgentID	HourlyRate	CommissionRate	*<<other fields>>*
1001	21.50	4.5 %	...
1002	25.75	3.0 %	...
1003	20.00	4.5 %	...

Figure 1-5 *An example of a One-to-One relationship.*

The selection of the table that will play the primary role in this type of relationship is purely arbitrary. One-to-One relationships are not very common and are usually found in cases where a table has been split into two parts for confidentiality purposes.

One-to-Many

When a pair of tables has a One-to-Many relationship, a single record in the first table can be related to *many* records in the second table, but a single record in the second table can be related to *only one* record in the first table. This relationship is established by taking the Primary Key of the table on the "One" side and inserting it into the table on the "Many" side, where it becomes a Foreign Key.

A typical One-to-Many relationship is shown in Figure 1-6. In this example, a single record in the Artists table can be related to *many* records in the Engagements table, but a single record in the Engagements table can be related to *only one* record in the Artists table. As you probably have already guessed, ArtistID is a Foreign Key in the Engagements table.

Artists

ArtistID	ArtistFirstName	ArtistLastName	GroupName	<<other fields>>
67001	Mike	Hernandez	The Mike Hernandez Trio	...
67002	Zachary	Ehrlich	Jazz Times	...
67003	Gerry	Greer	The Country Squires	...

Engagements

EngagementID	ArtistID	CustomerID	StartDate	EndDate	<<other fields>>
1001	67003	701	1998-09-10	1998-09-12	...
1002	67001	625	1998-09-11	1998-09-12	...
1003	67001	712	1998-09-15	1998-09-19	...

Figure 1-6 *An example of a One-to-Many relationship.*

Many-to-Many

A pair of tables bears a Many-to-Many relationship when a single record in the first table can be related to *many* records in the second table, and a single record in the second table can be related to *many* records in the first table. In order to establish this relationship properly you must create what is known as a *linking table*. This table provides an easy way to associate records from one table with those of the other and will help to ensure that you have no problems adding, deleting, or modifying any related data. You define a linking table by taking a copy of the Primary Key of each table in the relationship and using them to form the structure of the new table. These fields actually serve two distinct roles: Together they form the Composite Primary Key of the linking table, and separately they each serve as a Foreign Key.

A Many-to-Many relationship that has not been properly established is said to be "unresolved." Figure 1-7 on the next page shows a clear example of an unresolved Many-to-Many relationship. In this case, a single record in the Artists table can be related to many records in the Recordings table, *and* a single record in the Recordings table can be related to *many* records in the Artists table.

This relationship is unresolved because of the inherent problem with a Many-to-Many relationship. The issue is this: How do you easily associate records from the first table with records in the second table? To reframe the question

Artists

ArtistID	ArtistFirstName	ArtistLastName	GroupName	<<otherfields>>
67001	Mike	Hernandez	The Mike Hernandez Trio	...
67002	Zachary	Ehrlich	Jazz Times	...
67003	Gerry	Greer	The Country Squires	...

Recordings

RecordingID	Title	YearReleased	<<other fields>>
1102	Jazz 'Round Midnight	1995	...
1103	Until I Return	1998	...
1104	Love Me, Don't Leave Me	1995	...
1105	Midnight Breeze	1996	...
1106	No Puede Ver	1994	...

Figure 1-7 *An unresolved Many-to-Many relationship.*

in terms of the tables shown in Figure 1-7, how do you associate a single artist with several recordings or a specific recording with several artists? Do you insert a few Artist fields into the Recordings table? Or do you add several Recording fields to the Artists table? Either of these approaches is going to create a number of problems when you try to work with related data, not least of which regards data integrity. The solution to this dilemma is to create a linking table in the manner previously stated. By creating and using the linking table, you can properly resolve the Many-to-Many relationship. Figure 1-8 shows this solution in practice.

In Figure 1-8, a linking table was created by taking the ArtistID from the Artists table and the RecordingID from the Recordings table and using them as the basis for a new table. As with any other table in the database, the new linking table has its own name—Artist_Recordings. The real advantage of a linking table is that it allows you to associate any number of records from both tables in the relationship. As the example shows, you can now easily associate a given artist with any number of recordings or a specific recording with any number of artists.

As we stated earlier, understanding relationships will pay great dividends when you begin to work with multitable SQL queries, so be sure to revisit this section when you begin working on Part III of this book.

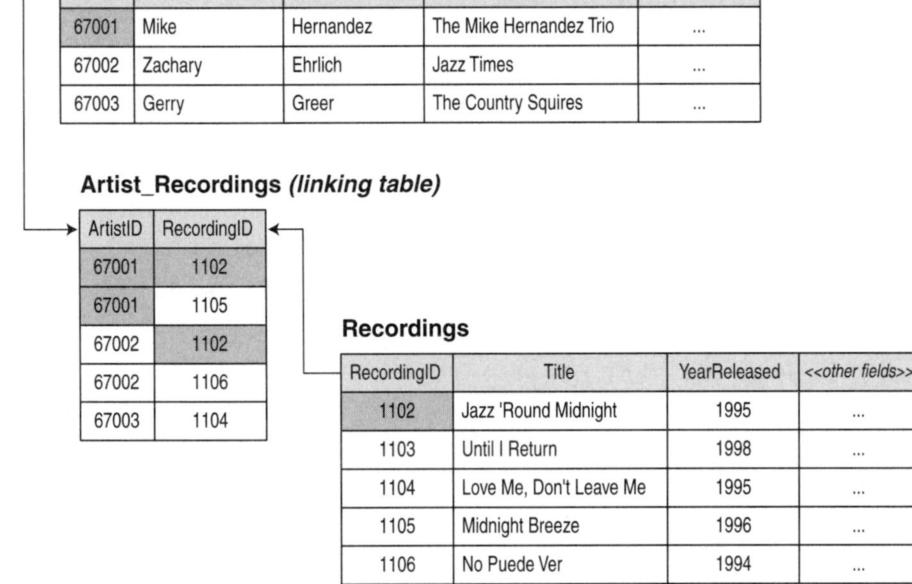

Artists

ArtistID	ArtistFirstName	ArtistLastName	GroupName	*<<other fields>>*
67001	Mike	Hernandez	The Mike Hernandez Trio	...
67002	Zachary	Ehrlich	Jazz Times	...
67003	Gerry	Greer	The Country Squires	...

Artist_Recordings ***(linking table)***

ArtistID	RecordingID
67001	1102
67001	1105
67002	1102
67002	1106
67003	1104

Recordings

RecordingID	Title	YearReleased	*<<other fields>>*
1102	Jazz 'Round Midnight	1995	...
1103	Until I Return	1998	...
1104	Love Me, Don't Leave Me	1995	...
1105	Midnight Breeze	1996	...
1106	No Puede Ver	1994	...

Figure 1-8 *A properly resolved Many-to-Many relationship.*

What's in It for Me?

Why should you be concerned with understanding Relational databases? Why should you even care what kind of environment you're using to work with your data? And aside from all this, what's really in it for you? Here's where the enlightenment starts and the fun begins.

The time you spend learning about Relational databases is an investment in time, and it is to your distinct advantage to do so. You should develop a good working knowledge of the Relational database because it's the most widely used data model in existence today. Forget what you read in the trades and what Harry over in the Information Technology Services department told you—a vast majority of the data being used by businesses and organizations is being collected, maintained, and manipulated in Relational databases. Yes, there have been proposed extensions to the model, the application programs that work with Relational databases have been injected with object orientation, and Relational databases have been integrated to some degree with the

Web. But no matter how you slice it, dice it, and spice it, it's still a Relational database! The Relational database has been around for over 25 years, it's still going strong, and it's not going be replaced any time in the foreseeable future.

Nearly all commercial database management application software used today is Relational. (However, folks such as Dr. Codd, C. J. Date, and Fabian Pascal might seriously question those claims!) If you want to be gainfully employed in the database field, you'd better know how to design a Relational database and how to implement it using one of the popular RDBMS programs. With the current push by many companies and corporations to Internet commerce, you'd better have some Web development experience under your belt as well.

Having a good working knowledge of Relational databases is helpful in many ways. For instance, the more you know about how Relational databases are designed, the easier it will be for you to develop end-user applications for a given database. You'll also be surprised how intuitive your RDBMS program will become because you'll understand why it provides the tools it does and how to use those tools to your best advantage. Your working knowledge will be a great asset as you learn how to use SQL because SQL is the standard language for creating, maintaining, and working with a Relational database.

"Where Do I Go from Here?"

Now that you know the importance of learning about Relational databases, you must understand that there is a difference between *database theory* and *database design*. Database theory involves the principles and rules that formulate the basis of the Relational database model. It is what is learned in the hallowed halls of academia and then quickly dismissed in the dark dens of the "real world." But theory is important, nonetheless, because it guarantees that the Relational database is structurally sound and that all actions taken on the data in the database have predictable results. On the other hand, database design involves the structured, organized set of processes used to design a Relational database. A good database design methodology will help you ensure the integrity, consistency, and accuracy of the data in the database and guarantee that any information you retrieve will be as accurate and up-to-date as possible.

If you want to design and create enterprise-wide databases, or develop Web-based Internet commerce databases, or begin to delve into data warehousing, you should seriously think about studying database theory. This applies even if you're not going to explore any of these areas but are considering becoming a high-end database consultant. For the rest of you who are going to design and create Relational databases on a variety of platforms (which, we believe, is the vast majority of those people reading this book), learning a good, solid database design methodology will serve you well. Always remember that designing a database is relatively easy, but *implementing* a database within a specific RDBMS program on a particular platform is another issue altogether. (Another story, another book, another time.)

There are a number of good database design books on the market. Some, such as Mike Hernandez's companion book *Database Design for Mere Mortals*, deal only with database design methodologies. Others, such as C. J. Date's *An Introduction to Database Systems*, mix both theory and design. (Be warned, though, that the books dealing with theory are not necessarily light reading.) Once you decide which direction you want to go, select and purchase the appropriate books, grab a Starbucks (or your beverage of choice), and dig right in. Once you become comfortable with Relational databases in general, you'll find that you will need to study and become very familiar with SQL.

And that's why you're reading this book.

SUMMARY

We began this chapter with a brief discussion of the different types of databases commonly found today. You learned that organizations working with dynamic data use an Operational database, ensuring that the information retrieved is always as accurate and up-to-the-minute as possible. You also learned that organizations working with static data use an Analytical database.

We then looked at a brief history of the Relational Database Model. We explained that Dr. E. F. Codd created the model based on specific branches of mathematics and that the model has been in existence for over 25 years. Database software, as you now know, has been developed for various computer environments and has steadily grown in power, performance, and capability since the 1970s. From the mainframe to the desktop to the Web, RDBMS programs are the backbone of many organizations today.

Next, we looked at an anatomy of a Relational database. We introduced you to its basic components and briefly explained their purpose. You learned about the three types of relationships and now understand their importance, not only in terms of the database structure itself, but also as they relate to your understanding of SQL.

Finally, we explained why it's to your advantage to learn about Relational databases and how to design them. You now know that the Relational database is the most common type of database in use today and that just about every database software program you're likely to encounter will be used to support a Relational database. You now have some ideas of how to pursue your education on Relational database theory and design a little further.

In the next chapter, you'll learn some techniques to fine-tune your existing database structures.

2

Ensuring Your Database Structure Is Sound

"We shape our buildings: thereafter they shape us."
—Sir Winston Churchill

Topics Covered in This Chapter

Most of you reading this book are probably working with an existing database structure implemented on your favorite (we hope) RDBMS program. It's hard for us to assume, at this point, whether or not you—or the person who developed the database—really had the necessary knowledge and skills or the time to design the database properly. Assuming the worst, you probably have a number of tables that could use some fine-tuning. Fortunately, you're about to learn some techniques that will help you get your database in shape and will ensure that you can easily retrieve the information you need from your tables.

Why Is This Chapter Here?

You may wonder why we're discussing database design topics in this book and why they're included in a beginning chapter. The reason is simple: If you have a poorly designed database structure, many of the SQL statements you'll learn to build in the remainder of the book will be, at best, difficult to implement or, at worst, relatively useless. However, if you have a well-designed database structure, the skills you learn in this book will serve you well.

This chapter will not teach you the intricacies of database design, but it will help you get your database in relatively good shape. We highly recommend that you read through this chapter so that you can make certain your table structures are sound.

❖ **Note** It is important to note that we are about to discuss the *logical* design of the database. We're not teaching you how to create or implement a database in SQL because, as we mentioned in the Introduction, these subjects are beyond the scope of this book.

Why Worry about Sound Structures?

If your database structure isn't sound, you'll have problems retrieving seemingly simple information from your database, it will be difficult to work with your data, and you'll cringe every time you need to add or delete fields in your tables. Other aspects of the database, such as data integrity, table relationships, and the ability to retrieve accurate information, are affected when you have poorly designed structures. These issues are just the tip of the iceberg. And it goes on! Make sure you have sound structures to avoid all this grief.

You can avoid many of these problems if you properly design your database from the beginning. Even if you've already designed your database, all is not lost. You can still apply the following techniques and gain the benefits of a sound structure. However, you must be aware that the quality of your final structures is in direct proportion to the amount of time you *invest* in fine-tuning them. The more care and patience you give to applying the techniques, the more you can guarantee your success.

Let's now turn to the first order of business in shaping up your structures: working with the fields.

Fine-tuning Fields

Because fields are the most basic structures in a database, you must ensure that they are in tip-top shape before you begin fine-tuning the tables as a whole. In many cases, fixing the fields will eliminate a number of existing problems with a given table and help you avoid any potential problems that might have arisen.

What's in a Name? (Part One)

As you know, a field represents a characteristic of the subject of the table to which it belongs. If you give the field an appropriate name, you should be able to identify the characteristic it's supposed to represent. A name that is ambiguous, vague, or unclear is a sure sign of trouble and suggests that the purpose of the field has not been carefully thought out. Use the following checklist to test each of your field names.

- *Is the name descriptive and meaningful to your entire organization?* If users in several departments are going to use this database, make certain you use a name that is meaningful to everyone who accesses this field. Semantics is a funny thing, and if you use a word that has a different meaning to different groups of people, you're just inviting trouble.
- *Is the field name clear and unambiguous?* PhoneNumber is a field name that can be very misleading. What kind of phone number is this field supposed to represent? A home phone? A work phone? A cellular phone? Learn to be specific. If you need to record each of these types of phone numbers, then create HomePhone, WorkPhone, and CellPhone fields.

  In addition to making your field names clear and unambiguous, be sure that you don't use the same field name in several tables. Let's say you have three tables called Customers, Vendors, and Employees. No doubt you will have City and State fields in each of these tables and the fields will have the same names in all three tables. There doesn't seem to be a problem with this until you have to refer to one particular field. How do you distinguish, let's say, between the City field in the Vendors table, the City field in the Customers table, and the City field in the Employees table? The answer is simple: add a short prefix to each of the field names. For example, use the name VendCity in the Vendors table, CustCity in the Customers table, and EmpCity in the Employees table. Now you can easily make a clear reference to any of these fields. (You can use this technique on any generic field such as FirstName, LastName, and Address.)

The main thing to remember: Make sure that each field in your database has a unique name and that it appears only once in the entire database structure. The only exception to this rule is when a field is being used to establish a relationship between two tables.

- *Did you use an acronym or abbreviation as a field name?* If you did, change it! Acronyms can be hard to decipher and are easily misunderstood. Imagine seeing a field named CAD_SW. How would you know what the field represents? Use abbreviations sparingly, and handle them with care. Only use an abbreviation if it supplements or enhances the field name in a positive manner; it shouldn't detract from the meaning of the field name.
- *Did you use a name that implicitly or explicitly identifies more than one characteristic?* These types of names are easy to spot because they typically use the words "and" or "or." Field names that contain a back slash (\), a hyphen (-), or an ampersand (&) are dead giveaways as well. If you have fields with names such as Phone\Fax or Area or Location, review the data that they store and determine if you need to deconstruct them into smaller, distinct fields.

❖ **Note** The SQL Standard defines a *regular identifier* as a name that must begin with a letter and can contain only letters, numbers, and the underscore character; spaces *are not* allowed. It also defines a *delimited identifier* as a name—surrounded with double quotes—that must start with a letter and can contain letters, numbers, the underscore character, spaces, and a very specific set of special characters. Because many SQL implementations implement only the regular identifier naming convention, we recommend that you use this naming convention exclusively for your field names.

After using this checklist to revise your field names, you have one task left: Make certain you use the singular form of the field name. A field with a plural name such as Categories implies that it may contain two or more values for any given record, which is not a good idea. A field name is singular because it represents a single characteristic of the subject of the table to which it belongs. A table name, on the other hand, is plural because it represents a collection of similar objects or events. You can distinguish table names from field names quite easily when you use this naming convention.

Smoothing Out the Rough Edges

Now that you've straightened out the field names, let's focus on the structure of the field itself. While you may be fairly sure that your fields are sound, there are a few things you can do to make certain they're built as efficiently as possible. Test your fields against the following checklist to determine whether or not your fields need a little more work.

- *Make sure the field represents a specific characteristic of the subject of the table.* The idea here is to determine whether the field truly belongs in the table. If it isn't germane to the table, remove it. The only exceptions to this rule occur when the field is being used to establish a relationship between this table and other tables in the database or when it has been added to the table in support of some task required by a database application. For example, in the Classes table in Figure 2-1, the

Staff

StaffID	StaffFirstName	StaffLastName	StaffStreetAddress	StaffCity	StaffState	*<<other fields>>*
98014	James	Leverling	722 Moss Bay Blvd.	Kirkland	WA	...
98019	Laura	Callahan	901 Pine Avenue	Portland	OR	...
98020	Albert	Buchanan	13920 S.E. 40th Street	Bellevue	WA	...
98021	Tim	Smith	30301- 166th Ave. N.E.	Seattle	WA	...
98022	Janet	Leverling	722 Moss Bay Blvd.	Kirkland	WA	...
98023	Alaina	Hallmark	Route 2, Box 203 B	Woodinville	WA	...

Classes

ClassID	Class	ClassroomID	StaffID	StaffLastName	StaffFirstName	*<<other fields>>*
1031	Art History	1231	98014	Leverling	James	...
1030	Art History	1231	98014	Leverling	James	...
2213	Biological Principles	1532	98021	Smith	Tim	...
2005	Chemistry	1515	98019	Callahan	Laura	...
2001	Chemistry	1519	98233	Hallmark	Alaina	...
1006	Drawing	1627	98020	Buchanan	Albert	...
2907	Elementary Algebra	3445	98022	Leverling	Janet	...

Figure 2-1 *A table with unnecessary fields.*

StaffLastName and StaffFirstName fields are unnecessary because of the presence of the StaffID field. StaffID is being used to establish a relationship between the Classes table and the Staff table, and you can view data from both tables simultaneously using a View or an SQL Select query. If you have such fields in your tables, you can either remove them completely or use them as the basis of a new table if they don't appear anywhere else in the database structure. (We'll show you how to do this later in this chapter.)

- *Make certain that the field contains only a single value*. A field that can potentially store several instances of the *same* values is known as a *multivalued* field. Likewise, a field that can potentially store two or more *distinct* values is known as a *multipart* field. Multivalued and multipart fields can wreak havoc in your database, especially when you try to edit, delete, or sort the data. When you ensure that each field stores only a single value, you go a long way toward guaranteeing data integrity and accurate information. But for the time being, just try to identify any multivalued or multipart fields and make note of them. You'll learn how to resolve them in the next section.
- *Make sure the field does not store the result of a calculation or concatenation.* Calculated fields are not allowed in a properly designed table. The issue here is the value of the calculated field itself. A field, unlike a cell in a spreadsheet, does not store an actual calculation. When the value of any part of the calculation changes, the result value stored in the field is not updated. The only ways to update the value are to do so manually or to write some procedural code that will do it automatically. Either way, it is incumbent on the user or you (the developer) to make certain the value is updated. The preferred way to work with calculations, however, is by incorporating them into a SELECT Statement. You'll learn the advantages of dealing with calculations in this manner when you get to Chapter 5: Getting More Than Simple Columns.
- *Make certain the field appears only once in the entire database.* If you've made the common mistake of inserting the same field (for example, CompanyName) into several tables within the database, you're going to have a problem with inconsistent data. This occurs when you change the value of this field in one table and forget to make the same

modification wherever else the field appears. Avoid this problem entirely by ensuring that a field appears only once in the entire database structure. (The only exception to this rule is when you're using a field to establish a relationship between two tables.)

Resolving Multipart Fields

As we mentioned earlier, multipart and multivalued fields will wreak havoc with data integrity, so you need to resolve them in order to avoid any potential problems. Deciding which to resolve first is purely arbitrary, so we'll begin with multipart fields.

You'll know if you have a multipart field by answering a very simple question: "Can I take the current value of this field and break it up into smaller, more distinct parts?" If your answer is "Yes," you have a multipart field. Figure 2-2 shows a poorly designed table with several multipart fields.

Customers

CustomerID	CustomerName	StreetAddress	PhoneNumber	<<*other fields*>>
1001	Suzanne Viescas	15127 NE 24th, #383, Redmond, WA 98052	425 555-2686	...
1002	Will Thompson	122 Spring River Drive, Duvall, Wa 98019	425 555-2681	...
1003	Gary Hallmark	Route 2, Box 203B, Auburn, WA 98002	253 555-2676	...
1004	Michael Davolio	672 Lamont Ave, Houston, TX 77201	713 555-2491	...
1005	Kenneth Peacock	4110 Old Redmond Rd., Redmond, WA 98052	425 555-2506	...
1006	John Viescas	15127 NE 24rh, #383, Redmond, WA 98052	425 555-2511	...
1007	Laura Callahan	901 Pine Avenue, Portland, OR 97208	503 555-2526	...
1008	Neil Patterson	233 West Valley Hwy, San Diego, CA 92199	619 555-2541	...

MULTIPART FIELDS

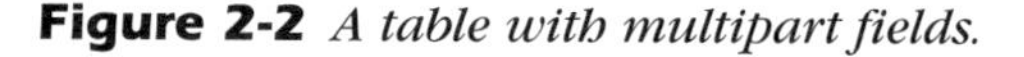

Figure 2-2 *A table with multipart fields.*

There are three multipart fields in this table: CustomerName, StreetAddress, and PhoneNumber. You can see that each field can be broken down into smaller fields. For example, CustomerName can be broken down into two distinct fields—CustFirstName and CustLastName. (Note that we're using the naming convention discussed earlier in this chapter when we add the prefix Cust to the FirstName and LastName fields.) When you identify a multipart field in a table, determine how many parts there are to the value it stores and then break the field down into as many smaller fields as appropriate. Figure 2-3 on the next page shows how to resolve the multivalued fields in the Customers table.

Customers

CustomerID	CustFirstName	CustLastName	CustAddress	CustCity	CustState	CustZipcode
1001	Suzanne	Viescas	15127 NE 24th, #383	Redmond	WA	98052
1002	Wil	Thompson	122 Spring River Drive	Duvall	WA	98019
1003	Gary	Hallmark	Route 2, Box 203B	Auburn	WA	98002
1004	Michael	Davolio	672 Lamont Ave	Houston	TX	77201
1005	Kenneth	Peacock	4110 Old Redmond Rd.	Redmond	WA	98052
1006	John	Viescas	15127 NE 24th, #383	Redmond	WA	98052
1007	Laura	Callahan	901 Pine Avenue	Portland	OR	97208
1008	Neil	Patterson	233 West Valley Hwy	San Diego	CA	92199

Figure 2-3 *The resolution of the multipart fields in the Customers table.*

❖ **Note** Along with breaking down StreetAddress, it's also a good idea to break down PhoneNumber into two distinct fields. Unfortunately, we couldn't demonstrate this in Figure 2-3 due to space limitations.

Sometimes you may have difficulty recognizing a multipart field. Take a look at the Instruments table shown in Figure 2-4. At first glance, there do not seem to be any multipart fields. On closer inspection, however, you will see that InstrumentID is actually a multipart field. The value stored in this field represents two distinct pieces of information: the category to which the instrument belongs—such as AMP (amplifier), GUIT (guitar), and MFX (multi-effects unit)—and its identification number. These two values should be separated and stored in their own fields to ensure data integrity. Imagine the difficulty of updating this field if the MFX category changed to MFU. You would have to write code to parse the value in this field and test for the existence of MFX and then replace it with MFU if it does exist within the parsed

Instruments

InstrumentID	Manufacturer	InstrumentDescription	*<<other fields>>*
GUIT2201	Fender	Fender Stratocaster	...
MFX3349	Zoom	Player 2100 Multi-Effects	...
AMP1001	Marshall	JCM 2000 Tube Super Lead	...
AMP5590	Crate	VC60 Pro Tube Amp	...
SFX2227	Dunlop	Cry Baby Wah-Wah	...
AMP2766	Fender	Twin Reverb Reissue	...

Figure 2-4 *An example of a subtle multipart field.*

value. It's not so much that you *couldn't* do this, but you'd definitely be working harder than necessary, and you shouldn't have to go through this at all if your database is properly designed. When you have fields such as the one in this example, break them up into smaller fields so that you will have sound, efficient field structures.

Resolving Multivalued Fields

Resolving multipart fields is not very hard at all, but resolving multivalued fields can be a little more difficult and will take some work. Fortunately, you'll know a multivalued field when you see one. Almost without exception, the data stored in this type of field contains a number of commas. The commas are used to separate the various values within the field itself. An example of a multivalued field is shown in Figure 2-5.

Pilots

PilotID	PilotFirstName	PilotLastName	HireDate	Certifications	<<*other fields*>>
25100	John	Leverling	1994-07-11	727, 737, 757, MD80	...
25101	David	Callahan	1994-05-01	737, 747, 757	...
25102	David	Smith	1994-09-11	757, MD80, DC9	...
25103	Kathryn	Patterson	1994-07-11	727, 737, 747, 757	...
25104	Michael	Hernandez	1994-05-01	737, 757, DC10	...
25105	Kendra	Bonnicksen	1994-09-11	757, MD80, DC9	...

Figure 2-5 *A table with a multivalued field.*

In this example, each pilot is certified to fly any number of planes and those certifications are stored in a single field called Certifications. The manner in which the data is stored in this field is very troublesome because you are bound to encounter the same type of data integrity problems associated with multipart fields. When you look at the data more closely, you'll see that it will be difficult for you to perform searches and sorts on this field in an SQL query. Before you can resolve this field in the appropriate manner, you must first understand the true relationship between a multivalued field and the table to which it is originally assigned.

The values in a multivalued field have a Many-to-Many relationship with every record in its parent table: One specific value in a multivalued field can be associated with any number of records in the parent table, and a single record in the parent table can be associated with any number of values in the multivalued field. In Figure 2-5, for example, a specific aircraft in the Certifications field can be associated with any number of pilots, and a single pilot can be associated with any number of aircraft in the Certifications field. You resolve this Many-to-Many relationship as you would any other Many-to-Many relationship within the database—with a linking table.

To create the linking table, use the multivalued field and a *copy* of the Primary Key field from the original table as the basis for the new table. Give the new linking table an appropriate name and designate both fields as a Composite Primary Key. (In this case, it is the combination of the values of both fields that will uniquely identify each record within the new table.) Now you can associate the values of both fields in the linking table on a One-to-One basis. Figure 2-6 shows an example of this process using the Pilots table shown in Figure 2-5.

Pilots

PilotID	PilotFirstName	PilotLastName	HireDate	*<<other fields>>*
25100	John	Leverling	1994-07-11	...
25101	David	Callahan	1994-05-01	...
25102	David	Smith	1994-09-11	...
25103	Kathryn	Patterson	1994-07-11	...
25104	Michael	Hernandez	1994-05-01	...
25105	Kendra	Bonnicksen	1994-09-11	...

Pilot Certifications *(linking table)*

PilotID	CertificationID
25100	8102
25100	8103
25100	8105
25100	8106
25101	8103
25101	8104
25101	8105

Certifications

CertificationID	TypeofAircraft	*<<other fields>>*
8102	Boeing 727	...
8103	Boeing 737	...
8104	Boeing 747	...
8105	Boeing 757	...
8106	McDonnell Douglas MD80	...

Figure 2-6 *Resolving a multivalued field using a linking table.*

Contrast the entries for John Leverling (Pilot ID 25100) in both the old Pilots table and the new Pilot_Certifications table. The major advantage of the new linking table is that you can now associate *any* number of certifications with a single pilot. Asking certain types of questions are now much easier as well. For example, you can determine which pilots are certified to fly a Boeing 747 aircraft or retrieve a list of certifications for a specific pilot. You'll also find that you can sort the data in any order you wish, without any adverse effects.

When you follow the procedures presented in this section, your fields will be in good shape. Now that you've refined the fields, let's turn to our second order of business and take a look at the table structures.

Fine-tuning Tables

Tables serve as the basis for any SQL query you create. You'll soon find that poorly designed tables pose data integrity problems and are difficult to work with when you create multitable SQL queries. Because of this, you must make certain that your tables are structured as efficiently as possible so that you can easily retrieve the information you need.

What's in a Name? (Part Two)

In the previous section, you learned how important it is for a field to have an appropriate name and why you give serious thought to naming your fields. In this section, you'll learn that the same applies to tables as well. By definition, a table should represent a single subject; if it represents more than one subject, it should be divided into smaller tables. The name of the table must clearly identify the subject the table represents. You can be confident that the subject of the table has not been carefully thought out if a table name is ambiguous, vague, or unclear. Make sure your table names are sound by checking them against the following checklist.

- *Is the name unique and descriptive enough to be meaningful to your entire organization?* Giving your table a unique name ensures that each table in the database represents a different subject and that everyone in the organization will understand what the table represents. Defining a unique and descriptive name does take some work on your part, but it's well worth the effort in the long run.

- *Does the name accurately, clearly, and unambiguously identify the subject of the table?* When the table name is vague or ambiguous, you can bet that the table represents more than one subject. "Dates" is a good example of a vague table name. It's hard to determine exactly what this table represents unless you have a description of the table at hand. For example, let's say this table appears in a database used by an entertainment agency. If you inspect this table closely, you'll probably find that it contains dates for client meetings and booking dates for the agency's stable of entertainers. This table clearly represents two subjects. In this case, divide the table into two new tables and give each table an appropriate name, such as Client_Meetings and Entertainer_Schedules.
- *Does the name contain words that convey physical characteristics?* Avoid using words such as "File," "Record," and "Table" in the table name because they introduce a level of confusion that you don't need. A table name that includes this type of word is very likely to represent more than one subject. Consider the name "Employee_Record." On the surface, there doesn't appear to be any problem with this name. But when you think about what an employee record is supposed to represent, you'll realize that there are potential problems with this name. The name contains a word that we're trying hard to avoid and it potentially represents three subjects: employees, departments, and payroll. With this in mind, split the original table (Employee_Record) into three new tables, one for each of the three subjects.
- *Did you use an acronym or abbreviation as a table name?* If the answer to this question is "Yes," change the name right now! Abbreviations rarely convey the subject of the table and acronyms are usually hard to decipher. For example, say your company database has a table named SC. How do you know what the table represents without knowing the meaning of the letters themselves? The fact is that you can't easily identify the subject of the table. What's more, you may find that the table means different things to different departments in the company. (Now, this is scary.) The folks in Personnel think it stands for Steering_Committees; the Information Systems staff believe it to be System_Configurations; and the people in Security insist that it represents Security_Codes. This example clearly illustrates why you should avoid using abbreviations and acronyms in a table name.

- *Did you use a name that implicitly or explicitly identifies more than one subject?* This is one of the most common mistakes you can make with a table name and it is relatively easy to identify. This type of name typically contains the words "and" or "or" and characters such as the back slash (\), hyphen (-), or ampersand (&); Facility\Building and Department or Branch are typical examples. When you name a table in this manner, you must clearly identify whether it truly represents more than one subject. If it does, then deconstruct it into smaller tables and then give the new tables appropriate names.

❖ **Note** Remember, the SQL Standard defines a *regular identifier* as a name that must begin with a letter and can contain only letters, numbers, and the underscore character; spaces *are not* allowed. It also defines a *delimited identifier* as a name—surrounded with double quotes—that must start with a letter and can contain letters, numbers, the underscore character, spaces, and a very specific set of special characters. Because many SQL implementations implement only the regular identifier naming convention, we recommend that you use this naming convention exclusively for your table names.

After you've finished revising your table names, you have one more task to perform: Check each table name once more and make certain you used the plural form of the name. You use the plural form because a table stores a *collection of instances* of the subject of the table. For example, an Employees table doesn't store the data for just one employee, but for many employees. Using the plural form also helps you to distinguish a table name from a field name.

Ensuring a Sound Structure

Let's focus on the table structures now that you've revised the table names. It's imperative that the tables are properly designed so that you can efficiently store data and retrieve accurate information. The time you spend ensuring your tables are well built will pay dividends when you need to create complex multitable SQL queries. Use the following checklist to determine whether your table structures are sound.

- *Make sure the table represents a single subject.* Yes, we know, we've said this a number of times already, but we can't overemphasize this point. As long as you guarantee that each of your tables represents a single subject, you greatly reduce the risk of potential data integrity problems. Also remember that the subject represented by the table can be an object or event. By "object" we mean something that is tangible, such as employees, vendors, machines, buildings, or departments. On the other hand, an "event" is something that happens at a given point in time that has characteristics that you want to record. The best example of an event that everyone can relate to is a doctor's appointment. While you can't explicitly touch a doctor's appointment, it does have characteristics that you need to record, such as the appointment date, the appointment time, the patient's blood pressure, and the patient's temperature.

- *Make certain each table has a Primary Key.* You must assign a Primary Key to each table for two reasons. The first is that it uniquely identifies each record within a table, and the second is that it is used in establishing table relationships. If you do not assign a Primary Key to each table, you will eventually have data integrity problems and problems with some types of multitable SQL queries. You'll learn some tips on how to define a proper Primary Key later in this chapter.
- *Make sure the table does not contain any multipart or multivalued fields.* Theoretically, you should have resolved these issues when you refined the field structures. Nonetheless, it's still a good idea to review the fields one last time to ensure that you've completely removed each and every one of them.
- *Make sure there are no calculated fields in the table.* While you might believe that your current table structures are free of calculated fields, you may have overlooked one or two during the field refinement process. This is a good time to take another look at the table structures and remove any calculated fields you may have missed.
- *Make certain the table is free of any unnecessary duplicate fields.* One of the hallmarks of a poorly designed table is the inclusion of duplicate fields from other tables. You might feel compelled to add duplicate fields to a table for one of two reasons: to provide "reference" information or to indicate multiple occurrences of a particular type of value. These duplicate fields raise various difficulties when you work with the data and attempt to retrieve information from the table. Let's now take a look at how to deal with duplicate fields.

Resolving Unnecessary Duplicate Fields

Possibly the hardest part of ensuring well-built structures is dealing with duplicate fields. Here are a couple of examples that demonstrate how you properly resolve tables that contain duplicate fields.

Figure 2-7 illustrates an example of a table containing duplicate fields that supply "reference" information.

In this case, StaffLastName and StaffFirstName appear in the Classes table so that a person viewing the table can see the name of the instructor for a given class. However, these fields are unnecessary because of the One-to-Many relationship that exists between the Classes and Staff tables. (A single staff member can teach any number of classes, but a single class is taught by a specific staff member.) StaffID establishes the relationship between these tables, and the relationship itself lets you view data from both tables simultaneously in an

Staff

StaffID	StaffFirstName	StaffLastName	StaffStreetAddress	StaffCity	StaffState	<<other fields>>
98014	James	Leverling	722 Moss Bay Blvd.	Kirkland	WA	...
98019	Laura	Callahan	901 Pine Avenue	Portland	OR	...
98020	Albert	Buchanan	13920 S.E. 40th Street	Bellevue	WA	...
98021	Tim	Smith	30301 166th Ave. N.E.	Seattle	WA	...
98022	Janet	Leverling	722 Moss Bay Blvd.	Kirkland	WA	...
98023	Alaina	Hallmark	Route 2, Box 203 B	Woodinville	WA	...

These fields are unnecessary

Classes

ClassID	Class	ClassroomID	StaffID	StaffLastName	StaffFirstName	<<other fields>>
1031	Art History	1231	98014	Leverling	James	...
1030	Art History	1231	98014	Leverling	James	...
2213	Biological Principles	1532	98021	Smith	Tim	...
2005	Chemistry	1515	98019	Callahan	Laura	...
2001	Chemistry	1519	98233	Hallmark	Alaina	...
1006	Drawing	1627	98020	Buchanan	Albert	...
2907	Elementary Algebra	3445	98022	Leverling	Janet	...

Figure 2-7 *A table with duplicate fields added for "reference" information.*

SQL query. With this in mind, you can confidently remove the StaffLastName and StaffFirstName fields from the Classes table without any adverse effects. Figure 2-8 shows the revised Classes table structure.

Staff

StaffID	StaffFirstName	StaffLastName	StaffStreetAddress	StaffCity	StaffState	*<<other fields>>*
98014	James	Leverling	722 Moss Bay Blvd.	Kirkland	WA	...
98019	Laura	Callahan	901 Pine Avenue	Portland	OR	...
98020	Albert	Buchanan	13920 S.E. 40th Street	Bellevue	WA	...
98021	Tim	Smith	30301- 166th Ave. N.E.	Seattle	WA	...
98022	Janet	Leverling	722 Moss Bay Blvd.	Kirkland	WA	...
98023	Alaina	Hallmark	Route 2, Box 203 B	Woodinville	WA	...

Classes

ClassID	Class	ClassroomID	StaffID	*<<other fields>>*
1031	Art History	1231	98014	...
1030	Art History	1231	98014	...
2213	Biological Principles	1532	98021	...
2005	Chemistry	1515	98019	...
2001	Chemistry	1519	98233	...
1006	Drawing	1627	98020	...
2907	Elementary Algebra	3445	98022	...

Figure 2-8 *Resolving the duplicate "reference" fields.*

Keeping these unnecessary fields in the table automatically introduces a major problem with inconsistent data. You must ensure that the values of the StaffLastName and StaffFirstName fields in the Classes table always match their counterparts in the Staff table. For example, say a female staff member marries and decides to use her married name as her legal name from this day forward. Not only do you have to be certain to make the appropriate change to her record in the Staff table, but you must ensure that every occurrence of her name in the Classes table changes as well. Again, it's possible to do this (at least, technically), but you're working much harder than is necessary. Besides, one of the major premises behind using a Relational database is that you should enter a piece of data only once in the entire database. (The only exception to this rule is when you're using a field to establish a relationship between two tables.) As always, the best course of action is to remove all duplicate fields from the tables in your database.

Another clear example of a table containing duplicate fields is shown in Figure 2-9. This example illustrates how duplicate fields are mistakenly used to indicate multiple occurrences of a particular type of value. In this case, the three Committee fields are ostensibly used to record the names of the committees in which the employee participates.

Employees

EmployeeID	EmpFirstName	EmpLastName	Committee1	Committee2	Committee3	*<<other fields>>*
7004	Peacock	Samuel	Steering			...
7005	Kennedy	John	Y2K Conformance	Safety		...
7006	Thompson	Sarah	Safety	Y2K Conformance	Steering	...
7007	Callahan	David				...
7008	Buchanan	Andrea	Y2K Conformance			...
7009	Smith	David	Steering	Safety	Y2K Conformance	...
7010	Patterson	Neil				...
7011	Viescas	Michael	Y2K Conformance	Steering	Safety	...

Figure 2-9 *A table with duplicate fields used to indicate multiple occurrences of a particular type of value.*

It's relatively easy to see why these duplicate fields will create problems. One problem concerns the actual number of Committee fields in the table. What if a few employees do end up belonging to four committees? For that matter, how can we really tell just how many Committee fields we're actually going to need? If it turns out that several employees are participating in more than three committees, you'll need to add more Committee fields to the table.

A second problem pertains to retrieving information from the table. How do you retrieve those employees who are currently in the Y2K Conformance committee? It's not impossible, but you'll have difficulty retrieving this information. You must execute three separate queries in order to answer the question accurately because you cannot be certain in which of the three Committee fields the value Y2K Conformance is stored. Now you're expending more time and effort than is truly necessary.

A third problem that arises concerns sorting the data. You cannot sort the data by Committee in any practical fashion, and there's no way that you'll get the committee names to line up correctly in alphabetical order. While these may seem like minor problems, they can be quite frustrating when you're trying to get an overall view of the data in some form of orderly manner.

If you study the Employees table in Figure 2-9 on the previous page closely, you'll soon realize that there is a Many-to-Many relationship between the employees and committees to which they belong. A single employee can belong to any number of committees, and a single committee can be composed of any number of employees. You can, therefore, resolve these duplicate fields in the same manner that you would resolve any other Many-to-Many relationship—by creating a linking table. In the case of the Employees table, create the linking table by using a copy of the Primary Key (EmployeeID) and a single Committee field. Give the new table an appropriate name, such as Committee_Members, designate both the EmployeeID and Committee fields as a Composite Primary Key, remove the Committee fields from the Employees table, and you're done. (You'll learn more about Primary Keys later in this chapter.) Figure 2-10 shows the revised Employees table and the new Committee_Members table.

Employees

EmployeeID	EmpFirstName	EmpLastName	EmpCity	*<<other fields>>*
7004	Peacock	Samuel	Chico	...
7005	Kennedy	John	Portland	...
7006	Thompson	Sarah	Lubbock	...
7007	Callahan	David	Salem	...
7008	Buchanan	Andrea	Medford	...
7009	Smith	David	Fremont	...
7010	Patterson	Neil	San Diego	...
7011	Viescas	Michael	Redmond	...

Committee_Members

EmployeeID	Committee
7004	Steering
7005	Y2K Conformance
7005	Safety
7006	Safety
7006	Y2K Conformance
7006	Steering
7008	Y2K Conformance
7009	Steering

Figure 2-10 *The revised Employees table and the new Committee_Members table.*

While you've resolved the duplicate fields that were in the original Employees table, you're not quite finished yet. Keeping in mind that there is a Many-to-Many relationship between the employees and the committees to which they belong, you might very well ask, "Where is the Committees table?" There isn't one—yet! Chances are that a committee has some other characteristics that you need to record, such as the name of the room where the committee meets and the day of the month that the meeting is held. So, you should create a real Committees table that includes fields such as CommitteeID, CommitteeName, MeetingRoom, and MeetingDay. When you finish creating the new table, replace the Committee field in the Committee_Members table with the CommitteeID field from the new Committees table. The final structures appear in Figure 2-11.

Employees

EmployeeID	EmpFirstName	EmpLastName	EmpCity	<<other fields>>
7004	Peacock	Samuel	Chico	...
7005	Kennedy	John	Portland	...
7006	Thompson	Sarah	Lubbock	...
7007	Callahan	David	Salem	...
7008	Buchanan	Andrea	Medford	...
7009	Smith	David	Fremont	...
7010	Patterson	Neil	San Diego	...
7011	Viescas	Michael	Redmond	...

Committee_Members

EmployeeID	CommitteeID
7004	103
7005	104
7005	102
7006	102
7006	104
7006	103
7008	104
7009	103

Committees

CommitteeID	CommitteeName	MeetingRoom	MeetingDay
100	Budget	11-C	Tuesday
101	Christmas	9-F	Monday
102	Safety	12-B	Monday
103	Steering	12-D	Tuesday
104	Y2K Compliance	Main-South	Wednesday

Figure 2-11 *The final Employees and Committees structures.*

You gain a real advantage by structuring the tables in this manner because you can now associate a single member with any number of committees or a single committee with any number of employees. You can then use an SQL query to view information from all three tables simultaneously.

You're now close to completing the process of fine-tuning your table structures. The last order of business is to make certain each record within a table can be uniquely identified and that the table itself can be identified throughout the entire database.

Identification Is the Key

As you learned in Chapter 1, the Primary Key is one of the most important keys in a table because it uniquely identifies each record within a table and officially identifies that table throughout the database. It also establishes a relationship between a pair of tables. You cannot underestimate the importance of the Primary Key—every table in your database must have one!

By definition, a Primary Key is a field or group of fields that uniquely identifies each record within a table. A Primary Key is known as a Simple Primary Key (or just Primary Key for short) when it is composed of a single field, and as a Composite Primary Key when it is composed of two or more fields. Define a Simple Primary Key when you can because it's more efficient and is much easier to use when establishing a table relationship. Use a Composite Primary Key only when it's appropriate (for example, to define and create a linking table).

You can use an existing field as a Primary Key as long as it satisfies all of the criteria on the following checklist. When the field you want to use as the Primary Key does not conform to *all* of the criteria, use a different field or define a new field to act as Primary Key for the table. Take some time now and use the following checklist to determine whether each Primary Key in your database is sound.

- *Does the field uniquely identify each record in the table?* Each record in a table represents an instance of the subject of the table. A good Primary Key ensures that you have a means of accurately identifying or referencing each record in this table from other tables in the database. It also helps you to avoid having duplicate records within the table.
- *Does this field contain unique values?* As long as the values of the Primary Key are unique, you have a means of ensuring that there are no duplicate records in the table.
- *Will this field ever contain unknown values?* This is a very important question because a Primary Key cannot contain unknown values. If you think this field has even the slightest possibility of containing unknown values, you should disqualify it immediately.
- *Can the value of this field ever be optional?* If the answer to this question is "Yes," you cannot use this field as the Primary Key. If the value of this field can be optional, it implies that it may be unknown at some point; as you learned in the previous item, a Primary Key cannot contain unknown values.
- *Is this a multipart field?* Although you should have eliminated all your multipart fields by now, you should ask yourself this question anyway. If

you missed a multipart field earlier, resolve it now and try to use another field as the Primary Key.

- *Can the value of this field ever be modified?* The values of a Primary Key field should remain static. That is, you should never change the value of a Primary Key unless you have a truly compelling reason to do so. When the value of the field is subject to arbitrary changes, it is difficult for the field to remain in conformance with the other points in this checklist.

As we stated earlier, a field must pass all the points on this checklist with flying colors before it can be used as a Primary Key. In Figure 2-12, PilotID serves as the Primary Key of the Pilots table. But the question is this: Does PilotID conform to all the points on the previous checklist? If it does, the Primary Key is sound. But if it doesn't, you must either modify it to conform with all the points on the checklist or select a different field as the Primary Key.

Pilots

PilotID	PilotFirstName	PilotLastName	HireDate	Position	PilotAreaCode	PilotPhone
25100	John	Leverling	1994-07-11	Captain	206	555-3982
25101	David	Callahan	1994-05-01	Captain	206	555-6657
25102	David	Smith	1994-09-11	FirstOfficer	915	555-1992
25103	Kathryn	Patterson	1994-07-11	Navigator	972	555-8832
25104	Michael	Hernandez	1994-05-01	Navigator	360	555-9901
25105	Kendra	Bonnicksen	1994-09-11	Captain	206	555-1106

Figure 2-12 *Is PilotID a sound Primary Key?*

As a matter of fact, PilotID is a sound Primary Key because it does conform to all the points on the checklist. But what happens when you don't have a field that can act as a Primary Key? Take the Employees table in Figure 2-13 on the next page, for example. Is there a field in this table that can act as a Primary Key?

It's very clear that this table doesn't contain a field (or group of fields) that can be used as a Primary Key. With the exception of EmpPhone, every field contains duplicate values. EmpZip, EmpAreaCode, and EmpPhone all contain unknown values. Because the value of every field in this table is subject to arbitrary change, it's evident that there is no field you can use as the Primary Key for this table. What do you do now? You create an Artificial Primary Key.

Employees

EmpFirstName	EmpLastName	EmpCity	EmpState	EmpZip	EmpAreaCode	EmpPhone	HireDate
Peacock	Samuel	Chico	CA	95926			1998-12-31
Kennedy	John	Portland	OR	97208	503	555-2621	1998-05-01
Thompson	Michael	Redmond	WA	98052	425	555-2626	1998-09-11
Callahan	David	Salem	OR				1998-12-27
Buchanan	Andrea	Medford	OR	97501	541	555-2641	1998-05-01
Smith	Michael	Fremont	CA	94538	510	555-2646	1998-09-11
Peacock	Neil	San Diego	CA	92199	619	555-2541	1998-05-01
Kennedy	John	Redmond	WA	98052	425	555-2511	1998-09-11

Figure 2-13 *Does this table have a Primary Key?*

This is an arbitrary field you define and add to the table for the sole purpose of using it as the table's Primary Key. The advantage of adding this arbitrary field is that you can ensure that it conforms to all the points on the checklist. Once you've added the field to the table, designate it as the Primary Key, and you're done! That's all there is to it. Figure 2-14 shows the Employees table with a new Artificial Primary Key called EmployeeID.

Employees

EmployeeID	EmpFirstName	EmpLastName	EmpCity	EmpState	EmpZip	*<<otherfields>>*
98001	Peacock	Samuel	Chico	CA	95926	...
98002	Kennedy	John	Portland	OR	97208	...
98003	Thompson	Michael	Redmond	WA	98052	...
98004	Callahan	David	Salem	OR		...
98005	Buchanan	Andrea	Medford	OR	97501	...
98006	Smith	Michael	Fremont	CA	94538	...
98007	Peacock	Neil	SanDiego	CA	92199	...
98008	Kennedy	John	Redmond	WA	98052	...

Figure 2-14 *The Employees table with the new Artificial Primary Key.*

At this point, you've done everything you can to strengthen and fine-tune your table structures. Now we'll take a look at how you can ensure that all your table relationships are sound.

Establishing Solid Relationships

In Chapter 1, you learned that a relationship exists between a pair of tables if records in the first table are in some way associated with records in the second table. You also learned that the relationship itself can be designated as one of three types: One-to-One, One-to-Many, and Many-to-Many. You also learned that each type of relationship is established in a specific manner. Let's review this for a moment.

- You establish a **One-to-One** relationship by taking the Primary Key from the "primary" table and inserting it into the "subordinate" table, where it becomes a Foreign Key. This is a special type of relationship because in many cases the Foreign Key will also act as the Primary Key of the "subordinate" table. You diagram this relationship as shown in Figure 2-15.

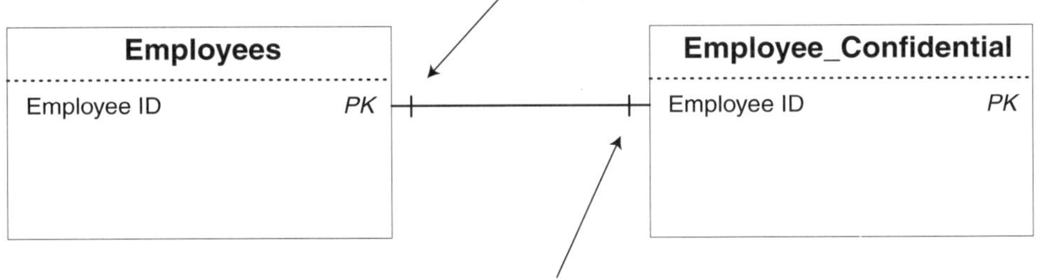

Figure 2-15 *Diagramming a One-to-One relationship.*

- You establish a **One-to-Many** relationship by taking the Primary Key of the table on the "One" side and inserting it into the table on the "Many" side, where it becomes a Foreign Key. Figure 2-16 on the next page shows how you diagram this type of relationship.

> ❖ **Note** The diagram symbols shown in this section are part of the diagramming method presented in Mike Hernandez's book *Database Design for Mere Mortals.*

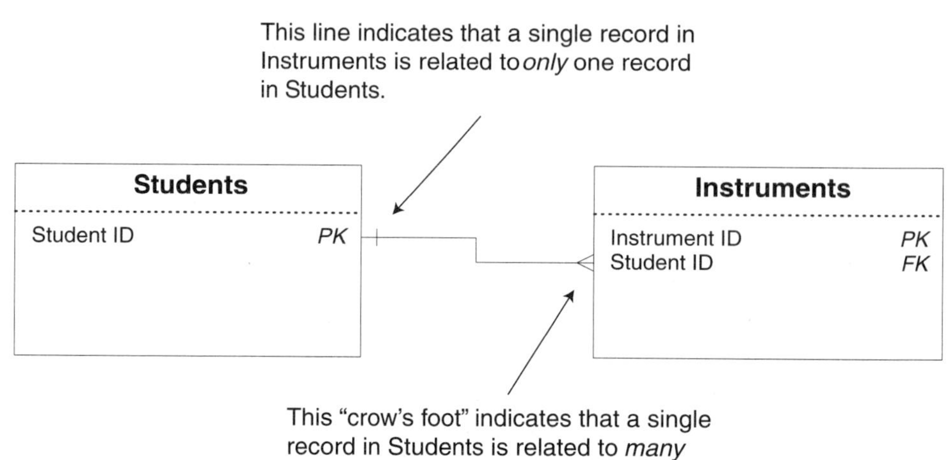

Figure 2-16 *Diagramming a One-to-Many relationship.*

- You establish a **Many-to-Many** relationship by creating a linking table. Define the linking table by taking a copy of the Primary Key of each table in the relationship and using them to form the structure of the new table. These fields commonly serve two distinct roles: together, they form the Composite Primary Key of the linking table; separately, they each serve as a Foreign Key. Diagram this relationship as shown in Figure 2-17.

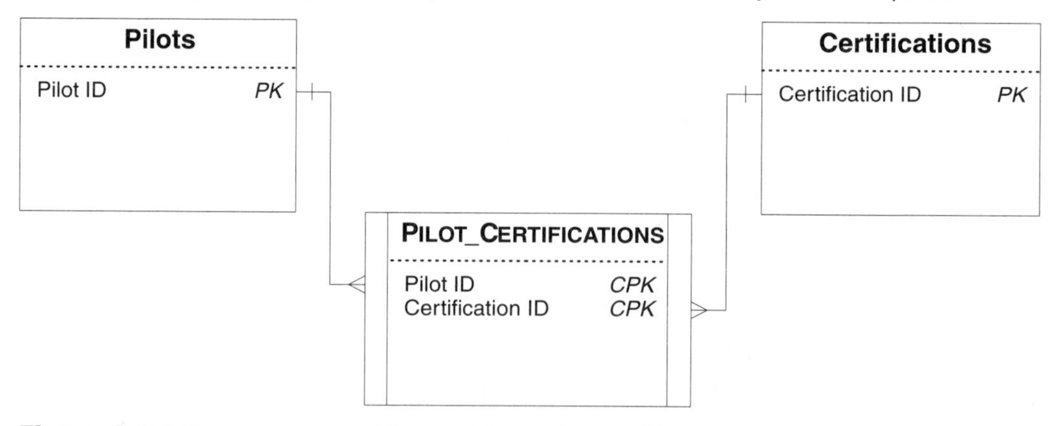

Figure 2-17 *Diagramming a Many-to-Many relationship.*

In order to make certain that the relationships among the tables in your database are really solid, you must establish relationship characteristics for each relationship. The characteristics you're about to define indicate what will occur when you delete a record, the type of participation a table has within the relationship, and to what degree each table participates within the relationship.

Before our discussion on relationship characteristics begins, we must make one point perfectly clear: We present the following characteristics within a generic and logical frame of reference. These characteristics are important because they allow you to enforce relationship integrity. However, the manner in which you implement them will vary from one database software program to another. You will have to study your database software's documentation to determine whether these characteristics are supported and, if so, how you can implement them.

Establishing a Deletion Rule

A *Deletion Rule* dictates what happens when a user makes a request to delete a record in the "primary" table of a One-to-One relationship or in the table on the "One" side of a One-to-Many relationship. You can guard against "orphaned" records by establishing this rule. (Orphaned records are those records in the "subordinate" table of a One-to-One relationship that don't have related records in the "primary" table, or records in the table on the "Many" side of a One-to-Many relationship that don't have related records in the table on the "One" side.)

You can set two types of Deletion Rules for a relationship: *Restrict* and *Cascade*.

- The **Restrict Deletion Rule** does not allow you to delete the requested record when there are related records in the "subordinate" table of a One-to-One relationship or in the table on the "Many" side of a One-to-Many relationship. You must delete any related records *prior* to deleting the requested record. You'll use this type of Deletion Rule as a matter of course.
- When the **Cascade Deletion Rule** is in force, you can delete the requested record as well as any related records in the "subordinate" table of a One-to-One relationship or in the table on the "Many" side of a One-

to-Many relationship. Use this rule very judiciously or you may wind up deleting records you really wanted to keep!

Regardless of the type of Deletion Rule you use, always examine your relationship very carefully in order to determine which type of rule is appropriate. You can use a very simple question to help you decide which type of rule to use. First, select a pair of tables and then ask yourself the following question: "If a record in [name of "primary" or "One" side table] is deleted, should related records in [name of "subordinate" or "Many" side table] be deleted as well?"

This question is framed in a generic sense so that you can understand the premise behind it. To apply this question in a real sense, substitute the phrases that are within the square brackets with table names. Your question will look something like this: "If a record in the Committees table is deleted, should related records in the Committee_Members table be deleted as well?"

Use a Restrict Deletion Rule if the answer to this question is "No"; otherwise, use the Cascade Deletion Rule. In the end, the answer to this question greatly depends on how you use the data stored within the database. This is why you must study the relationship carefully and make certain you choose the right rule. Figure 2-18 shows how you diagram the Deletion Rule for this relationship. Note that you'll use (R) for a Restricted Deletion Rule and (C) for a Cascade Deletion Rule.

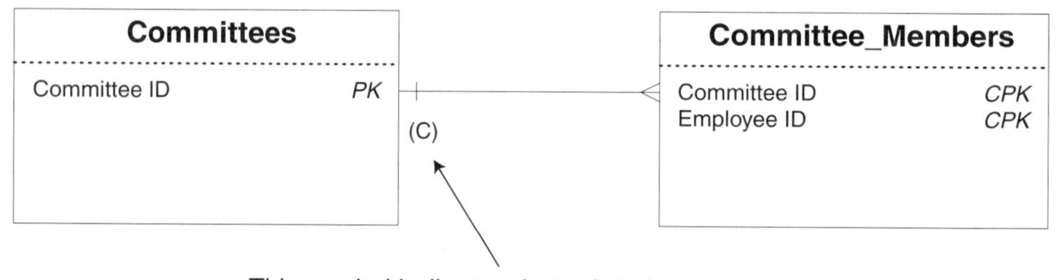

Figure 2-18 *Diagramming the Deletion Rule for the Committees and Committee_Members tables.*

Setting the Type of Participation

When you establish a relationship between a pair of tables, each table participates in a particular manner. The *Type of Participation* assigned to a given table determines whether a record must exist in that table before you can enter a record into the other table. There are two types of participation.

- **Mandatory**—At least one record must exist in this table before you can enter any records into the other table.
- **Optional**—There is no requirement for any records to exist in this table before you enter any records in the other table.

The Type of Participation you select for a pair of tables depends mostly on the business logic of your organization. For example, let's assume you work for a large company consisting of several departments. Let's also assume that you have an Employees table, a Departments table, and a Department_Employees table in the database you've created for your company. All relevant information about an employee is in the Employees table and all relevant information about a department is in the Departments table. The Department_Employees table is a linking table that allows you to associate any number of departments with a given employee. These tables are shown in Figure 2-19 on page 46.

In the last staff meeting, you were told to assign some of the staff to a new Research & Development department. Now here's the problem: You want to make certain you add the new department to the Departments table so that you can assign staff to that department in the Department_Employees table. This is where the Type of Participation characteristic comes into play. Set the Type of Participation for the Departments table to Mandatory and the Type of Participation for the Department_Employees table to Optional. By establishing these settings, you ensure that a department must exist in the Departments table before you can assign any employees to that department in the Department_Employees table.

As with the Deletion Rule, study each relationship carefully to determine the appropriate Type of Participation setting for each table in the relationship. You diagram the Type of Participation as shown in Figure 2-20 on page 47.

Setting the Degree of Participation

Now that you've determined *how* each table will participate in the relationship, you must figure out *to what degree* each will participate. You do this by

Employees

EmployeeID	EmpFirstName	EmpLastName	EmpCity	<<other fields>>
7004	Peacock	Samuel	Chico	...
7005	Kennedy	John	Portland	...
7006	Thompson	Sarah	Lubbock	...
7007	Callahan	David	Salem	...
7008	Buchanan	Andrea	Medford	...
7009	Smith	David	Fremont	...
7010	Patterson	Neil	San Diego	...
7011	Viescas	Michael	Redmond	...

Department_Employees

EmployeeID	DepartmentID	Position
7004	1000	Head
7005	1000	Floater
7005	1001	Floater
7007	1001	Staff
7008	1001	Head
7009	1003	Floater
7010	1002	Head
7011	1004	Head

Departments

DepartmentID	DepartmentName	Floor
1000	Accounting	5
1001	Administration	5
1002	HumanResources	7
1003	InformationServices	6
1004	Legal	7

Figure 2-19 *The Employees, Departments, and Department_Employees tables.*

determining the minimum and maximum number of records in one table that can be related to a single record in the other table. This process is known as identifying a table's *Degree of Participation*. The Degree of Participation for a given table is represented by two numbers that are separated with a comma and enclosed within parentheses. The first number indicates the minimum possible number of related records and the second number indicates the maximum possible number of related records. For example, a Degree of Participation such as "(1,12)" indicates that the minimum number of records that can be related is one and the maximum is twelve.

The Degree of Participation you select for various tables in your database largely depends on how your organization views and uses the data. Let's say

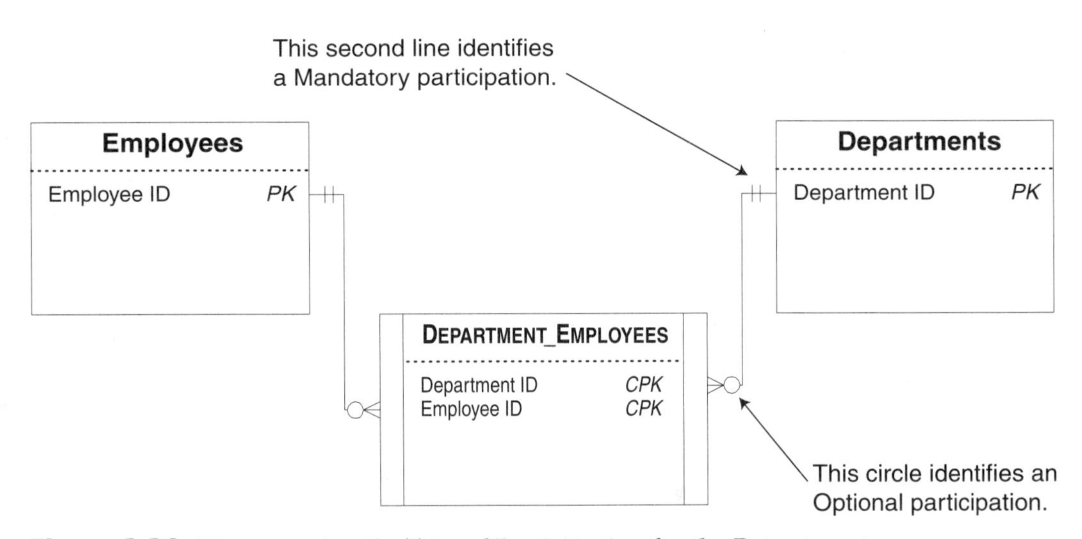

Figure 2-20 *Diagramming the Type of Participation for the Departments and Department_Employees tables.*

you're a booking agent for a talent agency and that two of the tables in your database are Agents and Entertainers. Let's further assume that there is a One-to-Many relationship between these tables—one record in the Agents table can be related to many records in the Entertainers table, but a single record in the Entertainers table can be related to only one record in the Agents table. In this case, we've ensured (in a general sense) that an entertainer is assigned to only one agent. (We definitely avoid the possibility of the entertainer playing one agent against another. This is a good thing.)

As it turns out, the boss wants to ensure that all his agents have a fair shake at making good commissions and wants to keep the in-fighting between agents down to a bare minimum. So he sets a new policy stating that a single agent can represent a maximum of six entertainers. (Although he thinks it may not work in the long run, he wants to try it anyway.) In order to implement his new policy, he sets the Degree of Participation for both tables to the following:

Agents	(1,1)—An entertainer can be associated with one and only one agent.
Entertainers	(0,6)—While an agent doesn't have to be associated with an entertainer at all, he or she cannot be associated with more than six entertainers at any given time.

Figure 2-21 shows how you diagram the Degree of Participation for these tables.

As with the other relationship characteristics, study each relationship carefully so that you can identify the proper Degree of Participation for each table. Let's assume you've set all the relationship characteristics for the Agents and Entertainers tables. Figure 2-22 shows how to add the Degree of Participation to your relationship diagram and how the diagram will look once it's complete. You can now use this diagram to identify the Type of Relationship, the Deletion Rule for the relationship, the Type of Participation for each table, and the Degree of Participation for each table.

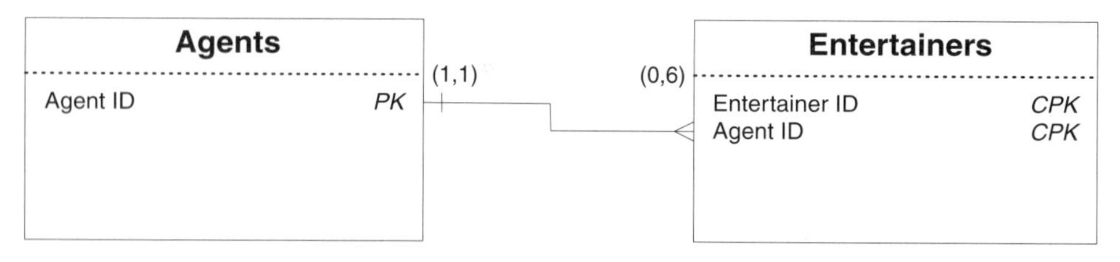

Figure 2-21 *Diagramming the Degree of Participation for the Agents and Entertainers tables.*

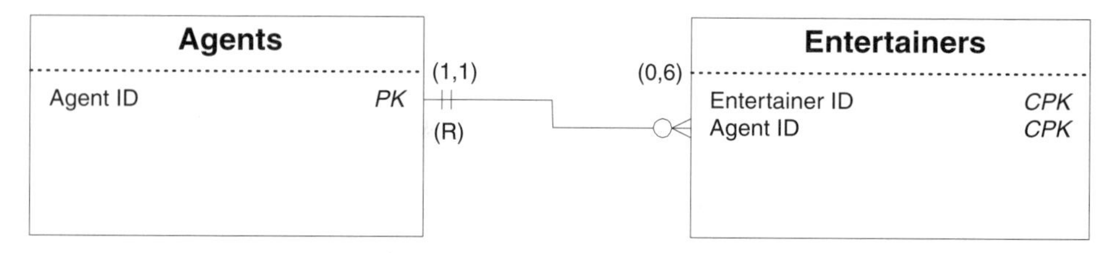

Figure 2-22 *Diagram of all relationship characteristics for the Agents and Entertainers tables.*

Is That All?

By using the techniques you learned in this chapter, you make the necessary beginning steps toward ensuring a fundamental level of data integrity in your database. The next step is to begin studying the manner in which your organization views and uses its data so that you can establish and impose Business Rules for your database. But to really get the most from your database, you should go back to the beginning and run it through a thorough database design process using a good design methodology. Unfortunately, these topics are beyond the scope of this book. However, you can learn a good design methodology from books such as *Database Design for Mere Mortals* by Michael J. Hernandez or *Handbook of Relational Database Design* by Barbara Von Halle and Candace C. Fleming. The point to remember is this: The more solid your database structure, the easier it will be both to extract information from the data in the database and to build applications programs for it.

SUMMARY

We opened this chapter with a short discussion on why you should be concerned with having sound structures in your database. You learned that poorly designed tables can cause numerous problems, not the least of which concern data integrity.

Next we discussed fine-tuning the fields in each table. You learned that giving your fields good names is very important because it ensures that each name is meaningful and actually helps you to find hidden problems with the field structure itself. You now know how to fine-tune your field structures by ensuring they conform to a few simple rules. These rules deal with issues such as guaranteeing that each field represents a single characteristic of the table's subject, contains only a single value, and never stores a calculation. We also discussed the problems found in multipart and multivalued fields, and you learned how to resolve them properly.

Fine-tuning the tables was the next issue we addressed. You learned that the table names are just as important an issue as field names for many of the same reasons. You now know how to give your tables meaningful names and ensure that each table represents only a single subject. We then discussed a set of rules you can use to make certain each table structure is sound. Although some of the rules seemed to duplicate some of the efforts you made in fine-tuning your field structures, you learned that the rules used for fine-tuning the table structures actually add an extra level of insurance in making sure that the table structures are as absolutely sound as they can be.

The next subject we tackled was Primary Keys. You learned the importance of establishing a Primary Key for each table in your database. You now know that a Primary Key must conform to a specific set of characteristics and that the field that will act as the Primary Key of a table must be chosen very carefully. You also learned that you can create an Artificial Primary Key if there is no field in the table that conforms to the complete set of characteristics for a Primary Key.

We closed this chapter with a discussion on establishing solid relationships. The three types of relationships were reviewed and you learned how to diagram each one. You then learned how to establish and diagram a Deletion Rule for the relationship. This rule is important because it helps you guard against "orphaned" records. The last two topics we discussed were the Type of Participation and Degree of Participation for each table within the relationship. You learned that a table's participation can be mandatory or optional and that you can set a specific range for the number of related records between each table.

In the next chapter, you'll learn a little bit about the history of SQL and how it evolved into its current version, SQL-92.

3

A Concise History of SQL

"There is only one religion, though there are many versions of it."
—George Bernard Shaw
Plays Pleasant and Unpleasant

Topics Covered in This Chapter

The Origins of SQL

Early Vendor Implementations

"... And Then There Was a Standard"

Evolution of the ANSI/ISO Standard

What the Future Holds

Why Should You Learn SQL?

Summary

The telling of history always involves vague and ambiguous accounts of various incidents, political intrigue, and human foibles. The history of SQL is no different than that of any other subject in this sense. SQL has been around in one form or another since just after the dawn of the Relational Model, and there are several detailed accounts of its long and spotty existence. In this chapter, however, we take a close look at the origin, evolution, and future of this database language. We have two goals: first, to give you an idea of how SQL matured into the language used by a majority of Relational database systems today and second, to give you a sense of why it is important for you to learn how to use SQL.

The Origins of SQL

As you learned in Chapter 1, Dr. E. F. Codd presented the Relational Database Model to the world in 1970. Soon after this landmark moment, organizations such as universities and research laboratories began efforts to develop a language that could be used as the foundation to a database system that supported the Relational Model. Initial work led to the development of several languages in the mid to early 1970s, and later efforts resulted in the development of SQL and the SQL-based databases in use today. But just where did SQL originate? How did it evolve? What is its future? For the answers to these questions, we must begin our story at IBM's Santa Teresa Research Laboratory in San Jose, California.

IBM began a major research project in the early 1970s called System/R. The goals of this project were to prove the viability of the Relational Model and to gain some experience in designing and implementing a Relational database. The researchers' initial endeavors between 1974 and 1975 proved successful, and they managed to produce a minimal prototype of a Relational database.

In addition to their efforts to develop a working Relational database, researchers were also working to define a database language. The work performed at this laboratory is arguably the most commercially significant of the initial efforts to define such a language. In 1974, Dr. Donald Chamberlin and his colleagues developed Structured English Query Language (SEQUEL). The language allowed users to query a Relational database using clearly defined English-style sentences. Dr. Chamberlin and his staff first implemented this new language in a prototype database called SEQUEL-XRM.

The initial feedback and success of SEQUEL-XRM encouraged Dr. Chamberlin and his staff to continue their research. They completely revised SEQUEL between 1976 and 1977 and named the new version SEQUEL/2. However, they subsequently had to change the name SEQUEL to SQL (Structured Query Language) for legal reasons—someone else had already used the acronym SEQUEL. To this day, many people still pronounce SQL as *sequel*, although the widely accepted "official" pronunciation is *es-cue-el*. SQL provided several new features, such as support for multitable queries and shared data access by multiple users.

Soon after the emergence of SQL, IBM began a new and more ambitious project aimed at producing a prototype database that would further substantiate the feasibility of the Relational Model. They called the new prototype "System R" and based it on a large subset of SQL. After much of the initial development work was completed, IBM installed System R in a number of internal sites and selected client sites for testing and evaluation. Many changes were made to System R and SQL based on the experiences and feedback of users at these sites. IBM closed the project in 1979 and concluded that the Relational Model was indeed a viable database technology with commercial potential.

❖ **Note** One of the more important successes attributed to this projct is the development of SQL. But SQL's roots are actually based in research language called SQUARE (Specifying Queries As Relational Expressions). This language was developed in 1975 (predating the System R project) and was designed to implement Relational Algebra with English-style sentences.

Early Vendor Implementations

The work done at the IBM research lab during the 1970s was followed with great interest in various technical journals, and the merits of the new Relational Model were briskly debated at database technology seminars. Toward the latter part of the decade, it became clear that IBM was keenly interested in and committed to developing products based on Relational database technology and SQL. This, of course, led many vendors to speculate how soon IBM would roll out its first product. Some vendors had the good sense to start work on their own products as quickly as possible and not wait around for IBM to lead the market.

In 1977, Relational Software, Inc. was formed by a group of engineers in Menlo Park, California, for the purpose of building a new Relational database product based on SQL. They called their product Oracle. Relational Software shipped its product in 1979, beating IBM's first product to market by two years and providing the first commercially available Relational Database Management System (RDBMS). One of Oracle's advantages was that it ran on Digital's VAX minicomputers instead of the more expensive IBM mainframes. Relational Software, Inc. has since been renamed to Oracle Corporation and is one of the leading vendors of RDBMS software.

Meanwhile, Michael Stonebraker, Eugene Wong, and several other professors at the University of California's Berkeley computer laboratories were also researching Relational database technology. Like the IBM team, they developed a prototype relational database and dubbed their product INGRES. INGRES included a database language called Query Language (QUEL) which, in comparison to SQL, was much more structured but made less use of English-like statements. INGRES was eventually converted to an SQL-based RDBMS when it became clear that SQL was emerging as the standard database language. Several professors left Berkeley in 1980 to form Relational Technology, Inc., and in 1981 they announced the first commercial version of INGRES. Relational Technology has gone through several transformations and is now part of Computer Associates International, Inc. INGRES is still one of the leading database products in the industry today.

Now we come full circle back to IBM. IBM announced its own RDBMS called SQL/Data System (SQL/DS) in 1981 and began shipping it in 1982. In 1983, they introduced a new version of SQL/DS for the VM/CMS operating system (one of several offered by IBM for their mainframe systems) and announced a new RDBMS product called Database 2 (DB2), which could be used on IBM mainframes using IBM's mainstream MVS operating system. First shipped in 1985, DB2 has become IBM's premiere RDBMS, and its technology has been incorporated into the entire IBM product line. By the way, IBM hasn't changed—it's still IBM.

During the course of more than 25 years, we've seen what began as research for the System R project become a force that impacts almost every level of business today and evolve into a multibillion dollar industry.

"...And Then There Was a Standard"

With the flurry of activity surrounding the development of database languages, you could easily wonder if anyone ever thought of standardization. While the idea was tossed about among the database community, there was never any consensus or agreement as to who should set the standard or which dialect it should be based upon. So each vendor continued to develop and improve its own database product in the hope that it—and by extension, its dialect of SQL—would become the industry standard.

Customer feedback and demand drove many vendors to include certain elements in their SQL dialect, and in time an unofficial standard emerged. It was a small specification by today's standards, as it encompassed only those elements that were similar across the various SQL dialects. However, this specification (such as it was) did provide database customers with a core set of criteria by which to judge the various database programs on the market, and it also gave users a small set of knowledge that they could leverage from one database program to another.

In 1982, American National Standards Institute (ANSI) responded to the growing need for an official Relational database language standard by commissioning its X3 organization's database technical committee, X3H2, to develop a proposal for such a standard. (X3 is one of many organizations overseen by ANSI.) In turn, X3H2 Database (X3H2) is just one of many technical committees that report to X3. X3H2 was and continues to be composed of database industry experts and representatives from almost every major SQL-based database vendor. In the beginning, the committee reviewed and debated the advantages and disadvantages of various proposed languages and also began work on a standard based on QUEL, the database language for INGRES. But market forces and the increasing commitment to SQL by IBM induced the committee to base their proposal on SQL instead.

The X3H2 committee's proposed standard was largely based on IBM's DB2 SQL dialect. The committee worked on several versions of its standard over the next two years and even improved SQL to some extent. However, an unfortunate circumstance arose as a result of these improvements: This new standard became incompatible with existing major SQL dialects. X3H2 soon realized that the changes made to SQL did not significantly improve it enough to warrant the incompatibilities, so the committee reverted to the original version of the standard.

ANSI ratified X3H2's standard in 1986 as "ANSI X3.135-1986 Database Language SQL," which became commonly known as "SQL/86." Although X3H2 made some minor revisions to its standard before it was adopted by ANSI, SQL/86 merely defined a minimal set of "least common denominator" requirements to which database vendors could conform. In essence, it conferred "official" status to the elements that were similar among the various SQL dialects and which had already been implemented by many database vendors. But the new standard finally provided a specific foundation from which the language and its implementations could be developed further.

The International Organization for Standardization (ISO) approved its own document (which corresponded exactly with ANSI SQL/86) as an international standard in 1987 and published it as "ISO 9075-1987 Database Language SQL." (Both standards are still often referred to as just SQL/86.) The international database vendor community could now work from the same standards as those vendors in the United States. Despite the fact that SQL gained the status of an official standard, the language was far from being complete.

Evolution of the ANSI/ISO Standard

SQL/86 was soon criticized in public reviews, by the government, and by industry pundits such as C. J. Date. Some of the problems cited by these critics included redundancy within the SQL syntax (there were several ways to define the same query), lack of support for certain relational operators, and lack of referential integrity. Although X3H2 knew of these problems even before SQL/86 was published, they decided that it was better to release a standard now (even though it still needed work) than to have no standard at all.

Both ISO and ANSI addressed the criticism pertaining to referential integrity by adopting refined versions of their standards. ISO published "ISO 9075:1989 Database Language SQL With Integrity Enhancements" in mid-1989, while ANSI adopted its "X3.135-1989 Database Language SQL With Integrity Enhancements," also often referred to as SQL/89, late that same year. But the ANSI committee's work for the year wasn't over just yet; X3H2 was still trying to address an important issue brought forth by the government.

Some government users complained that the specification explaining how to embed SQL within a conventional programming language was not an explicit component of the standard. (While the specification was included, it was relegated to an appendix.) Their concern was that vendors might not support portable implementations of embedded SQL because there was no specific requirement within the standard for them to do so. X3H2 responded by developing a second standard that required conformance to the embedding specification, and published it as "ANSI X3.168-1989 Database Language Embedded SQL." It's interesting to note that ISO chose not to publish a corresponding standard because of a lack of similar concern within the international community. This meant that ISO had no specification for embedding SQL within a programming language, a situation that would not change until ISO's publication of its SQL/92 standard.

SQL/86 and SQL/89 were far from being complete standards—they lacked some of the most fundamental features needed for commercial database systems. For example, neither standard specified a way to make changes to the database structure (including within the database system itself) once it was defined. No one could modify or delete any structural components (such as tables or columns) or make any changes to the security of the database. For example, you could CREATE a table, but the standard included no definition of the DROP command to delete a table or the ALTER command to change it. Also, you could GRANT security access to a table, but the standard did not define the REVOKE command to allow removal of access authority. Ironically, these capabilities were provided by all commercial SQL-based databases. They were not included in either standard, however, because each vendor implemented them in different ways. Other features were widely implemented among many SQL-based databases but omitted from the standards. Once again, it was an issue of varied implementations.

By the time SQL/89 was completed, both ANSI and ISO were already working on major revisions to SQL that would make it a complete and robust language. The new version would be referred to as SQL/92 (what else?) and would include features that had already been widely implemented by most major database vendors. But one of the main objectives of both ANSI and ISO was to avoid defining a "least common denominator" standard yet again. As a result, they decided to both include features that had not yet gained wide acceptance and add new features that were substantially beyond those currently implemented.

ANSI and ISO published their new SQL standards—"X3.135-1992 Database Language SQL" and "ISO/IEC 9075:1992 Database Language SQL," respectively—in October of 1992. (Work on these documents was completed in late 1991, but some final fine-tuning took place during the beginning of 1992.) The SQL/92 document is considerably larger than the one for SQL/89, but it's also much broader in scope. For example, it provides the means to modify the database structure after it has been defined, supports additional operations for manipulating character strings and dates and times, and defines additional security features. SQL/92 marks a major step forward from any of its predecessors.

Ironically, currently no database product fully supports and implements all of SQL/92. This is largely due to the complexity of many features in the new standard. But it would be unreasonable for us to think that vendors should be able to incorporate these features within one or two versions of their products. In addition to the fact that many of the complex features will take some time and effort to implement, database vendors have other pressing market-driven issues to address regarding their products, such as increasing performance, enhancing reliability, and providing enhanced system integration. This is not so much an excuse as it is an explanation of the way things work in the database industry.

Fortunately the standards committees anticipated this situation to some extent. In order to facilitate a smooth and gradual conformance to the new standard, ANSI and ISO defined SQL/92 on three levels.

ENTRY SQL	Similar to SQL/89, this level also includes features to make the transition from SQL/89 to SQL/92 easier as well as features that corrected errors in the SQL/89 standard. The idea was that this level would be the easiest to implement because most of its features had already been widely incorporated into existing products.
INTERMEDIATE SQL	This level encompasses most of the features in the new standard. Both committees' decisions to include certain features at this level were based upon several factors. The overall objectives were to enhance the standard so that SQL better supported the concepts in the Relational Model and to redefine syntax that was ambiguous or unclear. It was an easy decision to include features that were already implemented in some way by one or more vendors and that met these objectives. Features demanded by users of SQL database systems were given high consideration as long as they met these objectives and were relatively easy to implement by most vendors. This level was meant to ensure that it would be reasonably possible for a given product to have as robust an implementation as possible. As of this writing, this is still the level that most database vendors try to implement within their products.
FULL SQL	The entire SQL/92 specification is encompassed within this level. It obviously includes the more complex features that were omitted in the first two levels. This level includes features that, although considered important to meet customer demands or further "purify" the language, would be difficult to implement immediately by most vendors. Unfortunately, compliance with Full SQL is not yet a requirement, so it will be some time before we can expect database products to fully implement the standard.

Although many database vendors continue work on implementing the features in SQL/92, they also develop and implement features of their own. The additions they make to the SQL standard are known as *extensions*. For example, a vendor may provide more data types than the six specified in SQL/92. Although these extensions provide more functionality within a given product and allow vendors to differentiate themselves from one another, there are drawbacks. The main problem with adding extensions is that it causes each vendor's dialect of SQL to diverge further from the original standard. This, in turn, prevents database developers from creating portable applications that can be run from any SQL database. Perhaps this situation will change once the next version of the standard is released.

Other SQL Standards

The ANSI/ISO SQL/92 standard is the most widely accepted standard to date. This means, of course, that there are other standards in existence that incorporate SQL in one form or another. These are some of the more significant alternate standards.

X/OPEN — A group of European vendors (collectively known as X/OPEN) developed a set of standards that would help establish a portable application environment based on UNIX. The ability to "port" an application from one computer system to another without changing it is an important issue in the European market. Although they have adopted SQL as part of this set of standards, their version deviates from the ANSI/ISO standard in several areas.

SAA — IBM has always developed its own dialect of SQL, which they incorporated into their Systems Application Architecture (SAA) specification. Integrating IBM's SQL dialect into the complete line of IBM database products was one of the goals of the SAA specification. Although this goal has never been achieved, SQL still plays an important role in unifying IBM's database products.

FIPS — The National Institute of Standards and Technology (NIST) made SQL a Federal Information Processing Standard (FIPS) beginning in 1987. Originally published as "FIPS PUB 127," it specifies the level to which an RDBMS must conform to the ANSI/ISO standard. Since then, all Relational database products used by the U.S. Government have been required to conform to the current FIPS publication.

ODBC — In 1989 a group of database vendors formed the SQL Access Group to address the problem of database interoperability. Although their first efforts were somewhat unsuccessful, they widened their focus to include a way to bind an SQL database to a user-interface language. The result of their efforts was the Call-Level Interface specification (CLI) published in 1992. That same year, Microsoft published its Open Database Connectivity (ODBC) specification, which was based on the CLI standard. ODBC has since become the *de facto* means of accessing and sharing data among SQL databases that support it.

These standards continually evolve as newer versions of ANSI/ISO SQL are adopted, and they are sometimes independently developed as well.

Commercial Implementations

As you read earlier in this chapter, SQL first appeared in the mainframe environment. Products such as DB/2, INGRES, and Oracle have been around since 1979 and have legitimized the use of SQL as the preferred method of working with Relational databases. During the 1980s, Relational databases and SQL hit the desktop on personal computers, and products such as R:BASE, dBase IV, and Super Base put the power of SQL at the user's fingertips. The early 1990s heralded the advent of client/server computing, and RDBMS programs such as Microsoft SQL Server and Informix-SE have been designed to provide database services to users in numerous types of multiuser environments. Now, at the dawn of the new millennium, there is a concerted effort to make database information available via the Internet. Businesses are catching on to the idea of e-commerce, and many are moving quickly to establish a presence on the Web. As a result, database developers are demanding more powerful client/server databases and newer versions of long established mainframe RDBMS products that they can use to develop and maintain the databases needed for their Web sites.

What the Future Holds

Just before SQL/92 was published, the ANSI X3H2 committee was already embarking on yet another major revision of the standard. (Sounds exactly like the scenario that occurred when SQL/89 was released, doesn't it?) X3H2 departed from its traditional naming standard and dubbed its new specification

SQL3. One of the committee's major goals for the new version was support for a combination of both the Relational Model and the Object Model. This combination has been alternately referred to as the *Extended Relational Model* and the *Object-Relational Model*. The committee is also working on adding support for On-Line Analytical Processing (OLAP). However, the overall focus of the committee has been to greatly enhance the existing SQL/92 standard and to add support for features found in most object-relational database environments.

The work done on SQL3 so far is the result of an ambitious undertaking, to say the least. Not only have the goals mentioned previously been pursued, but the Standard has been divided into a number of parts. Several of these parts have been divided or consolidated at one point or another, and you sometimes need a good scorecard to keep track of what is or isn't in the new Standard.

Table 3.1 on the next two pages shows the name and description of each part of SQL3, as well as the status of each part at the time of this writing.

In 1997, ANSI's X3 organization was renamed National Committee for Information Technology Standards (NCITS), and the technical committee in charge of the SQL3 standard is now called ANSI NCITS-H2. Given the vast number of Relational database systems that exist in the world today, NCITS-H2 will continue work on SQL well into the foreseeable future. In fact, work on the next version has already begun.

Why Should You Learn SQL?

Learning SQL gives you the skills you need to retrieve information from any Relational database. It also helps you understand the mechanisms behind the graphical query interfaces found in many RDBMS products. Understanding SQL helps you craft complex queries and provides the knowledge required to troubleshoot queries when problems occur.

Because SQL is found in a wide variety of RDBMS products, you can utilize your skills across a variety of platforms. For example, once you learn SQL in Microsoft Access 2000, you can leverage your existing knowledge if your company decides to move to Sybase SQL Server. You won't have to relearn SQL—you'll just have to learn the differences between the Microsoft Access 2000 dialect and the Sybase SQL Server dialect. The same procedure applies if your company suddenly decides to move from Sybase SQL Server to IBM's DB/2.

Table 3.1 *Current structure of SQL3.*

Name	Status	Description
Part 1: SQL/Framework	Completed in 1999	Describes each part of the standard and contains information that is common to all parts.
Part 2: SQL/Foundation	Completed in 1999	Defines the syntax and semantics of the data definition and data manipulation portions of the SQL language.
SQL/OLAP (Online Analytical Processing)	In Process	Describes the functions and operations used for analytical processing. (This is intended as an amendment to SQL/Foundation.)
Part 3: SQL/CLI (Call-Level Interface)	Completed in 1999	Developed by the SQL Access group, this part corresponds to Microsoft's ODBC specification.
Part 4: SQL/PSM (Persistent Stored Modules)	Completed in 1999	Defines procedural language SQL statements that are useful in user-defined functions and procedures. (Support for stored procedures, stored functions, the Call statement, and routine invocation was eventually moved to SQL/Foundation.)
Part 5: SQL/Bindings	Completed in 1999	Specifies how SQL is embedded in non-object programming languages. This part will be merged into SQL/Foundation in the next version of SQL.
Part 6: Transaction (XA Specialization)	N/A	SQL specialization of the X-Open XA specification. This part was canceled.
Part 7: SQL/Temporal	On Hold	Defines support for storage and retrieval of temporal data. There has been some difference of opinion on the requirements and details of Temporal, so work has stalled over the last several years.
Part 8: SQL/Objects—Extended Objects	N/A	Defines how application-defined abstract data types are handled by the RDBMS. This part was merged back into SQL/Foundation, so it no longer exists.
Part 9: SQL/MED Management of External Data	In Process	Defines additional syntax and definitions to SQL/Foundation that allow SQL to access non-SQL data sources (files).
Part 10: SQL/OLB Object Language Bindings	Completed in 1998 (ANSI-only standard)	Specifies the syntax and semantics of embedding SQL in the Java programming language. This corresponds to another ANSI standard, SQLJ Part 0.

Table 3.1 *Continued*

Name	Status	Description
Part 11: SQL/Schemata	N/A	Information and Definition Schemas. This is currently part of SQL/Foundation but will be split into its own part in the next version of SQL.
SQL Routines using the Java™ Programming Language	Completed in 1999 (ANSI-only standard based on SQL/92)	Defines how Java code can be used within an SQL database.
Part 12: SQL/Replication	Work begins in 2000	Defines support and facilities for replicating a SQL database.

SQL is here to stay. Many vendors have invested huge amounts of money, time, and research in incorporating SQL into their RDBMS products, and a vast number of businesses and organizations have built much of their information technology infrastructures on those products. As you have probably surmised by what you've learned in this chapter, SQL will continue to evolve to meet the changing demands and requirements of the marketplace.

SUMMARY

We began this chapter with a discussion on the origins of SQL. You learned that SQL is a Relational database language that was created soon after the introduction of the Relational Model. We also explained that the early evolution of SQL was closely tied to the evolution of the Relational Model itself.

Next, we discussed the initial implementations of the Relational Model by various database vendors. You learned that the first Relational databases were implemented on mainframe computers. You also learned how IBM and Oracle came to be big players in the database industry.

We then discussed the origin of the ANSI SQL standard. You learned that there was an unofficial standard before ANSI decided to define an official one, and we discussed the ANSI X3H2 committee's initial work on the specification.

We explained that although the new standard was basically a set of "least common denominator" features, it did provide a foundation from which the language could be further developed. You also learned that the ISO published its own standard, which corresponded exactly with the ANSI specification.

The evolution of the ANSI/ISO standard was the next topic of discussion, and you learned that various people and organizations criticized the initial standards. We then discussed how ANSI/ISO responded to the criticisms by adopting several revisions to the standard. You learned how one version led to the next and how we arrived at the SQL/92 standard. We explained how the standard defines various conformance levels that allow vendors to implement the standard's features into their products as smoothly as possible. Next, we briefly discussed other standards that incorporate SQL in one form or another, and we took a quick look at the evolution of commercial SQL databases.

We closed the chapter with a short discussion on the future of SQL. You learned that SQL3 is a work in progress and that it will be a much more complex standard than SQL/92. We also explained why SQL will continue to be developed and gave you some good reasons for learning the language.

Part II

SQL Basics

4

Creating a Simple Query

"Think like a wise man but communicate in the language of the people."
—William Butler Yeats

Topics Covered in This Chapter

Introducing SELECT

The SELECT Statement

A Quick Aside: Data vs. Information

Translating Your Request into SQL

Eliminating Duplicate Rows

Sorting Information

Saving Your Work

Sample Statements

Summary

Problems for You to Solve

Now that you've learned a little bit about the history of SQL, it's time to jump right in and learn the language itself. As we mentioned in the Introduction, we'll be concerned only with the data manipulation portion of the language. So our entire focus will be on the true workhorse of SQL—the SELECT Statement.

Introducing SELECT

Above all other keywords, SELECT truly lies at the heart of SQL. It is the cornerstone of the most powerful and complex statement within the language and the means by which you retrieve information from the tables in your database. You use SELECT in conjunction with other keywords and clauses to find and view information in an almost limitless number of ways. Just about any question regarding who, what, where, when, or even what if and how many can be answered with SELECT. As long as you've designed your database properly and collected the appropriate data, you can get the answers you need to make sound decisions for your organization.

The SELECT operation in SQL can be broken down into three smaller operations, which we will refer to as the SELECT Statement, the SELECT Expression, and the SELECT Query. (Breaking the SELECT operation down in this manner will make it far easier to understand and to appreciate its complexity.) Each of these operations provides its own set of keywords and clauses, providing you with the flexibility to create a final SQL statement that is appropriate for the question you want to pose to the database. As you'll learn in later chapters, you can even combine the operations in various ways to answer very complex questions.

In this chapter, we'll begin our discussion of the SELECT Statement and take a brief look at the SELECT Query. We'll then examine the SELECT Statement in more detail as we work through to Chapter 6.

❖ **Note** You'll commonly see the terms table, record, and field used interchangeably with the terms table, row, and column in a variety of books and articles on the subject of Relational databases. However, the SQL Standard specifically uses the terms table, row, and column to refer to these particular elements of a database structure. We'll stay consistent with the SQL Standard and use these terms throughout the remainder of the book.

The SELECT Statement

The SELECT Statement forms the basis of every question you pose to the database. When you create and execute a SELECT Statement, you are "querying" the database. (We know it sounds a little obvious, but we want to make certain that everyone reading this starts from the same point of reference.) In fact, many RDBMS programs allow you to save a SELECT Statement as a *query*, *View*, or *stored procedure*. Whenever someone says she is going to query the database, you know that she's going to execute some sort of SELECT Statement. Depending on the RDBMS program, SELECT Statements can be executed directly from a command line window, from an interactive Query By Example (QBE) grid, or from within a block of programming code. Regardless of how you choose to define and execute it, the syntax of the SELECT Statement is always the same.

Major Clauses in a SELECT Statement

A SELECT Statement is composed of several distinct keywords, known as *clauses*. You define a SELECT Statement using various configurations of these clauses to retrieve the information you require. Some of these clauses are required, while others are optional. Additionally, each clause has one or more keywords that represent required or optional values. These values are used by the clause to help retrieve the information requested by the SELECT Statement as a whole. Figure 4-1 shows a diagram of the SELECT Statement and its clauses.

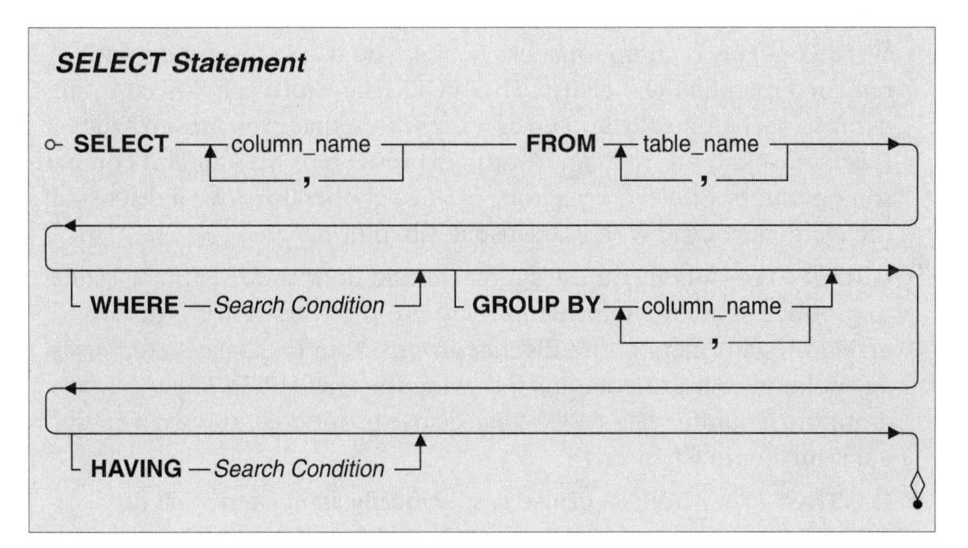

Figure 4-1 *A diagram of the SELECT Statement.*

> ❖ **Note** The syntax diagram in Figure 4.1 reflects a rudimentary SELECT Statement. We'll continue to update and modify the diagram as we introduce and work with new keywords and clauses. So for those of you who may have some previous experience with SQL statements, just be patient and bear with us for the time being.

Here's a brief summary of the clauses in a SELECT Statement.

- **SELECT**—This is the primary clause of the SELECT Statement and is absolutely required. You use it to specify the columns you want for the Result Set of your query. The columns themselves are drawn from the table or View you specify in the FROM clause. (You can also draw them from several tables simultaneously, but we'll discuss this later in Part III: Working with Multiple Tables.) You can also use aggregate functions, such as "Sum(HoursWorked)," or mathematical expressions, such as "Quantity × Price," in this clause.
- **FROM**—This is the second most important clause in the SELECT Statement and is also required. You use the FROM clause to specify the tables from which to draw the columns you've listed in the SELECT clause. You can use this clause in more complex ways, but we'll discuss this in later chapters.
- **WHERE**—This is an optional clause that you use to filter the rows returned by the FROM clause. The WHERE keyword is followed by an expression, technically known as a *Predicate*, that evaluates to True, False, or Unknown. You can test the expression using standard comparison operators, Boolean operators, or special operators. We'll discuss all the elements of the WHERE clause in Chapter 6.
- **GROUP BY**—When you use aggregate functions in the SELECT clause to produce summary information, you use the GROUP BY clause to divide the information into distinct groups. Your database system uses any column or list of columns following the GROUP BY keywords as grouping columns. The GROUP BY clause is optional, and we'll examine it further in Chapter 13.
- **HAVING**—The HAVING clause is specifically associated with the GROUP BY clause, and you use it to filter the grouped information. It is similar to the WHERE clause in that the HAVING keyword is followed by an expression that evaluates to True, False, or Unknown. You can test the expression using standard comparison operators, Boolean operators, or special operators. HAVING is also an optional clause, and we'll take a closer look at it in Chapter 14.

We're going to work with a very basic SELECT Statement at first, so we'll focus on the SELECT and FROM clauses. We'll add the other clauses, one by one, as we work through the other chapters and build a more complex SELECT Statement.

A Quick Aside: Data vs. Information

Before we pose the first query to the database, one thing must be perfectly clear: There is a distinct difference between *data* and *information*. In essence, data is what you store in the database, and information is what you retrieve from the database. This distinction is important for you to understand because it helps you to keep things in proper perspective. Remember that a database is designed to provide meaningful information to someone within your organization. However, the information can be provided only if the appropriate data exists in the database and if the database itself has been structured in such a way to support that information. Let's examine these terms in more detail.

The values that you store in the database are data. Data is static in the sense that it remains in the same state until you modify it by some manual or automated process. Figure 4-2 shows some sample data.

```
Katherine Ehrlich 89931  Active  79915
```

Figure 4-2 *An example of basic data.*

On the surface, this data is meaningless. For example, there is no easy way for you to determine what 89931 represents. Is it a zip code? Is it a part number? Even if you know it represents a customer identification number, is it associated with Katherine Ehrlich? There's just no way of knowing until the data is processed. Once you process the data so that it is meaningful and useful when you work with it or view it, the data becomes information. Information is dynamic in that it constantly changes relative to the data stored in the database and also in its ability to be processed and presented in an unlimited number of ways. You can show information as the result of a SELECT Statement, display it in a form on your computer screen, or print it on paper as a report. But the point to remember is that you must process your data in a manner that enables you to turn it into meaningful information.

Figure 4-3 on the next page shows the data from the previous example transformed into information on a customer screen. This illustrates how the data can be manipulated in such a way that it is now meaningful to anyone who views it.

When you work with a SELECT Statement, you use its clauses to manipulate *data*, but the statement itself returns *information*. Get the picture?

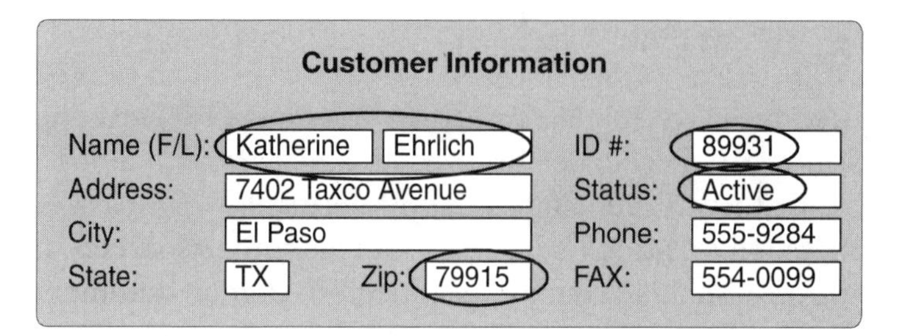

Figure 4-3 *An example of data processed into information.*

There's one last issue we need to address. When you execute a SELECT Statement, it usually retrieves one or more rows of information; the exact number depends on how you construct the statement. These rows are collectively known as a *Result Set*, which is the term we use throughout the remainder of the book. This name makes perfect sense because you always work with sets of data whenever you use a Relational database. (Remember that the Relational model is based, in part, on Set Theory.) You can easily view the information in a Result Set and, in many cases, you can modify its data. But, once again, it all depends on how you construct your SELECT Statement.

So let's get down to business and start using the SELECT Statement.

Translating Your Request into SQL

When you request information from the database, it's usually in the form of a question or a statement that implies a question. For example, you might formulate statements such as these:

"Which cities do our customers live in?"

"Show me a current list of our employees and their phone numbers."

"What kind of classes do we currently offer?"

"Give me the names of the folks on our staff and the dates they were hired."

Once you know what you want to ask, you can translate your request into a more formal statement. You compose the translation using this form:

Select <item> from the <source>

Start by looking at your request and replace words or phrases such as "list," "show me," "what," "which," and "who" with the word Select. Next, identify any nouns in your request and determine whether a given noun represents an item you want to see or if the noun is the name of a table in which an item might be stored. If it's an item, use it as a replacement for <item> in the translation statement; if it's a table name, use it as a replacement for <source>. If you translate the first question listed on the previous page, your statement looks something like this:

Select city from the customers table

Once you define your translation statement, you need to turn it into a full-fledged SELECT Statement using the SQL syntax shown in Figure 4-4. The first step, however, is to clean up your translation statement. You do so by crossing out any word that is not a noun representing the name of a column or table or that is not a word specifically used in the SQL syntax. Here's how the translation statement looks during the clean-up process:

Select city from ~~the~~ customers ~~table~~

Remove the words you've crossed out and you now have a complete SELECT Statement.

```
SELECT City FROM Customers
```

You can use the three-step technique we just presented on any request you pose to the database. In fact, we use this technique throughout most of the book and we encourage you to use it while you're beginning to learn how to build these statements. However, you'll eventually merge these steps into one seamless operation as you get more accustomed to writing SELECT Statements.

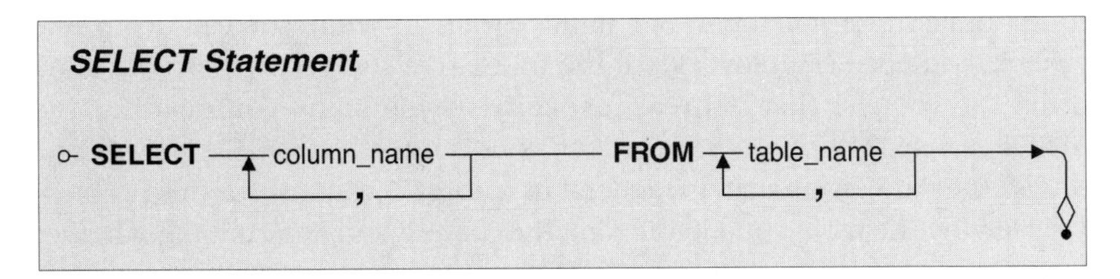

Figure 4-4 *The syntax of a simple SELECT Statement.*

Remember that you'll work mostly with columns and tables when you're beginning to learn how to use SQL. The syntax diagram in Figure 4-4 reflects this fact by using column_name in the SELECT clause and table_name in the FROM clause. In the next chapter, you'll learn how to use other terms in these clauses to create more complex SELECT Statements.

You probably noticed that the request we used in the previous example is relatively straightforward. It was easy to both redefine it as a translation statement and identify the column names that were present in the statement. But what if a request is not as straightforward and easy to translate, and it's difficult to identify the columns you need for the SELECT clause? The easiest course of action is to refine your request and make it more specific. For example, you can refine a request such as *"Show me the information on our clients"* by recasting it more clearly as *"List the name, city, and phone number for each of our clients."* If refining the request doesn't solve the problem, you still have two other courses of action. Your first alternative is to determine whether the table specified in the FROM clause of the SELECT Statement contains any column names that can help to clarify the request and thus make it easier to define a translation statement. Your second alternative is to examine the request more closely and determine whether a word or phrase it contains *implies* any column names. Whether you can use either or both alternatives is dependent on the request itself. Just remember that you do have techniques available when you find it difficult to define a translation statement. Let's take a look at an example of each technique and how you apply it in a typical scenario.

To illustrate the first technique, let's say you're trying to translate the following request.

> *"I need the names and addresses of all our employees."*

This looks like a straightforward request on the surface. But if you review this request once more, you'll find one minor problem: While you can determine the table you need (Employees) for the translation statement, there's nothing within the request that helps you specify the columns you need for the SELECT clause. Although the words "names" and "addresses" appear in the request, they are terms that are general in nature. You can solve this problem by reviewing the table you identified in the request and determining whether it contains any columns you can substitute for these terms. If so, use the column names in the translation statement. (You can opt to use generic versions of the column names in the translation statement if it will help you visualize the statement more clearly. However, you will need to use the actual column names in the SQL syntax.) In this case, look for column names in the Employees table that could be used in place of the words "name" and "addresses." Use the Employees table shown in Figure 4-5 and determine whether you can use any of its columns.

EMPLOYEES	
EmployeeID	*PK*
EmpLastName	
EmpFirstName	
EmpStreetAddress	
EmpCity	
EmpState	
EmpZipCode	
EmpPhoneNumber	

Figure 4-5 *The structure of the Employees table.*

You will indeed use six columns from this table. EmpFirstName and EmpLastName will both replace "names" in the request, while EmpStreetAddress, EmpCity, EmpState, and EmpZipCode will replace "addresses." Now, apply the entire translation process to the request, which we've repeated for your convenience. (We'll use generic forms of the column names for the translation statement and the actual column names in the SQL syntax.)

"I need the names and addresses of all our employees."

Translation Select first name, last name, street address, city, state, and zip code from the employees table

Clean Up Select first name, last name, street address, city, state, ~~and~~ zip code from ~~the~~ employees ~~table~~

SQL
```
SELECT EmpFirstName, EmpLastName, EmpStreet,
   EmpCity, EmpState, EmpZipCode
FROM Employees
```

❖ **Note** This example clearly illustrates how to use multiple columns in a SELECT clause. We'll discuss this technique in more detail later in this section.

The next example illustrates the second technique, which involves searching for implied columns within the request. Let's assume you're trying to put the following request through the translation process.

> *"What kind of classes do we currently offer?"*

At first glance, it may seem difficult to define a translation statement from this request. There are no column names indicated within the request, and without even one item to select, you can't create a complete translation statement. What do you do now? You take a closer look at each word in the request and determine whether there is one that *implies* a column name within the Classes table. Before you read any further, take a moment to study the request once again. Can you find such a word?

In this case, the word "kind" may imply a column name in the Classes table. Why? Because a kind of class can also be thought of as a category of class. If there is a category column in the Classes table, then you have the column name you need to complete the translation statement and, by inference, the SELECT Statement. Let's assume that there is a category column in the Classes table and take the request through the three-step process once again.

> *"What kind of classes do we currently offer?"*

Translation Select category from the classes table

Clean Up Select category from ~~the~~ classes ~~table~~

SQL

```
SELECT Category
FROM Classes
```

As the example shows, this technique involves using synonyms as replacements for certain words or phrases within the request. If you identify a word or phrase that might imply a column name, try to replace it with a synonym. The synonym you choose may indeed identify a column that exists in the database. However, if the first synonym that comes to mind doesn't work, try another. Continue this process until you either find a synonym that does identify a column name or until you're satisfied that neither the original word nor any of its synonyms represent a column name.

> ❖ **Note** Unless we indicate otherwise, all column names and table names used in the SQL syntax portion of the examples are drawn from the sample databases in Appendix B. This convention applies to all examples for the remainder of the book.

Expanding the Field of Vision

You can retrieve multiple columns within a SELECT Statement just as easily as you can retrieve a single column. List the names of the columns you want to use in the SELECT clause, and separate each name in the list with a comma. In the syntax diagram shown in Figure 4-6, the option to use more than one column is indicated by a line that flows from right to left beneath column_name. The comma in the middle of the line denotes that you must insert a comma before the next column name you want to use in the SELECT clause.

Figure 4-6 *Using multiple columns in a SELECT clause.*

The option to use multiple columns in the SELECT Statement provides you with the means to answer questions such as these.

"Show me a current list of our employees and their phone numbers."

Translation	Select the last name, first name, and phone number of all our employees from the employees table
Clean Up	Select ~~the~~ last name, first name, ~~and~~ phone number ~~of all our employees~~ from ~~the~~ employees ~~table~~
SQL	`SELECT EmpLastName, EmpFirstName, EmpPhoneNumber FROM Employees`

"What are the names and prices of the products we carry, and under what category is each item listed?"

Translation	Select the name, price, and category of every product from the products table

Clean Up	Select ~~the~~ name, price, ~~and~~ category ~~of every product~~ from ~~the~~ products ~~table~~
SQL	`SELECT ProductName, RetailPrice, Category` `FROM Products`

You gain the advantage of seeing a wider spectrum of information when you work with several columns in a SELECT Statement. Incidentally, the sequence of the columns in your SELECT clause is not important—you can list the columns in any order you wish. This gives you the flexibility to view the same information in a variety of ways.

For example, let's say you're working with the table shown in Figure 4-7, and you're asked to pose the following request to the database.

> *"Show me a list of subjects, the category each belongs to, and the code we use in our catalog. But I'd like to see the name first, followed by the category and then the code."*

SUBJECTS	
SubjectID	*PK*
CategoryID	*FK*
SubjectCode	
SubjectName	
SubjectDescription	

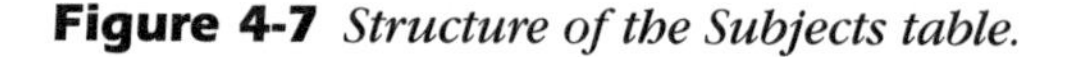

Figure 4-7 *Structure of the Subjects table.*

You can still transform this request into an appropriate SELECT Statement, even though the person making the request wants to see the columns in a specific order. Just list the column names in the order specified when you define the translation statement. Here's how the process looks when you transform this request into a SELECT Statement.

Translation	Select the subject name, category ID, and subject code from the subjects table
Clean Up	Select ~~the~~ subject name, category ID, ~~and~~ subject code from ~~the~~ subjects ~~table~~

There is no limit to the number of columns you can specify in the SELECT clause—in fact, you can list all of the columns from the source table. The following example shows the SELECT Statement you use to specify all of the columns from the Subjects table in Figure 4-7.

```
SQL        SELECT SubjectID, CategoryID, SubjectCode,
              SubjectName, SubjectDescription
           FROM Subjects
```

When you specify all the columns from the source table, you'll have a lot of typing to do if the table contains a number of columns! Fortunately, the SQL Standard specifies the asterisk as a shortcut you can use to shorten the statement considerably. The syntax diagram in Figure 4-8 shows that you can use the asterisk as an alternative to a list of columns in the SELECT clause.

Figure 4-8 *Syntax diagram showing the asterisk shortcut.*

Place the asterisk immediately after the SELECT clause when you want to specify all of the columns from the source table in the FROM clause. For example, here's how the preceding SELECT Statement looks when you use the shortcut.

```
SQL        SELECT *
           FROM Subjects
```

There's certainly less typing to do using this statement! However, one issue arises when you create SELECT Statements in this manner: The asterisk represents all of the columns that *currently exist* in the source table, and adding or deleting columns affects what you see in the Result Set of the SELECT Statement. (Oddly enough, the SQL Standard states that adding or deleting columns *should not* affect your Result Set.) This issue is important only if you must see the same columns in the Result Set consistently. Your database system will not warn you if columns have been deleted from the source table when you use the asterisk in the SELECT clause, but it will raise a warning when it can't find a column you *explicitly* specified. Although this does not pose a real problem for our purposes, it will be an important issue when you delve into the world of programming with SQL. Our rule of thumb is this: Use the asterisk only when you need to create a "quick and dirty" query to see all the information in a given table. Otherwise, specify all the columns you need for the query. In the end, the query will return exactly the information you need and will be more self-documenting.

The examples we've seen so far are based on simple requests that require columns from only one table. You'll learn how to work with more complex requests that require columns from several tables in Part III: Working with Multiple Tables.

Eliminating Duplicate Rows

When working with SELECT Statements, you'll inevitably come across Result Sets with duplicate rows. There is no cause for alarm if you see such a Result Set. Use the DISTINCT keyword in your SELECT Statement, and the Result Set will be free and clear of all duplicate rows. Figure 4-9 shows the syntax diagram for the DISTINCT keyword.

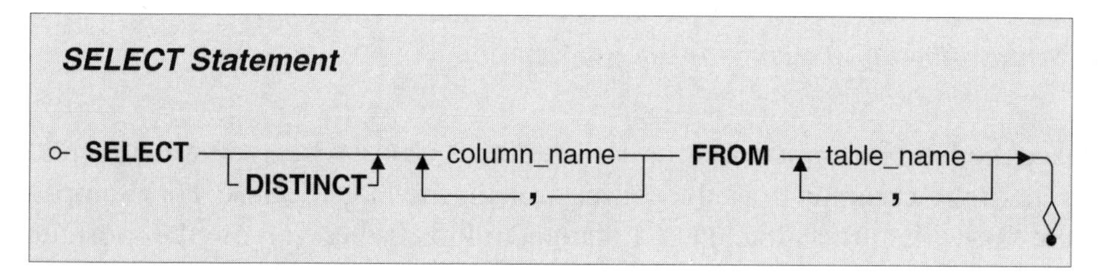

Figure 4-9 *The syntax for the DISTINCT keyword.*

As the diagram illustrates, DISTINCT is an optional keyword that precedes the list of columns specified in the SELECT clause. The DISTINCT keyword asks your database system to evaluate the values of all the columns *as a single unit* on a row-per-row basis and eliminate any redundancies it finds. The remaining unique rows are then returned to the Result Set. The following example shows what a difference the DISTINCT keyword can make under the appropriate circumstances.

Let's say you're posing the following request to the database.

"Which cities are represented by our bowling league membership?"

The question seems easy enough, so you take it through the translation process.

Translation Select city from the bowlers table

Clean Up Select city from ~~the~~ bowlers ~~table~~

SQL
```
SELECT City
FROM Bowlers
```

The problem is that the Result Set for this SELECT Statement shows *every occurrence* of each city name found in the Bowlers table. For example, if there are 20 people from Bellevue and 7 people from Kent and 14 people from Seattle, the Result Set displays 20 occurrences of Bellevue, 7 occurrences of Kent, and 14 occurrences of Seattle. Clearly, this redundant information is unnecessary; all you want to see is a *single* occurrence of each city name found in the Bowlers table. You resolve this problem by using the DISTINCT keyword in the SELECT Statement to eliminate the redundant information.

Let's run the request through the translation process once again using the DISTINCT keyword. Note that we now include the word "distinct" in both the translation step and the clean up step.

"Which cities are represented by our bowling league membership?"

Translation Select distinct city from the bowlers table

Clean Up Select distinct city from ~~the~~ bowlers ~~table~~

SQL
```
SELECT DISTINCT City
FROM Bowlers
```

The Result Set for this SELECT Statement displays exactly what you're looking for—a single occurrence of each distinct (or unique) city found in the Bowlers table.

You can use the DISTINCT keyword on multiple columns as well. Let's modify the previous example by requesting both the state and the city from the Bowlers table. Our new SELECT Statement looks like this.

```
SELECT DISTINCT State, City FROM Bowlers
```

This SELECT Statement returns a Result Set that contains unique records and shows definite distinctions between cities with the same name. For example, it shows the distinction between "Portland, ME," "Portland, OR," "Hollywood, CA," and "Hollywood, FL."

The DISTINCT keyword is a very useful tool under the right circumstances. Use it only when you really want to see unique rows in your Result Set.

Sorting Information

At the beginning of this chapter, we said that the SELECT Operation can be broken down into three smaller operations: the SELECT Statement, the SELECT Expression, and the SELECT Query. We also stated that you can combine these operations in various ways to answer complex requests. However, you also need to combine these operations in order to sort the rows of a Result Set.

By definition, the rows of a Result Set returned by a SELECT Statement are unordered; the sequence in which they appear is based upon their physical position in the table. The only way to sort the Result Set is to embed the SELECT Statement within a SELECT Query as shown in Figure 4-10. We define a SELECT Query as a SELECT Statement with an ORDER BY clause. It's the ORDER BY clause of the SELECT Query that lets you specify the sequence of rows in the final Result Set. As you'll learn in later chapters, you can actually embed a SELECT Statement within another SELECT Statement or SELECT Expression to answer very complex questions. However, the SELECT Query cannot be embedded at any level.

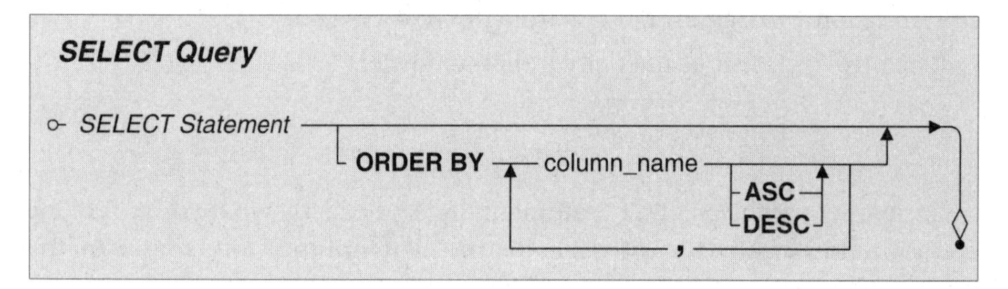

Figure 4-10 *The syntax diagram for the SELECT Query.*

> ❖ **Note** Throughout this book, we use the same terms you'll find in the ANSI SQL Standard or in common usage in most database systems. The ANSI SQL Standard, however, defines the ORDER BY clause only as part of a *Cursor*, which is an object that you define inside an application program. A complete discussion of Cursors is beyond the scope of this work. Because many implementations of SQL allow you to include an ORDER BY clause at the end of a SELECT Statement, we invented the term *SELECT Query* to describe this type of statement. This also allows us to discuss the concept of sorting the final output of a query for display online or for use in a report.

The ORDER BY clause allows you to sort the Result Set of the specified SELECT Statement by one or more columns and also provides the option of specifying an ascending or descending sort order for each column. The only columns you can use in the ORDER BY clause are those that are currently listed in the SELECT clause. (Although this requirement is specified in the SQL Standard, some vendor implementations allow you to disregard it completely. However, we comply with this requirement in all the examples used throughout the book.) When you use two or more columns in an ORDER BY clause, separate each column with a comma. The SELECT Query returns a final Result Set once the sort is complete.

❖ **Note** The ORDER BY clause *does not* affect the physical order of the rows in a table. If you do need to change the physical order of the rows, refer to your database software's documentation for the proper procedure.

First Things First: Collating Sequences

Before we look at some examples using the SELECT Query, a brief word on collating sequences is in order. (No pun intended!)

The manner in which the ORDER BY clause sorts the information depends on the collating sequence used by your database software. The collating sequence determines the order of precedence for every character listed in the current language character set specified by your operating system. For example, it identifies whether lowercase letters will be sorted before uppercase letters, or whether case will even matter. Check your database software's documentation, and perhaps consult your database administrator to determine the default collating sequence for your database.

Let's Now Come to Order

With the availability of the ORDER BY clause, you can present the information you retrieve from the database in a more meaningful fashion. This applies to simple requests as well as complex requests. You can now rephrase your requests so that they also indicate sorting requirements. For example, a question such as "*What are the categories of classes we currently offer?*" can be recast as *"List the categories of classes we offer and show them in alphabetical order."*

Before beginning to work with the SELECT Query, you need to adjust the way you define a translation statement. This involves adding a new section at the end of the translation statement to account for the new sorting requirements specified within the request. Use this new form to define the translation statement.

Select <item> from the <source> **and order by <column(s)>**

Now that your request will include phrases such as "sort the results by city," "show them in order by year," or "list them by last name and first name," study the request closely to determine which column or columns you need to use for sorting purposes. This is a simple exercise because most people use these types of phrases, and the columns needed for the sort are usually self-evident. Once you identify the appropriate column or columns, use them as a replacement for <column(s)> in the translation statement. Let's take a look at a simple request to see how this works.

"List the categories of classes we offer and show them in alphabetical order."

Translation Select category from the classes table and order by category

Clean Up Select category from ~~the~~ classes ~~table and~~ order by category

SQL
```
SELECT Category
FROM Classes
ORDER BY Category
```

In this example, you can assume that Category will be used for the sort because it's the only column indicated in the request. You can also assume that the sort should be in ascending order because there's nothing in the request to indicate the contrary. This is a safe assumption. According to the SQL Standard, ascending order is automatically assumed if you don't specify a sort order. However, if you want to be absolutely explicit, insert ASC after Category in the ORDER BY clause.

In the following request, the column needed for the sort is more clearly defined.

"Show me a list of vendor names in zip code order."

Translation Select vendor name and zip code from the vendors table and order by zip code

Clean Up Select vendor name ~~and~~ zip code from ~~the~~ vendors ~~table and~~ order by zip code

```
SQL         SELECT VendName, VendZipCode
            FROM Vendors
            ORDER BY VendZipCode
```

In general, most people will tell you if they want to see their information in descending order. When this situation arises and you need to display the Result Set in reverse order, insert the DESC keyword after the appropriate column in the ORDER BY clause. For example, here's how you modify the SELECT Statement in the previous example when you want to see the information sorted by zip code in descending order.

```
SQL         SELECT VendName, VendZipCode
            FROM Vendors
            ORDER BY VendZipCode DESC
```

The next example illustrates a more complex request that requires a multicolumn sort. The only difference between this example and the previous two examples is that this example uses more columns in the ORDER BY clause. Note that the columns are separated with commas, which is in accordance with the syntax diagram shown back in Figure 4-10.

"Display the names of our employees, including their phone number and ID number, and list them by last name and first name."

Translation — Select last name, first name, phone number, and employee ID from the employees table and order by last name and first name

Clean Up — Select last name, first name, phone number, ~~and~~ employee ID from ~~the~~ employees table ~~and~~ order by last name ~~and~~ first name

```
SQL         SELECT EmpLastName, EmpFirstName,
               EmpPhoneNumber, EmployeeID
            FROM Employees
            ORDER BY EmpLastName, EmpFirstName
```

One of the interesting things you can do with the columns in an ORDER BY clause is to specify a different sort order for each column. In the previous example, you can specify a descending sort for Last Name and an ascending sort for First Name. Here's how the SELECT Statement looks when you make the appropriate modifications.

```
SQL       SELECT EmpLastName, EmpFirstName, EmpPhoneNumber,
             EmployeeID
          FROM Employees
          ORDER BY EmpLastName DESC, EmpFirstName ASC
```

Although you don't need to use the ASC keyword explicitly, the statement is more self-documenting if you include it.

The previous example brings an interesting question to mind: Is there any importance placed on the sequence of the columns in the ORDER BY clause? The answer is "*Yes!*" The sequence is important because your database system will evaluate the columns in the ORDER BY clause from left to right. Also, the importance of the sequence grows in direct proportion to the number of columns you use. Always sequence the columns in the ORDER BY clause properly so that the result sorts in the appropriate order.

Saving Your Work

Save your SELECT Statements—every major database software program provides a way for you to save them! Saving your statements eliminates the need to recreate them every time you pose the same request to the database. When you save your SELECT Statement, assign a meaningful name that will help you remember what type of information the statement provides. And if your database software allows you to do so, write a concise description of the statement's purpose. The value of the description will become quite clear when you haven't seen a particular SELECT Statement for some time and you need to remember why you even constructed it in the first place.

A saved SELECT Statement is categorized as a Query in some database programs and as a View in others. Regardless of its designation, every database program provides you with a means to execute, or run, the saved statement and work with its Result Set.

> ❖ **Note** For the remainder of this discussion, we'll use the word "Query" to represent the saved SELECT Statement and "execute" to represent the method used to work with it.

There are two common methods used to execute a Query. The first is an interactive device (such as a toolbar or query grid), and the second is from within a block of programming code. You'll use the first method quite extensively; there's no need to worry about the second method until you begin working with your database software's programming language. While it's our job to teach you how to create and use SQL statements, it's your job to learn how to create, save, and execute them in your database software program.

Sample Statements

Now that we've covered the basic characteristics of the SELECT Statement and SELECT Query, let's take a look at some examples of how these operations are applied in different scenarios. These examples encompass each of the sample databases, and they illustrate the use of the SELECT Statement, the SELECT Query, and the two supplemental techniques used to establish columns for the translation statement. We've also included sample Result Sets that would be returned by these operations and placed them immediately after the SQL syntax line. The name that appears immediately above a Result Set has a twofold purpose: It is used to identify the Result Set itself, and it is the name assigned to the SQL statement in the example.

In case you're wondering why we assigned a name to each SQL statement, it's because we saved them! In fact, we've named and saved all of the SQL statements that appear in the examples here and throughout the remainder of the book. Each is stored in the appropriate sample database (as indicated within the example), and you can download the databases from the accompanying CD. This gives you the opportunity to see these statements in action before you try your hand at writing them yourself.

> ❖ **Note** Just a reminder that all of the column names and table names used in these examples are drawn from the sample database structures shown in Appendix B.

Sales Order Database

"Show me the names of all our vendors."

Translation: Select the vendor name from the vendors table

Clean Up: Select ~~the~~ vendor name from ~~the~~ vendors ~~table~~

SQL:

```
SELECT VendName
FROM Vendors
```

Vendor_Names (10 Rows)

VendName
Shinoman, Incorporated
Viscount
Nikoma of America
ProFormance
Kona, Incorporated
Big Sky Mountain Bikes
Dog Ear
Sun Sports Suppliers
Lone Star Bike Supply
Armadillo Brand

"What are the names and prices of all the products we carry?"

Translation: Select product name, retail price from the products table

Clean Up: Select product name, retail price from ~~the~~ products ~~table~~

SQL:

```
SELECT ProductName, RetailPrice
FROM Products
```

Product_Price_List (40 Rows)

ProductName	RetailPrice
Trek 9000 Mountain Bike	$1,200.00
Eagle FS-3 Mountain Bike	$1,800.00
Dog Ear Cyclecomputer	$75.00
Victoria Pro All Weather Tires	$54.95
Dog Ear Helmet Mount Mirrors	$7.45
Viscount Mountain Bike	$635.00
Viscount C-500 Wireless Bike Computer	$49.00
Kryptonite Advanced 2000 U-Lock	$50.00
Nikoma Lok-Tight U-Lock	$33.00
Viscount Microshell Helmet	$36.00
<< more rows here>>	

"Which states do our customers come from?"

Translation   Select distinct state from the customers table

Clean Up   Select distinct state from ~~the~~ customers ~~table~~

SQL

```
SELECT DISTINCT CustState
FROM Customers
```

Customer_States (4 Rows)

CustState
CA
OR
TX
WA

Entertainment Database

"List all entertainers, the cities they're based in, and sort it by city and name in ascending order."

Translation — Select city and stage name from the entertainers table and order by city and stage name

Clean Up — Select city ~~and~~ stage name from ~~the~~ entertainers ~~table and~~ order by city ~~and~~ stage name

SQL

```
SELECT EntCity, EntStageName
FROM Entertainers
ORDER BY EntCity ASC, EntStageName ASC
```

Entertainer_Locations (13 Rows)

EntCity	EntStageName
Auburn	Caroline Coie Cuartet
Auburn	Topazz
Bellevue	Albert Buchanan
Bellevue	Jazz Persuasion
Bellevue	Susan McLain
Redmond	Carol Peacock Trio
Redmond	JV & the Deep Six
Seattle	Coldwater Cattle Company
Seattle	Country Feeling
Seattle	Julia Schnebly
<< more rows here >>	

"Give me a unique list of engagement dates; I'm not concerned with how many engagements there are per date."

Translation Select distinct start date from the engagements table

Clean Up Select distinct start date from ~~the~~ engagements ~~table~~

SQL

```
SELECT DISTINCT StartDate
FROM Engagements
```

Engagement_Dates (66 Rows)

StartDate
1999-07-01
1999-07-10
1999-07-11
1999-07-15
1999-07-17
1999-07-18
1999-07-24
1999-07-29
1999-07-30
1999-07-31
<< *more rows here* >>

School Scheduling Database

"Can we view complete class information?"

Translation Select all columns from the classes table

Clean Up Select all ~~columns~~ from ~~the~~ classes ~~table~~

SQL
```
SELECT *
FROM Classes
```

Class_Information (76 Rows)

ClassID	Subject	Classroom	Credits	StartTime	Duration	<<other columns>>
1000	Introduction to Art	1231	5	10:00	50	...
1002	Design	1619	4	15:30	110	...
1004	Drawing	1627	4	08:00	50	...
1006	Drawing	1627	4	09:00	110	...
1012	Painting	1627	4	13:00	170	...
1020	Computer Art	3404	4	13:00	110	...
1030	Art History	1231	5	11:00	50	...
1031	Art History	1231	5	14:00	50	...
1156	Composition—Fundamentals	3443	5	08:00	50	...
1162	Composition—Fundamentals	3443	5	09:00	80	...
<<more rows here>>						

"Give me a list of the buildings on campus and the number of floors for each building. Sort the list by building in ascending order."

Translation Select building name and number of floors from the buildings table

Clean Up Select building name ~~and~~ number of floors from ~~the~~ buildings ~~table~~

SQL
```
SELECT BuildingName, NumberOfFloors
FROM Buildings
ORDER BY BuildingName ASC
```

Building_List (6 Rows)

BuildingNam	NumberOfFloors
Arts and Sciences	3
College Center	3
Instructional Building	3
Library	2
PE and Wellness	1
Technology Building	2

Bowling League Database

"Where are we holding our tourneys?"

Translation Select distinct tourney location from the tournaments table

Clean Up Select distinct tourney location from ~~the~~ tournaments ~~table~~

SQL
```
SELECT DISTINCT TourneyLocation
FROM Tournaments
```

Tourney_Locations (7 Rows)

TourneyLocation
Acapulco Lanes
Bolero Lanes
Imperial Lanes
Red Rooster Lanes
Sports World Lanes
Thunderbird Lanes
Totem Lanes

"Give me a list of all tourney dates and locations. I need the dates in descending order and the locations in alphabetical order."

Translation — Select tourney date and location from the tournaments table and order by tourney date in descending order and location in ascending order

Clean Up — Select tourney date ~~and~~ location from ~~the~~ tournaments ~~table~~ ~~and~~ order by tourney date ~~in~~ descending ~~order and~~ location ~~in~~ ascending ~~order~~

SQL

```
SELECT TourneyDate, TourneyLocation
FROM Tournaments
ORDER BY TourneyDate DESC, TourneyLocation ASC
```

Tourney_Dates (14 Rows)

TourneyDate	TourneyLocation
1999-09-04	Acapulco Lanes
1999-08-28	Totem Lanes
1999-08-21	Sports World Lanes
1999-08-14	Imperial Lanes
1999-08-07	Bolero Lanes
1999-07-31	Thunderbird Lanes
1999-07-24	Red Rooster Lanes
1999-07-17	Acapulco Lanes
1999-07-10	Totem Lanes
1999-07-03	Sports World Lanes
<<more rows here>>	

Recipe Database

"What types of recipes do we have, and what are the names of the recipes we have for each type? Can you sort the information by type and recipe name?"

Translation — Select recipe class ID and recipe title from the recipes table and order by recipe class ID and recipe title

Clean Up — Select recipe class ID ~~and~~ recipe title from ~~the~~ recipes ~~table~~ ~~and~~ order by recipe class ID ~~and~~ recipe title

SQL

```
SELECT RecipeClassID, RecipeTitle
FROM Recipes
ORDER BY RecipeClassID ASC, RecipeTitle ASC
```

Recipe_Classes_And_Titles (15 Rows)

RecipeClassID	RecipeTitle
1	Fettuccini Alfredo
1	Huachinango Veracruzana (Red Snapper, Veracruz style)
1	Irish Stew
1	Pollo Picoso
1	Roast Beef
1	Salmon Filets in Parchment Paper
1	Tourtière (French-Canadian Pork Pie)
2	Asparagus
2	Garlic Green Beans
3	Yorkshire Pudding
<<more rows here>>	

"Show me a list of unique recipe class IDs in the recipes table."

Translation Select distinct recipe class ID from the recipes table

Clean Up Select distinct recipe class ID from ~~the~~ recipes ~~table~~

SQL
```
SELECT DISTINCT RecipeClassID
FROM Recipes
```

Recipe_Class_Ids
(6 Rows)

RecipeClassID
1
2
3
4
5
6

SUMMARY

In this chapter, we introduced the SELECT operation and you learned that it is one of four data manipulation operations in SQL. We also discussed how the SELECT operation can be divided into three smaller operations: the SELECT Statement, the SELECT Expression, and the SELECT Query.

The discussion then turned to the SELECT Statement, where you were introduced to its component clauses. We covered the fact that the SELECT and FROM clauses are the fundamental clauses required to retrieve information from the database, and that the remaining clauses—WHERE, GROUP BY, and HAVING—are used to conditionally process and filter the information returned by the SELECT clause.

We briefly diverged into a discussion on the difference between data and information. You learned that the values stored in the database are data and that information is data that has been processed in a manner that makes it meaningful to the person viewing it. You also learned that the rows of information returned by a SELECT Statement are known as a Result Set.

Retrieving information was the next topic of discussion, and we began by presenting the basic form of the SELECT Statement. You learned how to build a proper SELECT Statement by using a three-step technique that involves taking a request and translating it into proper SQL syntax. You also learned that you could use two or more columns in the SELECT clause to expand the scope of information you retrieve from your database. We followed this section with a quick look at the DISTINCT keyword, and you learned that it is the means by which you eliminate duplicate rows from a Result Set.

Next, we looked at the SELECT Query and how it can be combined with a SELECT Statement to sort the SELECT Statement's Result Set. You learned that this is necessary because the SELECT Query is the only SELECT operation that contains an ORDER BY clause. We went on to show that the ORDER BY clause is used to sort the information by one or more columns and that each column can have its own ascending or descending sort specification. A brief discussion on saving your SELECT statements followed, and you learned that you can save your statement as a Query or a View for future use.

Finally, we presented a number of examples using various tables in the sample databases. The examples illustrated how the various concepts and techniques presented in this chapter are used in typical scenarios and applications. In the next chapter, we'll take a closer look at the SELECT clause and show you how to retrieve something besides information from a list of columns.

Problems for You to Solve

Below, we show you the request statement and the name of the solution query in the sample databases. If you want some practice, you can work out the SQL you need for each request and then check your answer with the query we saved in the samples. Don't worry if your syntax doesn't exactly match the syntax of the queries we saved—as long as your Result Set is the same.

Sales Order Database

1. *"Show me all the information on our employees."*
   You can find the solution in Employee_Information (8 rows).
2. *"Show me a list of cities, in alphabetical order, where our vendors are located, and include the names of the vendors we work with in each city."*
   You can find the solution in Vendor_Locations (10 rows).

Entertainment Database

1. *"Give me the names and phone numbers of all our agents, and list them in last name/ first name order."*
   You can find the solution in Agent_Phone_List (8 rows).
2. *"Give me the information on all our engagements."*
   You can find the solution in Engagement_Information (131 rows).
3. *"List all engagements and their associated start dates. Sort the records by date in descending order and by engagement in ascending order."*
   You can find the solution in Scheduled_Engagements (131 rows).

School Scheduling Database

1. *"Show me a complete list of all the subjects we offer."*
   You can find the solution in Subject_List (56 rows).
2. *"What kinds of titles are associated with our faculty?"*
   You can find the solution in Faculty_Titles (3 rows).
3. *"List the names and phone numbers of all our staff, and sort them by last name and first name."*
   You can find the solution in Staff_Phone_List (27 rows).

Bowling League Database

1. *"List all of the teams in alphabetical order."*
   You can find the solution in Team_List (8 rows).
2. *"Show me all the bowling score information for each of our members."*
   You can find the solution in Bowling_Score_Information (1344 rows).
3. *"Show me a list of bowlers with their current average and handicap, and sort it in alphabetical order."*
   You can find the solution in Bowler_Statistics (32 rows).

Recipe Database

1. *"Show me a list of all the ingredients we currently keep track of."*
   You can find the solution in Complete_Ingredients_List (79 rows).
2. *"Show me all the main recipe information, and sort it by the name of the recipe in alphabetical order."*
   You can find the solution in Main_Recipe_Information (15 rows).

5

Getting More Than Simple Columns

"Facts are stubborn things."
—Tobias Smollett
Gil Blas de Santillane

Topics Covered in This Chapter

The SELECT Clause: Take Two

Moving Beyond Basic Information

What Is an Expression?

What Are You Trying to Express?

Types of Expressions

Using Expressions in a SELECT Clause

That "Nothing" Value—Null

Sample Statements

Summary

Problems for You to Solve

In Chapter 4, you learned how to use a SELECT Statement to retrieve information from one or more columns in a table. This technique is useful if you're posing only simple requests to the database for some basic facts. However, you'll need to expand your SQL "vocabulary" when you begin working with complex requests. In this chapter, we'll discuss how the *type* of data stored in a column can have an important impact on your queries. You'll learn how to adjust the scope of information you retrieve from the database by using *expressions* to manipulate the data from which the information is drawn. We'll begin by revisiting the SELECT clause.

The SELECT Clause: Take Two

You retrieve information from the columns in a table by listing the appropriate column names in the SELECT clause of a SELECT Statement. For example, you would use the following SELECT Statement to retrieve the first name, last name, and phone number of each employee in an Employees table.

```
SQL        SELECT FirstName, LastName, PhoneNumber
           FROM Employees
```

This is the most basic method of retrieving information from a table. When you specify a column name in a SELECT clause, you are using what the SQL Standard defines as a *Column Reference*. Figure 5-1 shows the syntax diagram for this term.

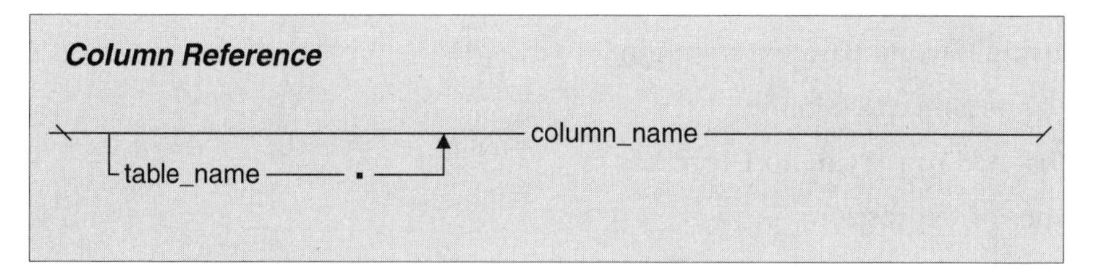

Figure 5-1 *The syntax diagram for a Column Reference.*

Although you can use just the column name itself in a SELECT clause, you may also explicitly qualify a column name with the name of its parent table. This is how you would rewrite the previous SELECT Statement to incorporate qualified column names.

```
SQL        SELECT Employees.FirstName, Employees.LastName,
              Employees.PhoneNumber
           FROM Employees
```

Although you needn't worry about qualifying each column name when you base a SELECT Statement on a single table, it does become more of an issue when you base a SELECT Statement on multiple tables. You'll learn more about this in Chapter 8.

Specifying Explicit Values

The SQL Standard provides flexibility for enhancing the information returned from a SELECT Statement by allowing use of values such as character strings, numbers, dates, times, or a suitable combination of these items, in any valid expression used within a SELECT Statement. The SQL Standard categorizes these types of values as *Literal Values* and specifies the manner in which they are defined.

Character String Literals

A *character string literal* is a sequence of individual characters enclosed in *single* quotes. Yes, we know that you are probably used to using double quotes to enclose character strings, but we're presenting these concepts as the SQL Standard defines them. Figure 5-2 shows the diagram for a character string literal.

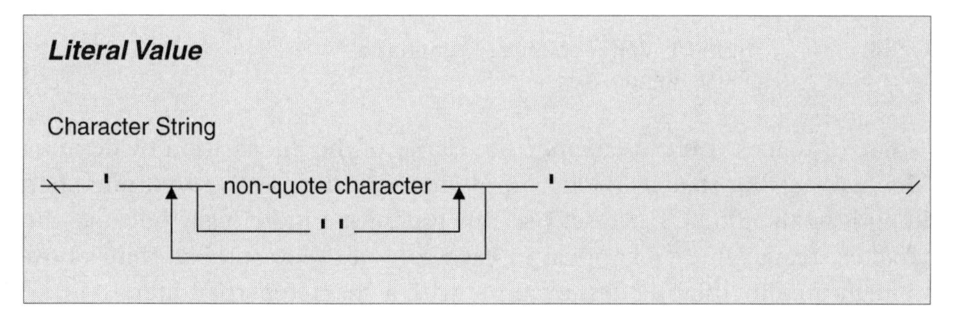

Figure 5-2 *Diagram of a character string literal value.*

Here are a few examples of the types of character string literals you can define.

```
'This is a sample character string literal.'
'Here''s yet another!'
'B-28'
'Seattle'
```

You probably noticed what seemed to be a double quote in both the diagram and the second line of the previous example. Actually, it's not a double quote but two consecutive single quotes with no space between the quotes. The SQL Standard states that a single quote embedded within a character string is represented by two consecutive single quotes. The SQL Standard defines it this way so that your database system can distinguish between a single quote that defines the beginning or end of a character string literal and a quote that you want included within the literal. The following two lines illustrate how this works.

SQL	`'The Vendor''s name is: '`
Displayed as	**The Vendor's name is:**

As we mentioned earlier, you can use character string literals to enhance the information returned by a SELECT Statement. Although the information you see in a Result Set is usually easy to understand, it's very likely that the information can be made clearer. For example, if you execute the following SELECT Statement, the information the Result Set displays is just the vendor's Web site address and the vendor's name.

```
SQL          SELECT VendWebPage, VendName
             FROM Vendors
```

In some instances you can enhance the clarity of the information by defining a character string that provides supplementary descriptive text and then adding it to the SELECT clause. Use this technique judiciously because the character string value will appear in each row of the Result Set. Here's how you might modify the previous example with a character string literal.

```
SQL          SELECT VendWebPage, 'is the web site for',
                VendName
             FROM Vendors
```

A row in the Result Set generated by this SELECT Statement looks like this.

www.datatexcg.com	is the web site for	DataTex Consulting Group

This somewhat clarifies the information displayed by the Result Set by identifying the actual purpose of the Web address. Although this is a simple example, it illustrates what you can do with character string literals. Later in this chapter, you'll see how you can use them in expressions.

❖ **Note** You'll find this technique especially useful when working with legacy databases that contain cryptic column names. However, you won't have to use this technique very often with your own databases when you follow the recommendations in Chapter 2.

Numeric Literals

A *numeric literal* is another type of literal you can use within a SELECT Statement. As the name implies, it consists of a signed number and can include a decimal place, the exponent symbol, and an exponential number. Figure 5-3 shows the diagram for a numeric literal.

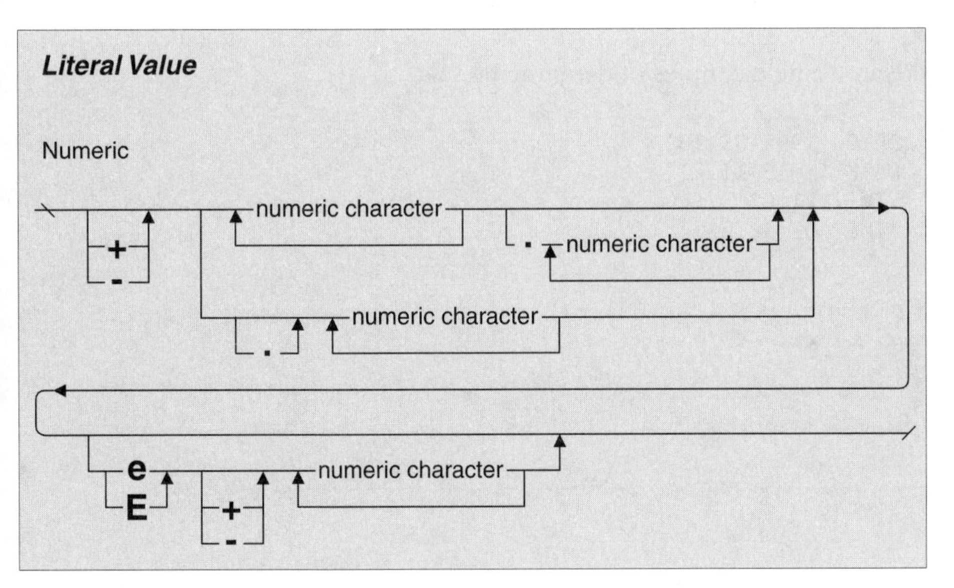

Figure 5-3 *Diagram of a numeric literal value.*

Examples of numeric literals include

```
427
-11.253
.554
0.3E-3
```

Numeric literals are most useful in expressions, so we'll postpone further discussion until later in this chapter.

Date and Time Literals

You can supply specific dates and times for use within a SELECT Statement by using *date literals* and *time literals*. The SQL Standard refers to these literals collectively as *datetime literals*. Defining these literals is a simple task, as Figure 5-4 shows. Bear in mind a couple of points, however, when using datetime literals.

DATE — The format for a date literal is year-month-day, which is the format we follow throughout the book. However, many SQL databases allow the more common month/day/year format (United States) or day/month/year format (most non-U.S. countries).

TIME — The hour format is based on a 24-hour clock. For example, 07:00 P.M. is represented as 19:00.

Here are some examples of datetime literals.

```
DATE '1999-05-16'
DATE '2016-11-22'
TIME '21:00'
TIME '03:30:25'
```

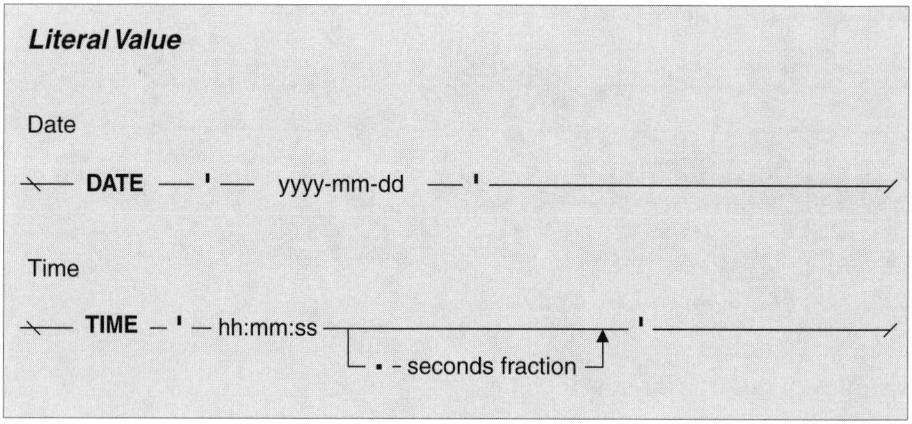

Literal Value

Date

DATE — ' — yyyy-mm-dd — '

Time

TIME — ' — hh:mm:ss — [. - seconds fraction] — '

Figure 5-4 *Diagram of a datetime literal value.*

Note that both literals are composed of a keyword and a string of characters indicating the desired value. Although the DATE and TIME keywords are defined in the SQL Standard as required components of date and time literals respectively, most database systems rarely support these keywords in this particular context and require only the character string portion of the literal. Therefore, we'll refrain from using either keyword and instead use single quotes to delimit a date or time literal that appears in any example throughout the remainder of the book. We show you how to use dates and times in expressions later in this chapter.

Moving Beyond Basic Information

The techniques you've learned so far will let you get answers to simple requests posed to the database. Now you'll begin to learn how to deal with more complex requests that are sure to come up as you work with your database.

The SQL Standard provides the tools you need to work with complex requests. Deciding which tool to use depends on the nature of the request itself. Here are several examples.

- To find the names of the instructors who teach a certain class, implement a *Search Condition* from within the WHERE clause of a SELECT Statement to get the answer. (See Chapter 6.)
- To view information on your staff of doctors and their patients, use one or more JOIN clauses to gather the information from the appropriate tables. (See Chapter 8.)
- To filter groups of data, implement a Search Condition in a HAVING clause of a SELECT Statement. (See Chapter 14.)

Don't worry—you'll learn how to use these techniques as you work through the book. We mention all of them here because they have something in common: Each technique requires the use of an *expression* in order to fulfill the request properly. Because an expression is a crucial component of any SQL statement used to answer a complex request, it is very important that you thoroughly understand expressions before learning any other techniques in this book.

What Is an Expression?

An expression is some form of operation involving numbers, character strings, or dates and times. It can use values drawn from specific columns in a table, literal values, or a combination of both. Once the operation defined by the expression has been completed, the expression returns a value to the SQL statement for further processing. You can use expressions to broaden or narrow the scope of the information you retrieve from the database. Expressions are especially useful when you are posing "what if" questions. Here's a sample of the types of requests you can answer using expressions.

What is the total amount for each line item?

Give me a list of employees, last name first.

Show me the start time and end time for each class.

Show the difference between the Handicap Score and the Raw Score for each bowler.

What is the estimated per-hour rate for each engagement?

What if we raised the prices of our products by 5 percent?

The type of data used in an expression impacts the value the expression returns, so let's first look at some of the data types the SQL Standard provides.

What Are You Trying to Express?

Every column in the database has an assigned *data type* that determines the kind of values the column can store. The data type also determines the operations that can be performed on the column's values. You can ensure that an expression is meaningful and will return a proper value if you know the data types of the columns you're using within the expression.

Data Types in SQL

The SQL Standard defines seven major data types within three general categories—character, numeric, and datetime. (Sounds slightly familiar, doesn't it?) In turn, each data type has one or more uniquely named variations also known as data types. Here's a brief look at each of these data types.

CHARACTER — This data type stores a fixed- or varying-length character string of one or more printable characters. The characters it accepts are usually based upon the American Standard Code for Information Interchange (ASCII) or the Extended Binary Coded Decimal Interchange Code (EBCDIC) character sets. A fixed-length Character data type is known as CHARACTER or CHAR, and a varying-length Character data type is known as

CHARACTER VARYING, CHAR VARYING, or VARCHAR. The size of a fixed-length Character data type is defined by the user, and the maximum size of a varying-length Character data type is defined by the database system. (This rule applies to the National Character data types as well.)

NATIONAL CHARACTER — The National Character data type is the same as the Character data type except that it draws its characters from ISO-defined foreign language character sets. NATIONAL CHARACTER, NATIONAL CHAR, and NCHAR are names used to refer to a fixed-length National Character, while NATIONAL CHARACTER VARYING, NATIONAL CHAR VARYING, and NCHAR VARYING are names used to refer to a varying-length National Character.

BIT — You can store strings of binary number sequences such as digitized images and sound waves in this data type. The database system defines the size of the Bit data type as a whole. This data type can be referred to as BIT or BIT VARYING.

EXACT NUMERIC — This data type stores whole numbers and numbers with decimal places. The precision (the number of significant digits) and the scale (number of digits to the right of the decimal place) of an Exact Numeric can be user-defined and can only be equal to or less than the maximum limits allowed by the database system. NUMERIC, DECIMAL, DEC, INTEGER, INT, and SMALLINT are all names used to refer to this data type. One point you must remember is that the SQL Standard—as well as most database systems—defines an INTEGER as having a greater range of values than a SMALLINT. Check your database system's documentation for the applicable ranges.

APPROXIMATE NUMERIC — This data type stores numbers with decimal places and exponential numbers. Names used to refer to this data type include FLOAT, REAL, and DOUBLE PRECISION. The Approximate Numeric doesn't have a precision and scale per se, but the SQL Standard does allow a user-defined precision only for a REAL data type. Any scale associated with these data types is always defined by the database system.

Note that the SQL Standard and most database systems define the range of values for a DOUBLE PRECISION data type to be greater than those of a REAL data type. Check your documentation for these ranges as well.

DATETIME — Dates, times, and combinations of both are stored in this data type. As we first mentioned in our discussion on Literal Values, the SQL Standard defines the date format as year-month-day and specifies time values as being based on a 24-hour clock. Although most database systems allow you to use the more common month/day/year or day/month/year date format and time values based on an A.M./P.M. clock, we use the date and time formats specified by the SQL Standard throughout the book. The three names used to refer to this data type are DATE, TIME, and TIMESTAMP. You can use the TIMESTAMP data type to store a combination of a date and time.

INTERVAL — This data type stores the quantity of time between two Datetime values, expressed either as year, month; year/month; day, time; or day/time. Most major database systems do not yet support this data type, so you needn't worry about it for now.

Many database systems provide additional data types known as *extended data types* beyond those specified by the SQL Standard. Examples of extended data types include MONEY/CURRENCY, BOOLEAN (for True or False values), SERIAL/ROWID (for unique row identifiers), and BYTE/BLOB (for unstructured binary data).

Because our sole focus is on the *data manipulation* portion of SQL, you need only be concerned with the appropriate range of values for each data type your database system supports. This knowledge will help ensure that the expressions you define will execute properly, so be sure to familiarize yourself with the data types provided by your RDBMS program.

Now that you're familiar with the various data types the SQL Standard provides, let's begin our discussion on building simple expressions.

Types of Expressions

You will generally use the following three types of expressions when working with SQL statements.

CONCATENATION	Combining two or more items into a single character string
MATHEMATICAL	Addition, subtraction, multiplication, and division
DATE/TIME ARITHMETIC	Applying addition or subtraction to dates and times

Concatenation

The SQL Standard defines two sequential vertical bars as the concatenation operator. You can concatenate two items by placing a single item on either side of the concatenation operator. The result is a single string of characters that is a combination of both items. Figure 5-5 shows the syntax diagram for the concatenation expression.

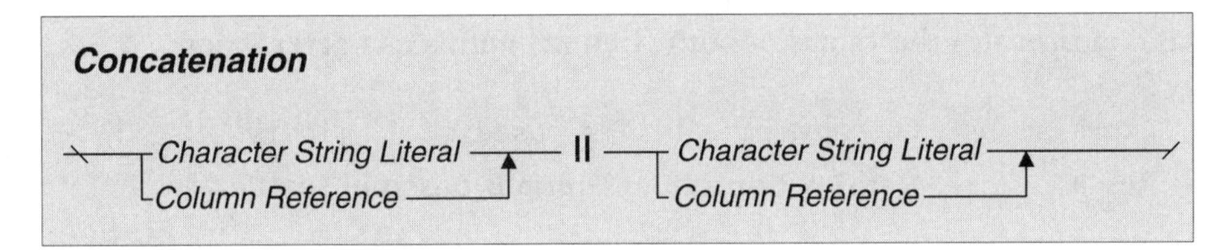

Figure 5-5 *Syntax diagram for the concatenation expression.*

Here's a general idea of how the concatenation operation works.

Expression `ItemOne || ItemTwo`

Result **ItemOneItemTwo**

Let's start with the easiest example in the world: concatenating two character string literals, such as a first and a last name.

Expression `'Mike' || 'Hernandez'`

Result **MikeHernandez**

There are two points to consider in this example: First, single quotes are required around each name because they are character string literals. Second, the first and last names are right next to each other. Although the operation combined them correctly, it may not be what you expected. The solution is to add a space between the names.

Expression `'Mike' || ' ' || 'Hernandez'`

Result **Mike Hernandez**

The previous example shows that you can concatenate additional character values by using more concatenation operators. There is no limit to the number of character values you can concatenate, but there is a limit to the length of the character string the concatenation operation returns. In general, the length of the character string returned by a concatenation operation can be no greater than the maximum length allowed for a varying-length Character data type. Your database system may handle this issue slightly differently, so check your documentation for further details.

Concatenating two or more character strings makes perfect sense, but you can also concatenate the values of two or more character columns in the same fashion. For example, suppose you have two columns called CompanyName and City. You can create an expression that concatenates the value of each column by using the column names within the expression. Here's an example that concatenates the values of both columns with a character string.

Expression	`CompanyName || ' is based in ' || City`
Result	**DataTex Consulting Group is based in Seattle**

There is no need to surround CompanyName or City with single quotes because they are Column References. (Remember Column Reference from the beginning of the chapter?) You can use a Column Reference in any type of expression, as you'll see in the examples throughout the remainder of the book.

You can concatenate dates or numbers with character strings as well, but you use the *CAST* function shown in Figure 5-6 to do so.

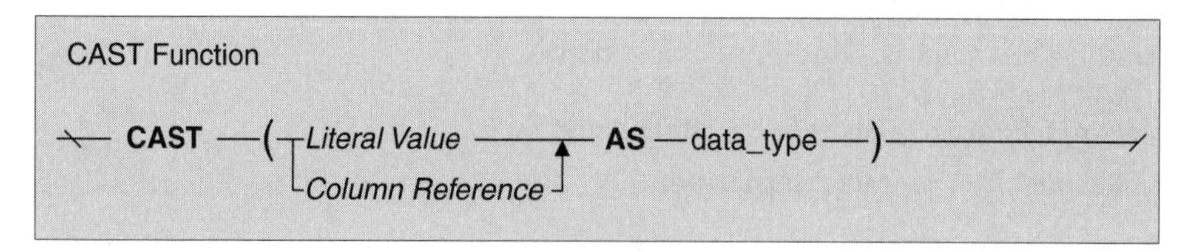

Figure 5-6 *Syntax diagram for the CAST function.*

The CAST function converts a literal value or the value of a column into a specific data type. This helps to ensure that the data types of the values in the expression are "compatible." All the values you use in an expression must be compatible in order for the operation defined within the expression to work properly. Otherwise, your database system is sure to raise an error message.

❖ **Note** Every database system has a function or set of functions that you can use to convert data types. Although the SQL Standard explicitly defines the CAST function, it may or may not be used in your particular RDBMS. Check your database system's documentation for details on the conversion functions your system provides.

Converting a literal value from one data type to another is a relatively intuitive and straightforward task. However, you'll have to keep the following restrictions in mind when you convert a column value from its original data type to a different data type.

- The value of a varying-length character column (VARCHAR) may be truncated if you convert it to a fixed-length character column (CHARACTER). Your database system should also give you a warning that the truncation is about to occur.
- You can convert a character column to any other data type, but the column's value must represent a legitimate literal value of the target data type. Note that the database system ignores any leading and/or trailing spaces when it converts a character column value to a numeric or datetime value.
- When you convert a numeric column's value to another Numeric data type, the database system will raise an error if the value doesn't fit the target data type. For example, you will likely get an error if you attempt to convert a REAL value greater than 32,767 to a SMALLINT. Additionally, numbers to the right of the decimal place will be truncated or rounded as appropriate when you convert a number that has a decimal fraction to an INTEGER or SMALLINT. The amount of truncation or rounding is determined by the database system.
- When you convert the value of a numeric column to a Character data type, one of three possible results will occur.
  1. It will convert successfully.
  2. It will be padded with blanks if its length is shorter than the defined length of the character column.
  3. The database system will raise an error if the character representation of the numeric value is longer than the defined length of the character column.

> ❖ **Note** Although the SQL Standard defines these restrictions, your database system may allow you some leeway when you convert a value from one data type to another. Refer to your database system's documentation for details.
>
> It's important to note that this list does not constitute the entire set of restrictions defined by the SQL Standard. We listed only those restrictions that apply to the data types we use in this book. For a more in-depth discussion on data types and data conversion issues, please refer to any of the books listed in Appendix C: Suggested Reading.

Now that you know the purpose of the CAST function, let's look at how to use it in a concatenation expression.

To concatenate a character string literal or the value of a character column with a date literal or the value of a date column, use the CAST function to convert the date value to a character string. Here's an example of using CAST to convert the value of a date column called DateEntered.

Expression `EntStageName|| ' was signed with our agency on ' || CAST(DateEntered as CHARACTER)`

Result **Modern Dance was signed with our agency on 1999-05-16**

You can also use the CAST function to concatenate a numeric literal or the value of a numeric column to a character data type. In the next example, we use CAST to convert the value of a numeric column called RetailPrice.

Expression `ProductName || ' sells for ' || CAST(RetailPrice AS CHARACTER)`

Result **Trek 9000 Mountain Bike sells for $1,200.00**

A concatenation expression can use character strings, datetime values, and numeric values simultaneously. The following example illustrates how you can use all three data types within the same expression.

Expression `'Order Number' || Cast(OrderNumber AS CHARACTER) || ' was placed on ' || CAST(OrderDate AS CHARACTER)`

Result **Order Number 1 was placed on 1999-07-04**

❖ **Note** The SQL Standard defines a variety of functions that you can use to extract information from a column or calculate a value across a range of rows. We'll cover some of these in more detail in Chapter 12.

Now that we've shown how to concatenate data from various sources into a single character string, let's look at the different types of expressions you can create using numeric data.

Mathematical

The SQL Standard defines addition, subtraction, multiplication, and division as the operations you can perform on numeric data. Yes, we know—this is quite a limited set of operations! Fortunately, most RDBMS programs provide a much wider variety of operations, including modulus, square root, exponential, and absolute power. They also provide a wide array of scientific, trigonometrical, statistical, and mathematical functions as well. For our purposes, however, we focus only on those operations defined by the SQL Standard.

The order in which the four mathematical operations are performed—known as the *order of precedence*—is an important issue when you create mathematical expressions. The SQL Standard gives equal precedence to multiplication and division and specifies that they should be performed before any addition or subtraction. This is slightly contrary to the order of precedence you probably learned back at school, where multiplication is done before division, division before addition, and addition before subtraction. In most database systems, however, mathematical expressions are evaluated from left to right by default. This could lead to some interesting results, depending on how you construct the expression! So, we strongly recommend that you make extensive use of parentheses in complex mathematical expressions to ensure that they evaluate properly.

If you remember how you created mathematical expressions back in school, then you already know how to create them in SQL. In essence, you use an optionally signed numeric value, a mathematical operator, and another optionally signed numeric value to create the expression. Figure 5-7 on the next page shows a diagram of this process.

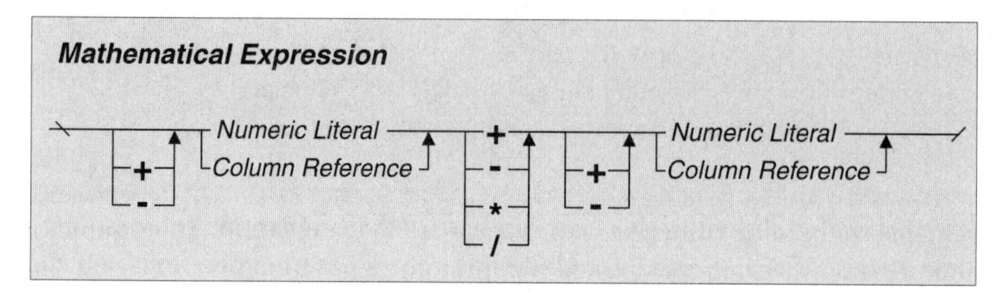

Figure 5-7 *Syntax diagram for a mathematical expression.*

Here are some examples of mathematical expressions using numeric literal values, column references, and combinations of both.

```
25 + 35
-12 * 22
RetailPrice * QuantityOnHand
TotalScore / GamesBowled
RetailPrice - 2.50
TotalScore / 12
```

As mentioned earlier, you need to use parentheses to ensure that a complex mathematical expression evaluates properly. Here's a simple example of how you might use parentheses in such an expression.

Expression	`(11 - 4) + (12 * 3)`
Result	**43**

Pay close attention to the placement of parentheses in your expression because it affects the expression's return value. The two expressions in the following example illustrate this quite clearly. Although both expressions have the exact same numbers and operators, the placement of the parentheses is entirely different and causes the expressions to return completely different values.

Expression	`(23 * 11) + 12`
Result	**265**

Expression	`23 * (11 + 12)`
Result	**529**

It's easy to see why you need to be careful with parentheses, but don't let this stop you from using them. They can be invaluable when working with complex expressions.

You can also use parentheses as a way to nest operations within an expression. When you use nested parenthetical operations, your database system evaluates them in an "innermost to outermost" fashion. Here's an example of an expression that contains nested parenthetical operations.

Expression	`(12 * (3 + 4)) - (24 / (10 + (6 - 4)))`
Result	**82**

Executing the operations within the expression is not really as difficult as it seems. Here's how your database system evaluates the expression.

1. (3+4) = **7**	
2. (6–4) = **2**	
3. (10+2) = **12**	*10 plus the result of the second operation*
4. (12*7) = **84**	*12 times the result of the first operation*
5. (24/12) = **2**	*24 divided by the result of the third operation*
6. 84–2 = **82**	*84 minus the result of the fifth operation*

Although we used numeric literals in the previous example, we could just as easily have used Column References or a combination of numeric literals and Column References as well. The key point to remember here is that you should plan and define your mathematical expressions carefully so that they return the results you seek.

When working with a mathematical expression, be sure that the values used in the expression are compatible. This is especially true of an expression that contains Column References. You can use the CAST function for this purpose just as you did within a concatenation expression. For example, say you have a column called TotalLength based on an INTEGER data type that stores whole numbers, and a column called Distance based on a REAL data type that stores numbers with decimal places. To add the value of the Distance column to the value of the TotalLength column, you must use the CAST function to convert the Distance column's value into an INTEGER data type or the TotalLength column's value into a REAL data type. The following is the expression you use to accomplish this.

Expression	`TotalLength + CAST(Distance AS INTEGER)`
Result	**483**

If you forget to ensure the compatibility of the column values within an expression, your database system may raise an error message and will probably cancel the execution of the operations within the expression as well. Most RDBMS programs are good about letting you know that it's a data type mismatch problem, so you'll know what you need to do to fix your expression. Many RDBMS systems handle such conversions automatically without warning you, but they usually convert all numbers to the most complex data type before evaluating the expression. In the previous example, your RDBMS might convert TotalLength to REAL. REAL is a more complex data type than INTEGER because all INTEGER values can be contained within the REAL data type. However, this may not be what you wanted.

As you just learned, creating mathematical expressions is a relatively easy task as long as you do a little planning and know how to use the CAST function to your advantage. In our last discussion for this section, we'll show you how to create expressions that add and subtract dates and times.

Date and Time Arithmetic

The SQL Standard defines addition and subtraction as the operations you can perform on dates and times. Contrary to what you might expect, many RDBMS programs differ in the way they implement these operations. Some database systems allow you to define these operations as you would in a mathematical expression, while others require you to use special "built-in" functions for these tasks. Refer to your database system's documentation for details on how your particular RDBMS handles these operations. For our purposes, we discuss date and time expressions only in general terms so that we can give you an idea of how these operations should work.

Date Expressions

Figure 5-8 shows the syntax for a date expression. As you can see, creating the expression is simple enough—take one value and add it to or subtract it from a second value. However, keep in mind a few points when creating date expressions.

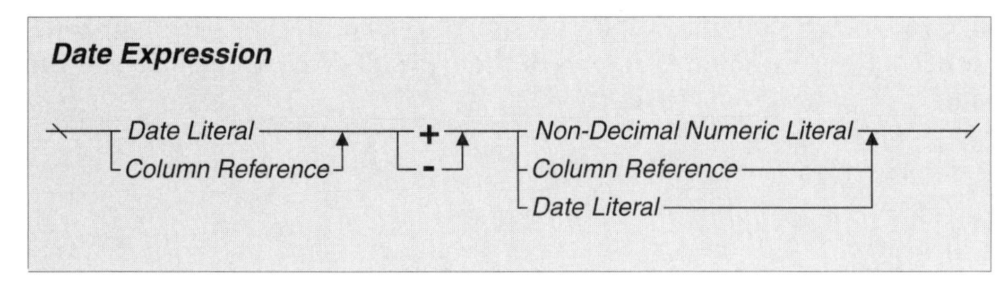

Figure 5-8 *Syntax diagram for a date expression.*

When you use a Column Reference, make certain it is based on a DATE data type or a *non-decimal numeric* data type. (INTEGER and SMALLINT are in this category.) Otherwise, you may have to use the CAST function to convert it into a DATE data type. It's interesting to note that the SQL Standard has no requirement for this conversion and leaves the matter entirely in the hands of the database vendors. Consequently, some database systems convert the column's values for you automatically, while others require you to convert the column explicitly. Your RDBMS will ultimately determine whether the conversion is required, so check your documentation.

The SQL Standard allows you to take a non-decimal numeric value and add it to or subtract it from a date. You can think of this as adding and subtracting days. This allows you to answer questions such as "What is the date nine days from now?" and "What was the date five days ago?" It certainly doesn't make sense to use a number with decimal places—how can you possibly get a date 3.5 days in the future?

While we're on this subject, here's another point to consider. You can subtract a date from another date, but you cannot *add* a date to another date. This is entirely logical when you think about it. Let's take a personnel database as an example. You may need to subtract a hire date from the current date to determine how long an employee has been with the company, but you would *add a number* to the current date to retrieve a date for the employee's next review.

The way you define a date expression determines whether it returns a date or a non-decimal numeric value. We can summarize date expressions as follows.

Date (Literal or Column) ± Non-Decimal Numeric (Literal or Column) = Date

Date (Literal or Column) - Date (Literal or Column) = Non-Decimal Numeric Value

Once you understand this simple concept, you can create any date expression you need. Here are some examples of the types of date expressions you can define.

```
'1999-05-16' - 5
'1999-11-14' + 12
ReviewDate + 90
EstimateDate - DaysRequired
'1999-07-22' - '1999-06-13'
ShipDate - OrderDate
```

❖ **Note** The SQL Standard states that you can add and subtract an INTERVAL data type from a DATE or TIME literal or a column containing a DATE or TIME value. However, most implementations do not support the INTERVAL data type defined in the SQL Standard, but they do allow you to add or subtract two DATE or TIME values. When you subtract one DATE or TIME value from another, you get the "interval" between the two dates or times, but as a DATE or TIME data type. When you add one DATE or TIME value to another, you get another DATE or TIME value. In all examples in this book, we assume that you can both add and subtract DATE and TIME values. Check your database documentation for details about how your system handles these expressions.

Time Expressions

You can create expressions using time values as well, and Figure 5-9 shows the syntax you use. Date and time expressions are very similar, and the same rules and restrictions that apply to a date expression also apply to a time expression.

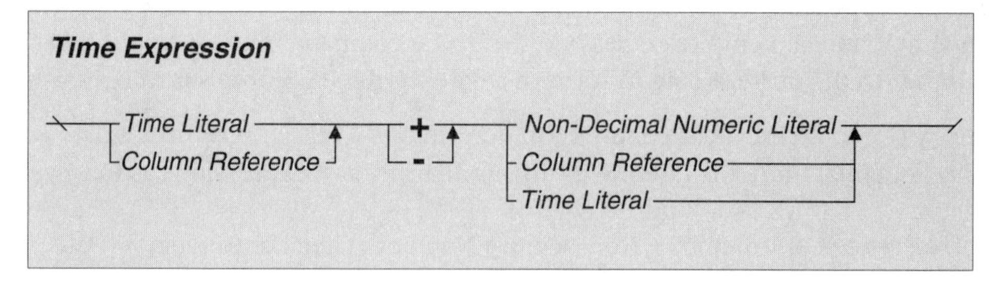

Figure 5-9 *Syntax diagram for a time expression.*

A time expression returns either a time or a non-decimal numeric value, depending upon how you define the expression itself. We can summarize time expressions as follows.

Time (Literal or Column) ± Non-Decimal Numeric (Literal or Column) = Time

Time (Literal or Column) - Time (Literal or Column) = Non-Decimal Numeric Value

Here are some general examples of time expressions.

```
'14:00' + '00:22'
'19:00' - '16:30'
StartTime + '00:19'
StopTime - StartTime
```

We said earlier that we would present date and time expressions only in general terms. Our goal was to make sure that you understood date and time expressions conceptually and that you had a general idea of the types of expressions you should be able to create. It is an unfortunate fact that most database systems do not implement the SQL Standard's specification for time expressions exactly and many only partially support the specification for the date expression. All database systems, however, provide one or more functions that allow you to work with dates and times, and we recommend that you study your database system's documentation to learn what type of functions your system provides. Although the syntax for these functions will be slightly different than what we've shown here, the general concepts we've taught regarding date and time arithmetic *will* apply.

Now that you know how to create the various types of expressions, the next step is to learn how to use them.

Using Expressions in a SELECT Clause

Knowing how to use expressions is arguably one of the most important concepts you'll learn in this book. You'll use expressions for a variety of purposes when working with SQL. For example, you use an expression to

- Create a calculated column in a query
- Search for a specific column value

- Filter the rows in a Result Set
- Connect two tables in a JOIN operation

We'll show you how to do this (and more) as we work through the rest of the book. We begin by showing you how to use basic expressions in a SELECT clause.

> ❖ **Note** Throughout this chapter, we use the "Request/Translation/Clean Up/SQL" technique introduced in Chapter 4.

You can use basic expressions in a SELECT clause to clarify information in a Result Set and to expand the Result Set's scope of information. For example, you can create expressions to concatenate first and last names, calculate the total price of a product, determine how long it took to complete a project, or specify a date for a patient's next appointment. Let's look at how you might use a concatenation expression, a mathematical expression, and a date expression in a SELECT clause. First, we'll work with the concatenation expression.

Working with a Concatenation Expression

Unlike mathematical and date expressions, you use concatenation expressions only to enhance the readability of the information contained in the Result Set of a SELECT Statement. Suppose you are posing the following request:

"Show me a current list of our employees and their phone numbers."

When translating this request into a SELECT Statement, you can improve the output of the Result Set somewhat by concatenating the first and last names into a single column. Here's one way you can translate this request.

Translation Select the first name, last name, and phone number of all our employees from the employees table

Clean Up Select ~~the~~ first name, last name, ~~and~~ phone number ~~of all our employees~~ from ~~the~~ employees ~~table~~

SQL

```
SELECT EmpFirstName || ' ' || EmpLastName,
   'Phone Number: ' || EmpPhoneNumber
FROM Employees
```

You probably noticed that aside from concatenating the first name column, a space, and the last name column together, we also concatenated the character literal string "Phone Number:" with the phone number column. This example clearly shows that you can easily use more than one concatenation expression in a SELECT clause to enhance the readability of the information in the Result Set. Remember that you can also concatenate values with different data types by using the CAST function. For instance, we concatenate a character column value with a numeric column value in the next example.

"Show me a list of all our vendors and their identification numbers."

Translation Select the vendor name and vendor ID from the vendors table

Clean Up Select ~~the~~ vendor name ~~and~~ vendor ID from ~~the~~ vendors ~~table~~

SQL

```
SELECT "The ID Number for " || VendName ||
   ' is ' || CAST(VendorID AS CHARACTER)
FROM Vendors
```

Although the concatenation expression is a useful tool in a SELECT Statement, it is one that you should use judiciously. When you use concatenation expressions containing long character string literals, keep in mind that the literals will appear in every row of the Result Set. You may end up cluttering the final result with repetitive information instead of enhancing it. Carefully consider your use of literals in concatenation expressions so that they work to your advantage.

Naming the Expression

When you use an expression in a SELECT clause, the Result Set includes a new column that displays the result of the operation defined in the expression. This new column is known as a calculated (or derived) column. For example, the Result Set for the following SELECT Statement will contain three columns—two "real" columns and one calculated column.

SQL

```
SELECT EmpFirstName || ' ' || EmpLastName,
   EmpPhoneNumber, EmpCity
FROM Employees
```

The two real columns are, of course, EmpPhoneNumber and EmpCity, and the calculated column is derived from the concatenation expression at the beginning of the SELECT clause.

According to the SQL Standard, you can optionally provide a name for the new column by using the AS keyword. Almost every database system, however, *requires* a name for a calculated column. Some database systems require you to provide the name explicitly, while others actually provide the name for you. Determine how your database system handles this before you work with the examples.

Figure 5-10 shows the syntax for defining a name for an expression. You can use any valid character string literal (enclosed in single quotes) for the name. Some database systems relax this requirement when you're naming an expression and require quotes only when your column name includes embedded spaces. However, we strongly recommend that you not use spaces in your names because the spaces can become problematic in some database programming languages.

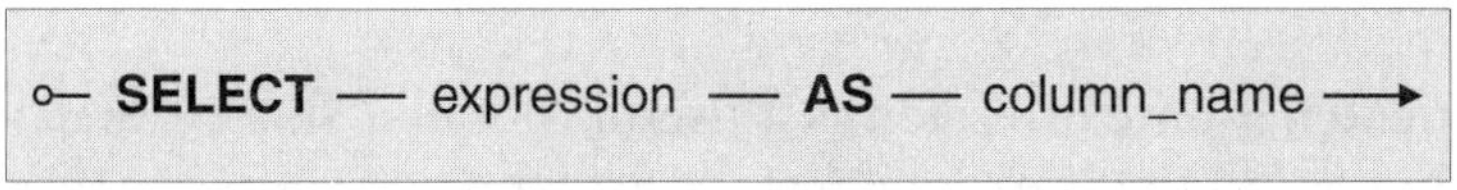

```
o— SELECT — expression — AS — column_name —→
```

Figure 5-10 *Naming an expression.*

Now we'll modify the SELECT Statement in the previous example and supply a name for the concatenation expression.

```
SQL        SELECT EmpFirstName || ' ' || EmpLastName AS
              EmployeeName, EmpPhoneNumber, EmpCity
           FROM Employees
```

The Result Set for this SELECT Statement will now contain three columns called EmployeeName, EmpPhoneNumber, and EmpCity.

Besides supplying a name for expressions, you can use the AS keyword to supply an "alias" for a real column name. Suppose you have a column called DOB and are concerned that some of your users or fellow workers may not be familiar with the meaning of the name. You can eliminate any possible misinterpretation of the name by using an alias. Here's an example of how you provide an alias for the DOB column.

```
SQL        SELECT EmpFirstName || ' ' || EmpLastName AS
              EmployeeName, DOB AS DateOfBirth
           FROM Employees
```

This SELECT Statement produces a Result Set with two columns called EmployeeName and DateOfBirth. You've now effectively eliminated any possible confusion of the information displayed in the Result Set.

Providing names for your calculated columns has a minor effect on the translation process. For example, here's one possible version of the translation process for the previous example.

"Give me a list of employee names and their dates of birth."

Translation Select first name and last name as EmployeeName and DOB as DateOfBirth from the employees table

Clean Up Select first name ~~and~~ || ‘‘ || last name as EmployeeName and DOB as DateOfBirth from ~~the~~ employees ~~table~~

```
SQL        SELECT EmpFirstName || ' ' || EmpLastName
              AS EmployeeName, DOB AS DateOfBirth
           FROM Employees
```

Once you get accustomed to using expressions, you won't need to state them quite as explicitly in your translation statements as we did here. You'll eventually be able to easily identify and define the expressions you need as you construct the SELECT Statement itself.

❖ **Note** Throughout the remainder of the book, we provide names for all calculated columns within an SQL statement, as appropriate.

Working with a Mathematical Expression

Mathematical expressions are arguably the most versatile of the three types of expressions, and you'll probably use them quite often. For example, you can use a mathematical expression to calculate a line item total, determine the average score from a given set of tests, calculate the difference between two lab results, and estimate the total seating capacity of a building. The real trick is to make certain your expression works, and that is just a function of doing a little careful planning.

Here's an example of how you might use a mathematical expression in a SELECT Statement.

"Give me a list of bowler names and their average scores."

Translation — Select first name and last name as bowler name and total score divided by games bowled as AverageScore from the bowlers table

Clean Up — Select first name and last name as BowlerName ~~and~~ total score ~~divided by~~ / games bowled as AverageScore from ~~the~~ bowlers ~~table~~

SQL

```
SELECT BowlerFirstName || ' ' || BowlerLastName
   AS BowlerName, TotalScore / GamesBowled AS
   AverageScore
FROM Bowlers
```

As the example shows, you're not limited to using a single type of expression in a SELECT Statement. Rather, you can use a variety of expressions to retrieve the information you need in the Result Set. Here's another way the previous SQL statement can be written.

SQL

```
SELECT BowlerFirstName || ' ' || BowlerLastName
   || ' has an average score of ' ||
   (CAST(TotalScore / GamesBowled AS
   CHARACTER)) AS BowlerAverages
FROM Bowlers
```

The information you can provide using mathematical expressions is virtually limitless, but you must properly plan your expressions and use the CAST function as appropriate.

Working with a Date Expression

Using a date expression is similar to using a mathematical expression in that you're simply adding or subtracting values. You can use date expressions for all sorts of tasks. For example, you can calculate an estimated ship date, project the number of days it will take to finish a project, or determine a follow-up appointment date for a patient. Here's an example of how you might use a date expression in a SELECT clause.

"How many days did it take to ship each order?"

Translation — Select the order number and ship date minus order date as DaysToShip from the orders table

Clean Up Select ~~the~~ order number ~~and~~ ship date ~~minus~~ - order date as DaysToShip from ~~the~~ orders ~~table~~

SQL
```
SELECT OrderNumber, ShipDate - OrderDate AS
   DaysToShip
FROM Orders
```

You can use time expressions in the same manner.

"What would be the start time for each class if we began each class ten minutes later than the current start time?"

Translation Select the start time and start time plus 10 as NewStartTime from the classes table

Clean Up Select ~~the~~ start time ~~and~~ start time ~~plus~~ + 10 as NewStartTime from ~~the~~ classes ~~table~~

SQL
```
SELECT StartTime, StartTime + '00:10'
   AS NewStartTime
FROM Classes
```

As we mentioned earlier, all database systems provide a function or set of functions for working with date values. We did want to give you an idea of how you might use dates and times in your SELECT Statements, however, and we again recommend that you refer to your database system's documentation for details on the date and time functions your database system provides.

A Brief Digression: Value Expressions

You now know how to use Column References, Literal Values, and expressions in a SELECT clause; you also know how to assign a name to a Column Reference or an expression. Now we'll show you how this all fits into the larger scheme of things.

The SQL Standard refers to a Column Reference, Literal Value, and expression collectively as a *Value Expression*. Figure 5-11 on the next page shows how a Value Expression is defined.

Let's take a closer look at the components of a Value Expression.

- The syntax begins with an optional plus or minus sign. You use either of these signs when you want the Value Expression to return a signed numeric value. The value itself can be a numeric literal, the value of a numeric column, a call to a function that returns a numeric value (we covered the CAST function earlier in this chapter), or the return value of a mathematical expression. You cannot use the plus or minus sign before an expression that returns a Character data type.

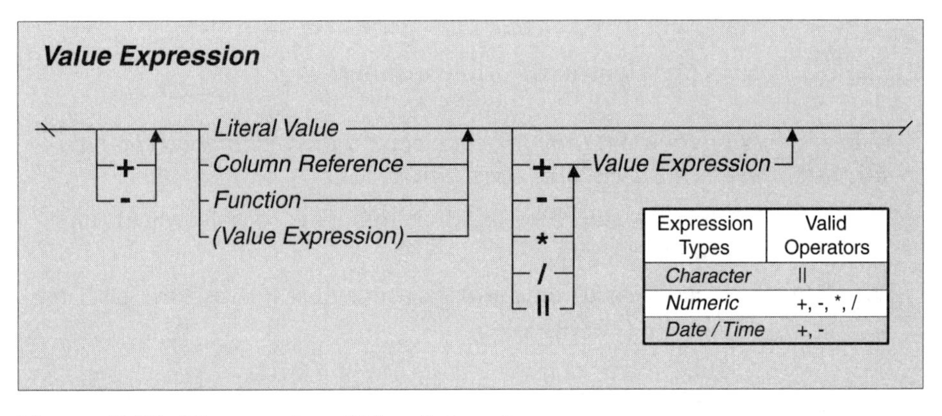

Figure 5-11 *Diagram for a Value Expression.*

- You can see that the first list also includes (Value Expression). This means that you can use a complex Value Expression comprised of other Value Expressions that include concatenation or mathematical operators of their own. The parentheses force the database system to evaluate this Value Expression first. We'll discuss order of precedence of operations in more detail in the next chapter.
- No, you're not seeing things: "Value Expression" does appear after the list of operators as well. The fact that you can use other Value Expressions within a Value Expression allows you to create very complex expressions.
- The next item in the syntax is a list of operators. As you can see in the inset box, the type of expression you use at the beginning of the syntax determines which operators you may select from this list.

By its very definition, a Value Expression returns a value that is used by some component of an SQL statement. The SQL Standard specifies the use of a Value Expression in a variety of statements and defined terms. No matter where you use it, you'll always define a Value Expression in the same manner as you've learned here.

We'll put this all into some perspective by showing you how a Value Expression is used in a SELECT Statement. Figure 5-12 shows a modified version of the final SELECT Statement syntax diagram presented in Chapter 4. This new syntax gives you the flexibility to use literals, Column References, expressions, or any combination of these within a single SELECT Statement. You can optionally name your Value Expressions with the AS keyword.

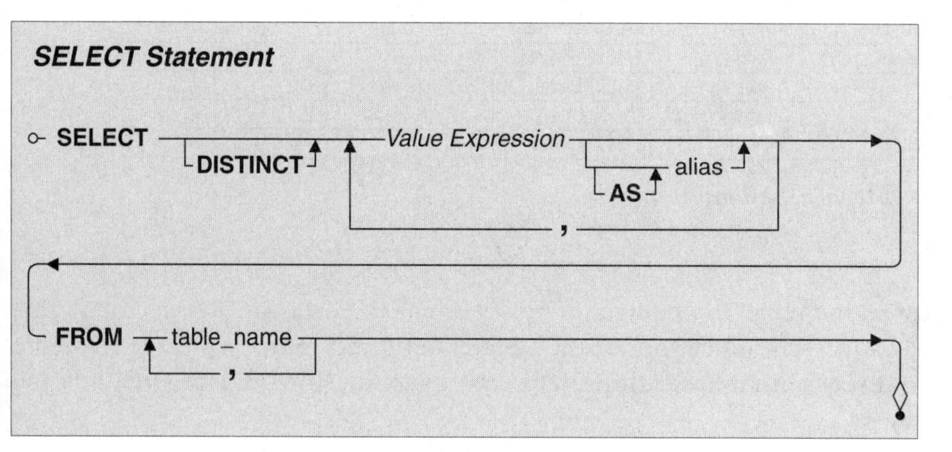

Figure 5-12 *The syntax diagram for the SELECT Statement.*

Throughout the remainder of the book, we use the term Value Expression to refer to a Column Reference, a Literal Value, or an expression as appropriate. In later chapters, we discuss how to use a Value Expression in other statements and show you a couple of other items that a Value Expression represents.

Now, back to our regularly scheduled program.

That "Nothing" Value—Null

As you know, a table consists of columns and rows. Each column represents a characteristic of the subject of the table, and each row represents a unique instance of the table's subject. You can also think of a row as one complete set of column values—each row contains exactly one value from each column in the table. Figure 5-13 on the next page shows an example of a typical table.

Thus far, we've shown how to retrieve information from the data in a table with a SELECT Statement and how to manipulate that data by using Value Expressions. All of this works just fine because we've continually made the assumption that each column in the table contains data. But as Figure 5-13 clearly illustrates, a column sometimes may not contain a value for a particular

Customers

CustomerID	CustFirstName	CustLastName	CustAddress	CustCity	CustCounty	CustState
1001	Suzanne	Viescas	15127 NE 24th, #383	Redmond	King	WA
1002	Wil	Thompson	122 Spring River Drive	Duvall	King	WA
1003	Gary	Hallmark	Route 2, Box 203B	El Paso	El Paso	TX
1004	Michael	Davolio	672 Lamont Ave	Marysville		WA
1005	Kenneth	Peacock	4110 Old Redmond Rd.	Fremont		CA
1006	John	Viescas	15127 NE 24th, #383	Redmond	King	WA
1007	Laura	Callahan	901 Pine Avenue	Washington		DC
1008	Neil	Patterson	233 West Valley Hwy	Everett	Snohomish	WA

Figure 5-13 *A typical Customers table.*

row in the table. Depending on how you use the data, the absence of a value may adversely affect your SELECT Statements and Value Expressions. Before we discuss any implications, let's first examine how SQL regards missing values.

Introducing Null

In SQL, a *Null* represents a *missing* or *unknown* value. You must understand from the outset that a Null *does not* represent a zero, a character string of one or more blank spaces, or a "zero-length" character string. The reasons are quite simple.

- A zero can have a very wide variety of meanings. It can represent the state of an account balance, the current number of available first-class ticket upgrades, or the current stock level of a particular product.
- Although a character string of one or more blank spaces is guaranteed to be meaningless to most of us, it is something that is definitely meaningful to SQL. A blank space is a valid character as far as SQL is concerned, and a character string composed of three blank spaces (`'   '`) is just as legitimate as a character string composed of three letters (`'abc'`).
- A "zero-length" string—two consecutive single quotes with no space in between (`''`)—can be meaningful under certain circumstances. In an Employee table, for example, a zero-length string value in a column called MiddleInitial may represent the fact that a particular employee does not have a middle initial in his name.

A Null is quite useful when used for its stated purpose, and the Customers table in Figure 5-13 shows a clear example of this. In the CustCounty column, each Null represents a missing or unknown county name for the row in which it appears. In order to use Nulls correctly, you must understand why they occur in the first place.

Missing values are commonly the result of human error. Consider the row for Michael Davolio, for example. If you're entering the data for Mr. Davolio and you fail to ask him for the name of the county he lives in, that data is considered missing and is represented in the row as a Null. Once you recognize the error, however, you can correct it by calling Mr. Davolio and asking him for the county name.

Unknown values appear in a table for a variety of reasons; one reason may be that a specific value you need for a column is as yet undefined. For example, you may have a Categories table in a School Scheduling database that doesn't have a category for a new set of classes that you want to offer beginning in the fall session. Another reason a table might contain unknown values is that the values are truly unknown. Let's use the Customers table in Figure 5-13 once again and consider the row for Kenneth Peacock. Say that you're entering the data for Mr. Peacock and you ask him for the name of the county he lives in. If he doesn't know the county name and you don't happen to know the county that includes the city in which he lives, then the value for the county column in his row is truly unknown and is represented in his row as a Null. Obviously, you can correct the problem once either of you determines the correct county name.

A column value may also be Null if none of its values apply to a particular row. Let's assume for a moment that you're working with an Employee table that contains a Salary column and an HourlyRate column. The value for one of these two columns is always going to be Null because an employee cannot be paid both a fixed salary and an hourly rate.

It's important to note that there is a very slim difference between "does not apply" and "is not applicable." In the previous example, the value of one of the two columns literally does not apply. But let's assume you're working with a Patient table that contains a column called HairColor and you're currently updating a row for an existing male patient. If that patient recently became bald, then the value for that column is definitely not applicable. Although you could just use a Null to represent a value that is not applicable, we recommend that you use a true value such as "N/A" or "Not Applicable." This will make the information clearer in the long run.

As you can see, whether you allow Nulls in a table depends on the manner in which you're using the data. Now that we've shown you the positive side of using Nulls, let's take a look at the negative implication of using Nulls.

The Problem with Nulls

The major drawback of Nulls is their adverse effect on mathematical operations. Any operation involving a Null evaluates to Null. This is logically reasonable—if a number is unknown then the result of the operation is necessarily unknown. Note how a Null alters the outcome of the operation in the next example.

```
(25 * 3) + 4 = 79
(Null * 3) + 4 = Null
(25 * Null) + 4 = Null
(25 *3) + Null = Null
```

The same result occurs when an operation involves columns containing Null values. For example, suppose you execute the following SELECT Statement and it returns the Result Set shown in Figure 5-14.

```
SQL        SELECT ProductID, ProductDescription, Category,
              Price, QuantityOnHand, Price *
              QuantityOnHand AS TotalValue
           FROM Products
```

Products

ProductID	ProductDescription	Category	Price	QuantityOnHand	TotalValue
70001	Shur-Lok U-Lock	Accessories		12	
70002	SpeedRite Cyclecomputer		65.00	20	1,300.00
70003	SteelHead Microshell Helmet	Accessories	36.00	33	1,118.00
70004	SureStop 133-MB Brakes	Components	23.50	16	376.00
70005	Diablo ATM Mountain Bike	Bikes	1,200.00		
70006	UltraVision Helmet Mount Mirrors		7.45	10	74.50

Figure 5-14 *Nulls involved in a mathematical expression.*

The operation represented by the TotalValue column is completed successfully as long as both the Price and QuantityOnHand columns are valid numeric values. Otherwise, TotalValue will contain a Null if either Price or QuantityOnHand contains a Null. The good news is that TotalValue will contain an appropriate value once you replace the Nulls in Price and QuantityOnHand with valid numeric values. You can avoid this problem completely by ensuring that the columns you use in a mathematical expression do not contain Null values.

This is not the only time we'll be concerned with Nulls. In Chapter 12, Simple Totals, we'll see how Nulls impact SELECT Statements that summarize information.

Sample Statements

Now that you know how to use various types of Value Expressions in the SELECT clause of a SELECT Statement, let's take a look, on the next eight pages, at some examples using the tables from each of the sample databases.

> ❖ **Note** We've combined the Translation and Clean Up steps in the following examples so that you can begin to learn how to consolidate the process. Although you'll still work with all three steps during the body of any given chapter, you'll get a chance to work with the consolidated process in each Sample Statements section.

Sales Order Database

"What is the inventory value of each product?"

Translation/ Clean Up: Select ~~the~~ product name, retail price ~~times~~ * quantity on hand as InventoryValue from ~~the~~ products ~~table~~

SQL

```
SELECT ProductName,
   RetailPrice * QuantityOnHand AS
   InventoryValue
FROM Products
```

Product_Inventory_Value (40 Rows)

ProductName	InventoryValue
Trek 9000 Mountain Bike	$7,200.00
Eagle FS-3 Mountain Bike	$14,400.00
Dog Ear Cyclecomputer	$1,500.00
Victoria Pro All Weather Tires	
Dog Ear Helmet Mount Mirrors	$89.40
Viscount Mountain Bike	$3,175.00
Viscount C-500 Wireless Bike Computer	$1,470.00
Kryptonite Advanced 2000 U-Lock	
<<more rows here >>	

"How many days elapsed between the order date and the ship date for each order?"

Translation/ Clean Up — Select ~~the~~ order number, order date, ship date, ship date ~~minus~~ - order date as DaysElapsed from ~~the~~ orders ~~table~~

SQL

```
SELECT OrderNumber, OrderDate, ShipDate,
   ShipDate-OrderDate AS DaysElapsed
FROM Orders
```

Shipping_Days_Analysis (944 Rows)

OrderNumber	OrderDate	ShipDate	DaysElapsed
1	1999-07-01	1999-07-04	3
2	1999-07-01	1999-07-03	2
3	1999-07-01	1999-07-04	3
4	1999-07-01	1999-07-03	2
5	1999-07-01	1999-07-01	0
6	1999-07-01	1999-07-05	4
7	1999-07-01	1999-07-04	3
8	1999-07-01	1999-07-01	0
9	1999-07-01	1999-07-04	3
10	1999-07-01	1999-07-04	3
<<more rows here>>			

Entertainment Database

"How long is each engagement due to run?"

Translation/ Clean Up	Select ~~the~~ engagement number, end date ~~minus~~ - start date ~~plus one~~ 1 as DueToRun from ~~the~~ engagements ~~table~~
SQL	SELECT EngagementNumber, CAST(EndDate - StartDate + 1 AS CHARACTER) || ' day(s)' AS DueToRun FROM Engagements

```
SELECT EngagementNumber, CAST(EndDate -
   StartDate + 1 AS CHARACTER) || ' day(s)'
   AS DueToRun
FROM Engagements
```

Engagement_Lengths (131 Rows)

EngagementNumber	DueToRun
1	4 day(s)
2	5 day(s)
3	6 day(s)
4	7 day(s)
5	4 day(s)
6	5 day(s)
7	8 day(s)
8	8 day(s)
9	11 day(s)
10	10 day(s)
<<more rows here>>	

❖ **Note** You have to add "1" to the date expression in order to account for each date in the engagement. Otherwise, you'll get "0 days(s)" for an engagement that starts and ends on the same date.

"What is the net amount for each of our contracts?"

Translation/ Clean Up: Select ~~the~~ engagement number, contract price, contract price ~~times~~ * 0.12 as OurFee, contract price ~~minus~~ - (contract price ~~times~~ * 0.12) as NetAmount from ~~the~~ engagements ~~table~~

SQL

```
SELECT EngagementNumber, ContractPrice,
   ContractPrice * 0.12 AS OurFee,
   ContractPrice -(ContractPrice * 0.12)
   AS NetAmount
FROM Engagements
```

Net_Amount_Per_Contract (131 Rows)

EngagementNumber	ContractPrice	OurFee	NetAmount
1	$170.00	$20.40	$149.60
2	$200.00	$24.00	$176.00
3	$590.00	$70.80	$519.20
4	$470.00	$56.40	$413.60
5	$1,130.00	$135.60	$994.40
6	$2,300.00	$276.00	$2,024.00
7	$770.00	$92.40	$677.60
8	$1,850.00	$222.00	$1,628.00
9	$1,370.00	$164.40	$1,205.60
10	$3,650.00	$438.00	$3,212.00
<<more rows here >>			

School Scheduling Database

"How many years has each staff member been with the school?"

Translation / Clean Up: Select last name || ',' || ~~and~~ first name ~~concatenated with a comma~~ as Staff, date hired, ~~and~~ (('1999-10-01' ~~minus~~ - date hired) ~~divided by~~ / 365) as YearsWithSchool from ~~the~~ staff ~~table~~

SQL:

```
SELECT StfLastName || ', ' || StfFirstName
   AS Staff, DateHired, CAST(('1999-10-01' -
   DateHired) / 365 AS INTEGER) AS YearsWithSchool
FROM Staff
ORDER BY StfLastName, StrFirstName
```

Length_Of_Service (27 Rows)

Staff	DateHired	YearsWithSchool
Black, Alastair	1988-12-11	10
Bonnicksen, Joyce	1986-03-02	13
Buchanan, Albert	1985-08-02	14
Buchanan, Amelia	1988-05-31	11
Callahan, David	1987-01-13	12
Callahan, Laura	1989-11-02	9
Coie, Caroline	1983-01-28	16
Davis, Allan	1989-08-20	10
Davolio, Michael	1989-02-09	10
Ehrlich, Katherine	1985-03-08	14
<<more rows here >>		

❖ **Note** The expression in this SELECT Statement is technically correct and works as expected, but it returns the wrong answer for any leap year. You can correct this problem by using the appropriate date arithmetic function provided by your database system. As mentioned earlier, most database systems provide their own methods of working with dates and times.

"Show me a list of staff members, their salaries, and a proposed 7% bonus for each staff member."

Translation/Clean Up — Select ~~the~~ last name || ',' || ~~and~~ first name as StaffMember, salary, ~~and~~ salary ~~times~~ * 0.07 as Bonus from ~~the~~ staff ~~table~~

SQL

```
SELECT StfLastName || ', ' || StfFirstName
   AS Staff, Salary, Salary * 0.07 AS Bonus
FROM Staff
```

Proposed_Bonuses (27 Rows)

Staff	Salary	Bonus
Black, Alastair	$60,000.00	$4,200.00
Bonnicksen, Joyce	$60,000.00	$4,200.00
Buchanan, Albert	$45,000.00	$3,150.00
Buchanan, Amelia	$48,000.00	$3,360.00
Callahan, David	$50,000.00	$3,500.00
Callahan, Laura	$45,000.00	$3,150.00
Coie, Caroline	$52,000.00	$3,640.00
Davis, Allan	$56,000.00	$3,920.00
Davolio, Michael	$49,000.00	$3,430.00
Ehrlich, Katherine	$45,000.00	$3,150.00
<<more rows here>>		

Bowling League Database

"What was each bowler's monthly average score for each of the four months in the tournament?"

Translation/ Clean Up
: Select last name || ‘,‘ || ~~and~~ first name ~~concatenated with a comma~~ as Bowler, total score, total score ~~divided by~~ / 4 as AverageScorePerMonth from ~~the~~ bowlers ~~table and~~ order by bowler

SQL

```
SELECT BowlerLastName || ', ' ||
   BowlerFirstName AS Bowler, TotalScore,
   TotalScore/4 AS AverageScorePerMonth
FROM Bowlers
ORDER BY Bowler
```

Average_Monthly_Score (32 Rows)

Bowler	TotalScore	AverageScorePerMonth
Black, Alastair	6319	1579.75
Cunningham, David	6702	1675.5
Ehrlich, Zachary	6208	1552
Fournier, Barbara	6242	1560.5
Fournier, David	6581	1645.25
Hallmark, Alaina	6622	1655.5
Hallmark, Bailey	6291	1572.75
Hallmark, Elizabeth	6379	1594.75
Hallmark, Gary	6593	1648.25
Hernandez, Kendra	6276	1569
<<more rows here>>		

"What was the point spread between a bowler's handicap and raw score for each match and game played?"

Translation/Clean Up: Select bowler ID, match ID, game number, handicap score, raw score, handicap score ~~minus~~ - raw score as PointDifference from ~~the~~ bowler scores ~~table~~ ~~and~~ order by bowler ID, match ID, game number

SQL

```
SELECT BowlerID, MatchID, GameNumber,
   HandiCapScore, RawScore,
   HandiCapScore-RawScore AS PointDifference
FROM Bowler_Scores
ORDER BY BowlerID, MatchID, GameNumber
```

Handicap_vs_RawScore (1344 Rows)

BowlerID	MatchID	GameNumber	HandiCapScore	RawScore	PointDifference
1	1	1	192	146	46
1	1	2	192	146	46
1	1	3	199	153	46
1	5	1	192	145	47
1	5	2	184	137	47
1	5	3	199	152	47
1	10	1	189	140	49
1	10	2	186	137	49
1	10	3	210	161	49
<<more rows here>>					

SUMMARY

We began the chapter by taking a look at using explicit values in your SELECT Statement. You learned that you can use character strings, numbers, dates, and times in a SELECT clause and that they are collectively known as literals. We then introduced you to the concept of using an expression to broaden or narrow the scope of information you retrieve from the database. We also explained that an expression is some form of operation involving numbers, character strings, or dates and times.

Our discussion then turned to the subject of data types, and we showed you that there are seven major data types in three general categories. We then went on to discuss each data type in some detail and explained that every data type has one or more uniquely named variations.

Next, we returned to the subject of expressions and provided a concise overview of each type of expression. We showed you how to concatenate strings of characters together and how to concatenate strings with other types of data using the CAST function. We then showed you how to create mathematical expressions, and we explained how the order of precedence affects a given mathematical operation. We closed this discussion with a look at date and time expressions. After showing you how the SQL Standard handles dates and times, we revealed that most database systems provide their own methods of working with dates and times.

We then proceeded to the subject of using expressions in a SELECT Statement, and we showed you how to incorporate expressions in the SELECT clause. We then showed you how to use both Literal Values and columns within an expression, as well as how to name the column that holds the result value of the expression. Before ending this discussion, we took a brief digression and introduced you to the Value Expression. We revealed that the SQL Standard uses this term to refer to a Column Reference, Literal Value, and expression collectively, and that you can use a Value Expression in various clauses of an SQL statement. (More on this in later chapters, of course!)

We closed this chapter with a discussion on Nulls. You learned that a Null represents a missing or unknown value. We showed you how to use a Null properly and explained that it can be quite useful under the right circumstances. But we also discussed how Nulls adversely affect mathematical operations. You now know that a mathematical operation involving a Null value returns a Null value. We also showed you how Nulls can make the information in a Result Set inaccurate.

In the next chapter, we'll discuss the idea of retrieving a very specific set of information. We'll then show you how to use a WHERE clause to filter the information retrieved by a SELECT Statement.

The following section presents a number of requests that you can work out on your own.

Problems for You to Solve

Below, we show you the request statement and the name of the solution query in the sample databases. If you want some practice, you can work out the SQL for each request and then check your answer with the query we saved in the samples. Don't worry if your syntax doesn't exactly match the syntax of the queries we saved—as long as your Result Set is the same.

Sales Order Database

1. *"What if we adjusted each product price by reducing it 5%?"*
   You can find the solution in Adjusted_Wholesale_Prices (90 rows).
2. *"Show me a list of orders made by each customer in descending date order."*
   (Hint: You may need to order by more than one column for the information to display properly.)
   You can find the solution in Orders_By_Customer_And_Date (944 rows).
3. *"Compile a complete list of vendor names and addresses in vendor name order."*
   You can find the solution in Vendor_Addresses (10 rows).

Entertainment Database

1. *"Give me the names of all our customers by city."*
   (Hint: You'll have to use an ORDER BY clause on one of the columns.)
   You can find the solution in Customers_By_City (15 rows).
2. *"List all entertainers and their Web sites."*
   You can find the solution in Entertainer_Web_Sites (13 rows).
3. *"Show the date of each agent's first six-month performance review."*
   (Hint: You'll need to use date arithmetic to answer this request.)
   You can find the solution in First_Performance_Review (8 rows).

School Scheduling Database

1. *"Give me a list of staff members, and show them in descending order of salary."*
   You can find the solution in Staff_List_By_Salary (27 rows).
2. *"Can you give me a staff member phone list?"*
   You can find the solution in Staff_Member_Phone_List (27 rows).
3. *"List the names of all our students, and order them by the cities they live in."*
   You can find the solution in Students_By_City (18 rows).

Bowling League Database

1. *"Show next year's tournament date for each tournament location."*
   You can find the solution in Next_Years_Tourney_Dates (14 rows).
2. *"List the name and phone number for each member of the league."*
   You can find the solution in Phone_List (32 rows).
3. *"Give me a listing of each team's lineup."*
   (Hint: Base this query on the Bowlers table.)
   You can find the solution in Team_Lineups (32 rows).

6

Filtering Your Data

"I keep six honest-serving men
(They taught me all I knew.)
Their names are What and Why and When
and How and Where and Who."
—Rudyard Kipling
"I keep six honest-serving men"

Topics Covered in This Chapter

In the previous two chapters, we discussed the techniques you use to see all the information in a given table. We also discussed how to create and use expressions to broaden or narrow the scope of that information. In this chapter, we'll show you how to "fine-tune" what you retrieve by filtering the information using a WHERE clause.

Refining What You See Using WHERE

The type of SELECT Statement we've worked with so far retrieves all the rows from a given table and uses them in the statement's Result Set. This is great if you really do need to see all the information the table has to offer. But what if you want to find only the rows that apply to a specific person, a specific place, a particular numeric value, or a range of dates? These are not unusual requests. In fact, they are the impetus behind many of the questions you commonly pose to the database. You may, for example, have a need to ask the following types of questions.

"Who are our customers in Seattle?"

"Show me a current list of our Bellevue employees and their phone numbers."

"What kind of music classes do we currently offer?"

"Give me a list of classes that earn three credits."

"Which entertainers maintain a Web site?"

"Give me a list of engagements for the Caroline Coie Trio."

"Give me a list of customers who placed orders in May."

"Give me the names of our staff members who were hired on May 16, 1985."

"What is the current tournament schedule for Red Rooster Lanes?"

"Which bowlers haven't been assigned to a team?"

In order to answer these questions, you'll have to expand your SQL vocabulary once again by adding another clause to our SELECT Statement: the WHERE clause.

The WHERE Clause

You use a WHERE clause in a SELECT Statement to filter the data the statement draws from a table. The WHERE clause contains a *Search Condition* that it uses as the filter, and it is this Search Condition that provides the mechanism needed to select only the rows you need or remove the ones you don't want. Your database system applies the Search Condition to each row in the logical table defined by the FROM clause. Figure 6-1 shows the syntax of the SELECT Statement with the WHERE clause.

A Search Condition contains one or more *Predicates*, each of which is an expression that tests one or more Value Expressions and returns a True, False, or Unknown answer. As you'll learn a bit later, you can combine multiple Pred-

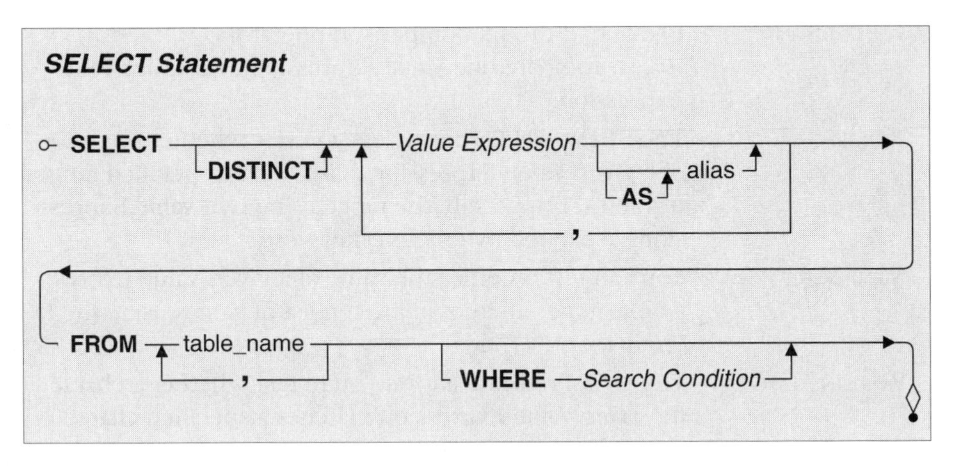

Figure 6-1 *SELECT Statement with a WHERE clause.*

icates into a Search Condition using AND or OR Boolean operators. When the entire Search Condition evaluates to True for a particular row, you will see that row in the final Result Set. Note that when a Search Condition contains only one Predicate, the terms "Search Condition" and "Predicate" are synonymous.

Remember from Chapter 5 that a Value Expression can contain column names, Literal Values, functions, or other Value Expressions. When you construct a Predicate, you will typically include at least one Value Expression that refers to a column from the tables you specify in the FROM clause.

The simplest and perhaps most commonly used Predicate compares one Value Expression (a column) to another (a literal). For example, if you want only the rows from the Customers table in which the value of the customer last name column is "Smith," you write a Predicate that compares the last name column to the Literal Value "Smith."

```
SQL        SELECT CustLastName
           FROM Customers
           WHERE CustLastName = 'Smith'
```

The Predicate in the WHERE clause is equivalent to asking this question for each row in the Customers table: "Does the customer last name equal "Smith"?" When the answer to this question is Yes (True) for any given row in the Customers table, that row appears in the Result Set.

The SQL Standard defines five basic Predicates: Comparison, BETWEEN, IN, LIKE, and IS NULL.

COMPARISON — Use one of the six comparison operators (=, <>, <, >, <=, >=) to compare one Value Expression to another Value Expression.

RANGE — The BETWEEN Predicate lets you test whether the value of a given Value Expression falls within a specified range of values. You specify the range using two Value Expressions separated by the AND keyword.

MEMBERSHIP — You can test whether the value of a given Value Expression matches an item in a given list of values using the IN Predicate.

PATTERN MATCH — The LIKE Predicate allows you to test whether a character string Value Expression matches a specified character string pattern.

NULL — Use the IS NULL Predicate to determine whether a Value Expression evaluates to Null.

Using a WHERE Clause

Before we explore each of the basic Predicates in the SQL Standard, let's first take a look at another example of how to construct a simple WHERE clause. This time, we'll give you a detailed walk-through of the steps to build your request.

> ❖ **Note** Throughout this chapter, we use the "Request/Translation/Clean Up/SQL" technique that we introduced in Chapter 4.

Suppose you're posing the following request to the database.

"What are the names of our customers who live in the state of Washington?"

When composing a translation statement for this type of request, you must try to indicate the information you want to see in the Result Set as explicitly and clearly as possible. You'll expend more effort to rephrase a request than you've been accustomed to so far, but the results will be well worth the extra work. Here's how you translate this particular request.

Translation — Select first name and last name from the customers table for those customers who live in Washington State

You'll clean up this translation in the usual fashion, but you'll also perform two extra tasks. First, look for any words or phrases that indicate or imply some type of restriction. A dead giveaway are the words "where," "who," and "for." Here are some examples of the types of phrases you're trying to identify.

"...who live in Bellevue."

"...for everyone whose zip code is 98125."

"...who placed orders in May."

"...for suppliers in California."

"...who were hired on May 16, 1985."

"...where the area code is 425."

"...for Mike Hernandez."

When you find such a restriction, you're ready for the second task. Study the phrase and try to determine which column is going to be tested, what value that column is going to be tested against, and how the column is going to be tested. The answers to these questions will help you formulate the Search Condition for your WHERE clause. Let's apply these questions to our translation statement.

- Which column is going to be tested? **State**
- What value is it going to be tested against? **'WA'**
- How is the column going to be tested? **Using the "equals" operator**

You need to be familiar with the structure of the table you're using to answer the request. If necessary, have a copy of the table structure handy before you begin to answer these questions.

❖ **Note** Sometimes the answers to these questions are evident, and other times the answers are implied. We'll show you how to make the distinction and decipher the correct answers as we work through other examples in this chapter.

After answering the questions, take them and create the appropriate condition. Next, cross out the original restriction and replace it with the word WHERE and the Search Condition you just created. Here's how your clean up statement will look after you've completed this task.

Clean Up	Select first name ~~and~~ last name from ~~the~~ customers ~~table for those customers who live in~~ where state ~~equals~~ = 'WA' ~~Washington State~~

Now you can turn this into a proper SELECT Statement.

```
SQL        SELECT CustFirstName, CustLastName
           FROM Customers
           WHERE CustState = 'WA'
```

The Result Set of our completed SELECT Statement will display only those customers who live in the state of Washington.

That's all there is to defining a WHERE clause. As we indicated at the beginning of this section, it's simply a matter of creating the appropriate Search Condition and placing it in the WHERE clause. The real work, however, is in defining the conditions.

Defining Search Conditions

Now that you have an idea of how to create a simple WHERE clause, let's take a closer look at the five basic types of Predicates you can define.

Comparison

The most common type of condition is one that uses a Comparison Predicate to compare two Value Expressions to each other. As you can see in Figure 6-2, you can define six different types of comparisons using the following Comparison Predicate operators.

= Equals	< Less Than	<= Less Than or Equal To
<> Not Equals	> Greater Than	>= Greater Than or Equal To

Comparing String Values: A Caution

You can easily compare numeric or date/time data, but you must pay close attention when you compare character strings. For example, you may not get the results you expect when you compare two seemingly similar strings such as "Mike" and "MIKE." The determining factor for all character string comparisons is the collating sequence used by your database system. The collating

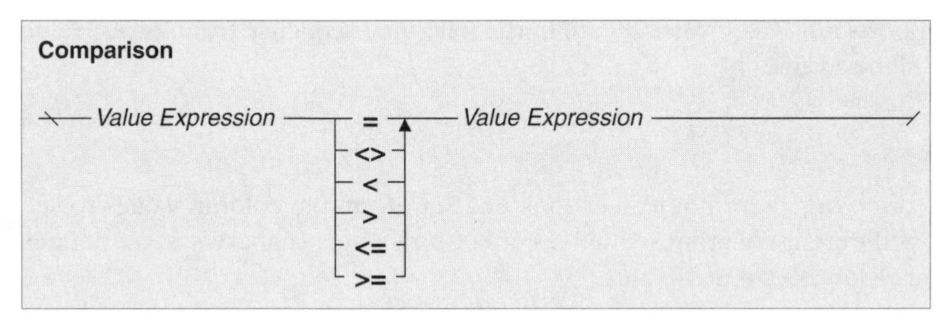

Figure 6-2 *Syntax diagram for the Comparison condition.*

sequence also determines how character strings are sorted and impacts how you use other comparison conditions as well.

Because many different vendors have implemented SQL on machines with different architectures and for many languages other than English, the SQL Standard does not define any default collating sequence for character string sorting or comparison. How characters are sorted from "lowest" to "highest" is dependent on the database software you are using and, in many cases, how the software was installed.

Many database systems use the ASCII collating sequence, which places numbers before letters and all uppercase letters before all lowercase letters. If your database supports the ASCII collating sequence, the characters are in the following sequence from lowest value to highest value.

"... 0123456789 ... ABC ... XYZ ... abc ... xyz ..."

Some systems, however, offer a "case insensitive" option; thus lowercase "a" is considered equal to uppercase "A." When your database supports this option using ASCII as a base, characters are in the following sequence from lowest value to highest value.

"... 0123456789 ... {Aa}{Bb}{Cc} ... {Xx}{Yy}{Zz} ..."

Note that the characters enclosed in braces ({}) are considered equal.

Database systems running on IBM mainframe systems use the IBM-proprietary EBCDIC sequence. In a database system that uses EBCDIC, all lowercase letters come first, then all uppercase letters, and finally numbers. If your database supports EBCDIC, characters are in the following sequence from lowest value to highest value.

"… abc … xyz … ABC … XYZ … 0123456789 …"

To drive this point home, let's look at a set of sample column values to see how different collating sequences affect how your database system defines higher, lower, or equal values.

Here is a table of column values sorted using the ASCII character set, case sensitive (numbers first, then uppercase, and then lowercase).

Company Name
3rd Street Warehouse
5th Avenue Market
Al's Auto Shop
Ashby's Cleaners
Zebra Printing
Zercon Productions
allegheny & associates
anderson tree farm
z-tech consulting
zorn credit services

Now, let's turn off case sensitivity so that lowercase letters and their uppercase equivalents are considered equal. The next table shows what happens.

Company Name
3rd Street Warehouse
5th Avenue Market
Al's Auto Shop
allegheny & associates
anderson tree farm
Ashby's Cleaners
z-tech consulting
Zebra Printing
Zercon Productions
zorn credit services

Finally, let's see how these values are sorted on an IBM system using the EBCDIC collating sequence (lowercase letters, uppercase letters, and then numbers).

Company Name
allegheny & associates
anderson tree farm
z-tech consulting
zorn credit services
Al's Auto Shop
Ashby's Cleaners
Zebra Printing
Zercon Productions
3rd Street Warehouse
5th Avenue Market

You can also encounter unexpected results when trying to compare two character strings of unequal length, such as "John" and "John " or "Mitch" and "Mitchell." Fortunately, the SQL Standard clearly specifies how the database system must handle this. Before your database compares two character strings of unequal length, it must add the special *default pad character* to the right of the smaller string until it is the same length as the larger string. (The default pad character is a space in most database systems.) Your database then uses its collating sequence to determine whether the two strings are now equal to each other. As a result, "John" and "John " are equal (once the padding takes place) and "Mitch " and "Mitchell" are unequal.

> ❖ **Note** Some database systems differ from the SQL Standard in that they *ignore* trailing blanks. Therefore, "John" and "John " are considered equal in some systems because the trailing blanks in the second item are completely disregarded. Be sure to test your database system to determine how it handles this type of comparison and if it returns the type of results you expect.

In summary, be sure to check your database system's documentation to determine how it collates uppercase letters, lowercase letters, and numbers.

Equality and Inequality

Although we've already seen a couple of examples, let's take another look at an equality comparison condition using the "equals" operator.

Assume we're posing this request to the database.

> *"Show me the first and last names of all the agents that were hired on March 14, 1977."*

Because we are going to search for a specific hire date, we can use an equality comparison condition with an "equals" operator to retrieve the appropriate information. Now we'll run this through the translation process to define the appropriate SELECT Statement.

Translation Select first name and last name from the agents table for all agents hired on March 14, 1977

Clean Up — Select first name ~~and~~ last name from ~~the~~ agents ~~table for all agents hired on~~ where date hired = ~~March 14, 1977~~ '1977-03-14'

SQL

```
SELECT AgtFirstName, AgtLastName
FROM Agents
WHERE DateHired = '1977-03-14'
```

In this example, we tested the values of a specific column to determine whether any values matched a given date value. In essence, we executed an *inclusive* process—a given row in the Agents table will be included in the Result Set *only* if the current value of the DateHired column for that row matches the specified date. But what if you wanted to do the exact opposite and *exclude* certain rows from the Result Set? In that case, you use a comparison condition with a "not equals" operator.

Suppose you submit the following request.

> *"Give me a list of vendor names and phone numbers for all our vendors, with the exception of those here in Bellevue."*

You've probably already determined that you need to exclude those vendors based in Bellevue and that you'll use a "not equals" condition for the task. The phrase "with the exception of" provides a clear indication that the "not equals" condition is appropriate for this request. Keep this in mind as you look at the translation process.

Translation — Select vendor name and phone number from the vendors table for all vendors except those based in 'Bellevue'

Clean Up — Select vendor name ~~and~~ phone number from ~~the~~ vendors ~~table for all vendors except those based in~~ where city <> 'Bellevue'

SQL

```
SELECT VendName, VendPhone
FROM Vendors
WHERE VendCity <> 'Bellevue'
```

❖ **Note** The SQL Standard uses the <> symbol for the "not equals" operator. Several RDBMS programs provide alternate notations, such as **!=** (supported by Microsoft SQL Server and Sybase) and **¬=** (supported by IBM's DB2). Be sure to check your database system's documentation for the appropriate notation of this operator.

You've effectively excluded all vendors from Bellevue with this simple condition. Later in this chapter, we'll show you a different method for excluding rows from a Result Set.

Less Than and Greater Than

Often you want rows returned where a particular value in a column is smaller or larger than the comparison value. This type of comparison employs the "less than" (<), "less than or equal to" (<=), "greater than" (>), or "greater than or equal to" (>=) comparison operators. The type of data you compare determines the relationship between those values.

CHARACTER STRINGS — This comparison determines whether the value of the first Value Expression "precedes" (<) or "follows" (>) the value of the second Value Expression in your database system's collating sequence. For example, you can interpret $a < c$ as "Does a precede c?" For details about collating sequences, see the previous section, Comparing String Values: A Caution.

NUMBERS — This comparison determines whether the value of the first Value Expression is "smaller" (<) or "larger" (>) than the value of the second Value Expression. For example, you can interpret $10 > 5$ as "Is *10* larger than *5*?"

DATES/TIMES — This comparison determines whether the value of the first Value Expression is "earlier" (<) or "later" (>) than the value of the second Value Expression. For example, you can interpret *'1999-05-16' < '1999-12-15'* as "Is May 16, 1999, earlier than December 15, 1999?" Dates and times are evaluated in chronological order.

Let's take a look at how you might use these Comparison Predicates to answer a request.

> *"Are there any orders where the ship date was accidentally posted earlier than the order date?"*

You'll use a "less than" comparison operator in this instance because you want to determine whether any ship date was posted earlier than its respective order date. Here's how you translate this request.

Translation Select order number from the orders table where the ship date is earlier than the order date

Clean Up Select order number from ~~the~~ orders ~~table~~ where ~~the~~ ship date ~~is earlier than the~~ < order date

SQL
```
SELECT OrderNumber
FROM Orders
WHERE Shipdate < OrderDate
```

The SELECT Statement's Result Set will include only those rows from the Orders table where the Search Condition is true.

The next example requires a "greater than" comparison operator to retrieve the appropriate information.

"Are there any classes that earn more than four credits?"

Translation Select class ID from the classes table for all classes that earn more than four credits

Clean Up Select class ID from ~~the~~ classes ~~table for all classes that earn more than four~~ where credits > 4

SQL
```
SELECT ClassID
FROM Classes
WHERE Credits > 4
```

The Result Set generated by this SELECT Statement includes only classes that earn five credits or more, such as Intermediate Algebra and Engineering Physics.

Now, let's take a look at some examples where you're interested not only in the values that may be greater than or less than but also equal to the comparison value.

"I need the names of everyone we've hired since January 1, 1989."

You use a "greater than or equal to" comparison for this request because you want to retrieve all hire dates from January 1, 1989, to the present, *including* employees hired on that date. As you run through the translation process, be sure to identify all the columns you need for the SELECT clause.

Translation Select first name and last name as EmployeeName from the employees table for all employees hired since January 1, 1989

Clean Up — Select first name ~~and~~ | ' ' | last name as EmployeeName from ~~the~~ employees ~~table for all employees hired since~~ where date hired >= ~~January 1, 1989~~ '1989-01-01'

SQL

```
SELECT FirstName || ' ' || LastName
   AS EmployeeName
FROM Employees
WHERE DateHired >= '1989-01-01'
```

Here's another request you might pose to the database.

"Show me a list of products with a retail price of fifty dollars or less."

As you've probably deduced, you'll use a "less than or equal to" comparison for this request. This ensures that the SELECT Statement's Result Set contains only those products that cost anywhere from one cent to exactly fifty dollars. Here's how you translate this request.

Translation — Select product name from the products table for all products with a retail price of fifty dollars or less

Clean Up — Select product name from ~~the~~ products ~~table for all products with a~~ where retail price ~~of~~ <= 50 ~~fifty dollars or less~~

SQL

```
SELECT ProductName
FROM Products
WHERE RetailPrice <= 50
```

The examples you've seen so far use only a single type of comparison. Later in this chapter, we'll show you how to combine comparisons using AND and OR.

Range

You can test the value of a Value Expression against a specific range of values with a range condition. Figure 6-3 shows the syntax for this condition.

The range condition tests the value of a given Value Expression against a range of values defined by two other Value Expressions. The BETWEEN... AND Predicate defines the range by using the value of the second Value Expression as the start point and the value of the third Value Expression as the end point; both the start point and end point are part of the range. A row is included in the Result Set only if the value of the first Value Expression falls within the specified range.

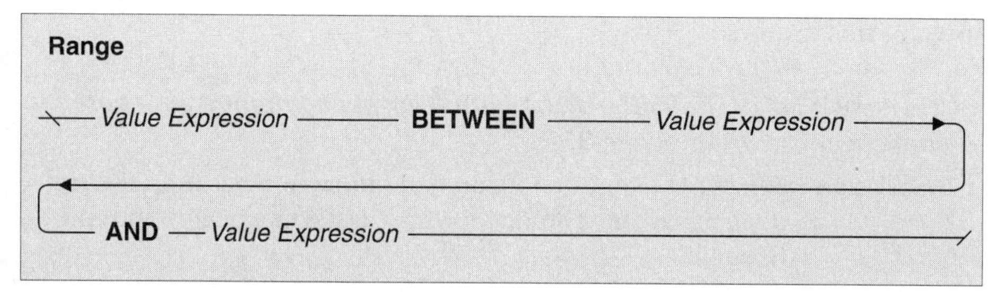

Figure 6-3 *Syntax diagram for the range condition.*

There's one "gotcha" about using BETWEEN ... AND. The SQL Standard dictates that Value1 BETWEEN Value2 AND Value3 is the same as Value1 >= Value2 AND Value1 <= Value3. This means that Value2 must be less than or equal to Value3 for the Predicate to work properly. However, some database systems allow Value2 to be greater than or equal to Value3. Check your database system documentation for details.

Here are a couple of examples that illustrate how you use a range condition.

> *"Which staff members were hired in July of 1986?"*

The range condition is appropriate here because you want to retrieve the names of everyone who was hired within a specific set of dates, in this case between July 1, 1986, and July 31, 1986. Let's now run this through the translation process and build the appropriate SELECT Statement.

Translation — Select first name and last name from the staff table where the date hired is between July 1, 1986, and July 31, 1986

Clean Up — Select first name ~~and~~ last name from ~~the~~ staff ~~table~~ where ~~the~~ date hired ~~is~~ between ~~July 1, 1986~~ '1986-07-01' and ~~July 31, 1986~~ '1986-07-31'

SQL

```
SELECT FirstName, LastName
FROM Staff
WHERE DateHired
BETWEEN '1986-07-01' AND '1986-07-31'
```

Notice that we stated the range of dates more explicitly in the translation statement than in the request. Use this technique to translate the request as clearly as possible and thus define the appropriate SELECT Statement.

You can also use a range condition on character string data quite effectively, as shown in this example.

> *"Give me a list of students—along with their phone numbers—whose last name begins with the letter B."*

Translation — Select last name, first name, and phone number from the students table for all students whose last name begins with the letter 'B'

Clean Up — Select last name, first name, ~~and~~ phone number from ~~the~~ students ~~table for all students whose name begins with the letter 'B'~~ where last name between 'b' and 'bz'

SQL

```
SELECT StudLastName, StudFirstName, StudPhoneNumber
FROM Students
WHERE StudLastName
BETWEEN 'b' AND 'bz'
```

When creating a range for character string data, think carefully about the values you want to include. For example, here are three possible ways you might have indicated the starting and ending points for the required range in this request. The results are quite different!

`BETWEEN 'a' AND 'c'` — We know that many of you would not have indicated "a" as the starting point because you know the range would then include everyone whose name begins with that letter. However, this is a fairly typical mistake.

`BETWEEN 'b' AND 'c'` — Indicating the starting and ending points in this manner probably returns the desired results for our example. However, you may get unexpected results based on the character data you're trying to compare. Remember that the BETWEEN operator *includes* the starting and ending points in the range. Consequently, a student whose last name is only the letter "c" will be included in the Result Set.

`BETWEEN 'b' AND 'bz'`	This is the clearest and most explicit method of indicating the starting and ending points; in most cases, it will return the desired results. In the end, you must understand your data in order to define the correct range.

So far, we've shown you how to narrow the scope of your request using a broad range of values and a more specific range of values. Now, let's take a look at how you can refine your requests even further by using an explicit list of values.

Set Membership

You'll use the membership condition to test the value of a Value Expression against a list of explicitly defined values. As you can see in Figure 6-4, the membership condition uses the IN Predicate to determine whether the value of the first Value Expression matches any value within a parenthetical list of values defined by one or more Value Expressions.

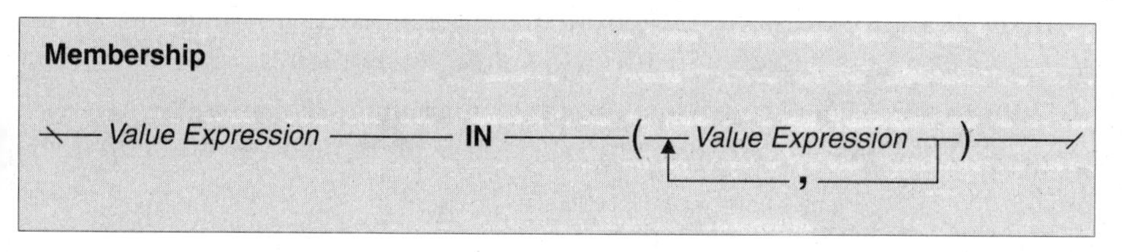

Figure 6-4 *Syntax diagram for the membership condition.*

Although theoretically you can include an almost limitless number of Value Expressions in the list, it makes more sense to use only a few; you already have two conditions at your disposal that you can use to indicate broader ranges of values. You can use the membership condition most effectively when you define a finite list of values, as you'll see in the following examples.

Here's a request you might pose to the database.

> *"I need to know which bowling lanes sponsored tournaments for the following 1999 dates: June 5, July 3, and August 7."*

This type of request lends itself to a membership condition because it focuses on searching for a specific set of values. If the request were not so explicit, you would most likely use a range condition instead. Here's how to translate this request.

Translation Select tourney location from the tournaments table where the tourney date is in this list of dates: June 5, 1999; July 3, 1999; August 7, 1999

Clean Up Select tourney location from ~~the~~ tournaments ~~table~~ where ~~the~~ tourney date ~~is~~ in ~~this list of dates:~~ (~~June 5, 1999;~~ '1999-06-05', ~~July 3, 1999;~~ '1999-07-03', ~~August 7, 1999~~ '1999-08-07')

SQL

```
SELECT TourneyLocation
FROM Tournaments
WHERE TourneyDate
IN ('1999-06-05', '1999-07-03', '1999-08-07')
```

Here's another request that requires a range condition for its answer.

"Which entertainers do we represent in Seattle, Redmond, and Bothell?"

Translation Select stage name from the entertainers table for all entertainers based in 'Seattle', 'Redmond', or 'Bothell'

Clean Up Select stage name from ~~the~~ entertainers ~~table for all entertainers based~~ where city in ('Seattle', 'Redmond', ~~or~~ 'Bothell')

SQL

```
SELECT EntStageName
FROM Entertainers
WHERE EntCity
IN ('Seattle', 'Redmond', 'Bothell')
```

You may have noticed that we used the word "or" in the translation statement's list of cities instead of "and" as it appears in the original request. The reason and logic for this is simple: There is only one entry in the EntCity column for a given entertainer. This may seem a trivial point, but using the proper words and phrases helps to clarify your translation and clean up statements and ensures that you define the most appropriate SELECT Statement for your request.

All the conditions you've learned so far use complete values as their criteria. Now we'll take a look at a condition that allows you to use partial values as a criterion.

Pattern Match

The pattern match condition is useful when you need to find values that are similar to a given pattern string or when you have only a partial piece of information to use as a search criterion. Figure 6-5 shows the syntax for this type of condition.

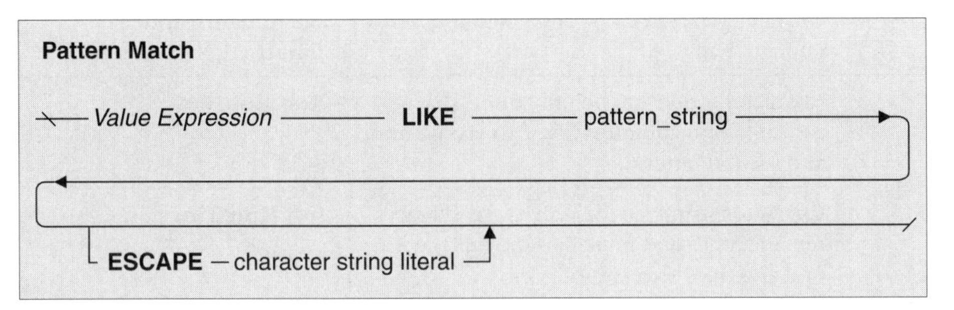

Figure 6-5 *Syntax diagram for the pattern match condition.*

This condition takes the value of a Value Expression and uses the LIKE Predicate to test whether the value matches a defined pattern string. A pattern string can consist of any logical combination of regular string characters and two special wildcard characters: the percent sign (%) and the underscore (_). The percent sign represents zero or more arbitrary regular characters, and the underscore represents a single arbitrary regular character. The manner in which you define the pattern string determines which values are retrieved from the Value Expression. Table 6.1 on the next page shows samples of the different types of pattern strings you can define.

Table 6.1 *Samples of defined pattern strings.*

Pattern String	Criterion Processed	Sample Return Values
'sha%'	Character string can be any length but must begin with "sha"	**Sha**nnon, **Sha**ron, **Sha**wn
'%son'	Character string can be any length but must end with "son"	Ben**son**, John**son**, Morri**son**
'%han%'	Character string can be any length but must contain "han"	Buc**han**an, **Han**del, Jo**han**sen, Nat**han**son
'ro_'	Character string can be only three characters in length and must have "ro" as the first and second letters	**Ro**b, **Ro**n, **Ro**y
'_im'	Character string can be only three characters in length and must have "im" as the second and third letters	J**im**, K**im**, T**im**
'_ar_'	Character string can be only four characters in length and must have "ar" as the second and third letters	B**ar**t, G**ar**y, M**ar**k
'_at%'	Character string can be any length but must have "at" as the second and third letters	G**at**es, M**at**thews, P**at**terson
'%ac_'	Character string can be any length but must have "ac" as the second and third letters from the end of the string	Apod**ac**a, Tr**ac**y, Wall**ac**e

Let's take a look at how you can use a pattern match condition by considering the following request.

"Give me a list of customers whose last names begins with 'Mar'."

Requests such as this one typically use phrases that indicate the need for a pattern match condition. Here are a few examples of the types of phrases you're likely to encounter.

"...begins with 'Her'."

"...starts with 'Ba'."

"...includes the word 'Park'."

"...contains the letters 'han'."

"...has 'ave' in the middle of it."

"... with 'son' at the end."

" ...ending in 'ez'."

As you can see, it can be relatively easy to determine the type of pattern string you need for a request. Once you know the type of pattern you need to create, you can continue with the translation process.

Translation — Select last name and first name from the customers table where the last name begins with 'Mar'

Clean Up — Select last name ~~and~~ first name from ~~the~~ customers ~~table~~ where ~~the~~ last name ~~begins with~~ like 'Mar%'

SQL

```
SELECT CustLastName, CustFirstName
FROM Customers
WHERE CustLastName LIKE 'Mar%'
```

The Result Set for this SELECT Statement includes names such as "Marks," "Marshall," "Martinez," and "Marx" because we were only concerned with matching the first three letters of the last name.

Here's how you might answer another request using a pattern match condition.

"Show me a list of vendor names where the word 'Forest' appears in the street address."

Translation — Select vendor name from the vendors table where the street address contains the word 'Forest'

Clean Up — Select vendor name from ~~the~~ vendors ~~table~~ where ~~the~~ street address ~~contains the word~~ like '%Forest%'

SQL

```
SELECT VendName
FROM Vendors
WHERE VendStreetAddress LIKE '%Forest%'
```

In this case, a row from the Vendors table is included in the Result Set only if the street address contains a street name such as "Forest Park Place," "Forest Ridge Avenue," "Evergreen Forest Drive," or "Black Forest Road."

Although you can search for any pattern string using the appropriate wildcard characters, you'll run into a problem if the values you want to retrieve include a percent sign or an underscore character. For example, you will have a problem trying to retrieve the value "MX_445" because it contains an underscore character. You can circumvent this potential dilemma by using the ESCAPE option of the LIKE Predicate, as shown in Figure 6-5 on page 161.

The ESCAPE option allows you to designate a *single* character string literal—known as an *escape character*—to indicate how the database system should interpret a percent sign or underscore character within a pattern string. Place the escape character after the ESCAPE keyword and enclose it within single quotes, as you would any character string literal. When the escape character precedes a wildcard character in a pattern string, the database system interprets that wildcard character *literally* within the pattern string.

Here's an example of how you might use the ESCAPE option.

"Show me a list of products that have product codes beginning with 'G_00' and ending in a single number or letter."

Translation	Select product name and product code from the products table where the product code begins with 'G_00' and ends in a single number or letter
Clean Up	Select product ~~name~~ and product code from ~~the~~ products ~~table~~ where ~~the~~ product code ~~begins with~~ like 'G_00_' ~~and ends in a single number or letter~~

SQL	`SELECT ProductName, ProductCode`
	`FROM Products`
	`WHERE ProductCode Like 'G\_00_' ESCAPE '\'`

It's evident that you need to use the ESCAPE option to help answer this request—otherwise, the database system interprets the underscore character in the pattern string as a wildcard character. Note that we included the escape character in the Clean Up statement. You should do so in your Clean Up statements as well because it ensures that you remember to use the ESCAPE option when you define your SELECT Statement.

This SELECT Statement will retrieve product codes such as G_002 and G_00X. Because we want to search for one of the two characters that are defined in the standard as a wildcard, we *must* include the ESCAPE clause. If we ask for `LIKE 'G_00_'`, the database system will return rows where the product code has a "G" for the first letter, *any* character in the second position (because of the wildcard character), zeros in the third and fourth positions, and any character in the fifth position. When we define "\" as the ESCAPE character, the database system ignores the escape character but interprets the first underscore character literally, not as a wildcard. Because we did not use the escape character just before the second underscore, the database system interprets the second underscore as a true wildcard character.

Keep in mind that the character you use as an escape character should not be part of the values you're trying to retrieve. It doesn't make sense to use "&" as an escape character if you're searching for values such as "Martin & Lewis," "Smith & Kearns," or "Hernandez & Viescas." Also remember that the escape character affects only the wildcard character that immediately follows it. However, you can use as many escape characters in your pattern sting as are appropriate.

Null

Now that you've learned how to search for complete values and partial values, let's discuss searching for *unknown* values. You learned in Chapter 5 that a Null *does not* represent a zero, a character string of one or more blank spaces, or a "zero-length" character string (a character string that has no characters in it) because each of these items can be meaningful in a variety of circumstances. You also learned a Null *does* represent a missing or unknown value. To retrieve Null values from a Value Expression, you use the *Null condition* shown in Figure 6-6.

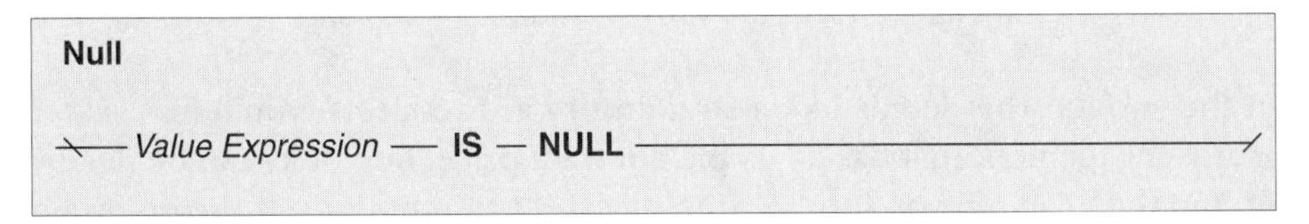

Figure 6-6 *Syntax diagram for the Null condition.*

This condition takes the value of the Value Expression and determines whether it is Null using the IS NULL Predicate; it's quite a straightforward operation. Let's take a look at how you might use this condition on the following examples.

"Give me a list of customers who didn't specify what county they live in."

Translation Select first name and last name as Customer from the customers table where the county name is unspecified

Clean Up Select first name || ' ' || ~~and~~ last name as Customer from ~~the~~ customers ~~table~~ where ~~the~~ county name is null ~~unspecified~~

SQL
```
SELECT CustFirstName || ' ' || CustLastName
   AS Customer
FROM Customers
WHERE CustCounty IS NULL
```

The only customers that appear in the Result Set for this SELECT Statement are those who didn't know or couldn't remember what county they live in, or those folks who live in Washington, DC. (Washington, by the way, is the only city in the entire United States that isn't situated within a county.)

Here's another request you might pose to the database.

"Which engagements do not yet have a contract price?"

Translation: Select engagement number and contract price from the engagements table for any engagement that does not have a contract price

Clean Up: Select engagement number ~~and~~ contract price from ~~the~~ engagements ~~table for any engagement that does not have a~~ where contract price is null

SQL
```
SELECT EngagementNumber, ContractPrice
FROM Engagements
WHERE ContractPrice IS NULL
```

On the surface, this seems like a straightforward request—you'll just search for any engagement that has "0" as the contract price. But looks can be deceiving, and they can lull you into making incorrect assumptions. If the entertainment agency in this example uses "0" as the contract price for any promotional engagement, then zero is a valid, meaningful value. Therefore, any contract price that is yet to be determined or negotiated is indeed (or should be) Null.

This example illustrates the fact that you do need to understand your data in order to pose meaningful, accurate requests to the database. If you execute a SELECT Statement and then think that the information you see in a Result Set is erroneous, don't panic. Your first impulse will probably be to rewrite the entire SELECT Statement because you believe you've made some disastrous mistake in the syntax. Before you do anything drastic, review the data you're working with and make certain you have a clear idea of how it's being used. Once you have a better understanding of the data, you'll often find that you need to make only minor changes to your SELECT Statement in order for it to retrieve the proper information.

> ❖ **Note** You must use the Null condition to search for Null values within a Value Expression. A condition such as `<ValueExpression> = Null` is invalid because the value of the Value Expression cannot be compared to something that is, by definition, unknown.

Excluding Rows with NOT

Up to this point, we've shown you how to *include* specific rows in a Result Set. Let's now take a look at how you *exclude* rows from a Result Set by using the NOT operator. We've already shown you one simple way to exclude rows from a Result Set by using an equality comparison condition with a "not equals" operator. You can also exclude rows with other types of conditions by using the NOT operator. As you can see in Figure 6-7 on the next page, this operator is an optional component of the BETWEEN, IN, LIKE, and IS NULL Predicates. A SELECT Statement will disregard any rows that meet the condition expressed by any of these Predicates when you include the NOT operator. The rows that will be in the Result Set instead are those that *did not meet* the condition.

The following examples illustrate how you can use NOT as part of a Search Condition.

> *"Show me a list of all the orders we've taken, except for those posted in July."*

A request such as this requires you to define a SELECT Statement that excludes rows meeting a specific criterion and commonly contains phrases that indicate the need for a NOT operator as part of the Search Condition. The types of phrases you'll encounter are similar to those listed here.

> *"...that don't begin with 'Her'."*
> *"...that aren't in the Administrative or Personnel departments."*
> *"...who has a fax number."*
> *"...who was hired before June 1 or after August 31."*

You have to perform a bit of deductive work sometimes in order to translate a phrase properly. Some phrases, such as the third phrase listed above, do not explicitly indicate the need for a NOT operator. In this case, the requirement

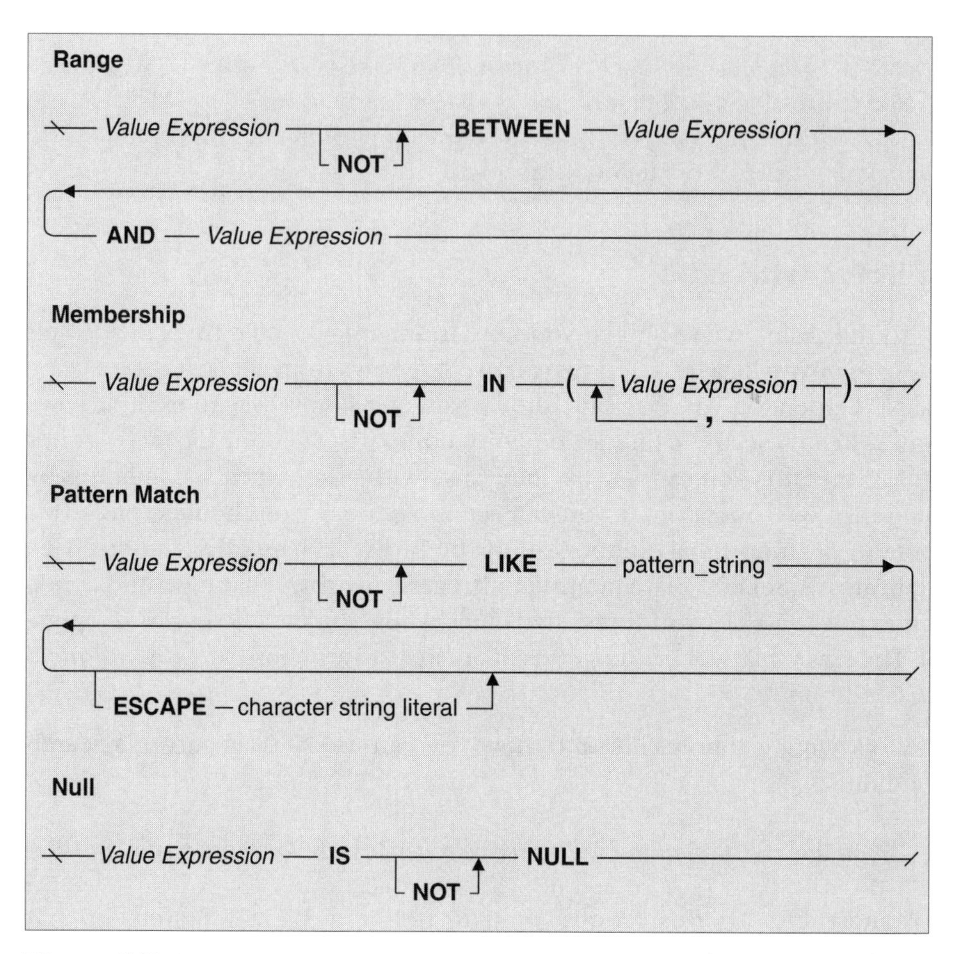

Figure 6-7 *Syntax for the NOT operator.*

is implied because you want to *exclude* everyone who *does not* have a fax number. As you begin to work with requests that contain these types of phrases, you'll often find that you need to analyze them carefully and possibly rewrite them in order to determine whether you need to exclude certain rows from the Result Set. There's no easy rule of thumb we can give you here, but with a little patience and practice it will become easier for you to determine whether you need a NOT operator for a specific request.

Once you've determined whether you need to exclude any information from the Result Set, you can continue with the translation process.

"Show me a list of all the orders we've taken, except for those posted in July."

Translation — Select order ID and order date from the orders table where the order date does not fall between July 1, 1999, and July 31, 1999

Clean Up — Select order ID ~~and~~ order date from ~~the~~ orders ~~table~~ where ~~the~~ order date ~~does~~ not ~~fall~~ between ~~July 1, 1999,~~ '1999-07-01' and ~~July 31, 1999~~ '1999-07-31'

SQL

```
SELECT OrderID, OrderDate
FROM Orders
WHERE OrderDate NOT BETWEEN '1999-07-01'
   AND '1999-07-31'
```

This SELECT Statement produces a Result Set that will *not* contain any orders posted between July 1, 1999, and July 31, 1999. It will, however, contain every other order in the Orders table (including, perhaps, rows in 1998 or 2000). You can further restrict the rows sent to the Result Set to just those orders taken in 1999 by using multiple conditions, which is an issue we'll cover in the next section.

Now let's assume you're working with the following request.

"I need the identification numbers of all faculty members who are not professors or associate professors."

Translation — Select staff ID and title from the faculty table where the title is not 'professor' or 'associate professor'

Clean Up — Select staff ID ~~and~~ title from ~~the~~ faculty ~~table~~ where ~~the~~ title ~~is~~ not in ('professor', ~~or~~ 'associate professor')

SQL

```
SELECT StaffID, Title
FROM Faculty
WHERE Title
NOT IN ('Professor', 'Associate Professor')
```

In this case, you need to exclude any staff member whose title is one of those specified within the request, so you use a membership condition with a NOT operator to send the correct rows to the Result Set.

Excluding rows from a Result Set becomes a relatively straightforward process once you get accustomed to analyzing and rephrasing your requests as the situation dictates. The real key, as you've seen so far, is being able to determine the type of condition you need to answer a given request.

Using Multiple Conditions

The requests we've worked with up to this point have been simple and have required only a single condition to supply the answer. Now we'll take a look at how you can answer complex requests using multiple conditions. Let's begin by considering the following request.

"Give me the first and last names of customers who live in Seattle and whose last name starts with the letter 'H'."

Based on the knowledge you've gained thus far, you can ascertain that this request requires an equality comparison condition and a pattern match condition to supply an answer. You've identified the conditions you need, but how do you combine them into one Search Condition? The answer lies in the way the SQL Standard defines the syntax for a Search Condition, as shown in Figure 6-8.

Introducing AND and OR

You combine two or more conditions by using the AND and OR operators, and the complete set of conditions you've combined to answer a given request constitutes a single Search Condition. As the diagram shows, you can also combine a complete Search Condition with other conditions by enclosing the Search Condition in parentheses. All this allows you to create very complex WHERE clauses that precisely control which rows are selected to be included in a Result Set.

Using AND

The first way you can combine two or more conditions is by using the AND operator. You use this operator when *all* of the conditions you combine must

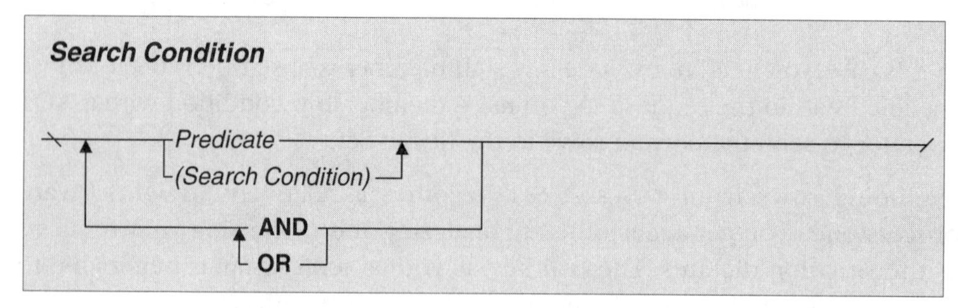

Figure 6-8 *Syntax diagram for the Search Condition.*

be met in order for a row to be included in a Result Set. Let's use the sample request we posed at the beginning of this section as an example and apply this operator during the translation process.

> *"Give me the first and last names of customers who live in Seattle and whose last name starts with the letter 'H'."*

Translation — Select first name and last name from the customers table where the city is 'Seattle' and the last name begins with 'H'

Clean Up — Select first name ~~and~~ last name from ~~the~~ customers ~~table~~ where ~~the~~ city ~~is~~ = 'Seattle' and ~~the~~ last name ~~begins with~~ like 'H%'

SQL

```
SELECT CustFirstName, CustLastName
FROM Customers
WHERE CustCity = 'Seattle'
AND CustLastName LIKE 'H%'
```

You've accounted for both the equality comparison condition and a pattern match condition required by the request, and you've ensured that they must both be met by using the AND operator. Any row that fails to meet either condition will be excluded from the Result Set.

You can chain any number of conditions you need to answer the request at hand. Just keep in mind that *all* the conditions you've combined with ANDs *must* be met in order for a row to be included in the Result Set. Remember that the entire Search Condition must evaluate to True for a row to appear in the Result Set. Figure 6-9 shows you the result when you combine two Predicate

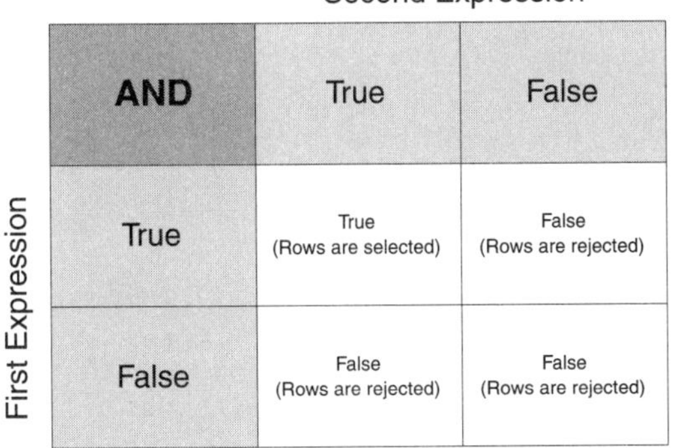

Second Expression / First Expression

AND	True	False
True	True (Rows are selected)	False (Rows are rejected)
False	False (Rows are rejected)	False (Rows are rejected)

Figure 6-9 *The result of combining two Predicate expressions with the AND operator.*

expressions using the AND operator. If *either* of the expressions evaluates to False, then the row is not selected.

Using OR

The second way to combine two or more conditions is by using the OR operator. You use this operator when *either* of the conditions you combine can be met in order for a row to be included in a Result Set. Here's an example of how you might use an OR operator in a Search Condition.

> *"I need the name, city, and state of every staff member who lives in Seattle or is from the state of Oregon.*

Translation	Select first name, last name, city, and state from the staff table where the city is 'Seattle' or the state is 'OR'
Clean Up	Select first name, last name, city, ~~and~~ state from ~~the~~ staff ~~table~~ where ~~the~~ city ~~is~~ = 'Seattle' or ~~the~~ state ~~is~~ = 'OR'
SQL	`SELECT StfFirstName, StfLastName, StfCity, StfState` `FROM Staff` `WHERE StfCity = 'Seattle' OR StfState = 'OR'`

In this case, you've accounted for both of the equality comparison conditions you need to answer this request, and you've ensured that *only one* of the conditions has to be met by using the OR operator. As long as a row fulfills either condition, it will be included in the Result Set. To help clarify the matter, Figure 6-10 shows you the result of combining two Predicate expressions with an OR operator.

Second Expression

OR	True	False
True	True (Rows are selected)	True (Rows are selected)
False	True (Rows are selected)	False (Rows are rejected)

First Expression

Figure 6-10 *The result of combining two Predicate expressions with the OR operator.*

Determining whether to use an AND operator to combine conditions is relatively easy and straightforward. However, determining whether to use an OR operator can be tricky sometimes. For example, consider the following request.

> *"Show me a list of vendor names and phone numbers for all vendors based in Washington and California."*

Your first impulse may be to use an AND operator because the condition is obvious—you want vendors in Washington *and* California. Unfortunately, you would be wrong. If you think about it, a vendor will be based in *either* Washington *or* California because *you can enter only one state value in the state column for that vendor*. The actual condition is much clearer now, isn't it? As we mentioned earlier in the chapter, you must get into the habit of studying and analyzing your requests as they become more complex and try to look for implied conditions as best as you can.

Let's continue and run this request through the translation process.

> *"Show me a list of vendor names and phone numbers for all vendors based in Washington and California."*

Translation — Select name, phone number, and state from the vendors table where the state is 'WA' or 'CA'

Clean Up — Select name, phone number, ~~and~~ state from ~~the~~ vendors ~~table~~ where ~~the~~ state ~~is~~ = 'WA' or state = 'CA'

SQL

```
SELECT VendName, VendPhoneNumber, VendState
FROM Vendors
WHERE VendState = 'WA' OR VendState = 'CA'
```

You've accounted for both equality comparison conditions and ensured that either one must be met by using the OR operator. Note, however, that "state" appears in the Search Condition of the Clean Up and SQL statements twice. This is necessary because each comparison condition follows the same syntax:

```
"Value Expression <comparison operator> Value Expression"
```

Remember that you cannot omit any clause, keyword, or defined term from the syntax unless it is explicitly defined as an optional item. Thus, a condition such as `WHERE VendState = 'WA' OR 'CA'` is completely invalid. You might ask why this is so. We'll explain more about the sequence in which expression operators get evaluated—the Order of Precedence—later. In this case, your database system evaluates the expression in strict left-to-right sequence. So, `VendState = 'WA'` will be evaluated first.

For any given row, the result will be True if the state is Washington, and False if it is not. Next, this True or False result gets "ORed" with the literal value `'CA'`—which is not a True or False value! Your database system may return an error at this point ('CA'—a character string literal—is an invalid data type for the OR operator), or it may return only the rows where "state" is Washington.

Always make certain that your conditions are completely and correctly defined; otherwise, the Search Condition for your SELECT Statement will fail.

> ❖ **Note** We used this example to illustrate a common trap you'll encounter when you use the OR operator. However, if you thought you could use a membership condition such as "WHERE VendState IN ('WA', 'CA')" to answer this request, you are absolutely correct. In some instances, you'll find that there's more than one way to express a condition.

Using AND and OR Together

You can use both AND and OR to answer particularly tricky requests. For example, you can answer this type of request using both operators.

> *"I need to see the names of staff members who have a 425 area code and a phone number that begins with 555, along with anyone who was hired between October 1 and December 31 of 1999."*

It should be easy for you to determine what types of conditions you need for this request by now. You've probably already determined that you need three conditions to answer this request: an equality comparison condition to find the area code, a pattern match condition to find the phone numbers, and a range condition to find those staff members hired between October and December. All you have to do now is determine how you're going to combine the conditions.

You need to combine the comparison and pattern match conditions with an AND operator because they identify the phone numbers you're searching for, and because both conditions must be met in order for a row to be included in the Result Set. You then treat this combination of conditions as a single unit and combine it with the range condition using an OR operator. Now, a row will be included in the Result Set as long as it meets *either* the combined condition or the range condition.

Here's the request again and the translation.

> *"I need to see the names of staff members who have a 425 area code and a phone number that begins with 555, along with anyone who was hired between October 1 and December 31 of 1999."*

Translation — Select first name, last name, area code, phone number, and date hired from the staff table where the area code is 425 and the phone number begins with '555' or the date hired falls between October 1, 1999, and December 31, 1999

Clean Up — Select first name, last name, area code, phone number, ~~and~~ date hired from ~~the~~ staff ~~table~~ where ~~the~~ area code ~~is~~ = 425 and ~~the~~ phone number ~~begins with~~ like '555%' or ~~the~~ date hired ~~falls~~ between ~~October 1, 1999,~~ '1999-10-01' and ~~December 31, 1999~~ '1999-12-31'

SQL

```
SELECT StfFirstName, StfLastName, StfAreaCode,
   StfPhoneNumber, DateHired
FROM Staff
WHERE (StfAreaCode = '425'
   AND StfPhoneNumber LIKE '555%')
OR DateHired
   BETWEEN '1999-10-01' AND '1999-12-31'
```

The previous example clearly demonstrates a situation where you can use a Search Condition within a Search Condition. Before you translated the request, we said that you needed to combine the comparison and pattern match conditions with an AND operator and then treat them as a single unit. When you treat a combined set of conditions as a single unit, by definition it becomes a Search Condition and you must enclose it in parentheses, just as we did in the example.

Here's another example using AND and OR.

> *"I need the name of every professor or associate professor who was hired on May 16, 1989."*

Translation — Select first name, last name, and date hired from the staff table where the title is 'professor' or 'associate professor' and the date hired is May 16, 1989

Clean Up	Select first name, last name, and date hired from ~~the~~ staff ~~table~~ where ~~the~~ title ~~is~~ = 'professor' or title = 'associate professor' and ~~the~~ date hired ~~is equals~~ = ~~May 16, 1989~~ '1989-05-16'
SQL	(see code below)

```
SELECT StfFirstName, StfLastName, Title, DateHired
FROM Staff
WHERE (Title = 'Professor' OR Title =
   'Associate Professor') AND DateHired =
   '1989-05-16'
```

You've probably guessed that the two conditions combined with the OR operator are being treated as a single Search Condition. This example merely reinforces the fact that you can define a Search Condition with either the AND or OR operator. But once again, the key is making certain that you enclose the Search Condition within parentheses.

Excluding Rows: Take Two

If you're feeling a bit of déjà vu, don't worry—we did discuss this already. Well, at least to some extent. You learned earlier in this chapter that the NOT operator is an option of the BETWEEN, IN, LIKE, and IS NULL Predicates. But as Figure 6-11 illustrates, NOT is also an option as the first keyword of a Search Condition, and it allows you to exclude rows from a Result Set just as you can by using NOT within a Predicate. You use this particular NOT operator *before* a single condition (Predicate) or embedded Search Condition. Once again, you can express the same condition in various ways.

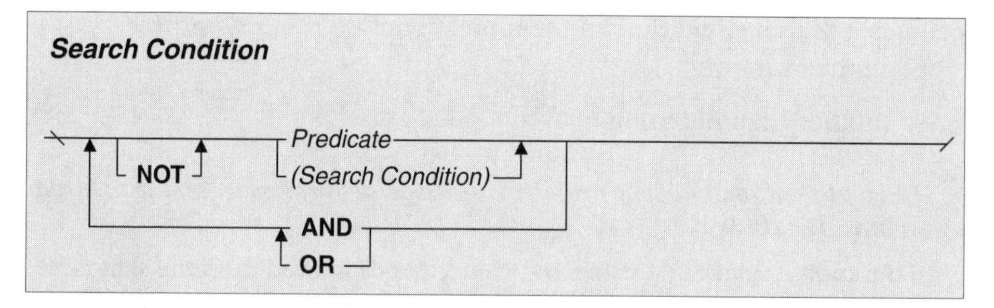

Figure 6-11 *Including the NOT operator in a Search Condition.*

Let's assume you're posing the following request to the database.

> *"Show me the location and date of any tournament not being held at Bolero Lanes, Imperial Lanes, or Thunderbird Lanes."*

You've probably already determined that you'll use a membership condition to answer this request. Now you just need to determine how you'll define it. One approach you can take is using the NOT operator within the Predicate.

```
WHERE TourneyLocation NOT IN ('Bolero Lanes',
   'Imperial Lanes', 'Thunderbird Lanes')
```

Another approach you might consider is using the NOT operator as the first keyword before the Search Condition.

```
WHERE NOT TourneyLocation IN ('Bolero Lanes', 'Imperial Lanes',
   'Thunderbird Lanes')
```

Either condition will exclude tournaments held at Bolero Lanes, Imperial Lanes, and Thunderbird Lanes from the Result Set. However, one advantage of using NOT before a Search Condition is that you can apply it to a comparison condition. (Remember that the syntax for a comparison condition does not include NOT as an optional operator.) But now you can use a comparison condition to exclude rows from a Result Set. The following example shows how you might use this type of condition.

> *"Show me the bowlers who live outside of Bellevue."*

Translation: Select first name, last name, and city from the bowlers table where the city is not 'Bellevue'

Clean Up: Select first name, last name, ~~and~~ city from ~~the~~ bowlers ~~table~~ where ~~the~~ city ~~is~~ not = 'Bellevue'

SQL:

```
SELECT BowlerFirstName, BowlerLastName, BowlerCity
FROM Bowlers
WHERE NOT BowlerCity = 'Bellevue'
```

Yes, we know that you could have expressed this condition as `WHERE BowlerCity <> 'Bellevue'`. This example simply emphasizes that you can express a condition in various ways.

Now that you've learned how to use a NOT operator within a single condition and a complete Search Condition, be aware of a problem that can occur when you define a Search Condition with two NOT operators that will *include* rows instead of *excluding* them. Here's an example.

"Which staff members are not a teacher or a teacher's aide?"

Translation — Select first name, last name, and title from the staff table where the title is not "teacher" or "teacher's aide"

Clean Up — Select first name, last name, ~~and~~ title from ~~the~~ staff ~~table~~ where ~~the~~ title ~~is~~ not in ("teacher", ~~or~~ "teacher's aide")

SQL

```
SELECT StfFirstName, StfLastName, Title
FROM Staff
WHERE NOT Title
NOT IN ('Teacher', 'Teacher''s Aide')
```

> ❖ **Note** We bet you're wondering about the two single quotes in the `'Teacher''s Aide'` character string literal. The SQL Standard dictates that you use a single quote to delimit a character string or date/time literal. When you need to embed a single quote within a character string literal, you must "clue in" your database system by entering the single quote twice. If you don't do that, the single quote acts as the end delimiter of the character string. The `"s Aide'"` that would occur after the second single quote would generate a syntax error!

We assume, of course, that one of the two NOT operators appears by mistake. You can still execute this SELECT Statement, but it will send the wrong rows to the Result Set. In this case, the two NOT operators cancel each other—just like a double-negative in arithmetic or in language—and the IN Predicate now determines which rows are sent to the Result Set. So instead of seeing anyone *other than* a teacher or teacher's aide in the Result Set, you'll see *only* teachers and teachers' aides. Although you would not consciously define a Search Condition in this manner, you could very well do it accidentally. Remember that it's often the simple mistakes that cause the most problems.

Order of Precedence

The SQL Standard specifies how a database system should evaluate single conditions within a Search Condition and the order in which those evaluations take place. You've already learned in this chapter *how* a database evaluates each type of condition. Now we'll show you how the database determines *when* to evaluate each single condition.

By default, the database evaluates conditions from left to right. This is particularly true in the case of simple conditions. In the following example, the SELECT Statement first searches for rows where the ship date is equal to the order date and then determines which rows contain customer number 1001. The rows that meet both conditions are then sent to the Result Set.

```
SQL        SELECT CustomerID, OrderDate, ShipDate
           FROM Orders
           WHERE ShipDate = OrderDate
              AND CustomerID = 1001
```

To have the SELECT Statement search for a specific customer number before evaluating the ship date, just switch the position of the conditions. We'll discuss why you might want to do this later in this section.

When a Search Condition contains various types of single conditions, the database evaluates them in a specific order based on the *operator* used in each condition. The SQL Standard defines the following order of precedence for operator evaluation.

Evaluation Order	Type of Operator
1	Positive Sign (+), Negative Sign (-)
2	Multiplication (*), Division (/)
3	Addition (+), Subtraction (-)
4	=, <>, <, >, <=, >=, BETWEEN, IN, LIKE, IS NULL
5	NOT
6	AND
7	OR

The SELECT Statement on the next page contains an example of the type of Search Condition that causes the database system to invoke the order of precedence. In this case, the database performs the addition operation, executes the comparisons, and determines whether either condition has been met. Any row that meets either condition is then sent to the Result Set.

```
SQL         SELECT CustomerID, OrderDate, ShipDate
            FROM Orders
            WHERE CustomerID = 1001 OR
               ShipDate = OrderDate + 4
```

Prioritizing Conditions

You can greatly increase the accuracy of your Search Conditions by understanding the order of precedence. This knowledge will help you formulate just the right condition for the request at hand. But you must be careful to avoid defining ambiguous conditions because they can produce unexpected results.

Let's use the following example to take a look at this potential problem.

```
SQL         SELECT CustFirstName, CustLastName, CustState,
               CustZipCode
            FROM Orders
            WHERE CustLastName = 'Patterson'
               AND CustState = 'CA'
               OR CustZipCode LIKE '%9'
```

In this instance, it's difficult to determine the true intent of the Search Condition because there are two ways you can interpret it.

1. You're looking for everyone named "Patterson" in the state of California *or* anyone with a zip code that ends with a 9.
2. You're specifically looking for everyone named "Patterson" *and* anyone who lives in California or has a zip code that ends with a 9.

You can avoid this ambiguity and make the Search Condition clearer by using parentheses to combine and prioritize certain conditions. For example, to follow the first interpretation of the Search Condition, you define the WHERE clause in this manner.

```
WHERE (CustLastName = 'Patterson' AND CustState = 'CA')
   OR CustZipCode LIKE '%9'
```

The parentheses ensure that the database analyzes and evaluates the two comparison conditions *before* it performs the same processes on the pattern match condition.

You could instead follow the second interpretation and define the WHERE clause in this manner.

```
WHERE CustLastName = 'Patterson' AND (CustState = 'CA'
   OR CustZipCode LIKE '%9')
```

In this case, the database analyzes and evaluates the first comparison condition *after* it performs those processes on the second comparison condition and the pattern match condition.

The idea of enclosing conditions in parentheses should be familiar to you by now. You learned how to do this when we discussed combining conditions earlier in this chapter. What we're trying to emphasize now is that the placement of the parentheses can have a serious impact on the outcome of the Search Condition.

You can define any number of parenthetical conditions and even embed them as necessary. Here's how the database handles parenthetical conditions.

- Parenthetical conditions are processed before non-parenthetical conditions.
- Two or more parenthetical conditions are processed from left to right.
- Embedded parenthetical conditions are processed from innermost to outermost.

Once the database begins to analyze a given parenthetical condition, it evaluates all expressions within the condition using the normal order of precedence. If you carefully translate your request and make effective use of parentheses within the Search Condition, you'll have better results.

Less Is Better Than More

We said at the beginning of this section that the database initially evaluates conditions from left to right and that it invokes the order of precedence when you define and use complex conditions. We also said that the manner in which you use parentheses in a Search Condition has a direct impact on its outcome. Now we'll pass along a simple, generic tip for speeding up the

Search Condition process: Ask for less. That is, select only those columns you need to fulfill the request and make the Search Condition as specific as you can so that your database processes the fewest rows possible. When you need to use multiple conditions, make certain that the condition that excludes the most rows from the Result Set is processed first. (Here's where your understanding of the order of precedence is really beneficial.)

We'll demonstrate this tip with an example we used earlier in this section.

```
SQL         SELECT CustomerID, OrderDate, ShipDate
            FROM Orders
            WHERE ShipDate = OrderDate
               AND CustomerID = 1001
```

In this instance, a row must fulfill both conditions in order for it to be included in the Result Set. Placing the Predicates in this order may influence your database to search for each ship date that is equivalent to its respective order date first; depending on the number of rows in the table, it could take the database quite some time to evaluate this condition. Then, the database will search the rows that met the first condition to identify which ones contain customer ID 1001.

Here's a better way to define the condition.

```
SQL         SELECT CustomerID, OrderDate, ShipDate
            FROM Orders
            WHERE CustomerID = 1001
               AND ShipDate = OrderDate
```

Now the database is more likely to search for the customer ID first. This condition is likely to produce a small number of rows, which means that the database will need less time to search for the rows that match the ship date Predicate.

You should make this technique a common practice and apply it when you define your Search Conditions. This will go a long way in helping to ensure that your SELECT Statements execute quickly and efficiently. Be sure to study your database system's documentation to learn what other techniques you can apply to optimize the SELECT Statement even further.

NULLs Revisited: A Cautionary Note

Now is as good a time as any to remind you about Nulls. You learned in Chapter 5 that a Null represents the absence of a value and that an expression processing a Null value will return a Null value. The same holds true for Search Conditions as well. A Predicate that evalutes a Null value *can never be true.* This may seem confusing, but the Predicate can never be False either! The SQL Standard defines the result of any Predicate that evaluates a Null as "Unknown." Remember that a Predicate must be True for a row to be selected, so a False or Unknown result will reject the row.

To help clarify the matter, let's reexamine in Figures 6-12 and 6-13 (see next page) the "truth" tables we first showed you in Figures 6-9 and 6-10 (pages 171 and 172); but this time, let's include the Unknown result you will get if a Null is involved.

Second Expression

AND	True	False	Unknown
True	True (Rows are selected)	False (Rows are rejected)	Unknown (Rows are rejected)
False	False (Rows are rejected)	False (Rows are rejected)	False (Rows are rejected)
Unknown	Unknown (Rows are rejected)	False (Rows are rejected)	Unknown (Rows are rejected)

First Expression

Figure 6-12 *The result of combining two Predicate expressions with the AND operator.*

You can see that an Unknown result from evaluating a Predicate on a Null column really throws a monkey wrench into the picture! For example, let's assume you have a simple Comparison Predicate: A = B. If either A or B for a given row is the Null value, then the result of the comparison is Unknown.

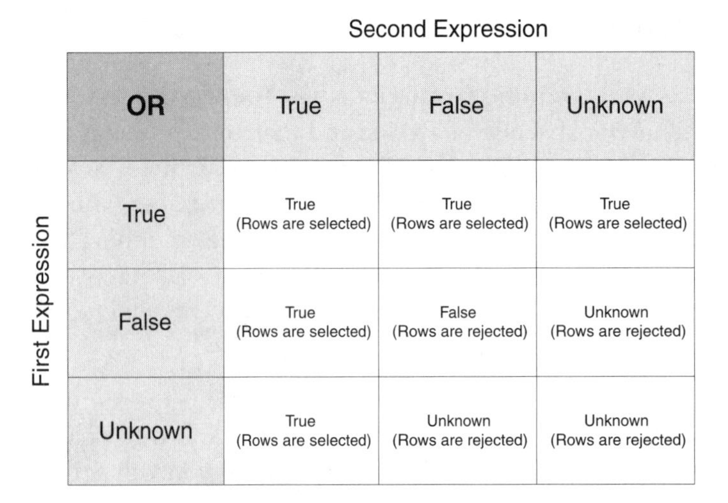

Second Expression / First Expression

OR	True	False	Unknown
True	True (Rows are selected)	True (Rows are selected)	True (Rows are selected)
False	True (Rows are selected)	False (Rows are rejected)	Unknown (Rows are rejected)
Unknown	True (Rows are selected)	Unknown (Rows are rejected)	Unknown (Rows are rejected)

Figure 6-13 *The result of combining two Predicate expressions with the OR operator.*

Because the result is not True, the row won't be selected. And if A = B is not True, you might also expect that NOT (A = B) would be True. NO! This is Unknown also. Figure 6-14 helps you understand how this is so.

(Expression)	NOT (Expression)
True	**False**
False	**True**
Unknown	**Unknown**

Figure 6-14 *The result of applying NOT to a True/False/Unknown value.*

Suppose you're posing this request to the database.

"Let me see the names and phone numbers of King county residents whose last name is Hernandez."

Translation Select first name, last name, and phone number from the customers table where the county name is 'King' and the last name is 'Hernandez'

Clean Up Select first name, last name, ~~and~~ phone number from ~~the~~ customers ~~table~~ where ~~the~~ county ~~name is~~ = 'King' and ~~the~~ last name ~~is~~ = 'Hernandez'

SQL
```
SELECT CustFirstName, CustLastName, CustPhoneNumber
FROM Customers
WHERE CustLastName = 'Hernandez'
   AND CustCounty = 'King'
```

As you know, a row must meet *both* conditions to be included in the Result Set. If either the county name or the last name is Null, the database disregards the row completely.

Let's now consider this request.

"Show me the names of all staff members who are graduate counselors or were hired on September 1, 1999."

Translation Select last name and first name from the staff table where the title is 'graduate counselor' or date hired is September 1, 1999

Clean Up Select last name ~~and~~ first name from ~~the~~ staff ~~table~~ where ~~the~~ title ~~is~~ = 'graduate counselor' or date hired ~~is~~ = ~~September 1, 1999~~ '1999-09-01'

SQL
```
SELECT StfLastName, StfFirstName
FROM Staff
WHERE Title = 'Graduate Counselor'
   OR DateHired = '1999-09-01'
```

Although you might expect Nulls to have the same effect on conditions combined with OR as they do on conditions combined with AND, that is not necessarily the case. A row still has a chance of being included in the Result Set as long as it meets *either* of these conditions. Take a look at Figure 6-13 again. Based on the values of Title and DateHired, Table 6-2 on the next page shows how the database determines whether to send a row to the Result Set when you combine the Predicates with OR.

Table 6-2 *Determining the Result Set with OR.*

Value of Title	Value of DateHired	Result
Graduate Counselor	**1999-09-01**	The row is included in the Result Set because it meets both conditions
Graduate Counselor	1999-11-15	The row is included in the Result Set because it meets the first condition
Registrar	**1999-09-01**	The row is included in the Result Set because it meets the second condition
Graduate Counselor	Null	The row is included in the Result Set because it meets the first condition
Null	**1999-09-01**	The row is included in the Result Set because it meets the second condition
Null	Null	The row is excluded from the Result Set because it does not meet either condition

When you suspect that a Result Set is displaying incorrect information, test any columns you're using as criteria with the Null condition. This will give you the opportunity to deal with any Null values as appropriate, and you can then execute your original SELECT Statement once again. For example, if you think there might be a few graduate counselors missing from the Result Set, you could execute the following SELECT Statement to determine if this is true.

```
SQL        SELECT StfLastName, StfFirstName, Title
           FROM Staff
           WHERE Title IS NULL
```

If there are Null values in the Title column, this SELECT Statement will produce a Result Set that contains the names of all staff members who do not have a title specified in the database. Now you can deal with this data as appropriate and then return to your original SELECT Statement.

The jury is still out on Nulls just yet. We'll revisit Nulls once more in Chapter 12 when we discuss SELECT Statements that summarize data.

Expressing Conditions in Different Ways

One side benefit to everything you've learned in this chapter is that you now have the ability to express a given condition in various ways. Let's take a look at this by considering the following request.

> *"Give me the name of every employee that was hired in October of 1999."*

You need to search for hire dates that fall between October 1, 1999, and October 31, 1999, in order to answer this request. Based on what you've already learned, you can define the condition in two ways.

```
DateHired BETWEEN '1999-10-01' AND '1999-10-31'
DateHired >= '1999-10-01' AND DateHired <= '1999-10-31'
```

Both of these conditions will send the same rows to the Result Set; the condition you choose to use is just a matter of preference. Some people find the first expression easier to understand, while others prefer the second expression.

Here are some other examples of equivalent conditions.

> *"Show me the vendors who are based in California, Oregon, or Washington."*

```
VendState IN ('CA', 'OR', 'WA')
VendState = 'CA' OR VendState = 'OR' OR VendState = 'WA'
```

> *"Give me a list of customers whose last name begins with 'H'."*

```
CustLastName >= 'H' AND CustLastName <= 'HZ'
CustLastName BETWEEN 'H' AND 'HZ'
CustLastName LIKE 'H%'
```

> *"Show me all the students who do not live in Seattle or Redmond."*

```
StudCity <> 'Seattle' AND StudCity <> 'Redmond'
StudCity NOT IN ('Seattle', 'Redmond')
NOT (StudCity = 'Seattle' OR StudCity = 'Redmond')
```

There's no "wrong" way for you to define a condition, but you can define a condition incorrectly by blatantly disregarding its syntax. (As you know, this will cause the condition to fail.) However, some database systems optimize certain types of conditions for speedy processing, making them preferable to other equivalent conditions. Check your database system's documentation to determine whether there are any preferred methods of defining conditions.

Sample Statements

You've now learned all the techniques you need to build solid Search Conditions. Let's take a look at some examples of various types of Search Conditions using the tables from each of the sample databases.

> ❖ **Note** We've combined the Translation and Clean Up steps for all the examples once again so that you can continue to learn how to consolidate the process.

Sales Order Database

"Show me all the orders for customer number 1001."

Translation/ Clean Up: Select ~~the~~ order number ~~and~~ customer ID from ~~the~~ orders ~~table~~ where ~~the~~ customer ID ~~is~~ = 1001

SQL:

```
SELECT OrderNumber, CustomerID
FROM Orders
WHERE CustomerID = 1001
```

Orders_for_Customer_1001 (44 Rows)

OrderNumber	CustomerID
2	1001
7	1001
16	1001
52	1001
55	1001
107	1001
137	1001
138	1001
151	1001
154	1001
<<more rows here>>	

"Show me an alphabetized list of products with names that begin with 'Dog'."

Translation/ Clean Up — Select ~~the~~ product name from ~~the~~ products ~~table~~ where ~~the~~ product name like 'Dog%' ~~and~~ order by product name

SQL

```
SELECT ProductName
FROM Products
WHERE ProductName LIKE 'Dog%'
ORDER BY ProductName
```

Products_That_Begin_With_DOG (4 Rows)

ProductName
Dog Ear Aero-Flow Floor Pump
Dog Ear Cyclecomputer
Dog Ear Helmet Mount Mirrors
Dog Ear Monster Grip Gloves

❖ **Note** We just wanted to remind you that you place the ORDER BY clause at *the end* of a SELECT Statement. If necessary, review the Sorting Information section in Chapter 4.

Entertainment Database

"Show me an alphabetical list of entertainers based in Bellevue, Redmond, or Woodinville."

Translation/ Clean Up: Select stage name, phone number ~~and~~ city from ~~the~~ entertainers ~~table~~ where ~~the~~ city ~~is~~ in ('Bellevue', 'Redmond', ~~or~~ 'Woodinville') ~~and~~ order by stage name

SQL

```
SELECT EntStageName, EntPhoneNumber, EntCity
FROM Entertainers
WHERE EntCity IN ('Bellevue', 'Redmond',
   'Woodinville')
ORDER BY EntStageName
```

Eastside_Entertainers (7 Rows)

EntStageName	EntPhoneNumber	EntCity
Albert Buchanan	555-2531	Bellevue
Carol Peacock Trio	555-2691	Redmond
Jazz Persuasion	555-2541	Bellevue
JV & the Deep Six	555-2511	Redmond
Katherine Ehrlich	555-0399	Woodinville
Modern Dance	555-2631	Woodinville
Susan McLain	555-2301	Bellevue

"Show me all the engagements that run for four days."

Translation/ Clean Up: Select engagement number, start date, ~~and~~ end date from ~~the~~ engagements ~~table~~ where the (end date ~~minus~~ - start date) ~~equals~~ = 3

SQL

```
SELECT EngagementNumber, StartDate, EndDate
FROM Engagements
WHERE (EndDate-StartDate) = 3
```

Four-Day Engagements (16 Rows)

EngagementNumber	StartDate	EndDate
1	1999-07-01	1999-07-04
5	1999-07-11	1999-07-14
13	1999-07-17	1999-07-20
17	1999-07-29	1999-08-01
21	1999-07-30	1999-08-02
56	1999-09-24	1999-09-27
58	1999-09-30	1999-10-03
59	1999-09-30	1999-10-03
63	1999-10-17	1999-10-20
70	1999-10-22	1999-10-25
<<more rows here>>		

❖ **Note** An engagement runs from the start date *through* the end date. When subtracting StartDate from EndDate, we get one less day than the total number of days for the engagement. For this reason, we compared the result of the calculation to 3, not 4.

School Scheduling Database

"Show me an alphabetical list of all the staff members and their salaries if they make between $40,000 and $50,000 a year."

Translation / Clean Up — Select first name, last name, and salary from ~~the~~ staff ~~table~~ where ~~the~~ salary ~~is~~ between 40000 and 50000, ~~then~~ order by last name, ~~and~~ first name

SQL

```
SELECT StfFirstName, StfLastName, Salary
FROM Staff
WHERE Salary BETWEEN 40000 AND 50000
ORDER BY StfLastname, StfFirstName
```

Staff_Salaries_40K_TO_50K (14 Rows)

StfLastName	StfFirstName	Salary
Buchanan	Albert	$45,000.00
Buchanan	Amelia	$48,000.00
Callahan	David	$50,000.00
Callahan	Laura	$45,000.00
Ehrlich	Katherine	$45,000.00
Fuller	Ann	$44,000.00
Leverling	Janet	$50,000.00
Maynez	Consuelo	$48,000.00
Patterson	Ann	$45,000.00
Piercy	Gregory	$45,000.00
<<more rows here >>		

"Show me a list of students whose last name is 'Kennedy' or who live in Seattle."

Translation/ Clean Up — Select first name, last name, ~~and~~ city from ~~the~~ students ~~table~~ where ~~the~~ last name ~~is~~ = 'Kennedy' or ~~the~~ city ~~is~~ = 'Seattle'

SQL

```
SELECT StdFirstName, StdLastName, StdCity
FROM Students
WHERE StdLastName = 'Kennedy' OR StdCity = 'Seattle'
```

Seattle_Students_And_Students_Named_Kennedy (5 Rows)

StudFirstName	StudLastName	StudCity
Sally	Callahan	Seattle
Sara	Kennedy	Portland
John	Kennedy	Portland
Kendra	Bonnicksen	Seattle
David	Nathanson	Seattle

Bowling League Database

"List the ID numbers of the teams that won one or more of the first ten matches in Game 3."

Translation / Clean Up — Select ~~the~~ team ID, match ID, ~~and~~ game number from ~~the~~ match_games ~~table~~ where ~~the~~ game number ~~is~~ = 3 and ~~the~~ match ID ~~is~~ between 1 and 10

SQL

```
SELECT WinningTeamID, MatchID, GameNumber
FROM Match_Games
WHERE GameNumber = 3 AND MatchID BETWEEN 1 AND 10
```

Game3_Top_Ten_Matches (10 Rows)

WinningTeamID	MatchID	GameNumber
1	1	3
3	2	3
5	3	3
7	4	3
3	5	3
4	6	3
5	7	3
8	8	3
2	9	3
1	10	3

"List the bowlers in teams 3, 4, and 5 who have a handicap of 40 or less."

Translation / Clean Up: Select first name, last name, team ID, ~~and~~ current handicap from ~~the~~ bowlers ~~table~~ where ~~the~~ team ID ~~is either~~ in (3, 4, ~~or~~ 5) and ~~the~~ current handicap ~~is less than or equal to~~ <= 40

SQL

```
SELECT BowlerFirstName, BowlerLastName, TeamID,
   CurrentHandicap
FROM Bowlers
WHERE TeamID IN (3, 4, 5) AND CurrentHandicap <= 40
```

Low_Handicap_Bowlers_Teams_3_Through_5 (6 Rows)

BowlerFirstName	BowlerLastName	TeamID	CurrentHandicap
David	Cunningham	3	36
Susan	McLain	3	33
Gary	Hallmark	4	39
Kathryn	Patterson	4	34
Michael	Hernandez	5	39
John	Viescas	5	29

SUMMARY

In this chapter, we introduced you to the idea of filtering the information you see in a Result Set by using a Search Condition in a WHERE clause. You learned that a Search Condition uses combinations of Predicates to filter the data that is sent to the Result Set, and that Predicates are specific tests you can apply to a Value Expression. We then introduced you to the five basic types of Predicates that you could define.

Our discussion continued with an in-depth look at each of the five basic types of Predicates you can define within a Search Condition of a WHERE clause. You learned how to compare values and how to test whether a value falls within a specified range of values. You also learned how to test whether a value matches one of a defined list of values or is part of a specific pattern string. Additionally, you learned that you could use the NOT operator to exclude rows from a Result Set.

We then discussed how to use multiple conditions by combining them with AND and OR operators. You learned that a row must meet all conditions combined with AND before it can be included in the Result Set, whereas it must meet *only one* of those conditions if the conditions are combined with OR. You also learned how to use AND and OR together to answer complex requests. We then took a second look at using NOT to exclude rows from a Result Set, and you learned that NOT can be used at two different levels in a Search Condition.

The order of precedence was the next topic of discussion, and you learned how the database analyzes and evaluates conditions. You now know that the database evaluates conditions in a specific order based upon the operator used in each condition. You also learned how to use parentheses to alter the order in which the database evaluates certain conditions and to ensure that you avoid defining ambiguous conditions.

We next took a brief detour to review Nulls. Here you learned that Nulls affect conditions in much the way that they affect expressions. You also know that you should test for Null values if you suspect that a Result Set is displaying incorrect information.

Finally, we discussed the fact that the same condition can be expressed in various ways. You now know, for example, that you can use three different types of conditions to search for people whose last name begins with the letter "H."

In the next part of the book, we'll introduce you to the idea of *sets* and the types of operations you can perform on them. Once you learn about sets, you'll be well on your way to learning how to define SELECT Statements using multiple tables.

The following section presents a number of requests that you can work out on your own.

Problems for You to Solve

Below, we show you the request statement and the name of the solution query in the sample databases. If you want some practice, you can work out the SQL you need for each request and then check your answer with the query we saved in the samples. Don't worry if your syntax doesn't exactly match the syntax of the queries we saved—as long as your Result Set is the same.

Sales Order Database

1. *"Give me the names of all vendors based in Ballard, Bellevue, and Redmond."*
   You can find the solution in Ballard_Bellevue_Redmond_Vendors (3 rows).
2. *"Show me an alphabetized list of products with a retail price of $125.00 or more."*
   (Hint: You'll alphabetize the list using a clause we discussed in a previous chapter.)
   You can find the solution in Products_Priced_Over_125 (13 rows).
3. *"Which vendors do we work with that don't have a Web site."*
   You can find the solution in Vendors_With_No_Website (4 rows).

Entertainment Database

1. *"Let me see a list of all engagements that occurred during August of 1999."*
   You can find the solution in August_1999_Engagements (21 rows).
2. *"Show me any engagements in August of 1999 that start between noon and 5 PM."*
   You can find the solution in August_Dates_Between_Noon_and_Five (17 rows).
3. *"List all the engagements that start and end on the same day."*
   (Hint: You'll need to use date arithmetic to answer this request.)
   You can find the solution in Single_Day_Engagements (6 rows).

School Scheduling Database

1. *"Show me which staff members use a post office box as their address."*
   You can find the solution in Staff_Using_POBoxes (6 rows).
2. *"Can you show me which students live outside of the Pacific Northwest?"*
   You can find the solution in Students_Residing_Outside_PNW (5 rows).
3. *"List all the subjects that have a subject code starting 'MUS'."*
   You can find the solution in Subjects_With_MUS_In_SubjectCode (4 rows).

Bowling League Database

1. *"Give me a list of the tournaments held during August 1999."*
   You can find the solution in August_1999_Tournament_Schedule (4 rows).
2. *"What are the tournament schedules for Bolero, Red Rooster, and Thunderbird Lanes?"*
   You can find the solution in Eastside_Tournaments (6 rows).
3. *"List the bowlers who live on the eastside (you know—Bellevue, Bothell, Duvall, Redmond, and Woodinville) and whose handicap is between 45 and 55."*
   You can find the solution in High_Handicap_Eastside_Bowlers (7 rows).

Part III

Working with Multiple Tables

7

Thinking in Sets

Small cheer and a great welcome makes a merry feast.
—William Shakespeare, *Comedy of Errors,* Act III, Scene i

Topics Covered in this Chapter

By now, you know how to create a set of information by asking for specific columns or expressions on columns (SELECT), how to sort the rows (ORDER BY), and how to restrict the rows returned (WHERE). Up to this point, we've been focusing on basic exercises involving a single table. But what if you want to know something about information contained in multiple tables? What if you want to compare or contrast sets of information from the same or different tables?

Creating a feast by peeling, slicing, and dicing a single pile of potatoes or a single bunch of carrots is easy. From here on out, most of the problems we're going to show you how to solve will involve getting data from *multiple* tables. We're not only going to show you how to put together a good stew—we're going to teach you how to be a chef!

Before digging into this chapter, you need to know that this chapter is all about the *concepts* you must understand in order to successfully link together two or more sets of information. We're also going to give you a brief overview of some specific syntax defined in the SQL Standard that directly supports the pure definition of these concepts. Be forewarned, however, that many current commercial implementations of SQL do not yet support this "pure" syntax. In later chapters, we'll show you how to implement the concepts you'll learn here using SQL syntax that is commonly supported by most major database systems. What we're after here is not the "letter of the law" but rather the "spirit of the law."

What Is a Set, Anyway?

If you were a teenager any time from the mid-1960s onward, you may have studied Set Theory in a mathematics course. (Remember "New Math?") If you were introduced to set algebra, you probably wondered why any of it would ever be useful.

Now you're trying to learn about Relational databases and this quirky language called SQL to build applications, solve problems, or just get answers to your questions. Were you paying attention in algebra class? If so, solving problems—particularly complex ones—in SQL will be much easier.

Actually, you've been working with sets from the beginning of this book. In Chapter 1, you learned about the basic structure of a Relational database—tables containing records that are made up of one or more fields. (Remember that in SQL, records are known as rows, and fields are known as columns.) Each table in your database is a *set* of information about one subject. In Chapter 2, you learned how to verify that the structure of your database is sound. Each table should contain the *set* of information related to one and only one subject or action.

In Chapter 4, you learned how to build a basic SELECT statement in SQL to retrieve a Result *Set* of information which contains specific columns from a single table and how to sort those Result Sets. In Chapter 5 you learned how to glean a new *set* of information from a table by writing expressions that operate on one or more columns. In Chapter 6 you learned how to restrict further the *set* of information you retrieve from your tables by adding a filter (WHERE clause) to your query.

As you can see, a set can be as little as the data from one column from one row in one table. Actually, you can construct a request in SQL that returns no rows—an empty set; sometimes it's useful to discover that something does *not* exist. A set can also be multiple columns (including columns you create with expressions) from multiple rows fetched from multiple tables. Each row in a Result Set is a *member* of the set. The values in the columns are specific *attributes* of each member—data items that describe the member of the set. In the next several chapters, we'll show how to ask for information from multiple sets of data and link these sets together to get answers to more complex questions. First, however, you need to understand a bit more about sets and the logical ways to combine them.

Operations on Sets

In Chapter 1 we discussed how Dr. E. F. Codd invented the Relational Model on which most modern databases and SQL are based. He based his new model on two branches of mathematics—Set Theory and First Order Predicate Logic.

Once you graduate beyond getting answers from only a single table, you need to learn how to use Result Sets of information to solve more complex problems. These complex problems usually require using one of the common set operations to link data from two or more tables. Sometimes, you'll need to get two different Result Sets from the same table and then combine them to get your answer.

The three most common set operations are as follows.

- **Intersection**—You use this to find the common elements in two or more different sets: "Show me the recipes that contain *both* lamb *and* rice." "Show me the customers who ordered *both* bicycles *and* helmets."
- **Difference**—You use this to find items that are in one set but not another: "Show me the recipes that contain lamb but *do not* contain rice." "Show me the customers who ordered a bicycle *but not* a helmet."
- **Union**—You use this to combine two or more similar sets: "Show me all the recipes that contain *either* lamb *or* rice." "Show me the customers who ordered *either* a bicycle *or* a helmet."

In the following three sections, we'll explain these basic set operations—the ones you should have learned in high school algebra. The SQL Set Operations section of this chapter gives an overview of how these operations are implemented in "pure" SQL.

Intersection

No, it's not your local street corner. An intersection of two sets contains the common elements of two sets. Let's take a look at an intersection both from the perspective of Set Theory and of solving business problems.

Intersection in Set Theory

An intersection is a very powerful mathematical tool often used by scientists and engineers. As a scientist, you might be interested in finding common points between two sets of chemical or physical sample data. For example, a pharmaceutical research chemist might have two compounds that seem to provide a certain beneficial effect. Finding the commonality (the intersection) between the two compounds might help discover what it is that makes the two compounds effective. Or, an engineer might be interested in finding the intersection between one alloy that is hard but brittle and another alloy that is soft but resilient.

Let's take a look at intersection in action by examining two sets of numbers. In this example, each single number is a member of the set. The first set of numbers is as follows.

1, 5, 8, 9, 32, 55, 78

The second set of numbers is as follows.

3, 7, 8, 22, 55, 71, 99

The intersection of these two sets of numbers is the numbers common to both sets. The answer is

8, 55

The individual entries—the members—of each set needn't be just single values. In fact, when solving problems with SQL, you'll probably deal with sets of rows.

According to Set Theory, when a member of a set is something more than a single number or value, each member (or object) of the set has multiple attributes or bits of data that describe the properties of each member. For example, your favorite stew recipe is a complex member of the set of all recipes that contains many different ingredients; each ingredient is an attribute of your complex stew member.

To find the intersection between two sets of complex set members, you have to find the members that match on all the attributes. Also, all the members in each set you're trying to compare must have the same number and type of attributes. For example, suppose you have a complex set like the one below in which each row represents a member of the set (a stew recipe), and each column denotes a particular attribute (an ingredient).

Potatoes	Water	Lamb	Peas
Rice	Chicken Stock	Chicken	Carrots
Pasta	Water	Tofu	Snap Peas
Potatoes	Beef Stock	Beef	Cabbage
Pasta	Water	Pork	Onions

A second set might look like the following.

Potatoes	Water	Lamb	Onions
Rice	Chicken Stock	Turkey	Carrots
Pasta	Vegetable Stock	Tofu	Snap Peas
Potatoes	Beef Stock	Beef	Cabbage
Beans	Water	Pork	Onions

The intersection of these two sets is the one member whose attributes all match in both sets.

Potatoes	Beef Stock	Beef	Cabbage

Intersection between Result Sets

If the previous examples look like rows in a table or a Result Set to you, you're on the right track! When you're dealing with rows in a set of data that you fetch with SQL, the attributes are the individual columns. For example, suppose you have a set of rows returned by a query like the one below. (These are recipes from John's cookbook.)

Recipe	Starch	Stock	Meat	Vegetable
Lamb Stew	Potatoes	Water	Lamb	Peas
Chicken Stew	Rice	Chicken Stock	Chicken	Carrots
Veggie Stew	Pasta	Water	Tofu	Snap Peas
Irish Stew	Potatoes	Beef Stock	Beef	Cabbage
Pork Stew	Pasta	Water	Pork	Onions

A second query Result Set might look like the following. (These are recipes from Mike's cookbook.)

Recipe	Starch	Stock	Meat	Vegetable
Lamb Stew	Potatoes	Water	Lamb	Peas
Turkey Stew	Rice	Chicken Stock	Turkey	Carrots
Veggie Stew	Pasta	Vegetable Stock	Tofu	Snap Peas
Irish Stew	Potatoes	Beef Stock	Beef	Cabbage
Pork Stew	Beans	Water	Pork	Onions

The intersection of these two sets is the two members whose attributes all match in both sets—that is, the two recipes that Mike and John have in common.

Recipe	Starch	Stock	Meat	Vegetable
Lamb Stew	Potatoes	Water	Lamb	Peas
Irish Stew	Potatoes	Beef Stock	Beef	Cabbage

Sometimes it's easier to see how intersection works using a set diagram. A set diagram is an elegant yet simple way to diagram sets of information and graphically represent how the sets intersect or overlap. You may also have heard this sort of diagram called a Euler or Venn Diagram. (By the way, Leonard Euler was an eighteenth century Swiss mathematician, and John Venn used this particular type of logic diagram in 1880 in a paper he wrote while a Fellow at Cambridge University. So you can see that "thinking in sets" is not a particularly modern concept!)

Let's assume you have a nice database containing all your favorite recipes. You really like the way onions enhance the flavor of beef, so you're interested in finding all recipes that contain both beef and onions. Figure 7-1 shows the set diagram that helps you visualize how to solve this problem.

The upper circle represents the set of recipes that contain beef. The lower circle represents the set of recipes that contain onions. Where the two circles overlap is where you'll find the recipes that contain both. As you can imagine, you first ask SQL to fetch all the recipes that have beef. In the second query, you ask SQL to fetch all the recipes that have onions. As you'll see a bit later, you can use a special SQL keyword—INTERSECT—to link the two queries to get the final answer.

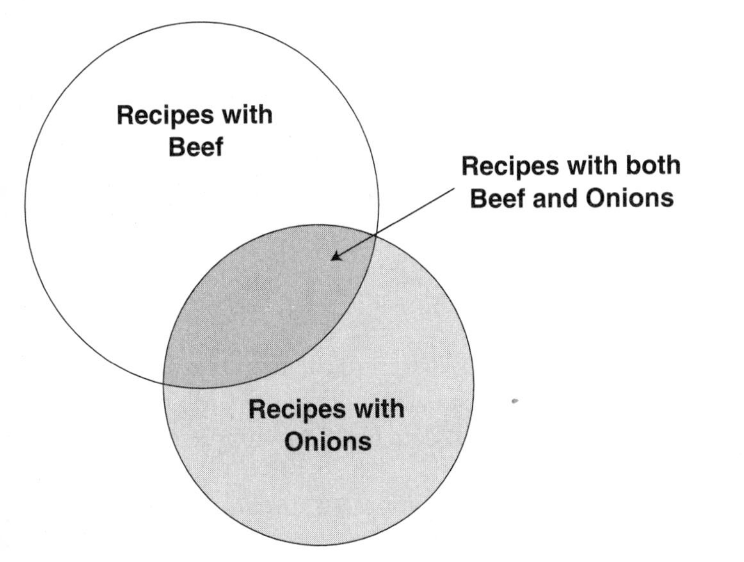

Figure 7-1 *Finding out which recipes have both beef and onions.*

Yes, we know what you're thinking. If your recipe table looks like the samples above, you could simply say

"Show me the recipes that have beef as the meat ingredient and onions as the vegetable ingredient."

Translation	Select the recipe name from the recipes table where meat ingredient is beef and vegetable ingredient is onions
Clean Up	Select ~~the~~ recipe name from ~~the~~ recipes ~~table~~ where meat ingredient ~~is~~ = beef and vegetable ingredient ~~is~~ = onions
SQL	`SELECT RecipeName FROM Recipes WHERE MeatIngredient = 'Beef' AND VegetableIngredient = 'Onions'`

Hold on now! If you remember the lessons you learned in Chapter 2, you know that a single Recipes table probably won't cut it. (Pun intended!) What about recipes that have ingredients other than meat and vegetables? What about the fact that some recipes have many ingredients and others have only a few? A correctly designed recipes database will have a separate Recipe_Ingredients table with one row per recipe per ingredient. Each ingredient row will have only one ingredient, so no single row can be both beef and onions at the same time. You'll need to first find all the beef rows, then find all the onions rows, and then intersect them on RecipeID. (If you're confused why we're criticizing the previous table design, be sure to go back and read Chapter 2!)

How about a bit more complex problem? Let's say you want to add carrots to the mix. A set diagram to visualize the solution might look like Figure 7-2.

Got the hang of it? The bottom line is that when you're faced with solving a problem involving complex criteria, a set diagram can be an invaluable way to see the solution expressed as the intersection of SQL Result Sets.

Problems You Can Solve with INTERSECT

As you might guess, you can use INTERSECT to find the matches between two or more sets of information. Here's just a small sample of the problems you can solve using an intersection technique with data from the sample databases.

"Show me customers and employees that have the same name."

"Find all the customers who ordered a bicycle who also ordered a helmet."

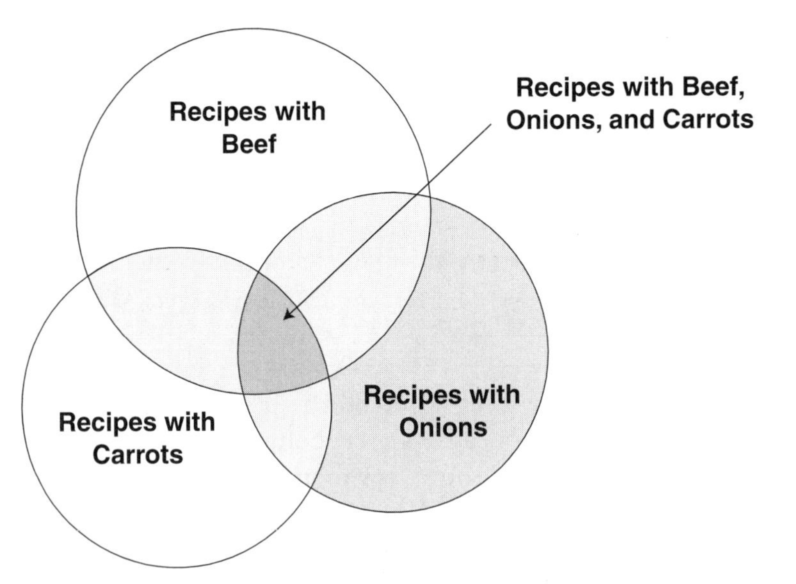

Figure 7-2 *Recipes with beef, onions, and carrots.*

> *"List the entertainers who played engagements for customers Bonnicksen and Rosales."*
>
> *"Show me the students who have an average score of 85 or better in Art and who also have an average score of 85 or better in Computer Science."*
>
> *"Find the bowlers who had a raw score of 155 or better at both Thunderbird Lanes and Bolero Lanes."*
>
> *"Show me the recipes that have beef and garlic."*

One of the limitations of using a pure intersection is that the values must match in all the columns in each Result Set. This works well if you're intersecting two or more sets from the same table—for example, customers who ordered bicycles and customers who ordered helmets. It also works well when you're intersecting sets from tables that have similar columns—for example, customer names and employee names. In many cases, however, you'll want to find solutions that require a match on only a few column values from each set. For this type of problem, SQL provides an operation called a JOIN—an intersect on key values. Here's a sample of problems you can solve with a JOIN.

> *"Show me customers and employees that live in the same city."* (JOIN on city name.)

"List customers and the entertainers they booked." (JOIN on engagement number.)

"Find the agents and entertainers that live in the same postal code." (JOIN on zip code.)

"Show me the students and their teachers who have the same first name." (JOIN on first name.)

"Find the bowlers who have the same average." (JOIN on current average.)

"Display all the ingredients for recipes that contain carrots." (JOIN on Ingredient ID.)

Never fear. In the next chapter we'll show you all about solving these problems (and more) using JOINs. And because so few commercial implementations of SQL support INTERSECT, we'll show how to use a JOIN to solve many problems that might otherwise require an INTERSECT.

Difference

What's the difference between 21 and 10? If you answered 11, you're on the right track! A Difference operation (sometimes also called Subtract, Minus, or Except) takes one set of values and removes the set of values from a second set. What remains is the set of values in the first set that are *not* in the second set. (As you'll see a bit later, EXCEPT is the keyword used in the SQL Standard.)

Difference in Set Theory

Difference is another very powerful mathematical tool. As a scientist, you might be interested in finding what's different about two sets of chemical or physical sample data. For example, a pharmaceutical research chemist might have two compounds that seem to be very similar, but one provides a certain beneficial effect and the other does not. Finding what's different about the two compounds might help uncover why one works and the other does not. As an engineer, you might have two similar designs, but one works better than the other. Finding the difference between the two designs could be crucial to eliminating structural flaws in future buildings.

Let's take a look at difference in action by examining two sets of numbers. The first set of numbers is as follows.

1, 5, 8, 9, 32, 55, 78

The second set of numbers is as follows.

3, 7, 8, 22, 55, 71, 99

The difference of the first set of numbers minus the second set of numbers is the numbers that exist in the first set but not the second. The answer is

1, 5, 9, 32, 78

Note that you can turn the previous difference operation around; thus, the difference of the second set minus the first set is

3, 7, 22, 71, 99

The members of each set needn't be single values. In fact, you'll most likely be dealing with sets of rows when trying to solve problems with SQL.

Earlier in this chapter we said that when a member of a set is something more than a single number or value, each member of the set has multiple attributes (bits of information that describe the properties of each member). For example, your favorite stew recipe is a complex member of the set of all recipes that contains many different ingredients. You can think of each ingredient as an attribute of your complex stew member.

To find the difference between two sets of complex set members, you have to find the members that match on all the attributes in the second set with members in the first set. Don't forget that all of the members in each set you're trying to compare must have the same number and type of attributes. Remove from the first set all the matching members you find in the second set, and the result is the difference. For example, suppose you have a complex set like the one below. Each row represents a member of the set (a stew recipe) and each column denotes a particular attribute (an ingredient).

Potatoes	Water	Lamb	Peas
Rice	Chicken Stock	Chicken	Carrots
Pasta	Water	Tofu	Snap Peas
Potatoes	Beef Stock	Beef	Cabbage
Pasta	Water	Pork	Onions

A second set might look like this.

Potatoes	Water	Lamb	Onions
Rice	Chicken Stock	Turkey	Carrots
Pasta	Vegetable Stock	Tofu	Snap Peas
Potatoes	Beef Stock	Beef	Cabbage
Beans	Water	Pork	Onions

The difference of these two sets is the objects in the first set that don't exist in the second set.

Potatoes	Water	Lamb	Peas
Rice	Chicken Stock	Chicken	Carrots
Pasta	Water	Tofu	Snap Peas
Pasta	Water	Pork	Onions

Difference between Result Sets

When you're dealing with rows in a set of data fetched with SQL, the attributes are the individual columns. For example, suppose you have a set of rows returned by a query like the one below. (These are recipes from John's cookbook.)

Recipe	Starch	Stock	Meat	Vegetable
Lamb Stew	Potatoes	Water	Lamb	Peas
Chicken Stew	Rice	Chicken Stock	Chicken	Carrots
Veggie Stew	Pasta	Water	Tofu	Snap Peas
Irish Stew	Potatoes	Beef Stock	Beef	Cabbage
Pork Stew	Pasta	Water	Pork	Onions

A second query Result Set might look like the following. (These are recipes from Mike's cookbook.)

Recipe	Starch	Stock	Meat	Vegetable
Lamb Stew	Potatoes	Water	Lamb	Peas
Turkey Stew	Rice	Chicken Stock	Turkey	Carrots
Veggie Stew	Pasta	Vegetable Stock	Tofu	Snap Peas
Irish Stew	Potatoes	Beef Stock	Beef	Cabbage
Pork Stew	Beans	Water	Pork	Onions

The difference between John's recipes and Mike's recipes is all the recipes in John's cookbook that *do not* appear in Mike's cookbook.

Recipe	Starch	Stock	Meat	Vegetable
Chicken Stew	Rice	Chicken Stock	Chicken	Carrots
Veggie Stew	Pasta	Water	Tofu	Snap Peas
Pork Stew	Pasta	Water	Pork	Onions

You can also turn this problem around. Suppose you want to find the recipes in Mike's cookbook that *are not* in John's cookbook. Here's the answer.

Recipe	Starch	Stock	Meat	Vegetable
Turkey Stew	Rice	Chicken Stock	Turkey	Carrots
Veggie Stew	Pasta	Vegetable Stock	Tofu	Snap Peas
Pork Stew	Beans	Water	Pork	Onions

Again, we can use a set diagram to help visualize how a difference operation works. Let's assume you have a nice database containing all your favorite recipes. You really do not like the way onions taste with beef, so you're interested in finding all recipes that contain beef but not onions. Figure 7-3 on the next page shows you the set diagram that helps you visualize how to solve this problem.

The upper full circle represents the set of recipes that contain beef. The lower full circle represents the set of recipes that contain onions. As you remember from the discussion about INTERSECT, where the two circles overlap is where

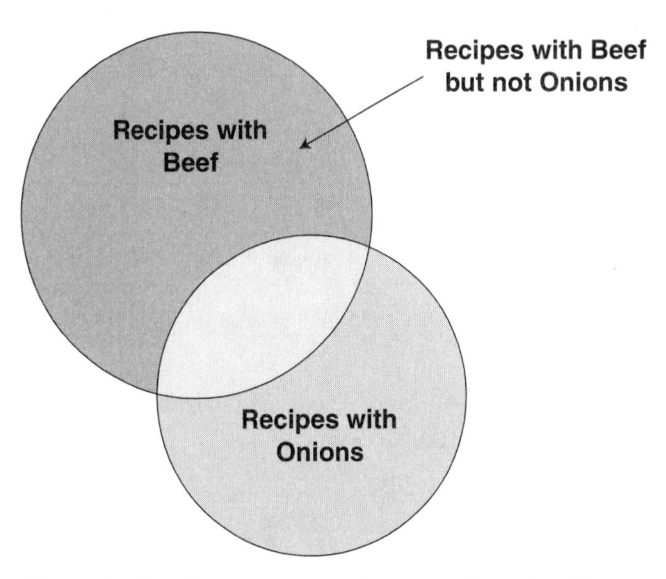

Figure 7-3 *Finding out which recipes have beef but not onions.*

you'll find the recipes that contain both. The dark-shaded part of the upper circle that's not part of the overlapping area represents the set of recipes that contain beef but do not contain onions. Likewise, the part of the lower circle that's not part of the overlapping area represents the set of recipes that contain onions but do not contain beef.

You probably know that you first ask SQL to fetch all the recipes that have beef. Next, you ask SQL to fetch all the recipes that have onions. (As you'll see a bit later in this chapter, the special SQL keyword EXCEPT links the two queries to get the final answer.)

Are you falling into the trap again? (You *did* read Chapter 2, didn't you?) If your recipe table looks like the samples above, you might think that you could simply say

> *"Show me the recipes that have beef as the meat ingredient and that do not have onions as the vegetable ingredient."*

Translation — Select the recipe name from the recipes table where meat ingredient is beef and vegetable ingredient is not onions

Clean Up — Select ~~the~~ recipe name from ~~the~~ recipes ~~table~~ where meat ingredient ~~is~~ = beef and vegetable ingredient ~~is not~~ <> onions

```
SQL        SELECT RecipeName FROM Recipes WHERE MeatIngredient
              = 'Beef' AND VegetableIngredient <> 'Onions'
```

Again, as you learned in Chapter 2, a single Recipes table isn't such a hot idea. (Pun intended!) What about recipes that have ingredients other than meat and vegetables? What about the fact that some recipes have many ingredients and others have only a few? A correctly designed Recipes database will have a separate Recipe_Ingredients table with one row per recipe per ingredient. Each ingredient row will have only one ingredient, so no one row can be both beef and onions at the same time. You'll need to first find all the beef rows, then find all the onions rows, then difference them on RecipeID.

How about a bit more complex problem? Let's say you hate carrots, too. A set diagram to visualize the solution might look like Figure 7-4.

First you need to find the set of recipes that have beef, then get the difference with either the set of recipes containing onions or the set containing carrots. Take that result and get the difference again with the remaining set (onions or carrots) to leave only the recipes that have beef but no carrots or onions (the light-shaded area in the upper circle).

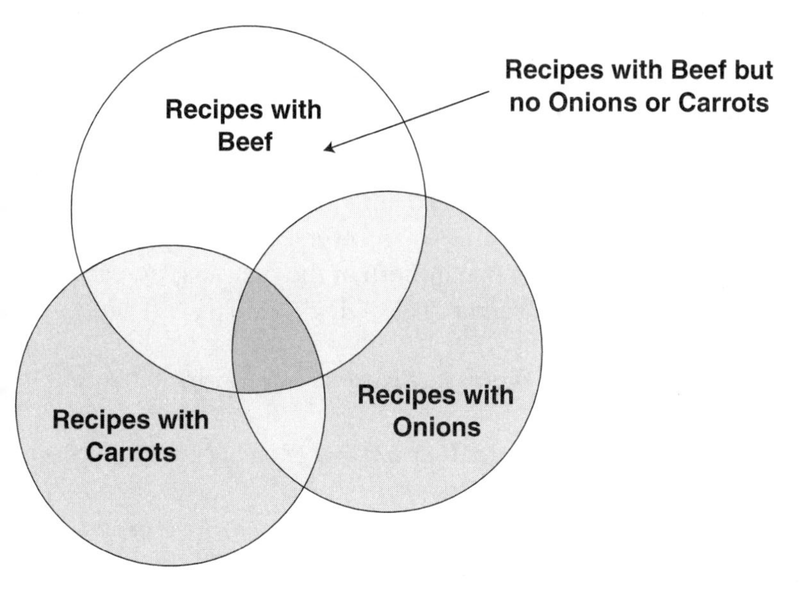

Figure 7-4 *Recipes with beef but no onions or carrots.*

Problems You Can Solve with Difference

Unlike intersection (which looks for common members of two sets), difference looks for members that are in one set but *not* in another set. Here's just a small sample of the problems you can solve using a difference technique with data from the sample databases.

> *"Show me customers whose names are not the same as any employee."*
>
> *"Find all the customers who ordered a bicycle but who did not order a helmet."*
>
> *"List the entertainers who played engagements for customer Bonnicksen but did not play any engagement for customer Rosales."*
>
> *"Show me the students who have an average score of 85 or better in Art but do not have an average score of 85 or better in Computer Science."*
>
> *"Find the bowlers who had a raw score of 155 or better at Thunderbird Lanes but not Bolero Lanes."*
>
> *"Show me the recipes that have beef but not garlic."*

One of the limitations of using a pure difference is that the values must match in all the columns in each Result Set. This works well if you're finding the difference between two or more sets from the same table—for example, customers who ordered bicycles and customers who ordered helmets. It also works well when you're finding the difference between sets from tables that have similar columns—for example, customer names and employee names.

In many cases, however, you'll want to find solutions that require a match on only a few column values from each set. For this type of problem, SQL provides an OUTER JOIN operation, which is an intersect on key values that includes the unmatched values from one or both of the two sets. Here's a sample of problems you can solve with an OUTER JOIN.

> *"Show me customers who do not live in the same city as any employees."* (OUTER JOIN on city name.)
>
> *"List customers and the entertainers they did not book."* (OUTER JOIN on engagement number.)
>
> *"Find the agents that are not in the same postal code as any entertainer."* (OUTER JOIN on zip code.)
>
> *"Show me the students who do not have the same first name as any teachers."* (OUTER JOIN on first name.)

> *"Find the bowlers who have an average of 150 or higher who have never bowled a game below 125."* (OUTER JOIN on Bowler ID from two different tables.)
>
> *"Display all the ingredients for recipes that do not have carrots."* (OUTER JOIN on Recipe ID.)

Don't worry! We'll show you all about solving these problems (and more) using OUTER JOINs in Chapter 9. Also, because few commercial implementations of SQL support EXCEPT, we'll show how to use an OUTER JOIN to solve many problems that might otherwise require an EXCEPT (difference).

Union

So far we've discussed finding the items that are common in two sets (intersection), and the items that are different (difference). The third type of set operation involves "adding" two sets (union).

Union in Set Theory

Union lets you combine two sets of similar information into one set. As a scientist, you might be interested in combining two sets of chemical or physical sample data. For example, a pharmaceutical research chemist might have two different sets of compounds that seem to provide a certain beneficial effect. The chemist can union the two sets to obtain a single list of all effective compounds.

Let's take a look at union in action by examining two sets of numbers. The first set of numbers is as follows.

1, 5, 8, 9, 32, 55, 78

The second set of numbers is as follows.

3, 7, 8, 22, 55, 71, 99

The union of these two sets of numbers is the numbers in both sets combined into one new set. The answer is

1, 5, 8, 9, 32, 55, 78, 3, 7, 22, 71, 99

Note that the values common to both sets, 8 and 55, appear only once in the answer. Also, the sequence of the numbers in the Result Set is not necessarily in any specific order. When you ask a database system to perform a UNION, the values returned won't necessarily be in sequence unless you explicitly include an ORDER BY clause. In SQL, you can also ask for a UNION ALL if you want to see the duplicate members.

The members of each set don't have to be just single values. In fact, you'll probably deal with sets of rows when working with SQL.

To find the union of two or more sets of complex members, all the members in each set you're trying to union must have the same number and type of attributes. For example, suppose you have a complex set like the one below. Each row represents a member of the set (a stew recipe), and each column denotes a particular attribute (an ingredient).

Potatoes	Water	Lamb	Peas
Rice	Chicken Stock	Chicken	Carrots
Pasta	Water	Tofu	Snap Peas
Potatoes	Beef Stock	Beef	Cabbage
Pasta	Water	Pork	Onions

A second set might look like the following.

Potatoes	Water	Lamb	Onions
Rice	Chicken Stock	Turkey	Carrots
Pasta	Vegetable Stock	Tofu	Snap Peas
Potatoes	Beef Stock	Beef	Cabbage
Beans	Water	Pork	Onions

The union of these two sets is the set of objects from both sets; duplicates are eliminated.

Potatoes	Water	Lamb	Peas
Rice	Chicken Stock	Chicken	Carrots
Pasta	Water	Tofu	Snap Peas
Potatoes	Beef Stock	Beef	Cabbage
Pasta	Water	Pork	Onions
Potatoes	Water	Lamb	Onions
Rice	Chicken Stock	Turkey	Carrots
Pasta	Vegetable Stock	Tofu	Snap Peas
Beans	Water	Pork	Onions

Combining Result Sets Using UNION

It's a small leap from sets of complex objects to rows in SQL Result Sets. When you're dealing with rows in a set of data that you fetch with SQL, the attributes are the individual columns. For example, suppose you have a set of rows returned by a query like the one below. (These are recipes from John's cookbook.)

Recipe	Starch	Stock	Meat	Vegetable
Lamb Stew	Potatoes	Water	Lamb	Peas
Chicken Stew	Rice	Chicken Stock	Chicken	Carrots
Veggie Stew	Pasta	Water	Tofu	Snap Peas
Irish Stew	Potatoes	Beef Stock	Beef	Cabbage
Pork Stew	Pasta	Water	Pork	Onions

A second query Result Set might look like the one on the next page. (These are recipes from Mike's cookbook).

Recipe	Starch	Stock	Meat	Vegetable
Lamb Stew	Potatoes	Water	Lamb	Peas
Turkey Stew	Rice	Chicken Stock	Turkey	Carrots
Veggie Stew	Pasta	Vegetable Stock	Tofu	Snap Peas
Irish Stew	Potatoes	Beef Stock	Beef	Cabbage
Pork Stew	Beans	Water	Pork	Onions

The union of these two sets is all the rows in both sets. Maybe John and Mike decided to write a cookbook together, too!

Recipe	Starch	Stock	Meat	Vegetable
Lamb Stew	Potatoes	Water	Lamb	Peas
Chicken Stew	Rice	Chicken Stock	Chicken	Carrots
Veggie Stew	Pasta	Water	Tofu	Snap Peas
Irish Stew	Potatoes	Beef Stock	Beef	Cabbage
Pork Stew	Pasta	Water	Pork	Onions
Turkey Stew	Rice	Chicken Stock	Turkey	Carrots
Veggie Stew	Pasta	Vegetable Stock	Tofu	Snap Peas
Pork Stew	Beans	Water	Pork	Onions

Let's assume you have a nice database containing all your favorite recipes. You really like recipes with either beef or onions, so you want a list of recipes that contain either ingredient. Figure 7-5 shows you the set diagram that helps you visualize how to solve this problem.

The upper circle represents the set of recipes that contain beef. The lower circle represents the set of recipes that contain onions. The union of the two circles gives you all the recipes that contain either ingredient, with duplicates eliminated where the two sets overlap. As you probably know, you first ask SQL to fetch all the recipes that have beef. In the second query, you ask SQL to fetch all the recipes that have onions. As you'll see a bit later, the SQL keyword UNION links the two queries to get the final answer.

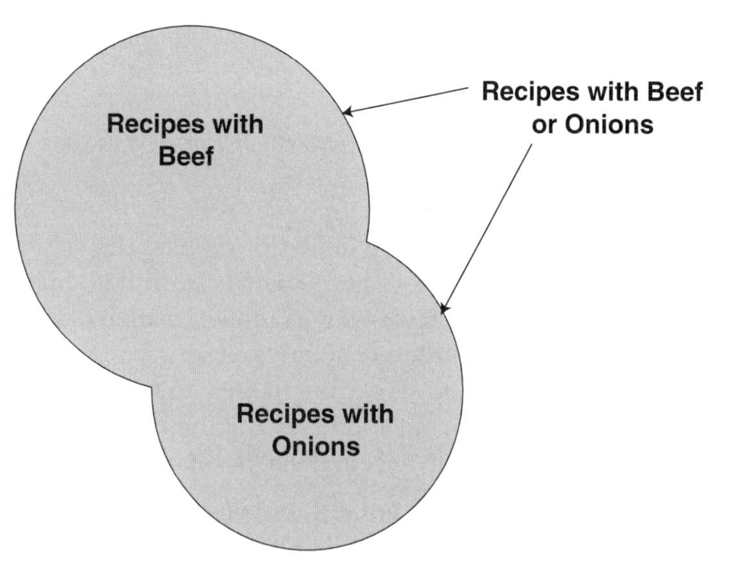

Figure 7-5 *Finding out which recipes have either beef or onions.*

By now you know that it's not a good idea to design a recipes database with a single table. Instead, a correctly designed recipes database will have a separate Recipe_Ingredients table with one row per recipe per ingredient. Each ingredient row will have only one ingredient, so no one row can be both beef or onions at the same time. You'll need to first find all the recipes that have a beef row, then find all the recipes that have an onions row, and then union them.

Problems You Can Solve with UNION

UNION lets you "mush together" rows from two similar sets—with the added advantage of no duplicate rows. Here's a sample of the problems you can solve using a union technique with data from the sample databases.

"Show me all the customer and employee names and addresses."

"List all the customers who ordered a bicycle combined with all the customers who ordered a helmet."

"List the entertainers who played engagements for customer Bonnicksen combined with all the entertainers who played engagements for customer Rosales."

"Show me the students who have an average score of 85 or better in Art together with the students who have an average score of 85 or better in Computer Science."

"Find the bowlers who had a raw score of 155 or better at Thunderbird Lanes combined with bowlers who had a raw score of 140 or better at Bolero Lanes."

"Show me the recipes that have beef together with the list of recipes that have garlic."

As with other "pure" set operations, one of the limitations is that the values must match in all the columns in each Result Set. This works well if you're unioning two or more sets from the same table—for example, customers who ordered bicycles and customers who ordered helmets. It also works well when you're performing a UNION on sets from tables that have like columns—for example, customer names and addresses and employee names and addresses. We'll explore the uses of UNION in detail in Chapter 10.

In many cases where you would otherwise union rows from the same table, you'll find that using DISTINCT (to eliminate the duplicate rows) with complex criteria on joined tables will serve as well. We'll show you all about solving problems this way using JOINs in Chapter 8.

SQL Set Operations

Now that you have a basic understanding of set operations, let's look briefly at how they're implemented in SQL.

"Classical" Set Operations vs. SQL

As noted earlier, not many commercial database systems yet support set INTERSECT or set difference directly. The current SQL Standard, however, clearly defines how these operations should be implemented. We feel that these set operations are important enough to at least warrant an overview of the syntax.

As promised, we'll show you alternative ways to solve an "intersect" or "difference" problem in later chapters using JOINs. Because most database systems do support UNION, Chapter 10 is devoted to its use. The remainder of this chapter gives you an overview of all three operations.

Finding Common Values—INTERSECT

Let's say you're trying to solve the following seemingly simple problem.

"Show me the orders that contain both a bike and a helmet."

Translation	Select the distinct order numbers from the order details table where the product number is in the list of bike and helmet product numbers
Clean Up	Select ~~the~~ distinct order numbers from ~~the~~ order details ~~table~~ where ~~the~~ product number ~~is~~ in ~~the list of~~ bike and helmet product numbers
SQL	`SELECT DISTINCT OrderNumber FROM Order_Details WHERE ProductNumber IN (1, 2, 6, 10, 11, 25, 26)`

> ❖ **Note** Readers familiar with SQL might ask why we didn't JOIN Order_Details to Products and look for bike or helmet product names. The simple answer is that we haven't introduced the concept of a JOIN yet, so we built the above example on a single table using IN and a list of known bike and helmet product numbers.

That seems to do the trick at first, but the answer includes orders that contain either a bike *or* a helmet, and you really want to find ones that contain *both* a bike *and* a helmet! If you visualize "Orders with Bicycles" and "Orders with Helmets" as two distinct sets, it's easier to understand the problem. Figure 7-6 shows one possible relationship between the two sets of orders using a set diagram.

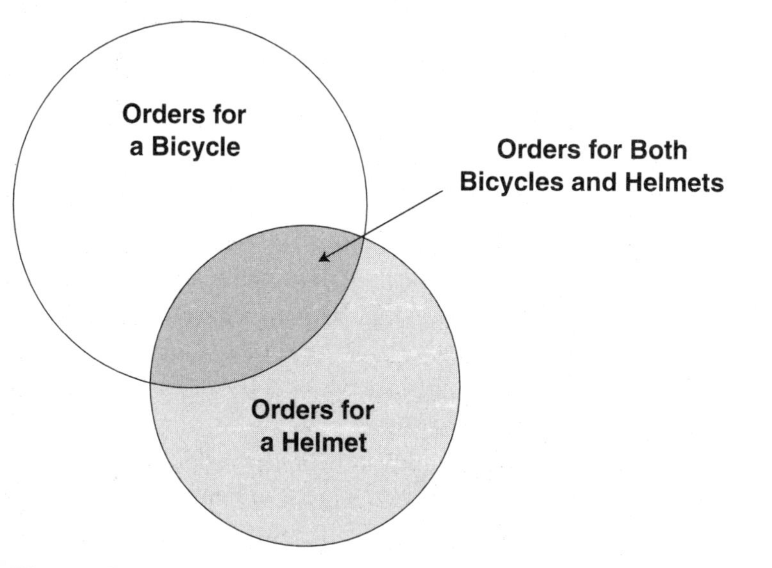

Figure 7-6 *One possible relationship between two sets of orders.*

Actually, there's no way to predict in advance what the relationship between two sets of data might be. In Figure 7-6, some orders have a bicycle in the list of products ordered, but no helmet. Some have a helmet, but no bicycle. The overlapping area, or intersection, of the two sets is where you'll find orders that have both a bicycle and a helmet. Figure 7-7 shows another case where *all* orders that contain a helmet also contain a bicycle, but some orders that contain a bicycle do not contain a helmet.

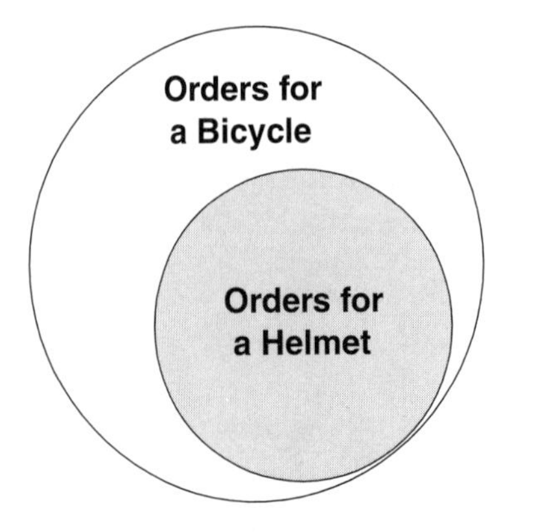

Figure 7-7 *All orders for a helmet also contain an order for a bicycle.*

Seeing "both" in your request suggests you're probably going to have to break the solution into separate sets of data and then link the two sets in some way. (Your request too needs to be broken up into two parts.)

"Show me the orders that contain a bike."

Translation	Select the distinct order numbers from the order details table where the product number is in the list of bike product numbers
Clean Up	Select ~~the~~ distinct order numbers from ~~the~~ order details ~~table~~ where ~~the~~ product number ~~is~~ in ~~the list of~~ bike product numbers
SQL	`SELECT DISTINCT OrderNumber FROM Order_Details WHERE ProductNumber IN (1, 2, 6, 11)`

"Show me the orders that contain a helmet."

Translation	Select the distinct order numbers from the order details table where the product number is in the list of helmet product numbers

Clean Up: Select ~~the~~ distinct order numbers from ~~the~~ order details ~~table~~ where ~~the~~ product number ~~is~~ in ~~the list of~~ helmet product numbers

SQL:

```
SELECT DISTINCT OrderNumber FROM Order_Details
WHERE ProductNumber IN (10, 25, 26)
```

Now you're ready to get the final solution by using—you guessed it—an *intersection* of the two sets. Figure 7-8 shows the SQL syntax diagram that handles this problem. (Note that you can use INTERSECT more than once to combine multiple SELECT Statements.)

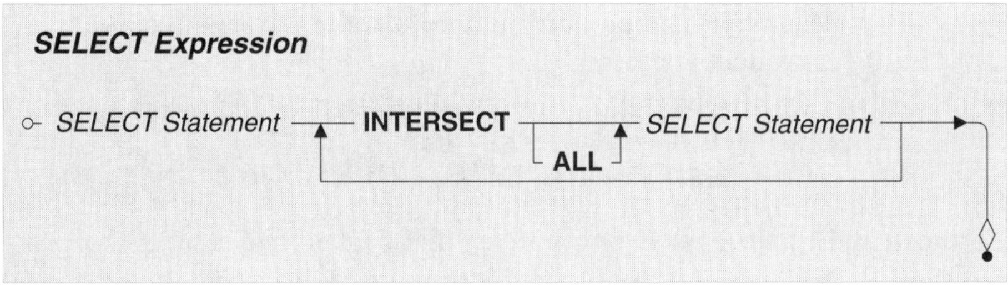

SELECT Expression

SELECT Statement — **INTERSECT** — [**ALL**] — *SELECT Statement*

Figure 7-8 *Linking two SELECT Statements with INTERSECT.*

You can now take the two parts of your request and link them together with an INTERSECT operator to get the correct answer.

SQL:

```
SELECT DISTINCT OrderNumber FROM Order_Details
WHERE ProductNumber IN (1, 2, 6, 11)
INTERSECT
SELECT DISTINCT OrderNumber FROM Order_Details
WHERE ProductNumber IN (10, 25, 26)
```

The sad news is that not many commercial implementations of SQL yet support the INTERSECT operator. But all is not lost! Remember that the Primary Key of a table uniquely identifies each row. (You don't have to match on all the fields in a row—just the Primary Key—to find unique rows that "intersect.") We'll show you an alternative method (JOIN) in Chapter 8 that can solve this type of problem in another way. The good news is most commercial implementations of SQL *do* support JOIN.

Finding Missing Values—EXCEPT (DIFFERENCE)

Okay, let's go back to the bicycles and helmets problem again. Let's say you're trying to solve this seemingly simple request as follows.

"Show me the orders that contain a bike but not a helmet."

Translation — Select the distinct order numbers from the order details table where the product number is in the list of bike product numbers and product number is not in the list of helmet product numbers

Clean Up — Select ~~the~~ distinct order numbers from ~~the~~ order details ~~table~~ where ~~the~~ product number ~~is~~ in ~~the list of~~ bike product numbers and product number ~~is~~ not in ~~the list of~~ helmet product numbers

SQL

```
SELECT DISTINCT OrderNumber FROM Order_Details
WHERE ProductNumber IN (1, 2, 6, 11)
AND ProductNumber NOT IN (10, 25, 26)
```

Unfortunately, the answer shows you orders that contain only a bike! The problem is the first IN clause finds detail rows containing a bicycle, but the second IN clause simply eliminates helmet rows. If you visualize "Orders with Bicycles" and "Orders with Helmets" as two distinct sets, you'll find this easier to understand. Figure 7-9 shows one possible relationship between the two sets of orders.

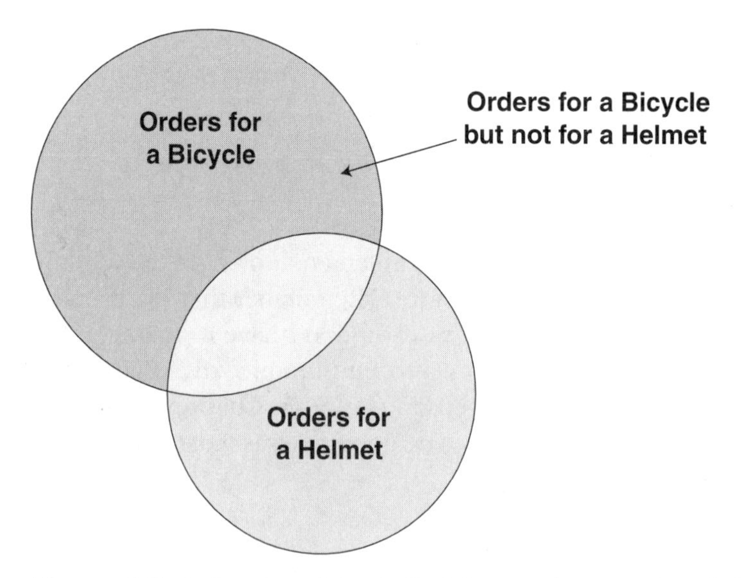

Figure 7-9 *Orders for a bicycle that do not also contain a helmet.*

Seeing "except" or "but not" in your request suggests you're probably going to have to break the solution into separate sets of data and then link the two sets in some way. (Your request too needs to be broken up into two parts.)

"Show me the orders that contain a bike."

Translation: Select the distinct order numbers from the order details table where the product number is in the list of bike product numbers

Clean Up: Select ~~the~~ distinct order numbers from ~~the~~ order details ~~table~~ where ~~the~~ product number ~~is~~ in ~~the list of~~ bike product numbers

SQL:
```
SELECT DISTINCT OrderNumber FROM Order_Details
WHERE ProductNumber IN (1, 2, 6, 11)
```

"Show me the orders that contain a helmet."

Translation: Select the distinct order numbers from the order details table where the product number is in the list of helmet product numbers

Clean Up: Select ~~the~~ distinct order numbers from ~~the~~ order details ~~table~~ where ~~the~~ product number ~~is~~ in ~~the list of~~ helmet product numbers

SQL:
```
SELECT DISTINCT OrderNumber FROM Order_Details
WHERE ProductNumber IN (10, 25, 26)
```

Now you're ready to get the final solution by using—you guessed it—a *difference* of the two sets. SQL uses the EXCEPT keyword to denote a difference operation. Figure 7-10 shows you the SQL syntax diagram that handles this problem.

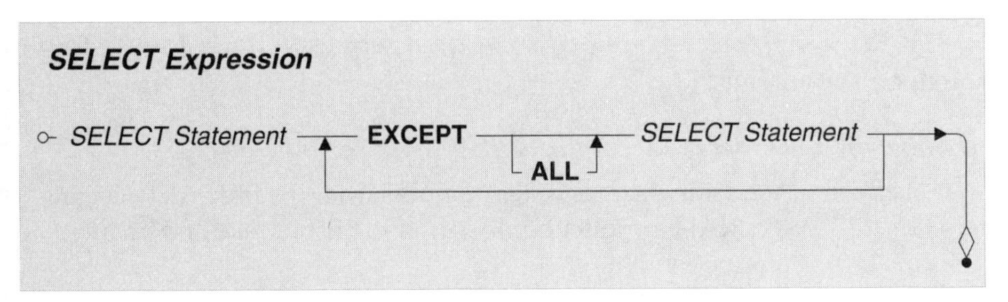

Figure 7-10 *Linking two SELECT Statements with EXCEPT.*

You can now take the two parts of your request and link them together with an EXCEPT operator to get the correct answer.

SQL

```
SELECT DISTINCT OrderNumber FROM Order_Details
WHERE ProductNumber IN (1, 2, 6, 11)
EXCEPT
SELECT DISTINCT OrderNumber FROM Order_Details
WHERE ProductNumber IN (10, 25, 26)
```

Remember from our earlier discussion about the difference operation that the sequence of the sets matters. In this case you're asking for bikes "except" helmets. If you want to find out the opposite case—orders for helmets that do not include bikes—you can turn it around as follows.

SQL

```
SELECT DISTINCT OrderNumber FROM Order_Details
WHERE ProductNumber IN (10, 25, 26)
EXCEPT
SELECT DISTINCT OrderNumber FROM Order_Details
WHERE ProductNumber IN (1, 2, 6, 11)
```

The sad news is that not many commercial implementations of SQL yet support the EXCEPT operator. Hang on to your helmet! Remember that the Primary Key of a table uniquely identifies each row. (You needn't match on all the fields in a row—just the Primary Key—to find unique rows that are "different.") We'll show you an alternative method (OUTER JOIN) in Chapter 9 that can solve this type of problem in another way. The good news is most commercial implementations of SQL *do* support OUTER JOIN.

Combining Sets—UNION

One more bicycles and helmets problem, then we'll pedal on to the next chapter. Let's say you're trying to solve this request, which looks simple enough on the surface.

"Show me the orders that contain either a bike or a helmet."

Translation: Select the distinct order numbers from the order details table where the product number is in the list of bike and helmet product numbers

Clean Up: Select ~~the~~ distinct order numbers from ~~the~~ order details ~~table~~ where ~~the~~ product number ~~is~~ in ~~the list of~~ bike and helmet product numbers

SQL

```
SELECT DISTINCT OrderNumber FROM Order_Details
WHERE ProductNumber IN (1, 2, 6, 10, 11, 25, 26)
```

Actually, that works just fine! So why use a UNION to solve this problem? The truth is, you probably would not. However, if we make the problem a bit more complicated—

> *"List the customers who ordered a bicycle together with the vendors who provide bicycles."*

—a UNION would be useful.

Unfortunately, answering this request involves creating a couple of queries using JOIN operations, then using UNION to get the final result. Because we haven't shown you how to do a JOIN yet, we'll save solving this problem for Chapter 10. Gives you something to look forward to, doesn't it?

Let's get back to the "bicycles or helmets" problem and solve it with a UNION. If you visualize "Orders with Bicycles" and "Orders with Helmets" as two distinct sets, then you'll find it easier to understand the problem. Figure 7-11 shows you one possible relationship between the two sets of orders.

Seeing "either," "or," or "together" in your request suggests that you'll need to break the solution into separate sets of data and then link the two sets with a UNION. This particular request can be broken up into two parts.

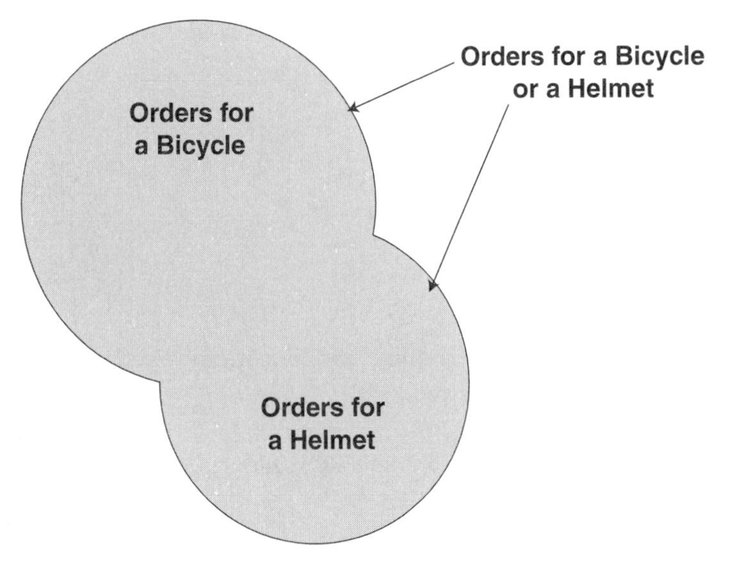

Figure 7-11 *Orders for bicycles or helmets.*

"Show me the orders that contain a bike."

Translation — Select the distinct order numbers from the order details table where the product number is in the list of bike product numbers

Clean Up — Select ~~the~~ distinct order numbers from ~~the~~ order details ~~table~~ where ~~the~~ product number ~~is~~ in ~~the list of~~ bike product numbers

SQL

```
SELECT DISTINCT OrderNumber FROM Order_Details
WHERE ProductNumber IN (1, 2, 6, 11)
```

"Show me the orders that contain a helmet."

Translation — Select the distinct order numbers from the order details table where the product number is in the list of helmet product numbers

Clean Up — Select ~~the~~ distinct order numbers from ~~the~~ order details ~~table~~ where ~~the~~ product number ~~is~~ in ~~the list of~~ helmet product numbers

SQL

```
SELECT DISTINCT OrderNumber FROM Order_Details
WHERE ProductNumber IN (10, 25, 26)
```

Now you're ready to get the final solution by using—you guessed it—a *union* of the two sets. Figure 7-12 shows the SQL syntax diagram that handles this problem.

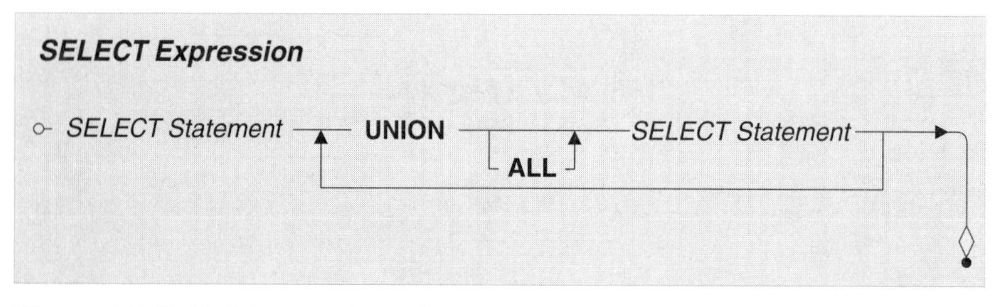

Figure 7-12 *Linking two SELECT Statements with UNION.*

You can now take the two parts of your request and link them together with a UNION operator to get the correct answer.

SQL

```
SELECT DISTINCT OrderNumber FROM Order_Details
WHERE ProductNumber IN (1, 2, 6, 11)
UNION
SELECT DISTINCT OrderNumber FROM Order_Details
WHERE ProductNumber IN (10, 25, 26)
```

The good news is that most commercial implementations of SQL support the UNION operator. As is perhaps obvious from the above examples, a UNION may be doing it the hard way when you want to get an "either-or" result from a single table. UNION is most useful for compiling a list from several similarly structured but different tables. We'll explore UNION in much more detail in Chapter 10.

SUMMARY

We began this chapter by discussing the concept of a set. Next, we discussed each of the major set operations implemented in SQL in detail—intersection, difference, and union. We showed how to use set diagrams to visualize the problem you're trying to solve. Finally, we introduced you to the basic SQL syntax and keywords (INTERSECT, EXCEPT, and UNION) for all three operations just to whet your appetite.

At this point you're probably saying, "Wait a minute, why did you show me three kinds of set operations—two of which I probably can't use?" Remember the title of the chapter: "Thinking in Sets." If you're going to be at all successful solving complex problems, you'll need to break down your problem into Result Sets of information that you then link back together.

So, if your problem involves "it must be this *and* it must be that," you may need to solve the "this" and then the "that" and then link them together to get your final solution. The SQL Standard defines a handy INTERSECT operation—but a JOIN may work just as well. Read on in Chapter 8.

Likewise, if your problem involves "it must be this *but it must not be* that," you may need to solve the "this" and then the "that" and then subtract the "that" from the "this" to get your answer. We showed you the SQL Standard EXCEPT operation, but an OUTER JOIN may also do the trick. Get the details in Chapter 9.

Finally, we showed you how to "add" sets of information using a UNION. As promised, we'll really get into UNION in Chapter 10.

8

INNER JOINs

"Do not quench your inspiration and your imagination, do not become the slave of your model."
—Vincent van Gogh

Topics Covered in This Chapter

What Is a JOIN?

The INNER JOIN

Uses for INNER JOINs

Sample Statements

Summary

Problems for You to Solve

Up to this point, we have primarily focused on solving problems using single tables. You now know how to get simple answers from one table. You also know how to get slightly more complex answers by using expressions or by sorting the Result Set. In other words, you now know how to draw the perfect eyes, chin, mouth, or nose. In this chapter, we'll show you how to link together or "join" multiple parts to form a portrait.

What Is a JOIN?

In Chapter 2, we emphasized the importance of separating the data in your tables into individual subjects. Most problems you need to solve in real life, however, require that you link together data from multiple tables—Customers and their Orders, Customers and the Entertainers they booked, Bowlers and their Scores, Students and the Classes they took, or Recipes and the Ingredients you need. To solve these more complex problems, you must link together, or "join," multiple tables to find your answer. You use the *JOIN* keyword to do so.

The previous chapter showed how useful it is to intersect two sets of data to solve problems. As you recall, however, an INTERSECT involves matching all the columns in both Result Sets to get the answer. A JOIN is also an intersect operation, but it's different because you ask your database system to perform a join only on the columns you specify. Thus, a JOIN lets you intersect two very dissimilar tables on matching column values. For example, you can use a JOIN to link Customers to their Orders by matching the CustomerID in the Customers table to the CustomerID in the Orders table.

As you'll see a bit later, you specify a JOIN as part of the FROM clause in an SQL statement. A JOIN defines a "logical table" that is the result of linking two tables or Result Sets. By placing the JOIN in a FROM clause, you define a linking of tables "from" which the query extracts the final Result Set. In other words, the JOIN replaces the single table name you learned to use in the FROM clause in earlier chapters. As you'll learn a bit later in this chapter, you can also specify multiple JOIN operations to create a complex Result Set on more than two tables.

The INNER JOIN

The SQL Standard defines several ways to perform a JOIN, the most common of which is the *INNER JOIN*. Imagine for a moment that you're linking students and the classes for which they registered. You might have some students who have been accepted to attend the school but who have not yet registered for any classes, and you might also have some classes that are on the schedule but do not yet have any students registered.

An INNER JOIN between the Students table and the Classes table returns Student rows linked with the related Classes rows (via the Student_Schedules table)—but it returns neither students who have not yet registered for any classes nor any classes for which no student is registered. An INNER JOIN returns only those rows where the linking values match in both of the tables or in Result Sets.

What's "Legal" to JOIN?

Most of the time, you specify the Primary Key from one table and the related Foreign Key from the second table as the link that JOIN uses. If you remember from Chapter 2, a Foreign Key must be the same data type as its related Primary Key. However, it's also "legal" to JOIN two tables or Result Sets on any columns that have what the SQL Standard calls "join eligible" data types.

In general, you can join a character column to another character column or expression, any type of number column (for example, an integer) to any other type of number column (perhaps a floating-point value), and any date column to another date column. This allows you, for example, to JOIN rows from the Customers table to rows from the Employees table on City or Zip Code columns (perhaps to find out which Customers and Employees live in the same city or postal region).

> ❖ **Note** Just because you *can* define a JOIN on any join eligible columns in two tables doesn't mean you *should*. The linking columns must have the same data meaning for the JOIN to make sense. For example, it doesn't make sense to JOIN Customer Name with Employee Address even though both columns are Character data type. You won't get any rows in the Result Set unless someone has put a name in the Employee Address column by mistake. Likewise, it doesn't make sense to JOIN Student ID with Class ID even though both are numbers. You may get some rows in the Result Set, but they won't make any sense.
>
> Even when it makes sense to JOIN linking columns, you may end up constructing a request that takes a long time to solve. For example, if you ask for a JOIN on columns for which your database administrator has not defined an index, your database system may have to do a lot of extra work. Also, if you ask for a JOIN on expressions—for example, a concatenation of first name and last name from two tables—your database system must not only form the result column from your expression for all rows but also may have to perform multiple scans of all the data in both tables to return the correct result.

Syntax

Now let's get out our palettes, start mixing up some colors, and examine the INNER JOIN syntax.

Using Tables

We'll start with something simple—an INNER JOIN on two tables. Figure 8-1 on the following page shows the syntax for creating the query.

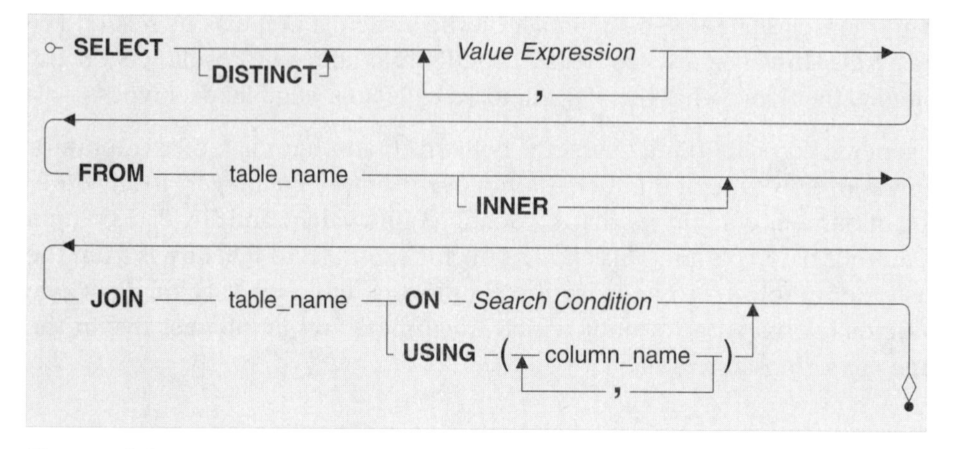

Figure 8-1 *A diagram of a query using an INNER JOIN on two tables.*

As you can see, the FROM clause is now just a bit more complicated. (We left out the WHERE and ORDER BY clauses for now to simplify things.) Instead of a single table name, you specify two table names and link them with the JOIN keyword. Note that the INNER keyword, which is optional, specifies the type of join. As you'll learn in the next chapter, you can also specify an OUTER JOIN. If you don't explicitly state the type of join you want, the default is INNER. We recommend that you always explicitly state the type of join you want so that the nature of your request is clear.

❖ **Note** Those who are following along with the complete syntax diagrams in Appendix A will find `table_name JOIN table_name` described as part of the *Joined Table* defined term. *Table Reference* includes *Joined Table*, and the FROM clause of a SELECT Statement uses *Table Reference*. We "rolled up" these complex definitions into a single diagram to make it easy to study a simple two-table join. We'll be using this same simplification technique in diagrams throughout the remainder of this chapter.

The critical part of an INNER JOIN is the ON or USING clause that follows the second table and tells your database system how to perform the join. To solve the join, your database system logically combines every row in the first table with every row in the second table. (This combination of all rows from one table with all rows from a second table is called a *Cartesian Product*.) It then applies the criteria in the ON or USING clauses to filter out the actual rows to be returned.

You learned about using *Search Condition* to form a WHERE clause in Chapter 6. You can use a Search Condition in the ON clause within a JOIN to specify a logical test that must be true in order to return any two linked rows. Keep in mind that it only makes sense to write a Search Condition that compares at least one column from the first table with at least one column from the second table. Although you can write a very complex Search Condition, you'll typically specify a simple equals comparison test on the Primary Key columns from one table with the Foreign Key columns from the second table.

Let's take a look at a simple example. In a well-designed database, you should break out complex classification names into a second table and then link the names back to the primary subject table via a simple key value. You do this to help prevent data entry errors. Anyone using your database chooses from a list of classification names rather than typing the name (and perhaps misspelling it) in each row. For example, in the Recipes sample database, Recipe_Classes appear in a table separate from Recipes. Figure 8-2 shows you the relationship between Recipe_Classes and Recipes.

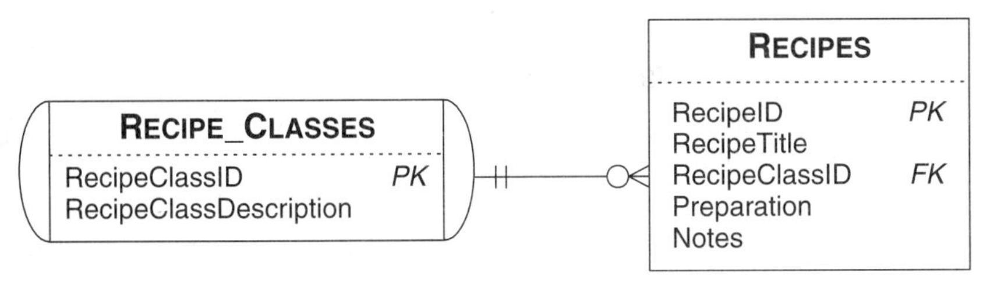

Figure 8-2 *Recipe class descriptions are in a separate table from Recipes.*

When you want to retrieve information about Recipes and the related Recipe Class Description from the database, you don't want to see the Recipe Class ID code numbers from the Recipes table. How to do that with a JOIN is described on the next page.

❖ **Note** Throughout this chapter, we'll be using the "Request/Translation/Clean Up/SQL" technique that we introduced in Chapter 4.

"Show me the recipe title, preparation, and recipe class description of all recipes in my database."

Translation: Select recipe title, preparation, and recipe class description from the recipe classes table joined with the recipes table on recipe class ID in the recipe classes table matching recipe class ID in the recipes table

Clean Up: Select recipe title, preparation, ~~and~~ recipe class description from ~~the~~ recipe classes ~~table~~ join~~ed with the~~ recipes ~~table~~ on recipe class ID ~~in the recipe classes table matching~~ = recipe class ID ~~in the recipes table~~

SQL:

```
SELECT RecipeTitle, Preparation,
   RecipeClassDescription
FROM Recipe_Classes
INNER JOIN Recipes
ON Recipe_Classes.RecipeClassID =
   Recipes.RecipeClassID
```

When beginning to use multiple tables in your FROM clause, you should always fully qualify each column name with the table name wherever you use it to make absolutely clear what column from what table you want. Note that we *had* to qualify the name of RecipeClassID in the ON clause because there are two columns named RecipeClassID—one in the Recipes table and one in the Recipe_Classes table. We didn't have to qualify RecipeTitle, Preparation, or RecipeClassDescription in the SELECT clause because each of these column names appears only once in all the tables. If we want to include RecipeClassID in the output, we must tell the database system *which* RecipeClassID we want—the one from Recipe_Classes or the one from Recipes. To write the query with all the names fully qualified, we should say

SQL:

```
SELECT Recipes.RecipeTitle,
   Recipes.Preparation,
   Recipe_Classes.RecipeClassDescription
FROM Recipe_Classes
INNER JOIN Recipes
ON Recipe_Classes.RecipeClassID =
   Recipes.RecipeClassID
```

❖ **Note** Although most commercial implementations of SQL support the JOIN keyword, some do not. If your database does not support JOIN, you can still solve the previous problem by listing all the tables you need in the FROM clause and then moving your *Search Condition* from the ON clause to the WHERE clause. In databases that do not support JOIN, you solve the above problem like this.

```
SELECT Recipes.RecipeTitle, Recipes.Preparation,
   Recipe_Classes.RecipeClassDescription
FROM Recipe_Classes, Recipes
WHERE Recipe_Classes.RecipeClassID =
   Recipes.RecipeClassID
```

For a beginner, this syntax is probably much more intuitive for simple queries. However, the SQL Standard syntax allows you to fully define the source for the final Result Set entirely within the FROM clause. Think of the FROM clause as fully defining a linked Result Set from which the database system obtains your answer. In the SQL Standard, you use the WHERE clause only to filter rows out of the Result Set defined by the FROM clause.

Not too difficult, is it? But what about the USING clause that we showed you in Figure 8-1 (page 236)? If the matching columns in the two tables have the same name and all you want to do is join on equal values, use the USING clause and list the column names. Let's do the previous problem again with USING.

"Show me the recipe title, preparation, and recipe class description of all recipes in my database."

Translation: Select recipe title, preparation, and recipe class description from the recipe classes table joined with the recipes table using recipe class ID

Clean Up: Select recipe title, preparation, ~~and~~ recipe class description from ~~the~~ recipe classes ~~table~~ join~~ed with the~~ recipes ~~table~~ using recipe class ID

SQL:

```
SELECT Recipes.RecipeTitle, Recipes.Preparation,
   Recipe_Classes.RecipeClassDescription
FROM Recipe_Classes
INNER JOIN Recipes
USING (RecipeClassID)
```

Some database systems do not yet support USING. If you find that you can't use USING with your database, you can always get the same result with an ON clause and an equal comparison.

❖ **Note** The SQL Standard also defines a NATURAL JOIN, which links the two specified tables by matching all the columns with the same name. If the only common columns are the linking columns and your database supports NATURAL JOIN, you can solve the above problem like this.

```
SELECT Recipes.RecipeTitle, Recipes.Preparation,
   Recipe_Classes.RecipeClassDescription
FROM Recipe_Classes
NATURAL INNER JOIN Recipes
```

Do not specify an ON or USING clause when using the NATURAL keyword.

As mentioned earlier in this section, your database system logically creates the combination of every row in the first table with every row in the second table and then applies the ON or USING criteria. This sounds like a lot of extra work for your database to first build all the combinations and then filter out the potentially few matching rows.

Rest assured that all modern relational database systems evaluate the entire JOIN clause before starting to fetch rows. In the example we have been using thus far, many database systems begin to solve this request by first fetching a row from Recipe_Classes. The database then uses an internal link—an index (if one has been defined by the designer of the tables)—to quickly find any matching Recipe rows for the first Recipe_Class before moving on to the next row in Recipe_Classes. In other words, your database uses a "smart" or "optimized" plan to fetch only the rows that match. This won't seem important when your database tables contain only a few hundred rows, but it makes a big difference when your database has to deal with hundreds of thousands of rows!

Assigning Correlation (Alias) Names to Tables

The SQL Standard defines a way to assign an "alias" name—known as a *correlation name* in the Standard—to any table you list in your FROM clause. This feature can be very handy for building complex queries using tables that have long, descriptive names. You can assign a short correlation name to a table to make it easier to explicitly reference columns in a table with a long name.

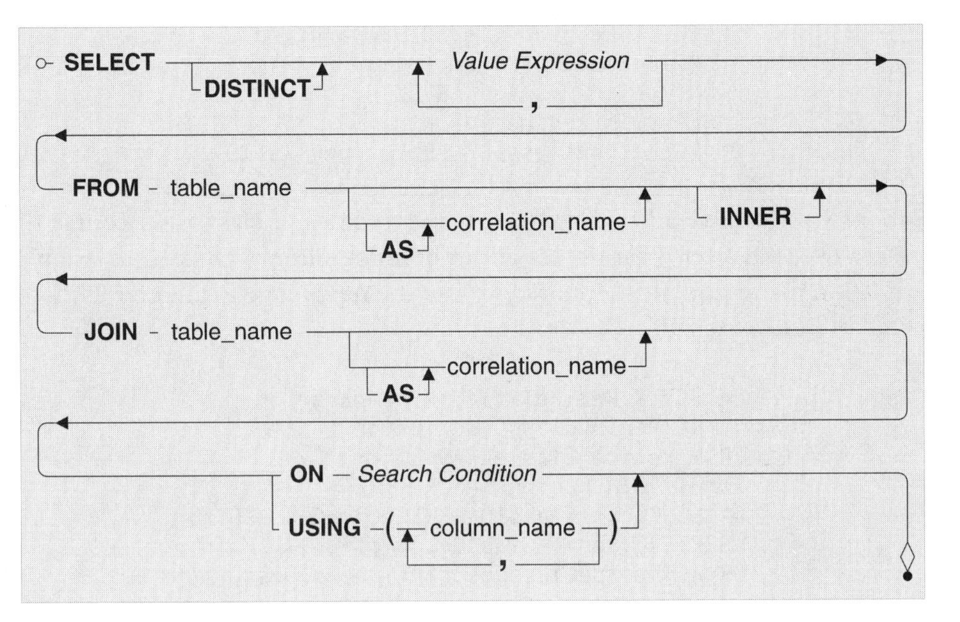

Figure 8-3 *Assigning a correlation (alias) name to a table in a FROM clause.*

Figure 8-3 shows you how to assign a correlation name to a table in a FROM clause.

To assign a correlation name to a table, follow the table name with the optional keyword AS and then the correlation name you wish to assign. (As with all optional keywords, we recommend including AS in order to make the query easier to read and understand.) Once you have assigned a correlation name to a table, you use that name in place of the original table name in all other clauses, including the SELECT clause, Search Conditions in the ON and WHERE clauses, and the ORDER BY clause. This can be a bit confusing because you tend to write the SELECT clause before you write the FROM clause. If you plan to give a table an alias in the FROM clause, you must use that alias when you qualify column names in the SELECT clause.

Let's reformulate the sample query we've been using with correlation names just to see what it looks like. The query using "R" as the correlation name for the Recipes table and "RC" as the correlation name for the Recipe_Classes table is shown on the next page.

```
SQL        SELECT R.RecipeTitle, R.Preparation,
              RC.RecipeClassDescription
           FROM Recipe_Classes AS RC
           INNER JOIN Recipes AS R
           ON RC.RecipeClassID = R.RecipeClassID
```

Suppose you want to add a filter to see only recipes of class Main course or Dessert. (See Chapter 6 for details about defining filters.) Once you assign a correlation name, you must continue to use the new name in all references to the table. Here's the SQL.

```
SQL        SELECT R.RecipeTitle, R.Preparation,
              RC.RecipeClassDescription
           FROM Recipe_Classes AS RC
           INNER JOIN Recipes AS R
           ON RC.RecipeClassID = R.RecipeClassID
           WHERE RC.RecipeClassDescription = 'Main course'
           OR RC.RecipeClassDescription = 'Dessert'
```

You don't have to assign a correlation name to all tables. In the previous example, we could have assigned a correlation name to only Recipes or Recipe_Classes, but not both.

In some cases, you *must* assign a correlation name to a table in a complex join. Let's hop over to the Bowling League database for a second to examine a case where this is true. Figure 8-4 shows you the relationship between the Teams and Bowlers tables.

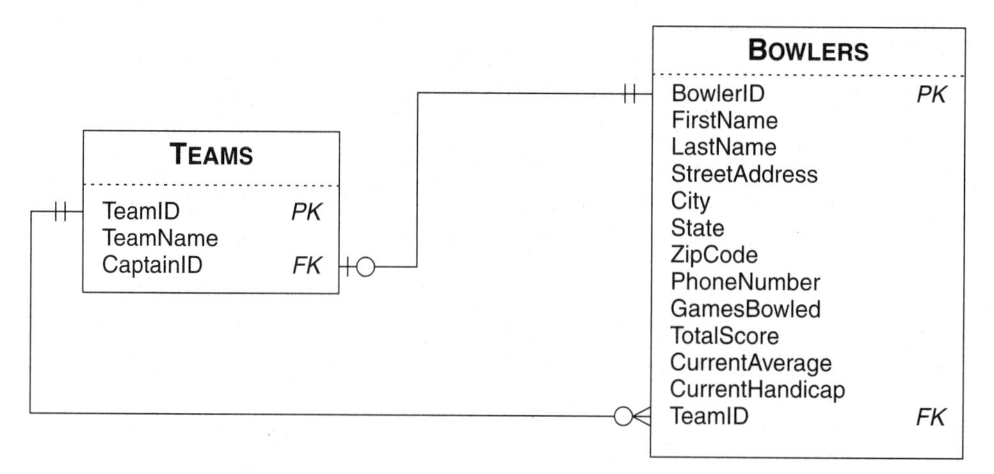

Figure 8-4 *The relationships between Teams and Bowlers.*

As you can see, TeamID is a Foreign Key in the Bowlers table that lets you find out the information for all bowlers on a team. One of the bowlers on a team is the team captain, so there's also a link from BowlerID in the Bowlers table to CaptainID in the Teams table.

If you want to list the team name, the name of the team captain, and the names of all the bowlers in one request, you must include *two* copies of the Bowlers table in your query—one to link to CaptainID to retrieve the name of the team captain and another to link on TeamID to get a list of all of the team members. In this case, you *must* assign an alias name to one or both copies of the Bowlers table so that your database system can differentiate between the copy that links in the captain's name and the copy that provides the list of all team members. Later in this chapter, we'll show an example that requires including multiple copies of one table and assigning alias names. You can find this example in the More Than Two Tables—Bowling League Database subsection of Sample Statements.

Embedding a SELECT Statement

Let's make it a bit more interesting. Instead of dabbing a bit of blue, then dabbing a bit of yellow on our painting to get green, let's mix up the shade of green we want on our paint palette first.

In most implementations of SQL, you can substitute an entire SELECT Statement for any table name in your FROM clause. Of course, you must assign a correlation name so that the result of evaluating your embedded query has a name. Figure 8-5 on the next page shows how to assemble a JOIN clause using embedded SELECT Statements.

Notice in the figure that a SELECT Statement can include all query clauses *except* an ORDER BY clause. Also, you can mix and match SELECT Statements with table names on either side of the INNER JOIN keywords.

Let's take a look at Recipes and Recipe Classes again. We'll assume that your request still needs only Main courses and Desserts. Here's the query again with the Recipe_Classes table filtered in a SELECT Statement that's part of the INNER JOIN.

```
SQL       SELECT R.RecipeTitle, R.Preparation,
             RCFiltered.ClassName
          FROM (SELECT RecipeClassID,
             RecipeClassDescription AS ClassName
          FROM Recipe_Classes AS RC
          WHERE RC.ClassName = 'Main course' OR
             RC.ClassName = 'Dessert') AS RCFiltered
          INNER JOIN Recipes AS R
          ON RCFiltered.RecipeClassID = R.RecipeClassID
```

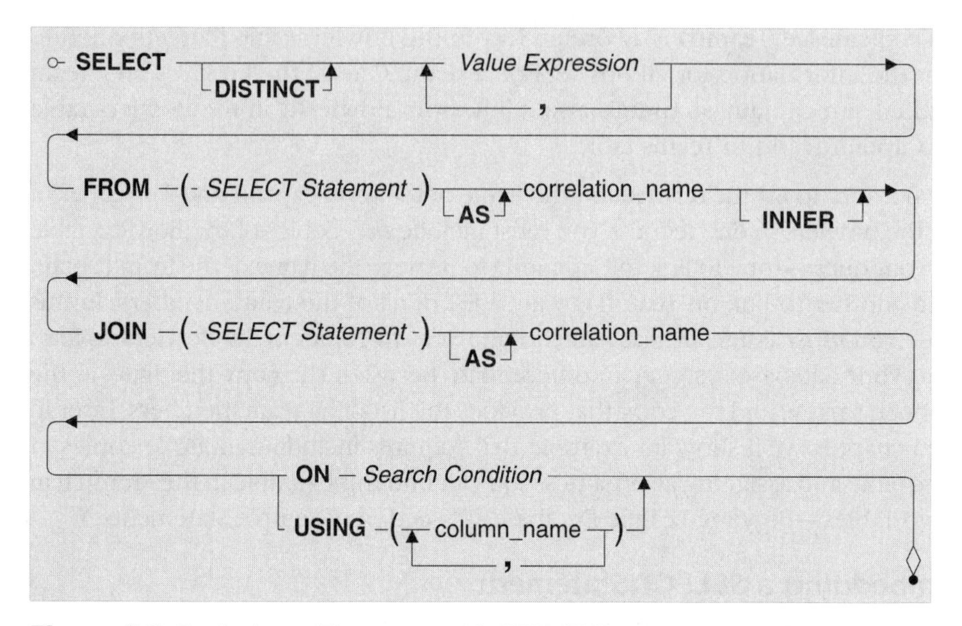

Figure 8-5 *Replacing table names with SELECT Statements in a JOIN.*

Watch out! There're a couple of "paint splatters" thrown in. First, when you decide to substitute a SELECT Statement for a table name, be sure to include not only the columns you want to appear in the final result but also any linking columns needed to perform the JOIN. That's why you see both RecipeClassID and RecipeClassDescription in the embedded statement. Just for fun, we gave RecipeClassDescription an alias name of "ClassName" in the embedded statement. As a result, the SELECT clause asks for ClassName rather than RecipeClassDescription. Note that the ON clause now references the correlation name of the embedded SELECT Statement—RCFiltered—rather than the original name of the table or the correlation name we assigned the table inside the embedded SELECT Statement.

If your database system has a very smart optimizer, defining your request this way should be just as fast as the previous example where the filter on Class Description was applied via a WHERE clause *after* the JOIN. You would like to think that your database system, in order to answer your request most efficiently, would first filter the rows from Recipe_Classes before attempting to find any matching rows in Recipes. It could be much slower to first join all rows from Recipe_Classes with matching rows from Recipes and *then* apply the filter. If you find it's taking longer to solve this request than it should, moving the WHERE clause into a SELECT Statement within the JOIN may force your database system to do the filtering on Recipe_Classes first.

Embedding JOINs within JOINs

Although you can solve many problems by linking just two tables, you'll often need to link three, four, or more tables to get all the data you require. For example, you might want to fetch all the relevant information about Recipes—the type of recipe, the recipe name, and all the ingredients for the recipe—in one query. Figure 8-6 shows the tables required to answer this request.

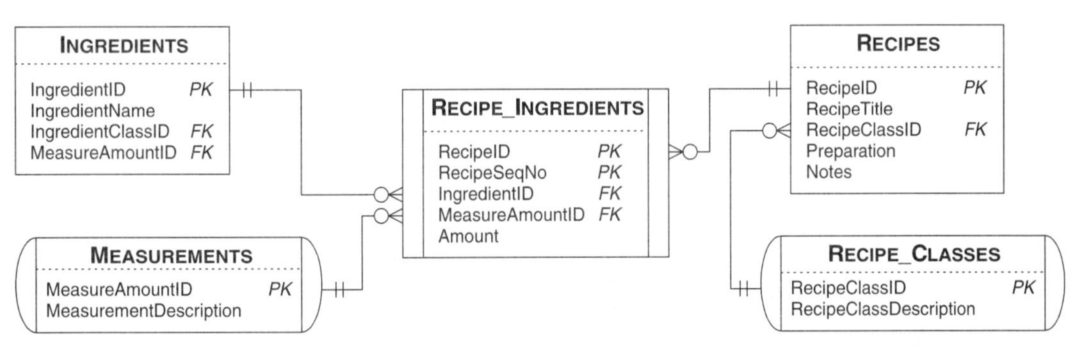

Figure 8-6 *The tables needed from the Recipes sample database to fetch all the information about recipes.*

Looks like you need to get data from *five* different tables! Never fear—you can do this by constructing a more complex FROM clause, embedding JOIN clauses within JOIN clauses. Here's the trick: Everywhere you can specify a table name, you can also specify an entire JOIN clause surrounded with parentheses. Figure 8-7 is a simplified version of Figure 8-3. (We've left off correlation name clauses and chosen the ON clause to form a simple join of two tables.)

To add a third table to the mix, just place an open parenthesis before the first table name, add a close parenthesis after the Search Condition, and insert INNER JOIN, a table name, the ON keyword, and another Search Condition. Figure 8-8 shows how to do this.

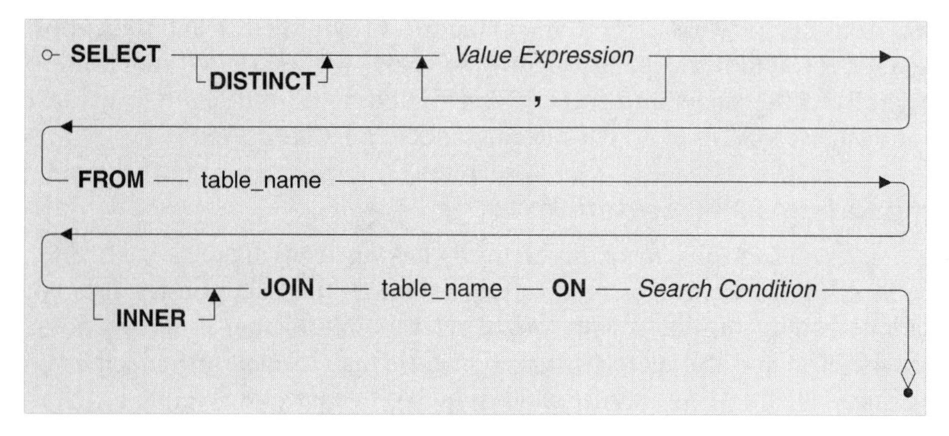

Figure 8-7 *A simple INNER JOIN of two tables.*

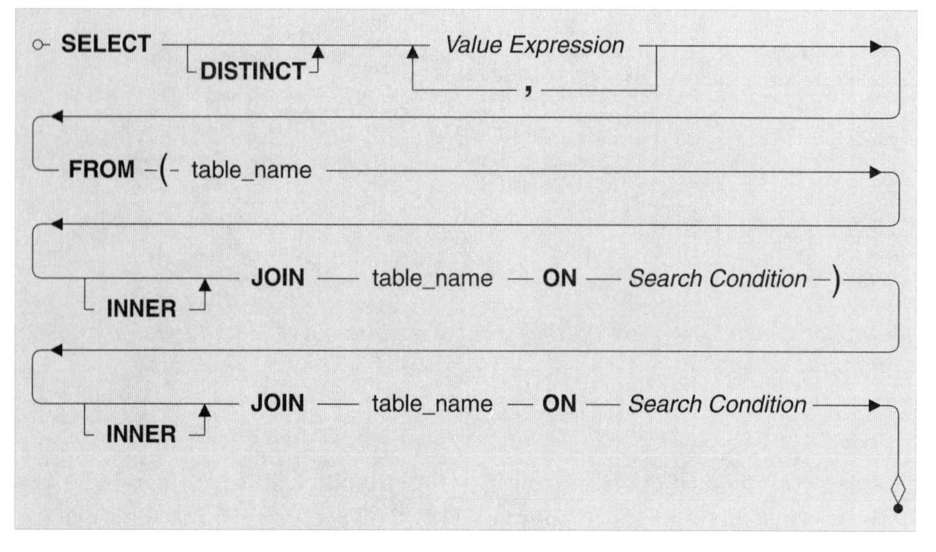

Figure 8-8 *A simple INNER JOIN of three tables.*

If you think about it, the INNER JOIN of two tables inside the parentheses forms a "logical" table, or inner Result Set. This Result Set now takes the place of the first simple table name in Figure 8-7. You can continue this process of enclosing an entire JOIN clause in parentheses and then adding another JOIN keyword, table name, ON keyword, and Search Condition until you have all the Result Sets you need. Let's make a request that needs data from all the tables you see in Figure 8-6 and see how it turns out.

"I need the recipe type, recipe name, preparation instructions, ingredient names, ingredient step number, ingredient quantities, and ingredient measurements from my Recipes database, sorted in step number sequence."

Translation Select the recipe class description, recipe title, preparation instructions, ingredient name, recipe sequence number, amount, and measurement description from the recipe classes table joined with the recipes table on recipe class ID, then joined with the recipe ingredients table on recipe ID, then joined with the ingredients table on ingredient ID, and then finally joined with the measurements table on measurement amount ID, order by recipe title and recipe sequence number

Clean up Select ~~the~~ recipe class description, recipe title, preparation ~~instructions~~, ingredient name, recipe sequence number, amount, ~~and~~ measurement description from ~~the~~ recipe classes ~~table~~ join~~ed with the~~ recipes ~~table~~ on recipe class ID~~, then~~ join~~ed with the~~ recipe ingredients ~~table~~ on recipe ID~~, then~~ join~~ed with the~~ ingredients ~~table~~ on ingredient ID~~, and then~~ ~~finally~~ join~~ed with the~~ measurements ~~table~~ on measurement amount ID~~,~~ order by recipe title ~~and~~ recipe sequence number

SQL

```
SELECT Recipe_Classes.RecipeClassDescription,
   Recipes.RecipeTitle, Recipes.Preparation,
   Ingredients.IngredientName,
   Recipe_Ingredients.RecipeSeqNo,
   Recipe_Ingredients.Amount,
   Measurements.MeasurementDescription
FROM (((Recipe_Classes
INNER JOIN Recipes
ON Recipe_Classes.RecipeClassID =
   Recipes.RecipeClassID)
INNER JOIN Recipe_Ingredients
ON Recipes.RecipeID =
   Recipe_Ingredients.RecipeID)
INNER JOIN Ingredients
ON Ingredients.IngredientID =
   Recipe_Ingredients.IngredientID)
INNER JOIN Measurements
ON Measurements.MeasureAmountID =
   Recipe_Ingredients.MeasureAmountID
ORDER BY RecipeTitle, RecipeSeqNo
```

Wow! Anyone care to jump in and add a filter for recipe class Main courses? If you said you need to add the WHERE clause just before the ORDER BY clause, you guessed the easiest way to do it.

In truth, you can substitute an entire JOIN of two tables anywhere you could otherwise place just a table name. In Figure 8-8, we implied that you must first join the first table with the second table and then join that result with the third table. You could also join the second and third tables first (as long as the third table is, in fact, related to the second table and not the first one) and then perform the final join with the first table. Figure 8-9 shows this alternate method.

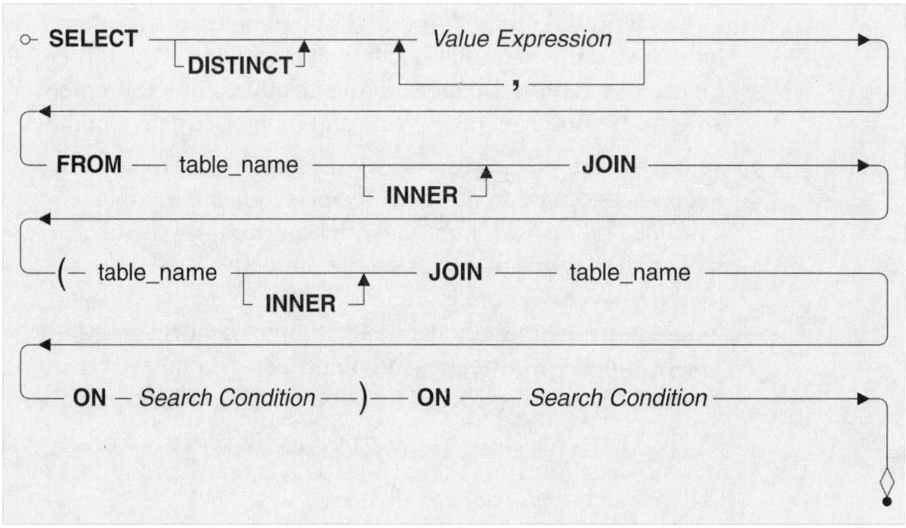

SELECT DISTINCT Value Expression ,
FROM table_name INNER JOIN
(table_name INNER JOIN table_name
ON Search Condition) ON Search Condition

Figure 8-9 *Joining more than two tables in an alternate sequence.*

Let's look at the problem from a painting perspective. If you're trying to get pastel green, the mixing sequence doesn't matter that much. You can mix white with blue to get pastel blue, and then mix in a bit of yellow; or you can mix blue with yellow to get green, and then add a bit of white to get the final color.

To solve the request we just showed you using five tables, we could also have stated the SQL as follows.

```
SQL         SELECT Recipe_Classes.RecipeClassDescription,
               Recipes.RecipeTitle, Recipes.Preparation,
               Ingredients.IngredientName,
               Recipe_Ingredients.RecipeSeqNo,
               Recipe_Ingredients.Amount,
               Measurements.MeasurementDescription
            FROM Recipe_Classes
            INNER JOIN (((Recipes
```

```
INNER JOIN Recipe_Ingredients
ON Recipes.RecipeID =
   Recipe_Ingredients.RecipeID)
INNER JOIN Ingredients
ON Ingredients.IngredientID =
   Recipe_Ingredients.IngredientID)
INNER JOIN Measurements
ON Measurements.MeasureAmountID =
   Recipe_Ingredients.MeasureAmountID)
ON Recipe_Classes.RecipeClassID =
   Recipes.RecipeClassID
ORDER BY RecipeTitle, RecipeSeqNo
```

You need to be aware of this feature because you may run into this sort of construction either in queries others have written or in the SQL built for you by query-by-example software. Also, the optimizers in some database systems are sensitive to the sequence of the JOIN definitions. If you find your query using many joins is taking a long time to execute on a large database, you may be able to get it to run faster by changing the sequence of JOINs in your SQL statement. For simplicity, we'll build most of the examples later in this chapter using a direct left-to-right construction of joins.

Check Those Relationships!

It should be obvious at this point that knowing the relationships between your tables is of utmost importance. When you find that the columns of data you need reside in different tables, you may need to construct a FROM clause as complicated as the one we just showed you to be able to gather together all the pieces in a way that logically makes sense. If you don't know the relationships between your tables and the linking columns that form the relationships, you'll paint yourself into a corner!

In many cases, you may have to follow a "path" through several relationships to get the data you want. For example, let's simplify the previous request and just ask for recipe name and ingredient names.

"Show me the names of all my recipes and the names of all the ingredients for each of those recipes."

Translation Select the recipe title and the ingredient name from the recipes table joined with the recipe ingredients table on recipe ID, and then joined with the ingredients table on ingredient ID

Clean Up — Select ~~the~~ recipe title ~~and the~~ ingredient name from ~~the~~ recipes ~~table~~ join~~ed with the~~ recipe ingredients ~~table~~ on recipe ID, ~~and then~~ join~~ed with the~~ ingredients table on ingredient ID

SQL

```
SELECT Recipes.RecipeTitle,
   Ingredients.IngredientName
FROM (Recipes
INNER JOIN Recipe_Ingredients
ON Recipes.RecipeID =
   Recipe_Ingredients.RecipeID)
INNER JOIN Ingredients
ON Ingredients.IngredientID =
   Recipe_Ingredients.IngredientID
```

Did you notice that even though you don't need *any* columns from the Recipe_Ingredients table you still must include it in the query? You must do so because the only way that Recipes and Ingredients are related is *through* the Recipe_Ingredients table.

Uses for INNER JOINs

Now that you have a basic understanding of the mechanics for constructing an INNER JOIN, let's look at some of the types of problems you can solve with it.

Find Related Rows

As you know, the most common use for an INNER JOIN is to link together tables so that you can fetch columns from different tables that are related. Following is a sample list of the kinds of requests you can solve from the sample databases using an INNER JOIN.

Sales Order Database

"Show me the vendors and the products they supply to us."

"List employees and the customers for whom they booked an order."

Entertainment Agency Database

"Display agents and the engagement dates they booked."

"List customers and the entertainers they booked."

"Find the entertainers who played engagements for customers Bonnicksen or Rosales."

School Scheduling Database

"Display buildings and all the classrooms in each building."

"List the faculty staff and the subject each teaches."

Bowling League Database

"Display bowling teams and the name of each team captain."

"List the bowling teams and all the team members."

Recipes Database

"Show me the recipes that have beef or garlic."

"Display all the ingredients for recipes that contain carrots."

We'll show how to construct queries to answer these requests (and more) in the Sample Statements section of this chapter.

Find Matching Values

A bit more esoteric use of an INNER JOIN is finding rows in two or more tables or Result Sets that match on one or more values that are *not* the related key values. Remember that in Chapter 7 we promised to show you how to perform the equivalent of an INTERSECT using an INNER JOIN. Following is a small sample of just some of the requests you can solve using this technique.

Sales Order Database

"Show me customers and employees that have the same name."

"Show me customers and employees that live in the same city."

"Find all the customers who ordered a bicycle who also ordered a helmet."

Entertainment Agency Database

"Find the agents and entertainers that live in the same postal code."

"List the entertainers who played engagements for customers Bonnicksen and *Rosales."*

School Scheduling Database

"Show me the students and their teachers who have the same first name."

"Show me the students who have an average score of 85 or better in Art and who also have an average score of 85 or better in Computer Science."

Bowling League Database

"Find the bowlers who have the same average."

"Find the bowlers who had a raw score of 155 or better at both Thunderbird Lanes and Bolero Lanes."

Recipes Database

"Find the ingredients that use the same default measurement amount."

"Show me the recipes that have beef and *garlic."*

The next section shows how to solve several of the previous problems.

Sample Statements

You now know the mechanics of constructing queries using INNER JOIN and have seen some of the types of requests you can answer with an INNER JOIN. Let's take a look at a fairly robust set of samples, all of which use INNER JOIN. These examples come from each of the sample databases, and they illustrate the use of the INNER JOIN on two tables, more than two tables, and joins on matching values.

> ❖ **Note** Because many of these examples use complex joins, your database system may choose a different way to solve these queries. For this reason, the first few rows we show you may not exactly match the result you obtain, but the total number of rows should be the same.
>
> To simplify the process, we have combined the Translation and Clean Up steps for all the following examples.

Two Tables

We'll start out with simple primary colors and show you sample requests that require an INNER JOIN on only two tables.

Sales Order Database

"Display all products and their categories."

Translation/ Clean Up: Select category description ~~and~~ product name from ~~the~~ categories ~~table~~ join~~ed with the~~ products ~~table~~ on category ID

SQL:

```
SELECT Categories.CategoryDescription,
   Products.ProductName
FROM Categories
INNER JOIN Products
ON Categories.CategoryID = Products.CategoryID
```

Products_And_Categories (40 rows)

CategoryDescription	ProductName
Accessories	Dog Ear Cyclecomputer
Accessories	Dog Ear Helmet Mount Mirrors
Accessories	Viscount C-500 Wireless Bike Computer
Accessories	Kryptonite Advanced 2000 U-Lock
Accessories	Nikoma Lok-Tight U-Lock
Accessories	Viscount Microshell Helmet
Accessories	Viscount CardioSport Sport Watch
Accessories	Viscount Tru-Beat Heart Transmitter
Accessories	Dog Ear Monster Grip Gloves
<<more rows here >>	

Entertainment Agency Database

"Show me entertainers, start and end dates of their contracts, and the contract price."

Translation/ Clean Up: Select entertainer stage name, start date, end date, ~~and~~ contract price from ~~the~~ entertainers ~~table~~ join~~ed with the~~ engagements ~~table~~ on entertainer ID

SQL

```
SELECT Entertainers.EntStageName,
   Engagements.StartDate, Engagements.EndDate,
   Engagements.ContractPrice
FROM Entertainers
INNER JOIN Engagements
ON Entertainers.EntertainerID =
   Engagements.EntertainerID
```

Entertainers_And_Contracts (131 rows)

EntStageName	StartDate	EndDate	ContractPrice
Carol Peacock Trio	1999-07-18	1999-07-26	$1,670.00
Carol Peacock Trio	1999-07-31	1999-08-06	$1,940.00
Carol Peacock Trio	1999-08-13	1999-08-14	$410.00
Carol Peacock Trio	1999-08-20	1999-08-20	$140.00
Carol Peacock Trio	1999-09-12	1999-09-18	$680.00
Carol Peacock Trio	1999-10-22	1999-10-25	$410.00
Carol Peacock Trio	1999-10-28	1999-11-06	$1,400.00
Carol Peacock Trio	1999-11-07	1999-11-07	$320.00
<<more rows here >>			

School Scheduling Database

"List the subjects taught on Wednesday."

Translation/ Clean Up: Select subject name from ~~the~~ subjects ~~table~~ join~~ed with the~~ classes ~~table~~ on subject ID where Wednesday schedule ~~is~~ = true

SQL:

```
SELECT DISTINCT Subjects.SubjectName
FROM Subjects
INNER JOIN Classes
ON Subjects.SubjectID = Classes.SubjectID
WHERE Classes.WednesdaySchedule = -1
```

❖ **Note** Because several sections of the same class may be scheduled on the same day of the week, we included the DISTINCT keyword to eliminate the duplicates. Some databases do support a "true" keyword, but we chose to use a more universal "integer with all bits on" value: -1. If your database system stores a true/false value as a single bit, you can also test for a "true" value of 1. A false value is always the number zero (0).

Subjects_On_Wednesday (45 rows)

SubjectName
Advanced English Grammar
Art History
Biological Principles
Business Tax Accounting
Chemistry
Composition—Fundamentals
Composition—Intermediate
Computer Art
Database Management
<<more rows here >>

Bowling League Database

"Display bowling teams and the name of each team captain."

Translation/ Clean Up: Select team name ~~and~~ captain full name from ~~the~~ teams ~~table~~ join~~ed with the~~ bowlers ~~table~~ on team captain ID ~~equals~~ = bowler ID

SQL:

```
SELECT Teams.TeamName, (Bowlers.BowlerLastName
   || ', ' || Bowlers.BowlerFirstName) AS CaptainName
FROM Teams
INNER JOIN Bowlers
ON Teams.CaptainID = Bowlers.BowlerID
```

Teams_And_Captains (8 rows)

TeamName	CaptainName
Marlins	Fournier, David
Sharks	Patterson, Ann
Terrapins	Morgenstern, Iris
Barracudas	Sheskey, Richard
Dolphins	Viescas, Suzanne
Orcas	Thompson, Sarah
Manatees	Viescas, Michael
Swordfish	Rosales, Joe

Recipes Database

"Show me the recipes that have beef or garlic."

Translation/ Clean Up: Select ~~unique~~ distinct recipe title from ~~the~~ recipes ~~table~~ join~~ed with the~~ recipe ingredients ~~table~~ on recipe ID where ingredient ID ~~is~~ in ~~the list of beef and garlic IDs~~ (1, 9)

SQL:

```
SELECT DISTINCT Recipes.RecipeTitle
FROM Recipes
INNER JOIN Recipe_Ingredients
ON Recipes.RecipeID = Recipe_Ingredients.RecipeID
WHERE Recipe_Ingredients.IngredientID IN (1, 9)
```

❖ **Note** Because some recipes might have both beef and garlic, we added the DISTINCT keyword to eliminate potential duplicate rows.

Beef_Or_Garlic_Recipes (5 rows)

RecipeTitle
Asparagus
Garlic Green Beans
Irish Stew
Pollo Picoso
Roast Beef

More Than Two Tables

Next, let's add some color to the palette by making requests that require a JOIN of more than two tables.

Sales Order Database

"Find all the customers who ever ordered a bicycle helmet."

Translation/ Clean Up: Select customer first name, customer last name from ~~the~~ customers ~~table~~ join~~ed with the~~ orders~~ table~~ on customer ID, ~~then~~ join~~ed with the~~ order details ~~table~~ on order number, ~~then~~ join~~ed with the~~ products~~ table~~ on product number where product name ~~contains~~ LIKE '%Helmet%'

SQL:

```
SELECT DISTINCT Customers.CustFirstName,
   Customers.CustLastName
FROM ((Customers
INNER JOIN Orders
ON Customers.CustomerID = Orders.CustomerID)
INNER JOIN Order_Details
ON Orders.OrderNumber =
   Order_Details.OrderNumber)
INNER JOIN Products
ON Products.ProductNumber =
   Order_Details.ProductNumber
WHERE Products.ProductName LIKE '%Helmet%'
```

> ❖ **Caution** If your database system is case-sensitive when performing searches in character fields, you must be careful that you enter the search criteria using the correct case for the letters. For example, in many database systems, 'helmet' is not the same as 'Helmet'.

> ❖ **Note** Because a customer may have ordered a helmet more than once, we included the DISTINCT keyword to eliminate duplicate rows.

Customers_Who_Ordered_Helmets (24 rows)

CustFirstName	CustLastName
Alaina	Hallmark
Allan	Davis
Amelia	Buchanan
Consuelo	Maynez
David	Callahan
David	Smith
Estella	Pundt
Gary	Hallmark
Gregory	Piercy
John	Viescas
<<more rows here >>	

Entertainment Agency Database

"Find the entertainers who played engagements for customers Bonnicksen or Rosales."

Translation/Clean Up: Select ~~unique~~ distinct entertainer stage name from ~~the~~ entertainers ~~table~~ join~~ed with the~~ engagements ~~table~~ on entertainer ID~~, then~~ join~~ed with the~~ customers ~~table~~ on customer ID where ~~the~~ customer last name ~~is~~ = 'Bonnicksen' or ~~the~~ customer last name ~~is~~ = 'Rosales'

SQL

```
SELECT DISTINCT Entertainers.EntStageName
FROM (Entertainers
INNER JOIN Engagements
ON Entertainers.EntertainerID =
   Engagements.EntertainerID)
INNER JOIN Customers
ON Customers.CustomerID =
   Engagements.CustomerID
WHERE Customers.CustLastName = 'Bonnicksen'
OR Customers.CustLastName = 'Rosales'
```

Entertainers_For_Bonnicksen_OR_Rosales (9 rows)

EntStageName
Carol Peacock Trio
Country Feeling
Julia Schnebly
JV & the Deep Six
Katherine Ehrlich
Modern Dance
Saturday Revue
Susan McLain
Topazz

Bowling League Database

"List all the tournaments, the tournament matches, and the game results."

Translation/ Clean Up: Select tourney ID, tourney location, match ID, lanes, odd lane team, even lane team, game number, game winner from ~~the~~ tournaments ~~table~~ join~~ed with the~~ tourney matches ~~table~~ on tourney ID~~, then~~ join~~ed with the~~ teams ~~table aliased~~ as odd lane team on odd lane team ID ~~equals~~ = team ID~~, then~~ join~~ed with the~~ teams ~~table aliased~~ as even lane team on even lane team ID ~~equals~~ = team ID~~, then~~ join~~ed with the~~ match games ~~table~~ on match ID~~, then~~ join~~ed with the~~ teams ~~table aliased~~ as winner on winning team ID ~~equals~~ = team ID

```
SQL        SELECT Tournaments.TourneyID AS Tourney,
              Tournaments.TourneyLocation AS Location,
              Tourney_Matches.MatchID,
              Tourney_Matches.Lanes,
              OddTeam.TeamName AS OddLaneTeam,
              EvenTeam.TeamName AS EvenLaneTeam,
              Match_Games.GameNumber AS GameNo,
              Winner.TeamName AS Winner
           FROM Teams AS Winner
           INNER JOIN (Teams AS EvenTeam
           INNER JOIN (Teams AS OddTeam
           INNER JOIN ((Tournaments
           INNER JOIN Tourney_Matches
           ON Tournaments.TourneyID =
              Tourney_Matches.TourneyID)
           INNER JOIN Match_Games
           ON Tourney_Matches.MatchID =
              Match_Games.MatchID)
           ON OddTeam.TeamID =
              Tourney_Matches.OddLaneTeamID)
           ON EvenTeam.TeamID =
              Tourney_Matches.EvenLaneTeamID)
           ON Winner.TeamID = Match_Games.WinningTeamID
```

❖ **Note** This is a really fun query because it requires *three* copies of one table (Teams) to get the job done. We had to assign correlation names to at least two of the tables to keep everything legal, but we went ahead and gave them all "alias" names to reflect their specific roles in the query. Also, when we constructed the SQL, we didn't exactly follow the structure of the Translation/Clean Up step. We did this to demonstrate that you can define the nested JOINs in any way you like as long as you keep the relationships straight.

Tournament_Match_Game_Results (168 rows)

Tourney	Location	MatchID	Lanes	OddLane Team	EvenLane Team	GameNo	Winner
1	Red Rooster Lanes	1	01-02	Marlins	Sharks	1	Marlins
1	Red Rooster Lanes	1	01-02	Marlins	Sharks	2	Sharks
1	Red Rooster Lanes	1	01-02	Marlins	Sharks	3	Marlins
1	Red Rooster Lanes	2	03-04	Terrapins	Barracudas	1	Terrapins
1	Red Rooster Lanes	2	03-04	Terrapins	Barracudas	2	Barracudas
1	Red Rooster Lanes	2	03-04	Terrapins	Barracudas	3	Terrapins
1	Red Rooster Lanes	3	05-06	Dolphins	Orcas	1	Dolphins
1	Red Rooster Lanes	3	05-06	Dolphins	Orcas	2	Orcas
1	Red Rooster Lanes	3	05-06	Dolphins	Orcas	3	Dolphins
<<more rows here >>							

Recipes Database

"Show me the main course recipes and list all the ingredients."

Translation/ Clean Up

Select recipe title, ingredient name, measurement description, ~~and~~ amount from ~~the~~ recipe classes ~~table~~ join~~ed with the~~ recipes ~~table~~ on recipe class ID~~, then~~ join~~ed with the~~ recipe ingredients ~~table~~ on recipe ID~~, then~~ join~~ed with the~~ ingredients ~~table~~ on ingredient ID~~, and finally~~ join~~ed with the~~ measurements ~~table~~ on measure amount ID~~,~~ where recipe class description ~~is~~ = 'main course'

SQL

```
SELECT Recipes.RecipeTitle,
   Ingredients.IngredientName,
   Measurements.MeasurementDescription,
   Recipe_Ingredients.Amount
FROM (((Recipe_Classes
INNER JOIN Recipes
ON Recipes.RecipeClassID =
   Recipe_Classes.RecipeClassID)
INNER JOIN Recipe_Ingredients
ON Recipes.RecipeID =
   Recipe_Ingredients.RecipeID)
INNER JOIN Ingredients
ON Ingredients.IngredientID =
   Recipe_Ingredients.IngredientID)
INNER JOIN Measurements
ON Measurements.MeasureAmountID =
   Recipe_Ingredients.MeasureAmountID
WHERE Recipe_Classes.RecipeClassDescription =
   'Main Course'
```

❖ **Caution** You can find a MeasureAmountID in both the Ingredients and the Recipe_Ingredients tables. If you define the final join on MeasureAmountID using the Ingredients table instead of the Recipe_Ingredients table, you'll get the "default" measurement for the ingredient rather than the one specified for the ingredient in the recipe.

Main_Course_Ingredients (53 rows)

RecipeTitle	IngredientName	MeasurementDescription	Amount
Irish Stew	Beef	Pound	1
Irish Stew	Onion	Whole	2
Irish Stew	Potato	Whole	4
Irish Stew	Carrot	Whole	6
Irish Stew	Water	Quarts	4
Irish Stew	Guinness Beer	Ounce	12
Fettuccini Alfredo	Fettuccini Pasta	Ounce	16
Fettuccini Alfredo	Vegetable Oil	Tablespoon	1
Fettuccini Alfredo	Salt	Teaspoon	3
<<more rows here >>			

Looking for Matching Values

Finally, let's add a third dimension to the picture. This last set of examples shows requests that utilize a join on common values from two or more Result Sets or tables. (If your database supports the INTERSECT keyword, you can also solve many of these problems by intersecting the Result Sets.)

Sales Order Database

"Find all the customers who ordered a bicycle and *who also ordered a helmet."*

The above request seems simple enough—perhaps too simple. Let's ask it a different way so it's clearer what we need the database to do.

"Find all the customers who ordered a bicycle, then find all the customers who ordered a helmet, and finally list the common customers so we know who ordered both a bicycle and a helmet."

Translation 1 Select customer first name and customer last name from those common to the set of customers who ordered bicycles and the set of customers who ordered helmets

Translation 2/ Clean Up

Select customer first name ~~and~~ customer last name from (Select unique customer names from ~~the~~ customers ~~table~~ join~~ed with the~~ orders ~~table~~ on customer ID~~, then~~ join~~ed with the~~ order details ~~table~~ on order number~~, then~~ join~~ed with the~~ products ~~table~~ on product number where product name ~~contains~~ LIKE '%Bike') join~~ed with~~ (Select unique customer names from ~~the~~ customers ~~table~~ join~~ed with the~~ orders ~~table~~ on customer ID~~, then~~ join~~ed with the~~ order details ~~table~~ on order number~~, then~~ join~~ed with the~~ products ~~table~~ on product number where product name ~~contains~~ LIKE '%Helmet') on customer ID

SQL

```
SELECT CustBikes.CustFirstName,
   CustBikes.CustLastName
FROM
(SELECT DISTINCT Customers.CustomerID,
   Customers.CustFirstName,
   Customers.CustLastName
FROM ((Customers
INNER JOIN Orders
ON Customers.CustomerID = Orders.CustomerID)
INNER JOIN Order_Details
ON Orders.OrderNumber =
   Order_Details.OrderNumber)
INNER JOIN Products
ON Products.ProductNumber =
   Order_Details.ProductNumber
WHERE Products.ProductName LIKE '%Bike')
AS CustBikes
INNER JOIN
(SELECT DISTINCT Customers.CustomerID
FROM ((Customers
INNER JOIN Orders
ON Customers.CustomerID = Orders.CustomerID)
INNER JOIN Order_Details
ON Orders.OrderNumber =
   Order_Details.OrderNumber)
INNER JOIN Products
ON Products.ProductNumber =
   Order_Details.ProductNumber
WHERE Products.ProductName LIKE '%Helmet')
AS CustHelmets
ON CustBikes.CustomerID =
   CustHelmets.CustomerID
```

❖ **Note** We simplified the second embedded SELECT Statement to fetch only the Customer ID because that's the only column we need for the INNER JOIN of the two sets to work. We could have actually eliminated the JOIN to the Customers table and fetched the CustomerID from the Orders table. You could also solve this problem as the INTERSECT of the two sets, but you would need to include all of the output columns in both of the Result Sets that you intersect.

Customers_Both_Bikes_And_Helmets (24 rows)

CustFirstName	CustLastName
Suzanne	Viescas
Will	Thompson
Gary	Hallmark
Michael	Davolio
Kenneth	Peacock
John	Viescas
Laura	Callahan
Neil	Patterson
Margaret	Peacock
<<more rows here >>	

Entertainment Agency Database

"List the entertainers who played engagements for both customers Bonnicksen and *Rosales."*

As you saw earlier, solving for Bonnicksen *or* Rosales is easy. Let's ask it a different way so it's clearer what we need the database to do for us.

"Find all the entertainers who played an engagement for Bonnicksen, then find all the entertainers who played an engagement for Rosales, and

finally list the common entertainers so we know who played an engagement for both."

Translation 1 — Select entertainer stage name from those common to the set of entertainers who played for Bonnicksen and the set of entertainers who played for Rosales

Translation 2/ Clean Up — Select entertainer stage name from (Select ~~unique~~ distinct entertainer stage names from ~~the~~ entertainers ~~table~~ join~~ed with the~~ engagements ~~table~~ on entertainer ID~~, then~~ join~~ed with the~~ customers ~~table~~ on customer ID where customer last name ~~is~~ = 'Bonnicksen') join~~ed with~~ (Select ~~unique~~ distinct entertainer stage names from ~~the~~ entertainers ~~table~~ join~~ed with the~~ engagements ~~table~~ on entertainer ID~~, then~~ join~~ed with the~~ customers ~~table~~ on customer ID where customer last name ~~is~~ = 'Rosales') on entertainer ID

SQL

```
SELECT EntBonnicksen.EntStageName
FROM
(SELECT DISTINCT Entertainers.EntertainerID,
   Entertainers.EntStageName
FROM (Entertainers
INNER JOIN Engagements
ON Entertainers.EntertainerID =
   Engagements.EntertainerID)
INNER JOIN Customers
ON Customers.CustomerID =
   Engagements.CustomerID
WHERE Customers.CustLastName = 'Bonnicksen')
AS EntBonnicksen
INNER JOIN
(SELECT DISTINCT Entertainers.EntertainerID,
   Entertainers.EntStageName
FROM (Entertainers
INNER JOIN Engagements
ON Entertainers.EntertainerID =
   Engagements.EntertainerID)
INNER JOIN Customers
ON Customers.CustomerID =
   Engagements.CustomerID
WHERE Customers.CustLastName = 'Rosales')
AS EntRosales
ON EntBonnicksen.EntertainerID =
   EntRosales.EntertainerID
```

Entertainers_Bonnicksen_AND_Rosales (4 rows)

EntStageName
Country Feeling
Katherine Ehrlich
Saturday Revue
Julia Schnebly

> ❖ **Note** This is another example of a request that can also be solved with INTERSECT.

School Scheduling Database

"Show me the students and teachers who have the same first name."

Translation/ Clean Up: Select student full name ~~and~~ staff full name from ~~the~~ students ~~table~~ join~~ed with the~~ staff ~~table~~ on first name

SQL

```
SELECT (Students.StudFirstName || ' ' ||
   Students.StudLastName) AS StudFullName,
   (Staff.StfFirstName || ' ' ||
   Staff.StfLastName) AS StfFullName
FROM Students
INNER JOIN Staff
ON Students.StudFirstName = Staff.StfFirstName
```

Students_Staff_Same_FirstName (5 rows)

StudFullName	StfFullName
John Kennedy	John Leverling
Michael Viescas	Michael Davolio
Michael Viescas	Michael Hernandez
David Nathanson	David Callahan
David Nathanson	David Smith

Bowling League Database

> *"Find the bowlers who had a raw score of 170 or better at both Thunderbird Lanes and Bolero Lanes."*

Yes, this is another "solve an intersection with a join" problem. Let's ask it a different way so that it's clearer what we need the database to do for us.

> *"Find all the bowlers who had a raw score of 170 or better at Thunderbird Lanes, then find all the bowlers who had a raw score of 170 or better at Bolero Lanes, and finally list the common bowlers so we know who had good scores at both bowling alleys."*

Translation 1
: Select bowler full name from those common to the set of bowlers who have a score of 170 or better at Thunderbird Lanes and the set of bowlers who have a score of 170 or better at Bolero Lanes

Translation 2/ Clean Up
: Select bowler full name from (Select ~~unique~~ distinct bowler ID ~~and~~ bowler full name from ~~the~~ bowlers ~~table~~ join~~ed with the~~ bowler scores ~~table~~ on bowler ID~~, then~~ join~~ed with the~~ tourney matches ~~table~~ on match ID~~, and finally~~ join~~ed with the~~ tournaments ~~table~~ on tourney ID where tourney location ~~is~~ = 'Thunderbird Lanes' and raw score ~~is greater than or equal to~~ >= 170) join~~ed with~~ (Select unique bowler ID ~~and~~ bowler full name from ~~the~~ bowlers ~~table~~ join~~ed with the~~ bowler scores ~~table~~ on bowler ID~~, then~~ join~~ed with the~~ tourney matches ~~table~~ on match ID~~, and finally~~ join~~ed with the~~ tournaments ~~table~~ on tourney ID where tourney location ~~is~~ = 'Bolero Lanes' and raw score ~~is greater than or equal to~~ >= 170) on bowler ID

SQL

```
SELECT BowlerTbird.BowlerFullName
FROM
(SELECT DISTINCT Bowlers.BowlerID,
   (Bowlers.BowlerLastName || ', ' ||
   Bowlers.BowlerFirstName) AS BowlerFullName
FROM ((Bowlers
INNER JOIN Bowler_Scores
ON Bowlers.BowlerID = Bowler_Scores.BowlerID)
INNER JOIN Tourney_Matches
ON Tourney_Matches.MatchID = Bowler_Scores.MatchID)
INNER JOIN Tournaments
ON Tournaments.TourneyID =
   Tourney_Matches.TourneyID
WHERE Tournaments.TourneyLocation =
   'Thunderbird Lanes'
```

```
AND Bowler_Scores.RawScore >= 170)
AS BowlerTbird
INNER JOIN
(SELECT DISTINCT Bowlers.BowlerID,
   (Bowlers.BowlerLastName || ', ' ||
   Bowlers.BowlerFirstName) AS BowlerFullName
FROM ((Bowlers
INNER JOIN Bowler_Scores
ON Bowlers.BowlerID = Bowler_Scores.BowlerID)
INNER JOIN Tourney_Matches
ON Tourney_Matches.MatchID = Bowler_Scores.MatchID)
INNER JOIN Tournaments
ON Tournaments.TourneyID =
   Tourney_Matches.TourneyID
WHERE Tournaments.TourneyLocation = 'Bolero Lanes'
AND Bowler_Scores.RawScore >= 170)
AS BowlerBolero
ON BowlerTbird.BowlerID = BowlerBolero.BowlerID
```

❖ **Note** Because a bowler may have had a high score at either bowling alley more than once, we added the DISTINCT keyword to eliminate the duplicates.

Good_Bowlers_TBird_And_Bolero (10 rows)

BowlerFullName
Kennedy, John
Patterson, Neil
McLain, Susan
Patterson, Kathryn
Viescas, John
Piercy, Greg
Thompson, Mary
Thompson, Will
Patterson, Rachel
Pundt, Steve

Recipes Database

"Display all the ingredients for recipes that contain carrots."

Translation/Clean Up: Select recipe ID, recipe title, ~~and~~ ingredient name from ~~the~~ recipes ~~table~~ join~~ed with the~~ recipe ingredients ~~table~~ on recipe ID, join~~ed with~~ ~~the~~ ingredients ~~table~~ on ingredient ID, then finally join~~ed with~~ (Select recipe ID from ~~the~~ ingredients ~~table~~ join~~ed with the~~ recipe ingredients ~~table~~ on ingredient ID where ingredient name ~~is~~ = 'carrot') on recipe ID

SQL

```
SELECT Recipes.RecipeID, Recipes.RecipeTitle,
   Ingredients.IngredientName
FROM ((Recipes
INNER JOIN Recipe_Ingredients
ON Recipes.RecipeID =
   Recipe_Ingredients.RecipeID)
INNER JOIN Ingredients
ON Ingredients.IngredientID =
   Recipe_Ingredients.IngredientID)
INNER JOIN
(SELECT Recipe_Ingredients.RecipeID
FROM Ingredients
INNER JOIN Recipe_Ingredients
ON Ingredients.IngredientID =
   Recipe_Ingredients.IngredientID
WHERE Ingredients.IngredientName = 'Carrot')
AS Carrots
ON Recipes.RecipeID = Carrots.RecipeID
```

❖ **Note** This request can be solved a bit more simply with a Subquery. We'll show you how to do that in Chapter 11.

Recipes_Containing_Carrots (16 rows)

RecipeID	RecipeTitle	IngredientName
1	Irish Stew	Beef
1	Irish Stew	Onion
1	Irish Stew	Potato
1	Irish Stew	Carrot
1	Irish Stew	Water
1	Irish Stew	Guinness Beer
14	Salmon Filets in Parchment Paper	Salmon
14	Salmon Filets in Parchment Paper	Carrot
14	Salmon Filets in Parchment Paper	Leek
14	Salmon Filets in Parchment Paper	Red Bell Pepper
14	Salmon Filets in Parchment Paper	Butter
<<more rows here >>		

SUMMARY

In this chapter, we thoroughly discussed how to link two or more tables or Result Sets on matching values. We began by defining the concept of a JOIN, then went into the details about forming an INNER JOIN. We discussed what is "legal" to use as the criteria for a JOIN, but cautioned you about making nonsensical joins.

We started out simply with examples joining two tables. We next showed how to assign correlation (alias) names to tables within your FROM clause. You may want to do this for convenience—or you may be required to assign correlation names when you include the same table more than once or use an embedded SELECT Statement.

We showed how to replace a reference to a table with a SELECT Statement within your FROM clause. We next showed how to extend your horizons by joining more than two tables or Result Sets. We wrapped up the discussion of the syntax of an INNER JOIN by re-emphasizing the importance of having a good database design and understanding how your tables are related.

We discussed a number of reasons why INNER JOINs are useful and gave you specific examples. The rest of the chapter provided more than a dozen examples of using INNER JOIN. We broke these examples into joins on two tables, joins on more than two tables, and joins on matching values. In the next chapter, we'll explore another variant of JOIN—an OUTER JOIN.

The following section presents a number of requests to work out on your own.

Problems for You to Solve

Below, we show you the request statement and the name of the solution query in the sample databases. If you want some practice, you can work out the SQL you need for each request and then check your answer with the query we saved in the samples. Don't worry if your syntax doesn't exactly match the syntax of the queries we saved—as long as your Result Set is the same.

Sales Order Database

1. *"List customers and the dates they placed an order, sorted in order date sequence."*
   (Hint: The solution requires a JOIN of two tables.)
   You can find the solution in Customers_And_OrderDates (944 rows).
2. *"List employees and the customers for whom they booked an order."*
   (Hint: The solution requires a JOIN of more than two tables.)
   You can find the solution in Employees_And_Customers (211 rows).
3. *"Display all orders, the products in each order, and the amount owed for each product, in order number sequence."*
   (Hint: The solution requires a JOIN of more than two tables.)
   You can find the solution in Orders_With_Products (4,196 rows).
4. *"Show me the vendors and the products they supply to us for products that cost less than $100."*
   (Hint: The solution requires a JOIN of more than two tables.)
   You can find the solution in Vendors_And_Products_Less_Than_100 (66 rows).
5. *"Show me customers and employees that have the same first name."*
   (Hint: The solution requires a JOIN on matching values.)
   You can find the solution in Customers_Employees_Same_FirstName (4 rows).

6. *"Show me customers and employees that live in the same city."*
(Hint: The solution requires a JOIN on matching values.)
You can find the solution in Customers_Employees_Same_City (11 rows).

Entertainment Agency Database

1. *"Display agents and the engagement dates they booked, sorted by booking start date."*
(Hint: The solution requires a JOIN of two tables.)
You can find the solution in Agents_Booked_Dates (131 rows).
2. *"List customers and the entertainers they booked."*
(Hint: The solution requires a JOIN of more than two tables.)
You can find the solution in Customers_Booked_Entertainers (93 rows).
3. *"Find the agents and entertainers that live in the same postal code."*
(Hint: The solution requires a JOIN on matching values.)
You can find the solution in Agents_Entertainers_Same_Postal (10 rows).

School Scheduling Database

1. *"Display buildings and all the classrooms in each building."*
(Hint: The solution requires a JOIN of two tables.)
You can find the solution in Buildings_Classrooms (44 rows).
2. *"List students and all the classes in which they are currently enrolled."*
(Hint: The solution requires a JOIN of more than two tables.)
You can find the solution in Student_Enrollments (35 rows).
3. *"List the faculty staff and the subject each teaches."*
(Hint: The solution requires a JOIN of more than two tables.)
You can find the solution in Staff_Subjects (111 rows).
4. *"Show me the students who have a grade of 85 or better in art and who also have a grade of 85 or better in any computer course."*
(Hint: The solution requires a JOIN on matching values.)
You can find the solution in Good_Art_CS_Students (1 row).

Bowling League Database

1. *"List the bowling teams and all the team members."*
(Hint: The solution requires a JOIN of two tables.)
You can find the solution in Teams_And_Bowlers (32 rows).
2. *"Display the bowlers, the matches they played in, and the bowler game scores."*
(Hint: The solution requires a JOIN of more than two tables.)
You can find the solution in Bowler_Game_Scores (1,344 rows).

3. *"Find the bowlers who have the same average."*
   (Hint: The solution requires a JOIN on matching values.)
   You can find the solution in Bowlers_Same_Average (70 rows).

Recipes Database

1. *"List all the recipes for salads."*
   (Hint: The solution requires a JOIN of two tables.)
   You can find the solution in Salads (1 row).
2. *"List all recipes that contain a Dairy ingredient."*
   (Hint: The solution requires a JOIN of more than two tables.)
   You can find the solution in Recipes_Containing_Dairy (2 rows).
3. *"Find the ingredients that use the same default measurement amount."*
   (Hint: The solution requires a JOIN on matching values.)
   You can find the solution in Ingredients_Same_Measure (628 rows).
4. *"Show me the recipes that have beef* and *garlic."*
   (Hint: The solution requires a JOIN on matching values.)
   You can find the solution in Beef_And_Garlic_Recipes (1 row).

9

OUTER JOINs

"The only difference between a problem and a solution is people understand the solution."
—Charles Franklin Kettering
Inventor, 1876–1958

Topics Covered in This Chapter

In the previous chapter, we covered all the "ins" of joins—linking two or more tables or Result Sets using INNER JOIN to find all the rows that match. Now it's time to talk about the "outs"—linking tables and finding out not only the rows that match but also the rows that don't match.

What Is an OUTER JOIN?

As we explained in the previous chapter, the SQL Standard defines several types of JOIN operations to link two or more tables or Result Sets. An OUTER JOIN asks your database system to return not only the rows that match on the criteria you specify but also to include unmatched rows from either one or both of the two sets you want to link.

Let's suppose, for example, that you want to fetch information from the School Scheduling database about students and the classes for which they're registered. As you learned in Chapter 8, an INNER JOIN returns only students who have registered for a class and classes for which a student has registered. It won't return any students who have been accepted at the school but haven't signed up for any classes yet, nor will it return any classes that are on the schedule but for which no student has yet shown an interest.

What if you want to list *all* students and the classes for which they are registered, if any? Conversely, suppose you want a list of *all* the classes and the students who have registered for those classes, if any. To solve this sort of problem, you need to ask for an OUTER JOIN.

Figure 9-1 shows one possible relationship between students and classes using a set diagram. As you can see, a few students haven't registered for a class yet, and a few classes do not yet have any students signed up to take the class.

If you ask for *all* students and the classes for which they are registered, you'll get a Result Set resembling Figure 9-2.

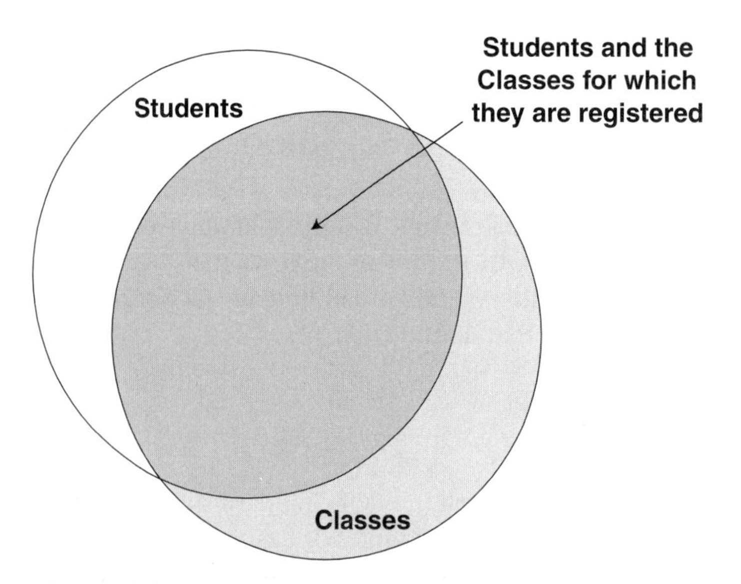

Figure 9-1 *A possible relationship between students and classes.*

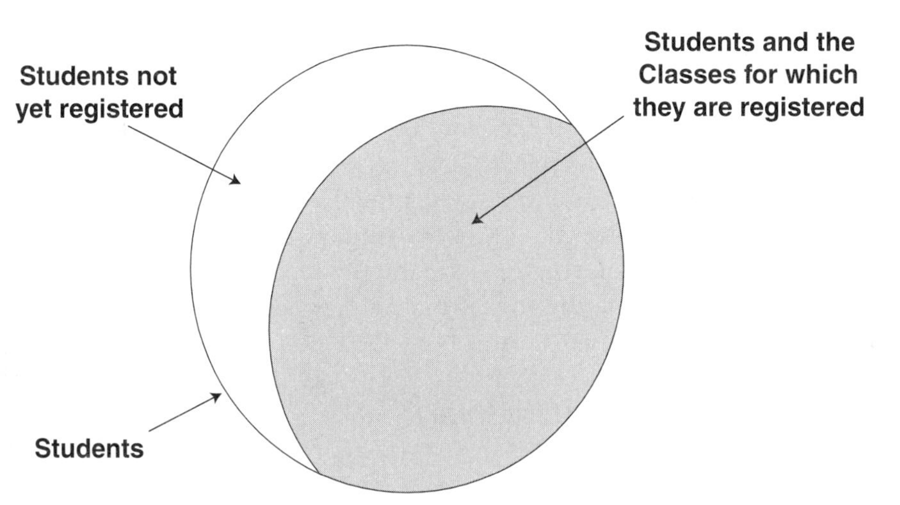

Figure 9-2 *All students and the classes for which they are registered.*

You might ask, "What will I see for the students who haven't registered for any classes?" If you remember the concept of a Null or "nothing" value discussed in Chapter 5, you know what you'll see: When you ask for all students joined with any classes, your database system returns a Null value in all columns from the Classes table when it finds a student who is not yet registered for any classes. If you think about the concept of a difference between two sets (discussed in Chapter 7), the rows with a Null value in the columns from the Classes table represent the difference between the set of all students and the set of students who have registered for a class.

Likewise, if you ask for all classes and any students who registered for classes, the rows with Null values in the columns from the Students table represent the difference between the set of all classes and the set of classes for which students have registered. As we promised, using an OUTER JOIN with a test for Null values is an alternate way to discover the difference between two sets. Unlike a true EXCEPT operation that matches on entire rows from the two sets, you can specify the match in a JOIN operation on just a few specific (usually the Primary Key and Foreign Key) columns.

The LEFT/RIGHT OUTER JOIN

You'll generally use the OUTER JOIN form that asks for all the rows from one table or Result Set and any matching rows from a second table or Result

Set. To do this, you specify either a LEFT OUTER JOIN or a RIGHT OUTER JOIN.

What's the difference between "LEFT" and "RIGHT"? Remember from the previous chapter that to specify an INNER JOIN on two tables, you name the first table, include the JOIN keyword, and then name the second table. When you begin building queries using OUTER JOIN, the SQL Standard considers the first table you name as the one on the "left," and the second table is the one on the "right." So if you want all the rows from the first table and any matching rows from the second table, you'll use a LEFT OUTER JOIN. Conversely, if you want all the rows from the second table and any matching rows from the first table, you'll specify a RIGHT OUTER JOIN.

Syntax

Let's examine the syntax needed to build either a LEFT or RIGHT OUTER JOIN.

Using Tables

We'll start simply with defining an OUTER JOIN using tables. Figure 9-3 shows the syntax diagram for creating a query with an OUTER JOIN on two tables.

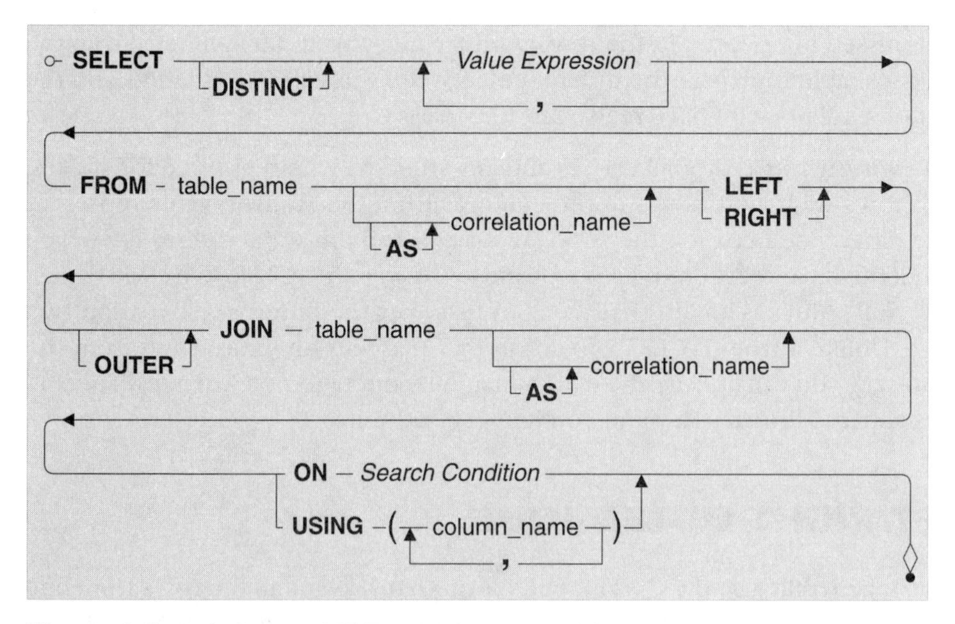

Figure 9-3 *Defining an OUTER JOIN on two tables.*

Just like INNER JOIN, all the action happens in the FROM clause. (We left out the WHERE and ORDER BY clauses for now to simplify things.) Instead of a single table name, you specify two table names and link them with the JOIN keyword. If you do not specify the type of JOIN you want, your database system assumes you want an INNER JOIN (covered in Chapter 8). In this case because you want an OUTER JOIN, you must explicitly state that you want either a LEFT OUTER or RIGHT OUTER JOIN.

❖ **Note** For those of you following along with the complete syntax diagrams in Appendix A, you can find `table_name JOIN table_name` described as part of the *Joined Table* defined term. *Table Reference* includes *Joined Table*, and the FROM clause of a SELECT Statement uses *Table Reference.* We "rolled up" these complex definitions into a single diagram to make it easy to study a simple two-table join. We'll be using this same simplification technique in diagrams throughout the remainder of this chapter.

The critical part of any JOIN is the ON or USING clause that follows the second table and tells your database system how to perform the join. To solve the join, your database system logically combines every row in the first table with every row in the second table. (This combination of all rows from one table with all rows from a second table is called a *Cartesian Product.*) It then applies the criteria in the ON or USING clauses to find the matching rows to be returned. Because you asked for an OUTER JOIN, your database system also returns the unmatched rows from either the "left" or "right" table.

You learned about using *Search Condition* to form a WHERE clause in Chapter 6. You can use a Search Condition in the ON clause within a join to specify a logical test that must be true in order to return any two linked rows. It only makes sense to write a Search Condition that compares at least one column from the first table with at least one column from the second table. Although you can write a very complex Search Condition, you can usually specify a simple equals comparison test on the Primary Key columns from one table with the Foreign Key columns from the second table.

To keep things simple, let's start with the same Recipe_Classes and Recipes example we used in the last chapter. Remember that in a well-designed database, you should break out complex classification names into a second table and then link the names back to the primary subject table via a simple key value. In the Recipes sample database, Recipe_Classes appear in a table separate from Recipes. Figure 9-4 shows you the relationship between Recipe_Classes and Recipes.

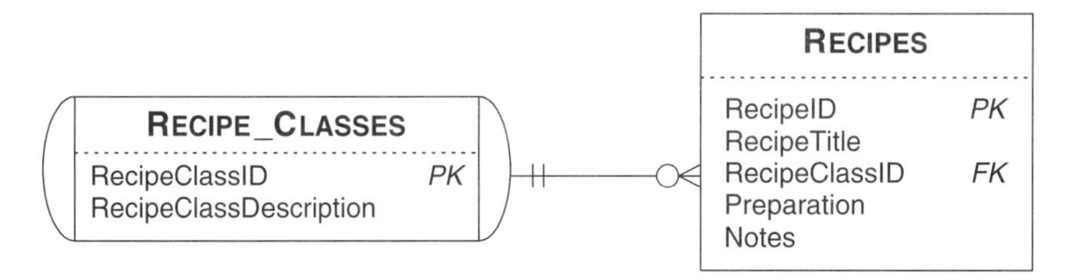

Figure 9-4 *Recipe Classes are in a separate table from Recipes.*

When you originally set up the kinds of recipes to save in your database, you might have started by entering all the recipe classes that came to mind. Now that you've entered a number of recipes, you might be interested in finding out which classes don't have any recipes entered yet. You might also be interested in listing *all* of the recipe classes along with the names of recipes entered thus far for each class. You can solve either problem with an OUTER JOIN.

> ❖ **Note** Throughout this chapter, we'll be using the "Request/Translation/Clean Up/SQL" technique that we introduced in Chapter 4.

"Show me all of the recipe types and any matching recipes in my database."

Translation — Select recipe class description and recipe title from the recipe classes table outer joined with the recipes table on recipe class ID in the recipe classes table matching recipe class ID in the recipes table

Clean Up — Select recipe class description ~~and~~ recipe title from ~~the~~ recipe classes ~~table~~ outer join~~ed with the~~ recipes ~~table~~ on recipe class ID ~~in the recipe classes table matching~~ = recipe class ID~~ in the recipes table~~

SQL
```
SELECT Recipe_Classes.RecipeClassDescription,
   Recipes.RecipeTitle
FROM Recipe_Classes
LEFT OUTER JOIN Recipes
ON Recipe_Classes.RecipeClassID =
   Recipes.RecipeClassID
```

When using multiple tables in your FROM clause, remember to qualify fully each column name with the table name wherever you use it so that it's absolutely clear which column from which table you want. Note that we *had* to qualify the name of RecipeClassID in the ON clause because there are two columns named RecipeClassID—one in the Recipes table and one in the Recipe_Classes table.

❖ **Note** Although most commercial implementations of SQL support OUTER JOIN, some do not. If your database does not support OUTER JOIN, you can still solve the problem by listing all the tables you need in the FROM clause, then moving your *Search Condition* from the ON clause to the WHERE clause. You must consult your database documentation to learn the specific non-standard syntax that your database requires to define the OUTER JOIN. For example, earlier versions of Microsoft SQL Server support this syntax (notice the asterisk in the WHERE clause).

```
SELECT Recipe_Classes.RecipeClassDescription,
   Recipes.RecipeTitle
FROM Recipe_Classes, Recipes
WHERE Recipe_Classes.RecipeClassID *=
   Recipes.RecipeClassID
```

If you're using Oracle, the syntax is as follows (notice the plus sign in the WHERE clause).

```
SELECT Recipe_Classes.RecipeClassDescription,
   Recipes.RecipeTitle
FROM Recipe_Classes, Recipes
WHERE Recipe_Classes.RecipeClassID =
   Recipes.RecipeClassID(+)
```

For a beginner, these syntaxes may be more intuitive for simple queries. However, the SQL Standard syntax allows you to fully define the source for the final Result Set entirely within the FROM clause. Think of the FROM clause as fully defining a linked Result Set from which the database system obtains your answer. In the Standard, you use the WHERE clause only to filter rows out of the Result Set defined by the FROM clause. Also, because the specific syntax for defining an OUTER JOIN via the WHERE clause varies by product, you may have to learn several different syntaxes if you work with multiple non-standard products.

If you execute the above query in the Recipes sample database, you should see 16 rows returned. Because we didn't enter any Soup recipes in the database, you'll get a Null value for RecipeTitle in the row where RecipeClassDescription is Soup. To find only this one row, use this approach.

"List the recipe classes that do not yet have any recipes."

Translation: Select recipe class description from the recipe classes table outer joined with the recipes table on recipe class ID where recipe ID is empty

Clean Up: Select recipe class description from ~~the~~ recipe classes ~~table~~ outer join~~ed with the~~ recipes ~~table~~ on recipe class ID where recipe ID is ~~empty~~ NULL

SQL

```
SELECT Recipe_Classes.RecipeClassDescription
FROM Recipe_Classes
LEFT OUTER JOIN Recipes
ON Recipe_Classes.RecipeClassID =
   Recipes.RecipeClassID
WHERE Recipes.RecipeID IS NULL
```

If you think about it, we've just done a DIFFERENCE or EXCEPT operation (see Chapter 7) using a JOIN. It's a bit like saying, "Show me all the recipe classes EXCEPT the ones that already appear in the recipes table." The set diagram in Figure 9-5 should help you visualize what's going on.

In Figure 9-5, all recipes have a recipe class, but some recipe classes exist for which no recipe has yet been defined. When we add the IS NULL test, we're

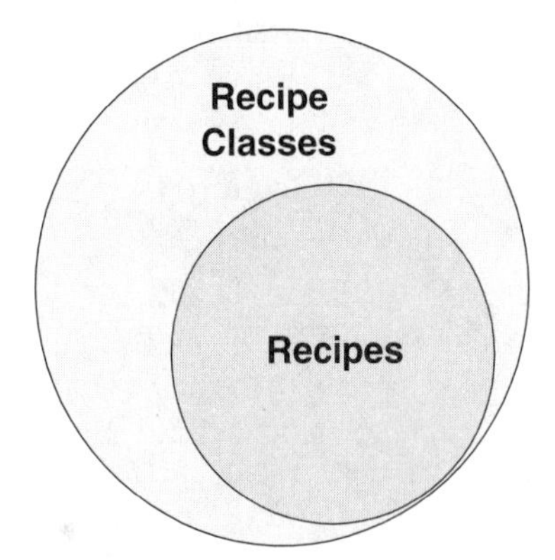

Figure 9-5 *A possible relationship between recipe classes and recipes.*

asking for all the rows in the lighter outer circle that don't have any matches in the set of recipes represented by the darker inner circle.

Notice that the diagram for an OUTER JOIN on tables in Figure 9-3 (on page 278) also has the optional USING clause. If the matching columns in the two tables have the same name and you just want to join on equal values, you can use the USING clause and list the column names. Let's do the previous problem again with USING.

"Display the recipe classes that do not yet have any recipes."

Translation: Select recipe class description from the recipe classes table outer joined with the recipes table using recipe class ID where recipe ID is empty

Clean Up: Select recipe class description from ~~the~~ recipe classes ~~table~~ outer join~~ed with the~~ recipes ~~table~~ using recipe class ID where recipe ID is ~~empty~~ NULL

SQL:

```
SELECT Recipe_Classes.RecipeClassDescription
FROM Recipe_Classes
LEFT OUTER JOIN Recipes
USING (RecipeClassID)
WHERE Recipes.RecipeID IS NULL
```

The USING syntax is a lot simpler, isn't it? Be aware, however, that some database systems do not yet support USING. If you find that you can't use USING with your database, you can always get the same result with an ON clause and an equal comparison.

❖ **Note** The SQL Standard also defines a type of JOIN operation called a NATURAL JOIN. A NATURAL JOIN links the two specified tables by matching all the columns with the same name. If the only common columns are the linking columns and your database supports NATURAL JOIN, you can solve the above problem like this.

```
SELECT Recipe_Classes.RecipeClassDescription
FROM Recipe_Classes
NATURAL LEFT OUTER JOIN Recipes
WHERE Recipes.RecipeID IS NULL
```

Do not specify an ON or USING clause if you use the NATURAL keyword.

Embedding a SELECT Statement

As you recall from Chapter 8, most SQL implementations let you substitute an entire SELECT Statement for any table name in your FROM clause. Of course, you must then assign a correlation name (see the section on assigning alias names in Chapter 8) so that the result of evaluating your embedded query has a name. Figure 9-6 shows how to assemble an OUTER JOIN clause using embedded SELECT Statements.

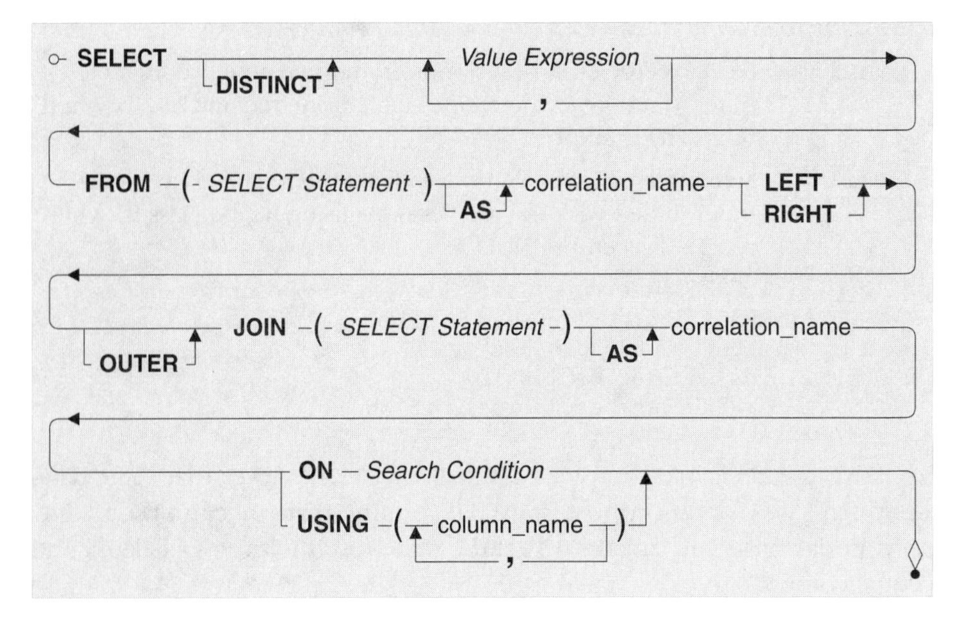

Figure 9-6 *An OUTER JOIN using SELECT Statements.*

Note that a SELECT Statement can include all query clauses *except* an ORDER BY clause. Also, you can mix and match SELECT Statements with table names on either side of the OUTER JOIN keywords.

Let's look at Recipes and Recipe Classes again. For this example, let's also assume that you are interested only in classes Salads, Soups, and Main courses. Here's the query with the Recipe_Classes table filtered in a SELECT Statement that's part of the INNER JOIN.

```
SQL        SELECT RCFiltered.ClassName, R.RecipeTitle
           FROM
           (SELECT RecipeClassID, RecipeClassDescription
           AS ClassName
           FROM Recipe_Classes AS RC
```

```
WHERE RC.ClassName = 'Salads'
OR RC.ClassName = 'Soup'
OR RC.ClassName = 'Main Course') AS RCFiltered
LEFT OUTER JOIN Recipes AS R
ON RCFiltered.RecipeClassID = R.RecipeClassID
```

You must be careful when using a SELECT Statement in a FROM clause. First, when you decide to substitute a SELECT Statement for a table name, you must be sure to include not only the columns you want to appear in the final result but also any linking columns you need to perform the JOIN. That's why you see both RecipeClassID and RecipeClassDescription in the embedded statement. Just for fun, we gave RecipeClassDescription an alias name of "ClassName" in the embedded statement. As a result, the SELECT clause asks for ClassName rather than RecipeClassDescription. Note that the ON clause now references the correlation name of the embedded SELECT Statement—RCFiltered—rather than the original name of the table or the correlation name we assigned the table inside the embedded SELECT Statement.

As the query is stated above for the actual Recipes sample database, you see one row with RecipeClassDescription of Soup with a Null value returned for RecipeTitle because there are no soup recipes in the sample database. We could just as easily have built a SELECT Statement on the Recipes table on the right side of the OUTER JOIN. For example, we could have asked for recipes that contain the word "beef" in their title, as in the following statement.

```
SQL       SELECT RCFiltered.ClassName, R.RecipeTitle
          FROM
          (SELECT RecipeClassID, RecipeClassDescription
          AS ClassName
          FROM Recipe_Classes AS RC
          WHERE RC.ClassName = 'Salads'
          OR RC.ClassName = 'Soup'
          OR RC.ClassName = 'Main Course') AS RCFiltered
          LEFT OUTER JOIN
          (SELECT Recipes.RecipeClassID,
             Recipes.RecipeTitle
          FROM Recipes
          WHERE Recipes.RecipeTitle LIKE '%beef%') AS R
          ON RCFiltered.RecipeClassID = R.RecipeClassID
```

Keep in mind that the LEFT OUTER JOIN asks for *all* rows from the Result Set or table on the left side of the JOIN, regardless of whether any matching rows exist on the right side. The previous query not only returns a Soup row with a Null RecipeTitle (because there are no soups in the database at all) but also a Salad row with a Null. You might conclude that there are no salad recipes in the database. Actually, there *are* salads in the database but no salads with "beef" in the title of the recipe!

❖ **Note** You may have noticed that you can enter a full *Search Condition* as part of the ON clause in a JOIN. This is absolutely true, so it is perfectly legal in the SQL Standard to solve the above problem as follows.

```
SELECT Recipe_Classes.RecipeClassDescription,
   Recipes.RecipeTitle
FROM Recipe_Classes
LEFT OUTER JOIN Recipes
ON Recipe_Classes.RecipeClassID =
   Recipes.RecipeClassID
AND
   (Recipe_Classes.RecipeClassDescription = 'Salads'
OR Recipe_Classes.RecipeClassDescription = 'Soup'
OR Recipe_Classes.RecipeClassDescription =
   'Main Course')
AND Recipes.RecipeTitle LIKE "%beef%"
```

Unfortunately, we have discovered that some major implementations of SQL solve this problem incorrectly or do not accept this syntax at all! Therefore, we recommend that you always enter in the *Search Condition* in the ON clause only criteria that compare columns from the two tables or Result Sets. If you want to filter the rows from the underlying tables, do so with a separate *Search Condition* in a WHERE clause in an embedded SELECT Statement.

Embedding JOINs within JOINs

Although you can solve many problems by linking just two tables, many times you'll need to link three, four, or more tables to get all the data to solve your request. For example, you might want to fetch all the relevant information about recipes—the type of recipe, the recipe name, and all the ingredients for the recipe—in one query. Now that you understand what you can do with an OUTER JOIN, you might also want to list *all* Recipe Classes—even those that have no recipes defined yet, and all the details about recipes and their ingredients. Figure 9-7 shows all the tables needed to answer this request.

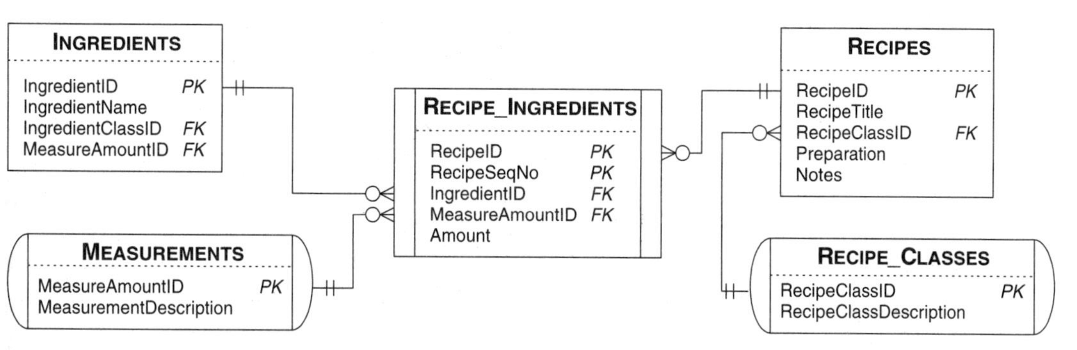

Figure 9-7 *The tables you need from the Recipes sample database to fetch all the information about recipes.*

Looks like you need data from *five* different tables! Just as in Chapter 8, you can do this by constructing a more complex FROM clause, embedding JOIN clauses within JOIN clauses. Here's the trick: Everywhere you can specify a table name, you can also specify an entire JOIN clause surrounded with parentheses. Figure 9-8 shows a simplified version of joining two tables. (We've left off the correlation name clauses and chosen the ON clause to form a simple INNER or OUTER JOIN of two tables.)

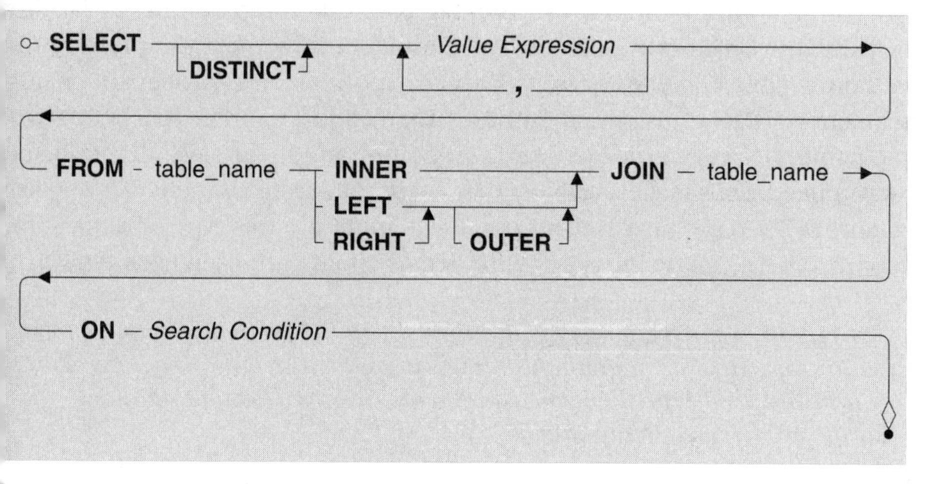

Figure 9-8 *A simple JOIN of two tables.*

To add a third table to the mix, just place an open parenthesis before the first table name, add a close parenthesis after the Search Condition, and then insert another JOIN, a table name, the ON keyword, and another Search Condition. Figure 9-9 shows how to do this.

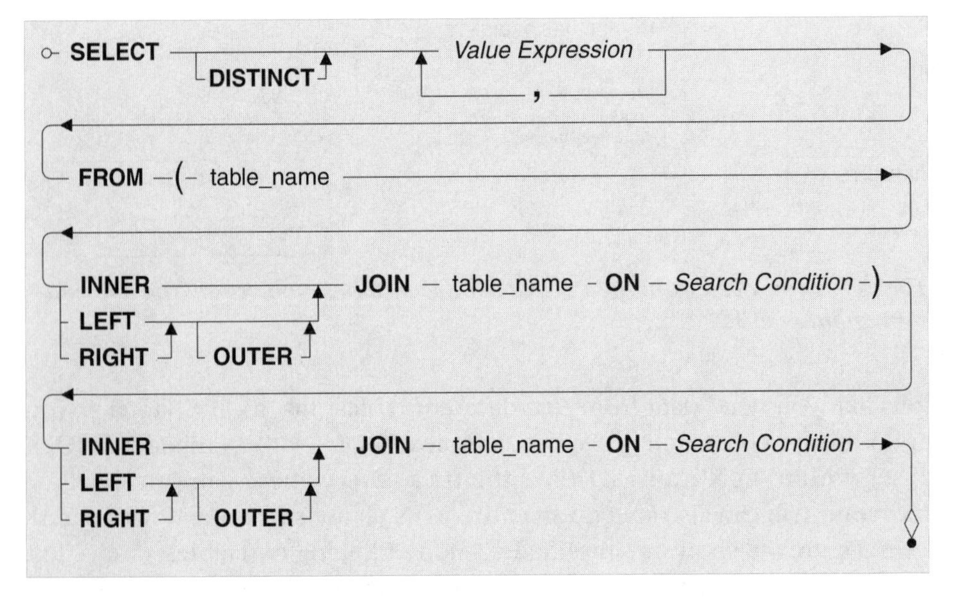

Figure 9-9 *A simple JOIN of three tables.*

If you think about it, the JOIN of two tables inside the parentheses forms a "logical" table, or inner Result Set. This Result Set now takes the place of the first simple table name in Figure 9-8. You can continue this process of enclosing an entire JOIN clause in parentheses, then adding another JOIN keyword, table name, ON keyword, and Search Condition until you have all the Result Sets you need. Let's make a request that needs data from all the tables you see in Figure 9-7 and see how it turns out. (You might use this type of request for a report that lists all recipe types with details about recipes in each type.)

"I need all of the recipe types, and then the matching recipe name, preparation instructions, ingredient names, ingredient step number, ingredient quantities, and ingredient measurements from my Recipes database, sorted in step number sequence."

Translation Select the recipe class description, recipe title, preparation instructions, ingredient name, recipe sequence number, amount, and measurement description from the recipe classes table left outer joined with the recipes table on recipe class ID, then joined with the recipe ingredients table on recipe ID, then joined with the ingredients table on ingredient ID, and then finally joined with the measurements table on measurement amount ID, order by recipe title and recipe sequence number

Clean Up — Select ~~the~~ recipe class description, recipe title, preparation ~~instructions~~, ingredient name, recipe sequence number, amount, ~~and~~ measurement description from ~~the~~ recipe classes ~~table~~ left outer join~~ed with the~~ recipes ~~table~~ on recipe class ID~~, then~~ join~~ed with the~~ recipe ingredients ~~table~~ on recipe ID~~, then~~ join~~ed with the~~ ingredients ~~table~~ on ingredient ID~~, and then finally~~ join~~ed with the~~ measurements ~~table~~ on measurement amount ID~~,~~ order by recipe title ~~and~~ recipe sequence number

SQL

```
SELECT Recipe_Classes.RecipeClassDescription,
   Recipes.RecipeTitle, Recipes.Preparation,
   Ingredients.IngredientName,
   Recipe_Ingredients.RecipeSeqNo,
   Recipe_Ingredients.Amount,
   Measurements.MeasurementDescription
FROM (((Recipe_Classes
LEFT OUTER JOIN Recipes
ON Recipe_Classes.RecipeClassID =
   Recipes.RecipeClassID)
INNER JOIN Recipe_Ingredients
ON Recipes.RecipeID =
   Recipe_Ingredients.RecipeID)
INNER JOIN Ingredients
ON Ingredients.IngredientID =
   Recipe_Ingredients.IngredientID)
INNER JOIN Measurements
ON Measurements.MeasureAmountID =
   Recipe_Ingredients.MeasureAmountID
ORDER BY RecipeTitle, RecipeSeqNo
```

In truth, you can substitute an entire JOIN of two tables anywhere you might otherwise place just a table name. In Figure 9-9, we implied that you must first join the first table with the second table and then join that result with the third table. You could also join the second and third tables first (as long as the third table is, in fact, related to the second table and not the first one) and then perform the final join with the first table. Figure 9-10 on the next page shows you this alternate method.

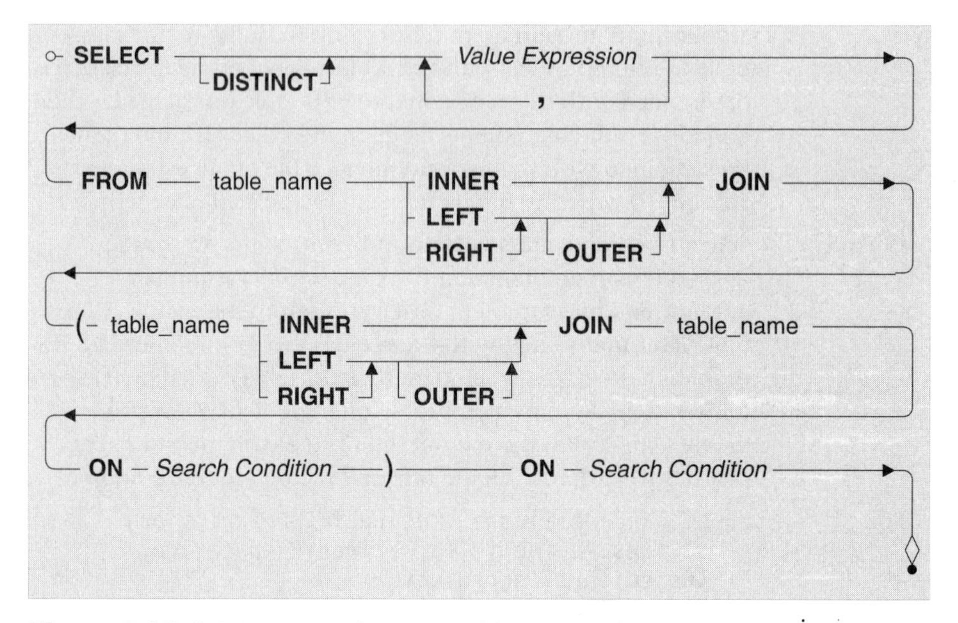

Figure 9-10 *Joining more than two tables in an alternate sequence.*

To solve the request we just showed you using five tables, we could have also stated the SQL as follows.

```
SQL       SELECT Recipe_Classes.RecipeClassDescription,
             Recipes.RecipeTitle, Recipes.Preparation,
             Ingredients.IngredientName,
             Recipe_Ingredients.RecipeSeqNo,
             Recipe_Ingredients.Amount,
             Measurements.MeasurementDescription
          FROM Recipe_Classes
          LEFT OUTER JOIN
          (((Recipes INNER JOIN Recipe_Ingredients
          ON Recipes.RecipeID = Recipe_Ingredients.RecipeID)
          INNER JOIN Ingredients
          ON Ingredients.IngredientID =
             Recipe_Ingredients.IngredientID)
          INNER JOIN Measurements
          ON Measurements.MeasureAmountID =
             Recipe_Ingredients.MeasureAmountID)
          ON Recipe_Classes.RecipeClassID =
             Recipes.RecipeClassID
          ORDER BY RecipeTitle, RecipeSeqNo
```

Remember that the optimizers in some database systems are sensitive to the sequence of the JOIN definitions. If your query with many JOINs is taking a long time to execute on a large database, it may run faster if you change the sequence of JOINs in your SQL statement.

You may have noticed that we used only one OUTER JOIN in the previous multiple-join examples. You're probably wondering whether it's possible or even makes sense to use more than one OUTER JOIN in a complex JOIN. Let's assume that not only are there some Recipe_Classes that don't have matching Recipes rows but also there are recipes that don't have any ingredients defined yet. In the previous example, you won't see any rows from the Recipes table that do not have any matching rows in the Recipe_Ingredients table because the INNER JOIN eliminates them. Let's ask for all recipes as well.

> *"I need all of the recipe types, and then all of the recipe names, preparations, and instructions, and then any matching ingredient names, ingredient step number, ingredient quantities, and ingredient measurements from my Recipes database, sorted in step number sequence."*

Translation: Select the recipe class description, recipe title, preparation instructions, ingredient name, recipe sequence number, amount, and measurement description from the recipe classes table left outer joined with the recipes table on recipe class ID, then left outer joined with the recipe ingredients table on recipe ID, then joined with the ingredients table on ingredient ID, and then finally joined with the measurements table on measurement amount ID, order by recipe title and recipe sequence number

Clean Up: Select ~~the~~ recipe class description, recipe title, preparation ~~instructions~~, ingredient name, recipe sequence number, amount, ~~and~~ measurement description from ~~the~~ recipe classes ~~table~~ left outer join~~ed with the~~ recipes ~~table~~ on recipe class ID~~, then~~ left outer join~~ed with the~~ recipe ingredients ~~table~~ on recipe ID~~, then~~ join~~ed with the~~ ingredients ~~table~~ on ingredient ID~~, and then finally~~ join~~ed with the~~ measurements ~~table~~ on measurement amount ID~~,~~ order by recipe title ~~and~~ recipe sequence number

SQL:

```
SELECT Recipe_Classes.RecipeClassDescription,
   Recipes.RecipeTitle, Recipes.Preparation,
   Ingredients.IngredientName,
   Recipe_Ingredients.RecipeSeqNo,
   Recipe_Ingredients.Amount,
   Measurements.MeasurementDescription
FROM (((Recipe_Classes
LEFT OUTER JOIN Recipes
ON Recipe_Classes.RecipeClassID =
   Recipes.RecipeClassID)
```

(continued)

```
LEFT OUTER JOIN Recipe_Ingredients
ON Recipes.RecipeID =
   Recipe_Ingredients.RecipeID)
INNER JOIN Ingredients
ON Ingredients.IngredientID =
   Recipe_Ingredients.IngredientID)
INNER JOIN Measurements
ON Measurements.MeasureAmountID =
   Recipe_Ingredients.MeasureAmountID
ORDER BY RecipeTitle, RecipeSeqNo
```

Be careful! This sort of multiple OUTER JOIN works as expected only if you're following a path of one-to-many relationships. Let's look at the relationship between Recipe_Classes, Recipes, and Recipe_Ingredients again, as shown in Figure 9-11.

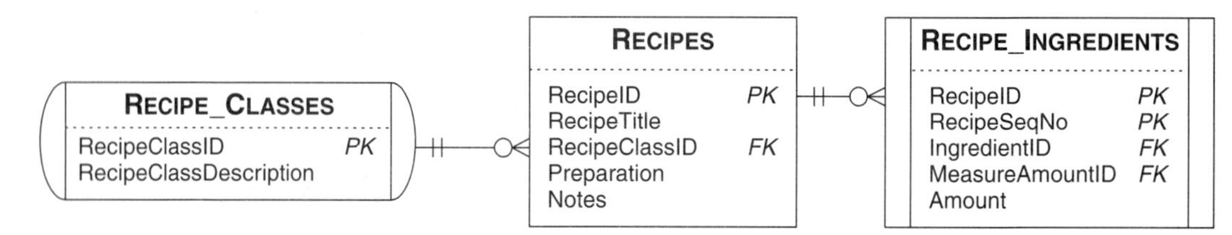

Figure 9-11 *The relationships between Recipe_Classes, Recipes, and Recipe_Ingredients tables.*

You may see a one-to-many relationship sometimes called a "parent-child" relationship. Each "parent" row (on the one side of the relationship) may have zero or more "children" rows (on the many side of the relationship). Unless you have "orphaned" rows on the many side (for example, a row in Recipes that has a Null in its RecipeClassID column), *every* row in the "child" table should have a matching row in the "parent" table. So it makes sense to say Recipe_Classes LEFT JOIN Recipes to pick up any "parent" rows in Recipe_Classes that don't have any "children" yet in Recipes. Recipe_Classes RIGHT JOIN Recipes should (barring any "orphaned" rows) give you the same result as an INNER JOIN.

Likewise, it makes sense to ask for Recipes LEFT JOIN Recipe_Ingredients because you may have some recipes for which no ingredients have yet been entered. Recipes RIGHT JOIN Recipe_Ingredients doesn't work because the linking column (RecipeID) in Recipe_Ingredients is also part of that table's Primary Key; therefore, you are guaranteed to have no "orphan" rows in Recipe_Ingredients because no column in a Primary Key can contain a Null value.

Now, let's take it one step further and ask for all ingredients, including those not yet included in any recipes. First, take a close look at the relationships between the tables, including the Ingredients table, as shown in Figure 9-12.

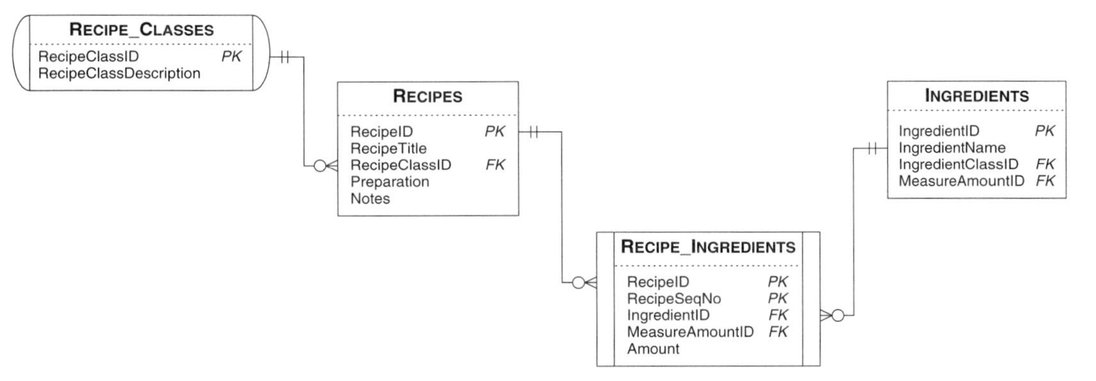

Figure 9-12 *The relationships between Recipe_Classes, Recipes, Recipe_Ingredients, and Ingredients tables.*

Let's try this request. (Caution: There's a trap here!)

"I need all the recipe types, and then all the recipe names, preparations, and instructions, and then any matching ingredient step numbers, ingredient quantities, and ingredient measurements, and finally all ingredient names from my Recipes database sorted in step number sequence."

Translation: Select the recipe class description, recipe title, preparation instructions, ingredient name, recipe sequence number, amount, and measurement description from the recipe classes table left outer joined with the recipes table on recipe class ID, then left outer joined with the recipe ingredients table on recipe ID, then joined with the measurements table on measurement amount ID, and then finally right outer joined with the ingredients table on ingredient ID, order by recipe title and recipe sequence number

Clean Up: Select ~~the~~ recipe class description, recipe title, preparation ~~instructions~~, ingredient name, recipe sequence number, amount, ~~and~~ measurement description from ~~the~~ recipe classes ~~table~~ left outer join~~ed with the~~ recipes ~~table~~ on recipe class ID, then left outer joined with the recipe ingredients ~~table~~ on recipe ID~~, then~~ join~~ed with the~~ measurements ~~table~~ on measurement amount ID~~, and then finally~~ right outer join~~ed~~

~~with the~~ ingredients ~~table~~ on ingredient ID, order by recipe title ~~and~~ recipe sequence number

SQL

```
SELECT Recipe_Classes.RecipeClassDescription,
   Recipes.RecipeTitle, Recipes.Preparation,
   Ingredients.IngredientName,
   Recipe_Ingredients.RecipeSeqNo,
   Recipe_Ingredients.Amount,
   Measurements.MeasurementDescription
FROM (((Recipe_Classes
LEFT OUTER JOIN Recipes
ON Recipe_Classes.RecipeClassID =
   Recipes.RecipeClassID)
LEFT OUTER JOIN Recipe_Ingredients
ON Recipes.RecipeID =
   Recipe_Ingredients.RecipeID)
INNER JOIN Measurements
ON Measurements.MeasureAmountID =
   Recipe_Ingredients.MeasureAmountID)
RIGHT OUTER JOIN Ingredients
ON Ingredients.IngredientID =
   Recipe_Ingredients.IngredientID
ORDER BY RecipeTitle, RecipeSeqNo
```

Do you think this will work? Actually, the answer is a resounding NO! Most database systems analyze the entire FROM clause and then try to determine the most efficient way to assemble the table links. Let's assume, however, that the database decides to fully honor how we've grouped the JOINs within parentheses. This means that the database system will work from the innermost JOIN first (Recipe_Classes joined with Recipes) and then work outward.

Because some rows in Recipe_Classes may not have any matching rows in Recipes, this first JOIN returns rows that have a Null value in RecipeID. Looking back at Figure 9-12, you can see that there's a one-to-many relationship between Recipe_Classes and Recipes. Unless some recipes exist that haven't been assigned a Recipe_Class, we should get *all* the rows from the Recipes table anyway! The next JOIN with the Recipe_Ingredients table also asks for a LEFT OUTER JOIN. We want all the rows, regardless of any Null values, from the previous JOIN (of Recipe_Classes with Recipes) and any matching rows in Recipe_Ingredients. Again, because some rows in Recipe_Classes may not have matching rows in Recipes or some rows in Recipes may not have Recipe_Ingredients, several of the rows may have a Null in the IngredientID column from the Recipe_Ingredients table. What we're doing with both

JOINs is "walking down" the one-to-many relationships from Recipe_Classes to Recipes and then from Recipes to Recipe_Ingredients. So far, so good. (By the way, the final INNER JOIN with Measurements is inconsequential—we know that all Ingredients have a valid MeasureAmountID.)

Now the trouble starts. The final RIGHT OUTER JOIN asks for all the rows from Ingredients and *any matching* rows from the result of the previous JOINs. Remember from Chapter 5 that a Null is a very special value; it cannot ever be equal to any other value, not even another Null. When we ask for *all* the rows in Ingredients, the IngredientID in all these rows has a non-Null value. None of the rows from the previous JOIN that have a Null in IngredientID will match at all, so the final JOIN throws them away! You will see any ingredient that isn't used yet in any recipe, but you won't see recipe classes that have no recipes or recipes that have no ingredients.

If your database system decides to solve the query by performing the JOINs in a different order, you may see recipe classes that have no recipes and recipes that have no ingredients, but you won't see ingredients not yet used in any recipe because of the Null matching problem. Some database systems may recognize this logic problem and refuse to solve your query at all—you'll see something like an "ambiguous OUTER JOINs" error message. The problem we're now experiencing results from trying to "walk back up" a many-to-one relationship with an OUTER JOIN going in the other direction. Walking down the hill is easy, but walking back up the other side requires special tools. What's the solution to this problem? Read on to the next section to find out!

The FULL OUTER JOIN

A FULL OUTER JOIN is neither "left" nor "right"—it's both! It includes *all* the rows from both of the tables or Result Sets participating in the JOIN. When no matching rows exist for rows on the "left" side of the JOIN, you see Null values from the Result Set on the "right." Conversely, when no matching rows exist for rows on the "right" side of the JOIN, you see Null values from the Result Set on the "left."

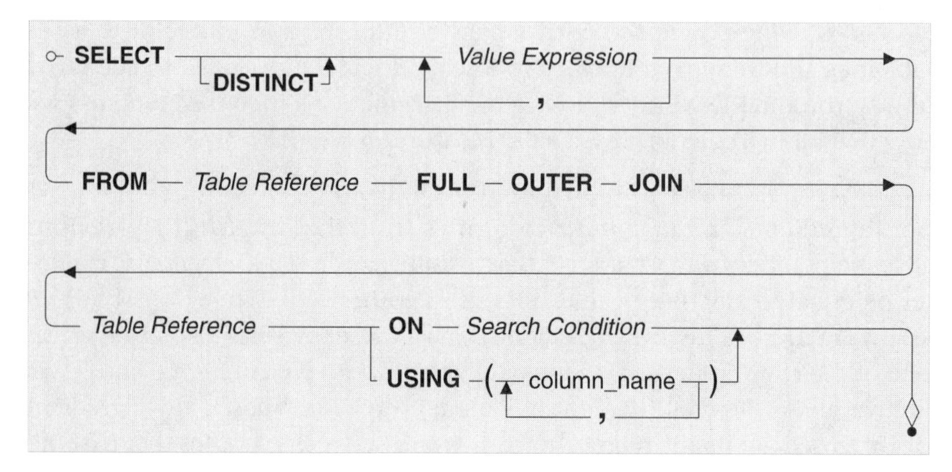

Figure 9-13 *A FULL OUTER JOIN.*

Syntax

Now that you've been working with JOINs for a bit, the syntax for a FULL OUTER JOIN should be pretty obvious. You can study the syntax diagram for a FULL OUTER JOIN in Figure 9-13.

To simplify things, we're now using the term *Table Reference* in place of a table name, SELECT Statement, or the result of another JOIN. Let's take another look at the problem we introduced at the end of the previous section. We can now solve it properly using a FULL OUTER JOIN.

"I need all of the recipe types, and then all of the recipe names, preparations, and instructions, and then any matching ingredient step numbers, ingredient quantities, and ingredient measurements, and finally all ingredient names from my Recipes database sorted in step number sequence."

Translation Select the recipe class description, recipe title, preparation instructions, ingredient name, recipe sequence number, amount, and measurement description from the recipe classes table full outer joined with the recipes table on recipe class ID, then left outer joined with the recipe ingredients table on recipe ID, then joined with the measurements table on measurement amount ID, and then finally full outer joined with the ingredients table on ingredient ID, order by recipe title and recipe sequence number

Clean Up: Select ~~the~~ recipe class description, recipe title, preparation ~~instructions~~, ingredient name, recipe sequence number, amount, ~~and~~ measurement description from ~~the~~ recipe classes ~~table~~ full outer join~~ed with the~~ recipes ~~table~~ on recipe class ID, then left outer join~~ed with the~~ recipe ingredients ~~table~~ on recipe ID~~, then~~ join~~ed with the~~ measurements ~~table~~ on measurement amount ID~~, and then finally~~ full outer join~~ed with the~~ ingredients ~~table~~ on ingredient ID, order by recipe title ~~and~~ recipe sequence number

SQL

```
SELECT Recipe_Classes.RecipeClassDescription,
   Recipes.RecipeTitle, Recipes.Preparation,
   Ingredients.IngredientName,
   Recipe_Ingredients.RecipeSeqNo,
   Recipe_Ingredients.Amount,
   Measurements.MeasurementDescription
FROM Recipe_Classes
FULL OUTER JOIN (((Recipes
LEFT OUTER JOIN Recipe_Ingredients
ON Recipes.RecipeID =
   Recipe_Ingredients.RecipeID)
INNER JOIN Measurements
ON Measurements.MeasureAmountID =
   Recipe_Ingredients.MeasureAmountID)
FULL OUTER JOIN Ingredients
ON Ingredients.IngredientID =
   Recipe_Ingredients.IngredientID)
ON Recipe_Classes.RecipeClassID =
   Recipes.RecipeClassID
ORDER BY RecipeTitle, RecipeSeqNo
```

The first and last JOINs now ask for *all* rows from both sides of the JOIN, so the problem with Nulls not matching is solved. You should now see not only recipe classes for which there are no recipes, and recipes for which there are no ingredients, but also ingredients that haven't been used in a recipe yet. You might get away with using a LEFT OUTER JOIN for the first JOIN, but because you can't predict in advance how your database system decides to nest the JOINs, you should ask for a FULL OUTER JOIN on both ends to ensure the right answer.

> ❖ **Note** As you might expect, database systems that do not support the SQL Standard syntax for LEFT OUTER JOIN or RIGHT OUTER JOIN also have a special syntax for FULL OUTER JOIN. You must consult your database documentation to learn the specific non-standard syntax that your database requires to define the OUTER JOIN. For example, earlier versions of Microsoft SQL Server support this syntax (notice the asterisks in the WHERE clause).

```
SELECT Recipe_Classes.RecipeClassDescription,
   Recipes.RecipeTitle
FROM Recipe_Classes, Recipes
WHERE Recipe_Classes.RecipeClassID *=* Recipes.RecipeClassID
```

> Products that do not support any FULL OUTER JOIN syntax but do support LEFT or RIGHT OUTER JOIN yield an equivalent result by performing a UNION on a LEFT and RIGHT OUTER JOIN. We'll discuss UNION in more detail in the next chapter. Since the specific syntax for defining a FULL OUTER JOIN via the WHERE clause varies by product, you may have to learn several different syntaxes if you work with multiple non-standard products.

FULL OUTER JOIN on Non-Key Values

Thus far, we have been discussing using OUTER JOINs to link tables or Result Sets on related key values. You can, however, solve some interesting problems by using an OUTER JOIN on non-key values. For example, the previous chapter showed how to find students and staff who have the same first name in the School Scheduling database. Suppose you're interested in listing *all* staff members and *all* students and showing the ones who have the same first name as well. You can do that with a FULL OUTER JOIN.

"Show me all of the students and all of the teachers and list together those who have the same first name."

Translation: Select student full name and staff full name from the students table full outer joined with the staff table on first name

Clean Up: Select student full name ~~and~~ staff full name from ~~the~~ students ~~table~~ full outer join~~ed with the~~ staff ~~table~~ on first name

SQL:

```
SELECT (Students.StudFirstName || ' ' ||
   Students.StudLastName) AS StudFullName,
   (Staff.StfFirstName || ' ' ||
   Staff.StfLastName) AS StfFullName
FROM Students
FULL OUTER JOIN Staff
ON Students.StudFirstName = Staff.StfFirstName
```

UNION JOIN

No discussion of OUTER JOINs would be complete without at least an honorable mention to UNION JOIN. In the SQL Standard, a UNION JOIN is a FULL OUTER JOIN with the matching rows removed. Figure 9-14 shows you the syntax.

As you might expect, not many commercial implementations support a UNION JOIN. Quite frankly, we're hard pressed to think of a good reason why you would want to do a UNION JOIN.

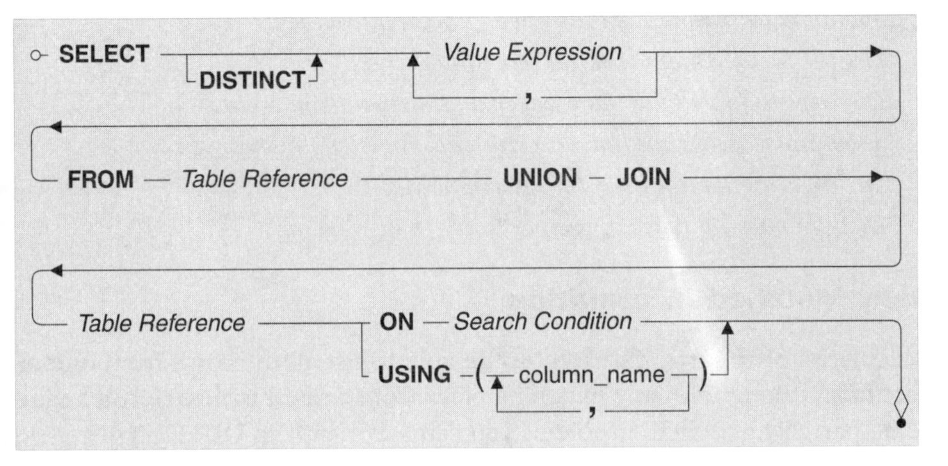

Figure 9-14 *The SQL syntax for a UNION JOIN.*

Uses for OUTER JOINs

Because an OUTER JOIN lets you see not only the matched rows but also the unmatched ones, it's great for finding out which, if any, rows in one table do not have a matching related row in another table. It also helps you find rows that have matches on a few rows, but not on all. In addition, it's useful for creating input to a report where you want to show "all" categories (regardless of whether matching rows exist in other tables) or "all" customers (regardless of whether a customer has placed an order). Following is a small sample of the kinds of requests you can solve with an OUTER JOIN.

Find Missing Values

Sometimes, you just want to find what's "missing." You do so by using an OUTER JOIN with a test for Null. Here's some "missing value" problems you can solve.

"What products have never been ordered?"

"Show me customers who haven't ever ordered a helmet."

"List entertainers who have never been booked."

"Display agents who haven't booked an entertainer."

"Show me tournaments that haven't been played yet."

"List the faculty members not teaching a class."

"Display students who have never withdrawn from a class."

"Show me classes that have no students enrolled."

"List ingredients not used in any recipe yet."

"Display missing types of recipes."

Find Partially Matched Information

Particularly for reports, it's useful to be able to list all the rows from one or more tables along with any matching rows from related tables. Here's a sample of "partially matched" problems you can solve with an OUTER JOIN.

"List all products and the dates for any orders."

"Display all customers and any orders for bicycles."

"Show me all entertainment styles and the customers who prefer those styles."

"List all entertainers and any engagements they have booked."

"List all bowlers and any games they bowled over 160."

"Display all tournaments and any matches that have been played."

"Show me all subject categories and any classes for all subjects."

"List all students and the classes for which they are currently enrolled."

"Display all faculty and the classes they are scheduled to teach."

"List all recipe types, all recipes, and any ingredients involved."

"Show me all ingredients and any recipes they're used in."

Sample Statements

You now know the mechanics of constructing queries using OUTER JOIN and have seen some of the types of requests you can answer with an OUTER JOIN. Let's look at a fairly robust set of samples, all of which use OUTER JOIN. These examples come from each of the sample databases, and they illustrate the use of the OUTER JOIN to find either missing values or partially matched values.

> ❖ **Note** Because many of these examples use complex joins, the optimizer for your database system may choose a different way to solve these queries. For this reason, the first few rows may not exactly match the result you obtain, but the total number of rows should be the same. To simplify the process, we have combined the Translation and Clean Up steps for all the following examples.

Sales Order Database

"What products have never been ordered?"

Translation/Clean Up: Select product number ~~and~~ product name from ~~the~~ products ~~table~~ left outer join~~ed with the~~ order details ~~table~~ on product ID where ~~the~~ order detail order number is null

SQL

```
SELECT Products.ProductNumber,
   Products.ProductName
FROM Products LEFT JOIN Order_Details
ON Products.ProductNumber =
   Order_Details.ProductNumber
WHERE Order_Details.OrderNumber IS NULL
```

Products_Never_Ordered (2 rows)

ProductNumber	ProductName
4	Victoria Pro All Weather Tires
23	Ultra-Pro Rain Jacket

"Display all customers and any orders for bicycles."

Translation 1 — Select customer full name, order date, product name, quantity ordered, and quoted price from the customers table left outer joined with the orders table on customer ID, then joined with the order details table on order number, then joined with the products table on product number, then finally joined with the categories table on category ID where category description is 'Bikes'

Translation 2/ Clean Up — Select customer full name, order date, product name, quantity ordered, ~~and~~ quoted price from ~~the~~ customers ~~table~~ left outer join~~ed with~~ (Select customer ID, order date, product name, quantity ordered, ~~and~~ quoted price from ~~the~~ orders ~~table~~ join~~ed with the~~ order details ~~table~~ on order number~~, then~~ join~~ed with the~~ products ~~table~~ on product number~~, then finally~~ join~~ed with the~~ categories ~~table~~ on category ID where category description ~~is~~ = 'Bikes') on customer ID

> ❖ **Note** Because we're looking for specific orders (bicycles), we split the Translation process into two steps to show that the orders need to be filtered before applying an OUTER JOIN.

SQL

```
SELECT Customers.CustFirstName || ' ' ||
   Customers.CustLastName AS CustFullName,
   RD.OrderDate, RD.ProductName,
   RD.QuantityOrdered, RD.QuotedPrice
FROM Customers
LEFT OUTER JOIN
(SELECT Orders.CustomerID, Orders.OrderDate,
   Products.ProductName,
   Order_Details.QuantityOrdered,
   Order_Details.QuotedPrice
FROM ((Orders
INNER JOIN Order_Details
ON Orders.OrderNumber =
   Order_Details.OrderNumber)
INNER JOIN Products
ON Order_Details.ProductNumber =
   Products.ProductNumber)
INNER JOIN Categories
ON Categories.CategoryID = Products.CategoryID
WHERE Categories.CategoryDescription = 'Bikes')
   AS RD
ON Customers.CustomerID = RD.CustomerID
```

> ❖ **Note** This request is really tricky because you want to list *all* customers OUTER JOINed with only the orders for bikes. If you turn Translation 1 directly into SQL, you won't find any of the customers who have not ordered a bike! An OUTER JOIN from Customers to Orders *will* return all customers and any orders. When you add the filter to select only bike orders, that's all you will get—customers who ordered bikes.
>
> Translation 2 shows you how to do it correctly—create an inner Result Set that returns only orders for bikes, then OUTER JOIN that with Customers to get the final answer.

All_Customers_And_Any_Bike_Orders (913 rows)

CustFullName	OrderDate	ProductName	QuantityOrdered	QuotedPrice
Suzanne Viescas				
Will Thompson	1999-10-22	Trek 9000 Mountain Bike	5	$1,164.00
Will Thompson	1999-11-14	Trek 9000 Mountain Bike	6	$1,164.00
Will Thompson	1999-08-10	Viscount Mountain Bike	2	$635.00
Will Thompson	1999-08-04	Viscount Mountain Bike	5	$615.95
Will Thompson	1999-11-14	Trek 9000 Mountain Bike	4	$1,200.00
Will Thompson	1999-08-10	Trek 9000 Mountain Bike	3	$1,200.00
Will Thompson	1999-11-06	Trek 9000 Mountain Bike	2	$1,200.00
<<more rows here>>				

(Looks like Will Thompson is a really good customer!)

Entertainment Agency Database

"List entertainers who have never been booked."

Translation/ Clean Up: Select entertainer ID ~~and~~ entertainer stage name from ~~the~~ entertainers ~~table~~ left outer join~~ed with the~~ engagements ~~table~~ on entertainer ID where engagement number is null

SQL

```
SELECT Entertainers.EntertainerID,
   Entertainers.EntStageName
FROM Entertainers
LEFT JOIN Engagements
ON Entertainers.EntertainerID =
   Engagements.EntertainerID
WHERE Engagements.EngagementNumber IS NULL
```

Entertainers_Never_Booked

EntertainerID	EntStageName
1009	Katherine Ehrlich

"Show me all musical styles and the customers who prefer those styles."

Translation/ Clean Up: Select style ID, style name, customer ID, customer first name, ~~and~~ customer last name from ~~the~~ musical styles ~~table~~ left outer join~~ed with~~ (~~the~~ musical preferences ~~table~~ inner join~~ed with the~~ customers ~~table~~ on customer ID) on style ID

SQL

```
SELECT Musical_Styles.StyleID,
   Musical_Styles.StyleName,
   Customers.CustomerID,
   Customers.CustFirstName,
   Customers.CustLastName
FROM Musical_Styles
LEFT OUTER JOIN (Musical_Preferences
INNER JOIN Customers
ON Musical_Preferences.CustomerID =
   Customers.CustomerID)
ON Musical_Styles.StyleID =
   Musical_Preferences.StyleID
```

All_Styles_And_Any_Customers (41 rows)

StyleID	StyleName	CustomerID	CustFirstName	CustLastName
1	40s Ballroom Music	10015	David	Nathanson
1	40s Ballroom Music	10011	Joyce	Bonnicksen
2	50s Music			
3	60s Music	10002	Ann	Fuller
4	70s Music	10007	Amelia	Buchanan
5	80s Music	10014	Mark	Rosales
6	Country	10009	Sarah	Thompson
7	Classical	10005	Elizabeth	Hallmark
<<more rows here >>				

(Looks like nobody likes 50s music!)

❖ **Note** We very carefully phrased the FROM clause to influence the database system to first perform the INNER JOIN between Musical_Preferences and Customers, and then OUTER JOIN that with Musical_Styles. If your database tends to process joins from left to right, you might have to state the FROM clause with the INNER JOIN first followed by a RIGHT OUTER JOIN to Musical_Styles. In Microsoft Access, we had to state the INNER JOIN as an embedded SELECT Statement to get it to return the correct answer.

Bowling League Database

"Show me tournaments that haven't been played yet."

Translation/ Clean Up
: Select tourney ID, tourney date, ~~and~~ tourney location from ~~the~~ tournaments ~~table~~ left outer join~~ed with the~~ tourney matches ~~table~~ where match ID is null

SQL

```
SELECT Tournaments.TourneyID,
   Tournaments.TourneyDate,
   Tournaments.TourneyLocation
FROM Tournaments
LEFT JOIN Tourney_Matches
ON Tournaments.TourneyID =
   Tourney_Matches.TourneyID
WHERE Tourney_Matches.MatchID IS NULL
```

Tourney_Not_Yet_Played (6 rows)

TourneyID	TourneyDate	TourneyLocation
15	2001-05-01	Red Rooster Lanes
16	2001-05-08	Thunderbird Lanes
17	2001-05-15	Bolero Lanes
18	2001-05-22	Sports World Lanes
19	2001-05-29	Imperial Lanes
20	2001-06-05	Totem Lanes

"List all bowlers and any games they bowled over 180."

Translation 1
: Select bowler name, tourney date, tourney location, match ID, and raw score from the bowlers table left outer joined with the bowler scores table on bowler ID, then inner joined with the tourney matches table on match ID, then finally inner joined with the tournaments table on tournament ID where raw score in the bowler scores table is greater than 180

Translation 2/ Clean Up
: Select bowler name, tourney date, tourney location, match ID, ~~and~~ raw score from ~~the~~ bowlers ~~table~~ left outer join~~ed with~~ (Select tourney date, tourney location, match ID, bowler ID, ~~and~~ raw score from ~~the~~ bowler scores ~~table~~ inner join~~ed with the~~ tourney matches ~~table~~ on bowler ID~~, then~~ join~~ed with the~~ tournaments ~~table~~ on tournament ID where raw score ~~is greater than~~ > 180) on bowler ID

SQL

```
SELECT Bowlers.BowlerLastName || ', ' ||
   Bowlers.BowlerFirstName AS BowlerName,
   TI.TourneyDate, TI.TourneyLocation,
   TI.MatchID, TI.RawScore
FROM Bowlers
LEFT JOIN
(SELECT Tournaments.TourneyDate,
   Tournaments.TourneyLocation,
   Bowler_Scores.MatchID,
   Bowler_Scores.BowlerID,
   Bowler_Scores.RawScore
FROM (Bowler_Scores
INNER JOIN Tourney_Matches
ON Bowler_Scores.MatchID =
   Tourney_Matches.MatchID)
INNER JOIN Tournaments
ON Tournaments.TourneyID =
   Tourney_Matches.TourneyID
WHERE Bowler_Scores.RawScore>180) AS TI
ON Bowlers.BowlerID = TI.BowlerID
```

All_Bowlers_And_Scores_Over_180 (106 rows)

BowlerName	TourneyDate	TourneyLocation	MatchID	RawScore
Fournier, Barbara				
Fournier, David				
Kennedy, John	1999-07-10	Totem Lanes	21	189
Kennedy, John	1999-09-04	Acapulco Lanes	53	191
Kennedy, John	1999-08-14	Imperial Lanes	41	188
Kennedy, John	1999-06-26	Imperial Lanes	13	182
Kennedy, John	1999-06-05	Red Rooster Lanes	1	191
Kennedy, John	1999-07-24	Red Rooster Lanes	29	182
<<more rows here >>				

❖ **Note** You guessed it! This is another example where you must build the filtered INNER JOIN Result Set first and then OUTER JOIN that with the table from which you want "all" rows.

School Scheduling Database

"List the faculty members not teaching a class."

Translation/ Clean Up: Select staff first name ~~and~~ staff last name from ~~the~~ staff ~~table~~ left join~~ed with the~~ faculty classes ~~table~~ on staff ID where class ID is null

SQL

```
SELECT Staff.StfFirstName, Staff.StfLastName,
FROM Staff
LEFT JOIN Faculty_Classes
ON Staff.StaffID = Faculty_Classes.StaffID
WHERE Faculty_Classes.ClassID IS NULL
```

Staff_Not_Teaching (4 rows)

StfFirstName	StfLastName
Jeffrey	Smith
Tim	Smith
Kathryn	Patterson
Joe	Rosales III

"Display students who have never withdrawn from a class."

Translation/ Clean Up: Select student full name from ~~the~~ students ~~table~~ left outer join~~ed with~~ (Select student ID from ~~the~~ student schedules ~~table~~ inner join~~ed with the~~ student class status ~~table~~ on class status where class status description ~~is~~ = 'withdrew') on student ID where ~~the~~ student_schedules.student ID~~ in the student schedules table~~ is null

SQL

```
SELECT Students.StudLastName || ', ' ||
   Students.StudFirstName AS StudFullName
FROM Students
LEFT OUTER JOIN
(SELECT Student_Schedules.StudentID
FROM Student_Class_Status
INNER JOIN Student_Schedules
ON Student_Class_Status.ClassStatus =
   Student_Schedules.ClassStatus
WHERE Student_Class_Status.ClassStatusDescription =
   'withdrew') AS Withdrew
ON Students.StudentID = Withdrew.StudentID
WHERE Withdrew.StudentID IS NULL
```

Students_Never_Withdrawn (15 rows)

StudFullName
Fuller, Andrew
Leverling, Sarah
Peacock, Carol
Callahan, Sally
Buchanan, Steven
Hallmark, Elizabeth
Kennedy, Sara
Fuller, Mary
<<more rows here>>

"Show me all subject categories and any classes for all subjects."

Translation/ Clean Up: Select category description, subject name, classroom ID, start time, ~~and~~ duration from ~~the~~ categories ~~table~~ left outer join~~ed with the~~ subjects ~~table~~ on category ID~~, then~~ left outer join~~ed with the~~ classes ~~table~~ on subject ID

SQL

```
SELECT Categories.CategoryDescription,
   Subjects.SubjectName, Classes.ClassRoomID,
   Classes.StartTime, Classes.Duration
FROM (Categories
LEFT OUTER JOIN Subjects
ON Categories.CategoryID = Subjects.CategoryID)
LEFT OUTER JOIN Classes
ON Subjects.SubjectID = Classes.SubjectID
```

❖ **Note** We were very careful again to construct the sequence and nesting of joins to be sure we got the answer we expected.

All_Categories_All_Subjects_Any_Classes (82 rows)

CategoryDescription	SubjectName	Classroom	StartTime	Duration
Accounting	Financial Accounting Fundamentals I	3313	9:00	50
Accounting	Financial Accounting Fundamentals I	3313	13:00	50
Accounting	Financial Accounting Fundamentals II	3415	8:00	50
Accounting	Fundamentals of Managerial Accounting	3415	10:00	50
Accounting	Intermediate Accounting	3315	11:00	50
Accounting	Business Tax Accounting	3313	14:00	50
Art	Introduction to Art	1231	10:00	50
Art	Design	1619	15:30	110
<<more rows here >>				

Further down in the Result Set, you'll find no classes scheduled for Developing a Business Plan, Computer Programming, and American Government. You'll also find no subjects scheduled for categories Psychology, French, or German.

Recipes Database

"List ingredients not used in any recipe yet."

Translation/ Clean Up — Select ingredient name from ~~the~~ ingredients ~~table~~ left outer join~~ed with the~~ recipe ingredients ~~table~~ on ingredient ID where recipe ID is null

SQL

```
SELECT Ingredients.IngredientName
FROM Ingredients
LEFT OUTER JOIN Recipe_Ingredients
ON Ingredients.IngredientID =
   Recipe_Ingredients.IngredientID
WHERE Recipe_Ingredients.RecipeID IS NULL
```

Ingredients_Not_Used
(20 rows)

IngredientName
Halibut
Chicken, Fryer
Bacon
Iceberg Lettuce
Butterhead Lettuce
Scallop
Vinegar
Red Wine
<<more rows here >>

"I need all the recipe types, and then all the recipe names, and then any matching ingredient step numbers, ingredient quantities, and ingredient measurements, and finally all ingredient names from my Recipes database."

Translation/Clean up: Select ~~the~~ recipe class description, recipe title, ingredient name, recipe sequence number, amount, ~~and~~ measurement description from ~~the~~ recipe classes ~~table~~ full outer join~~ed with the~~ recipes table on recipe class ID~~, then~~ left outer join~~ed with the~~ recipe ingredients ~~table~~ on recipe ID~~, then~~ join~~ed with the~~ measurements ~~table~~ on measurement amount ID~~, and then finally~~ full outer join~~ed with the~~ ingredients ~~table~~ on ingredient ID

SQL

```
SELECT Recipe_Classes.RecipeClassDescription,
   Recipes.RecipeTitle,
   Ingredients.IngredientName,
   Recipe_Ingredients.RecipeSeqNo,
   Recipe_Ingredients.Amount,
   Measurements.MeasurementDescription
FROM Recipe_Classes
FULL OUTER JOIN
   (((Recipes
LEFT OUTER JOIN Recipe_Ingredients
ON Recipes.RecipeID =
   Recipe_Ingredients.RecipeID)
INNER JOIN Measurements
ON Measurements.MeasureAmountID =
   Recipe_Ingredients.MeasureAmountID)
FULL OUTER JOIN Ingredients
ON Ingredients.IngredientID =
   Recipe_Ingredients.IngredientID)
ON Recipe_Classes.RecipeClassID =
   Recipes.RecipeClassID
```

❖ **Note** The above sample is a request you saw us solve in the section on FULL OUTER JOIN. We decided to include it here so that you can see the actual result. You won't find this query saved in the Microsoft Access version of the sample database because Microsoft Access does not support a FULL OUTER JOIN.

All_Recipe_Classes_All_Recipes (109 rows)

RecipeClass Description	RecipeTitle	Ingredient Name	RecipeSeq No	Amount	Measurement Description
Main course	Irish Stew	Beef	1	1	Pound
Main course	Irish Stew	Onion	2	2	Whole
Main course	Irish Stew	Potato	3	4	Whole
Main course	Irish Stew	Carrot	4	6	Whole
Main course	Irish Stew	Water	5	4	Quarts
Main course	Irish Stew	Guinness beer	6	12	Ounce
Hors d'oeuvres	Salsa Buena	Jalapeño	1	6	Whole
Hors d'oeuvres	Salsa Buena	Tomato	2	2	Whole
<<more rows here >>					

SUMMARY

In this chapter, we led you through the world of OUTER JOINs. We began by defining an OUTER JOIN and comparing it to the INNER JOIN you learned about in Chapter 8.

We next explained how to construct a LEFT or RIGHT OUTER JOIN, beginning with simple examples using two tables, then progressing on to embedding SELECT Statements and constructing statements using multiple JOINs. We showed how an OUTER JOIN combined with a Null test is equivalent to the DIFFERENCE operation we covered in Chapter 7. We also discussed some of the difficulties you may encounter when constructing statements using multiple OUTER JOINs. We closed the discussion of the LEFT and RIGHT OUTER JOIN with a problem requiring multiple OUTER JOINs that can't be solved with only LEFT or RIGHT.

In our discussion of FULL OUTER JOIN, we showed how you may need to use this type of join in combination with other INNER and OUTER JOINs to get the correct answer. We also briefly explained a variant of the FULL OUTER JOIN—the UNION JOIN.

We explained how OUTER JOINs are useful and listed a variety of requests that you can solve using OUTER JOINs. The rest of the chapter shows nearly a dozen examples of how to use OUTER JOIN. We provided several examples for each of the sample databases and showed you the logic behind constructing the solution statement for each request.

The following section presents a number of requests that you can work out on your own.

Problems for You to Solve

Below, we show you the request statement and the name of the solution query in the sample databases. If you want some practice, you can work out the SQL you need for each request and then check your answer with the query we saved in the samples. Don't worry if your syntax doesn't exactly match the syntax of the queries we saved—as long as your Result Set is the same.

Sales Order Database

1. *"Show me customers who haven't ever ordered a helmet."*
   (Hint: This is another request where you must first build an INNER JOIN to find all orders containing helmets and then do an OUTER JOIN with Customers.)
   You can find the solution in Customers_No_Helmets (2 rows).
2. *"Display customers who have no sales rep (employees) in the same zip code."*
   You can find the solution in Customers_No_Rep_Same_Zip (20 rows).
3. *"List all products and the dates for any orders."*
   You can find the solution in All_Products_Any_Order_Dates (2,682 rows).

Entertainment Agency Database

1. *"Display agents who haven't booked an entertainer."*
   You can find the solution in Agents_No_Contracts (1 row).
2. *"List customers with no bookings."*
   You can find the solution in Customers_No_Bookings (2 rows).
3. *"List all entertainers and any engagements they have booked."*
   You can find the solution in All_Entertainers_And_Any_Engagements (112 rows).

Bowling League Database

1. *"Display matches with no game data."*
   You can find the solution in Matches_Not_Played_Yet (1 row).

2. *"Display all tournaments and any matches that have been played."*
   You can find the solution in All_Tourneys_Match_Results (174 rows).

School Scheduling Database

1. *"Show me classes that have no students enrolled."*
   (Hint: You need only "enrolled" rows from Student_Classes, not "completed" or "withdrew.")
   You can find the solution in Classes_No_Students_Enrolled (63 rows).
2. *"Display subjects with no faculty assigned."*
   You can find the solution in Subjects_No_Faculty (1 row).
3. *"List students not currently enrolled in any classes."*
   (Hint: You need to find which students have an "enrolled" class status in student schedules and then find the students who are not in this set.)
   You can find the solution in Students_Not_Currently_Enrolled (2 rows).
4. *"Display all faculty and the classes they are scheduled to teach."*
   You can find the solution in All_Faculty_And_Any_Classes (79 rows).

Recipes Database

1. *"Display missing types of recipes."*
   You can find the solution in Recipe_Classes_No_Recipes (1 row).
2. *"Show me all ingredients and any recipes they're used in."*
   You can find the solution in All_Ingredients_Any_Recipes (108 rows).

10

UNIONs

"I beseech those whose piety will permit them reverently to petition, that they will pray for this union."
—Sam Houston, *Texas hero*

Topics Covered in This Chapter

What Is a UNION?

Writing Requests with UNION

Uses for UNION

Sample Statements

Summary

Problems for You to Solve

In Chapter 7, we introduced three fundamental set operations—Intersection, Difference, and Union. Chapter 8 showed how to perform the equivalent of an Intersect operation by linking Result Sets on key values using INNER JOIN. Chapter 9 discussed how to ask for a set difference by using an OUTER JOIN and testing for the Null value. This chapter explains how to do the third operation, a UNION.

What Is a UNION?

A UNION lets you SELECT the rows from two or more similar Result Sets and combine them into a single Result Set. Notice that we said "rows," not "columns." In Chapters 8 and 9, you learned how to bring together columns from two or more Result Sets using a JOIN. When you ask for a JOIN, the columns from the Result Sets appear side-by-side. For example, if you ask for the

RecipeClassDescription from the Recipe_Classes table and the RecipeTitle from the Recipes table with a JOIN, you get a Result Set that looks like Figure 10-1.

RecipeClassDescription	RecipeTitle
Main course	Irish Stew
Main course	Fettuccini Alfredo
Main course	Pollo Picoso
Main course	Roast Beef
Main course	Huachinango Veracruzana (Red Snapper, Veracruz style)
Main course	Tourtière (French-Canadian Pork Pie)
Main course	Salmon Filets in Parchment Paper
Vegetable	Garlic Green Beans
<<more rows here >>	

Figure 10-1 *Fetching data from two tables using a JOIN.*

Let's first take a quick look at the syntax for a basic UNION as shown in Figure 10-2.

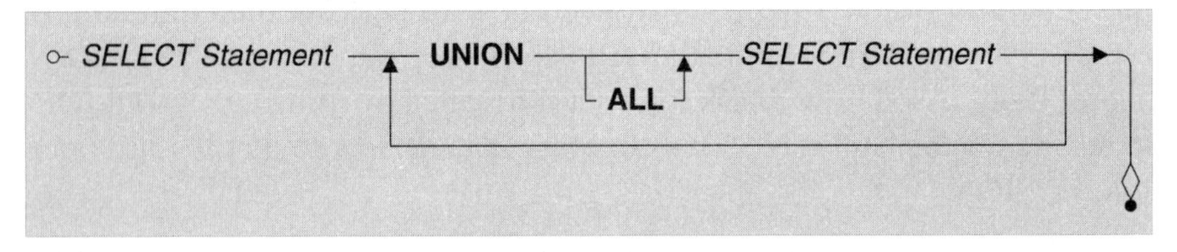

Figure 10-2 *The diagram for a basic UNION Statement.*

A UNION interleaves the rows from one Result Set together with the rows from another Result Set. You define each Result Set by writing a SELECT Statement that can include not only a complex JOIN in the FROM clause but also WHERE, HAVING, and GROUP BY clauses. You then link them with the UNION keyword. If you ask for RecipeClassDescription from the Recipe_Classes table UNION RecipeTitle from the Recipes table, you get an answer that looks like Figure 10-3.

RecipeClassDescription
Asparagus
Coupe Colonel
Dessert
Fettuccini Alfredo
Garlic Green Beans
Hors d'oeuvres
Huachinango Veracruzana (Red Snapper, Veracruz style)
Irish Stew
<<more rows here >>

Figure 10-3 *Fetching data from two tables using a UNION.*

Notice that we get only one column in the Result Set. The name of the column is inherited from the column in the first table we chose to include in the SELECT Expression, but it includes both RecipeTitle information (Asparagus) and RecipeClassDescriptions (Dessert). Instead of appearing side-by-side, the data from the two columns is interleaved vertically.

If you studied the diagram in Figure 10-2, you're probably wondering what the optional keyword ALL is about. When you leave out that keyword, your database system eliminates any rows that have duplicate values. For example, if there's a RecipeClassDescription of Dessert and a RecipeTitle of Dessert, you get only one Dessert row in the final Result Set. Conversely, when you include the ALL keyword, no duplicate rows are removed.

To perform a UNION, the two Result Sets must meet certain requirements. First, each of the two SELECT Statements that you're linking with a UNION must have the same number of output columns specified after the SELECT keyword so that the Result Set will have the same number of columns. Secondly, each corresponding column must be what the SQL Standard calls "comparable."

> ❖ **Note** The full SQL-92 Standard allows you to UNION dissimilar sets; however, most commercial implementations support the basic or "Entry Level" standard we're describing here. You may find that your database system allows you to use UNION in more creative ways.

As discussed in Chapter 6, you should compare only character values with character values, number values with number values, or date/time values with date/time values. Although some database systems allow mixing data types in a comparison, it really doesn't make sense to compare a character value such as "John" to a numeric value like 55. If it makes sense to compare two columns in a WHERE clause, then the columns are "comparable." This is what the Standard means when it requires that a column from one Result Set that you want to UNION with a column from another Result Set must be of a "comparable" data type.

Writing Requests with UNION

In the previous chapters on INNER JOIN and OUTER JOIN, we studied constructing a SELECT Statement using the SELECT, FROM, and WHERE clauses. The focus of those two chapters was on constructing complex JOINs within the FROM clause. To construct a UNION, you now have to graduate to a *SELECT Expression* that links two or more SELECT Statements with the UNION operator. Each SELECT Statement can have as simple or complex a FROM clause as you need to get the job done.

Using Simple SELECT Statements

Let's start simply by creating a UNION of two simple SELECT Statements that use a single table in the FROM clause. Figure 10-4 shows the syntax diagram for a UNION of two simple SELECT Statements.

Unlike when you ask for a JOIN, all of the action happens in the UNION operator that you specify to combine the two SELECT Statements. As mentioned earlier, if you leave out the optional ALL keyword, your database system eliminates any duplicate rows it finds. This means that the Result Set from your request may have fewer rows than the sum of the number of rows returned from each Result Set participating in the UNION. On the other hand, if you

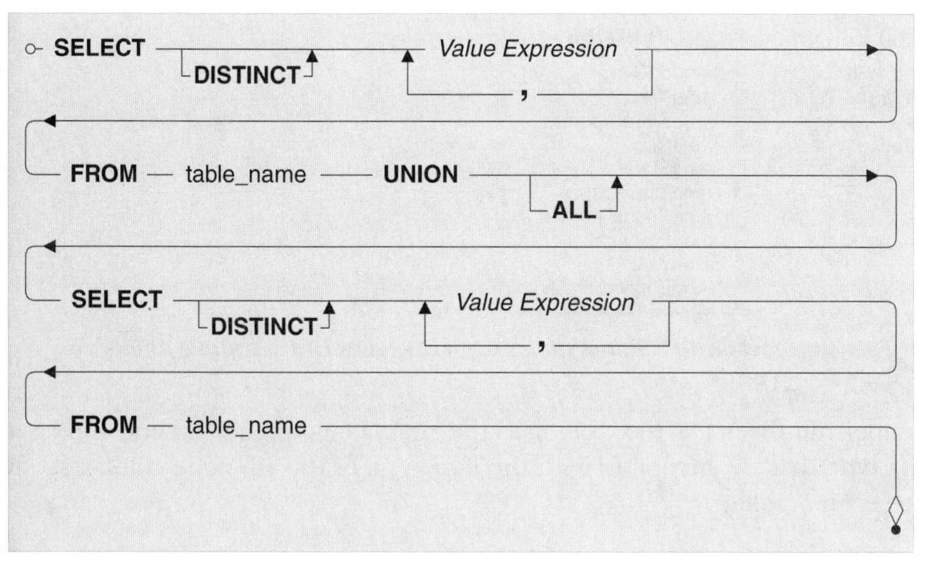

Figure 10-4 *Using a UNION to combine two simple SELECT Statements.*

include the ALL keyword, the number of rows in the Result Set will be equal to the sum of the number of rows in the two participating Result Sets.

> ❖ **Note** The SQL Standard also defines a CORRESPONDING clause that you can place after the UNION keyword to indicate that you want the UNION performed by comparing columns that have the same name in each Result Set. You can also further restrict the comparison set by including a specific list of column names after the CORRESPONDING keyword. We could not find a major commercial implementation of this feature, but you may find it supported in future releases of the product you use.

Let's create a simple UNION—a mailing list for customers and vendors from the Sales Order sample database. Figure 10-5 on the next page shows the two tables needed.

Notice that there's no "natural" relationship between these two tables, but they do both contain columns that have similar meanings and data types. In a mailing list, you need a name, street address, city, state, and zip code. Because all these fields in both tables are comparable character data, we don't need to worry about data types. (Some database designers might make zip code a

CUSTOMERS	
CustomerID	PK
CustFirstName	
CustLastName	
CustStreetAddress	
CustCity	
CustState	
CustZipCode	
CustPhoneNumber	

VENDORS	
VendorID	PK
VendName	
VendStreetAddress	
VendCity	
VendState	
VendZipCode	
VendPhoneNumber	
VendFaxNumber	
VendWebPage	
VendEmailAddress	

Figure 10-5 *The Customers and Vendors tables from the Sales Order sample database.*

number, but that's OK too, as long as the zip code column from one table is a data type that's comparable with the data type of the zip code column from the second table.)

One problem is that the name in the Vendors table is a single column, but there are two name fields in Customers: CustFirstName and CustLastName. In order to come up with the same number of columns from both tables, we need to build an expression on the two columns from Customers to create a single column expression to UNION with the single name column from Vendors. Let's build the query.

> ❖ **Note** Throughout this chapter, we'll be using the "Request/Translation/Clean Up/SQL" technique that we introduced in Chapter 4.

"Build a single mailing list that consists of the name, address, city, state, and zip for customers and the name, address, city, state, and zip for vendors."

Translation — Select customer full name, customer address, customer city, customer state, and customer zip code from the customers table combined with vendor name, vendor address, vendor city, vendor state, and vendor zip code from the vendors table

Clean Up — Select customer full name, customer address, customer city, customer state, ~~and~~ customer zip code from ~~the~~ customers ~~table combined with~~ UNION vendor name, vendor address, vendor city, vendor state, ~~and~~ vendor zip code from ~~the~~ vendors ~~table~~

SQL
```
SELECT Customers.CustLastName || ', ' ||
   Customers.CustFirstName AS MailingName,
   Customers.CustStreetAddress, Customers.CustCity,
   Customers.CustState, Customers.CustZipCode
```

```
FROM Customers
UNION
SELECT Vendors.VendName,
   Vendors.VendStreetAddress, Vendors.VendCity,
   Vendors.VendState, Vendors.VendZipCode
FROM Vendors
```

Notice that each SELECT Statement generates five columns, but we had to use an expression to combine the two name columns in the Customers table into a single column. All the columns from both SELECT Statements are character data, so we have no problem with their being comparable.

You might be wondering: "What are the names of the columns that are output from this query?" Good question! The SQL Standard specifies that when the names of respective columns are the same (for example, the name of the fourth column of the first SELECT Statement is the same as the name of the fourth column of the second SELECT Statement), that's the name of the output column. If the column names are different (as in the example we just constructed), the SQL Standard states that the name "is implementation-dependent and different from the <column name> of any column, other than itself, of any table ... contained in the SQL-statement."

What that means in plain English is your database system decides what names to assign to the output columns. Your system is compliant with the SQL Standard as long as the name doesn't appear in some other column position in one of the Result Sets participating in the UNION. Most commercial database systems default to the names of the columns in the first SELECT Statement. For the previous example, this means that you'll see column names of MailingName, CustStreetAddress, CustCity, CustState, and CustZipCode.

Notice that we did not include the ALL keyword in the UNION. Although it is unlikely that a customer last name and first name will match a vendor name (never mind the address, city, state, and zip), we wanted to avoid duplicate mailing addresses. If you're certain that you won't have any duplicates in two or more UNION sets, you can include the ALL keyword. Using ALL most likely will cause the request to run faster because your database system won't have to do extra work attempting to remove duplicates.

Combining Complex SELECT Statements

As you might imagine, the SELECT Statements you combine with a UNION operator can be as complex as you need to get the job done. The only restriction is that both SELECT Statements must ultimately provide the same number of columns, and the columns in each relative position must be comparable data types.

Suppose you want a list of all the customers and the bikes they ordered combined with all the vendors and the bikes they supply. First, let's identify all the tables we need. Figure 10-6 shows the tables needed to link customers to products.

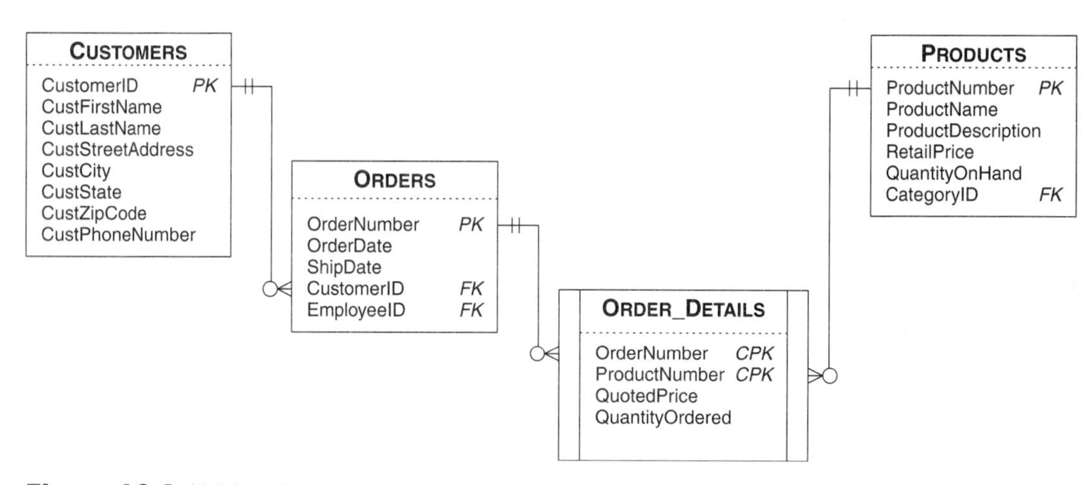

Figure 10-6 *Table relationships to link customers to the products they ordered.*

Looks like we need to JOIN four tables. If we want to find vendors and the products they sell, we need the tables shown in Figure 10-7.

As discussed in Chapter 8, you can nest multiple JOIN clauses to link several tables together to gather the information you need to solve a complex problem. For review, Figure 10-8 shows the nesting for three tables.

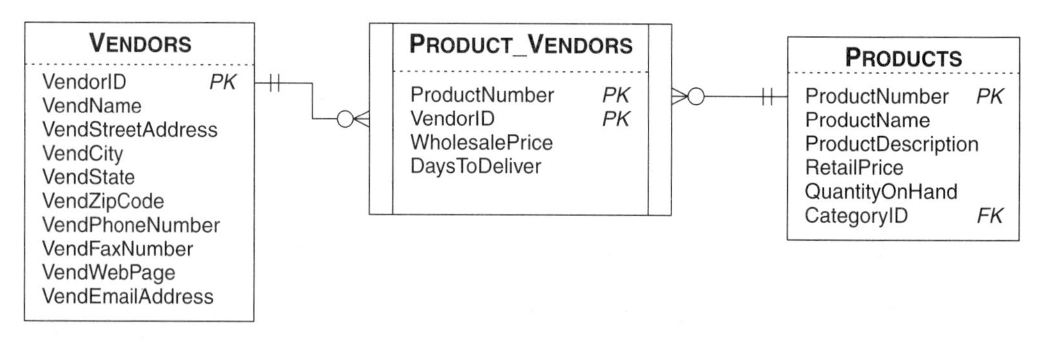

Figure 10-7 *Table relationships to link vendors to the products they sell.*

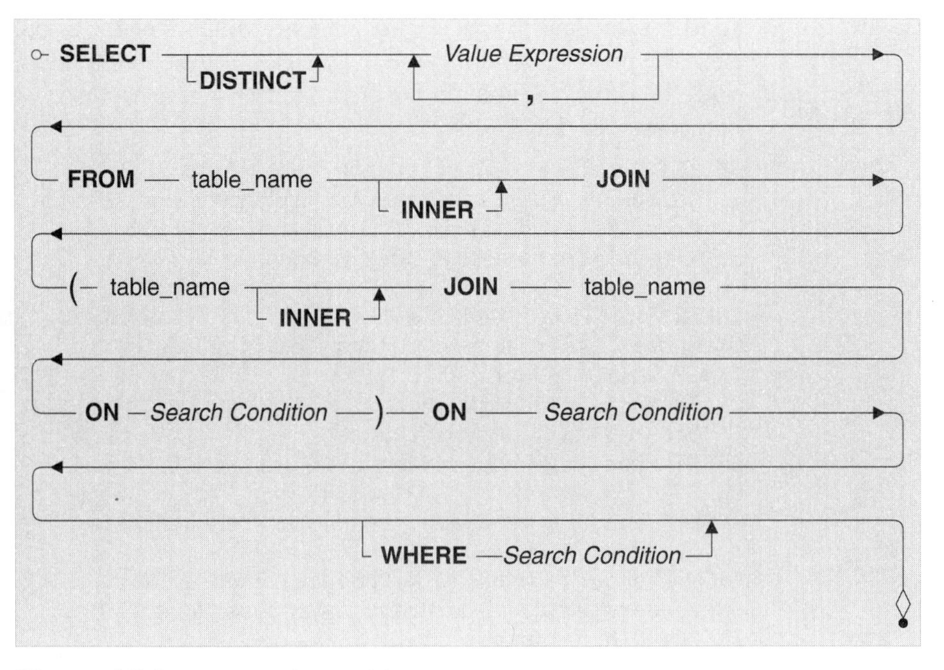

Figure 10-8 *JOINing three tables.*

We now have all the pieces needed to solve the puzzle. We can build a compound INNER JOIN to fetch the customer information, insert a UNION keyword, and then build the compound INNER JOIN for the vendor information.

"List customers and the bikes they ordered combined with vendors and the bikes they sell."

Translation: Select customer full name and product name from the customers table joined with the orders table on customer ID, then joined with the order details table on order number, and then joined with the products table on product number where product name contains 'bike', combined with select vendor name and product name from the vendors table joined with the product vendors table on vendor ID, and then joined with the products table on product number where product name contains 'bike'

Clean Up: Select customer full name ~~and~~ product name from ~~the~~ customers ~~table~~ join~~ed with the~~ orders ~~table~~ on customer ID~~, then~~ join~~ed with the~~ order details ~~table~~ on order number~~, and then~~ join~~ed with the~~ products ~~table~~ on product number where product name ~~contains~~ LIKE '%bike%'~~, combined with~~ UNION select vendor name ~~and~~ product name from ~~the~~ vendors ~~table~~ join~~ed~~ ~~with the~~ product vendors ~~table~~ on vendor ID~~, and then~~ join~~ed~~ ~~with the~~ products ~~table~~ on product number where product name ~~contains~~ LIKE '%bike%'

SQL

```
SELECT Customers.CustLastName || ', ' ||
   Customers.CustFirstName AS FullName,
   Products.ProductName, 'Customer' AS RowID
FROM ((Customers INNER JOIN Orders
ON Customers.CustomerID = Orders.CustomerID)
INNER JOIN Order_Details
ON Orders.OrderNumber = Order_Details.OrderNumber)
INNER JOIN Products
ON Products.ProductNumber =
   Order_Details.ProductNumber
WHERE Products.ProductName LIKE '%bike%'
UNION
SELECT Vendors.VendName, Products.ProductName,
   'Vendor' AS RowID
FROM (Vendors INNER JOIN Product_Vendors
ON Vendors.VendorID = Product_Vendors.VendorID)
INNER JOIN Products
ON Products.ProductNumber =
   Product_Vendors.ProductNumber
WHERE Products.ProductName LIKE '%bike%'
```

Well, that's about the size of the King Ranch, but it gets the job done! Notice that we also threw in a character string literal that we named RowID in both SELECT Statements so that it will be easy to see which rows originate from customers and which ones come from vendors. You might be tempted to insert a DISTINCT keyword in the first SELECT Statement because a really good customer may have ordered a particular bike model more than once. Because we didn't use the ALL keyword on the UNION, the request will eliminate any duplicates anyway. If you add DISTINCT, you may be asking your database system to eliminate duplicates twice!

When you need to build a UNION query, we recommend that you build the separate SELECT Statements first. It's easy then to copy and paste the syntax for each SELECT Statement into a new query, separating each statement with the UNION keyword.

Using UNION More Than Once

So far, we have shown you only how to use a UNION to combine two Result Sets. In truth, you can follow the second SELECT Statement specification with another UNION keyword and another SELECT Statement. Although some implementations have a limitation on the number of Result Sets that can be combined with UNION, in theory you can keep adding UNION SELECT to your heart's content.

Suppose you need to build up a single mailing list from three different tables—Customers, Employees, and Vendors—perhaps to create a combined list for holiday greeting labels. Figure 10-9 shows a diagram of the syntax to build this list.

You can see that you need to create one SELECT Statement to fetch all the names and addresses from the Customers table, UNION that with a SELECT Statement for the same information from the Employees table, and finally UNION that with a SELECT Statement for names and addresses from the Vendors table.

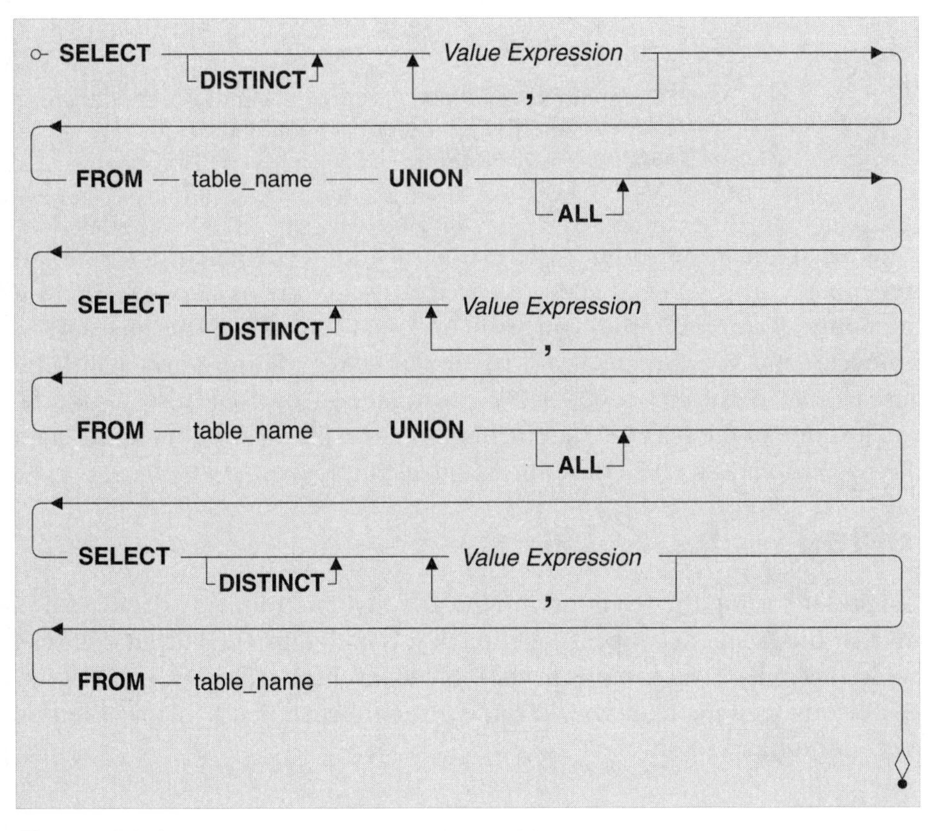

Figure 10-9 *Creating a UNION of three tables.*

"Create a single mailing list for customers, employees, and vendors."

Translation/ Clean Up: Select customer full name, customer street address, customer city, customer state, ~~and~~ customer zip code from ~~the~~ customers ~~table combined with~~ UNION Select employee full name, employee street address, employee city, employee state, ~~and~~ employee zip code from ~~the~~ employees ~~table combined with~~ UNION Select vendor name, vendor street address, vendor city, vendor state, ~~and~~ vendor zip code from ~~the~~ vendors ~~table~~

SQL
```
SELECT Customers.CustFirstName || ' ' ||
   Customers.CustLastName AS CustFullName,
   Customers.CustStreetAddress, Customers.CustCity,
   Customers.CustState, Customers.CustZipCode
FROM Customers
UNION
SELECT Employees.EmpFirstName || ' ' ||
   Employees.EmpLastName AS EmpFullName,
   Employees.EmpStreetAddress, Employees.EmpCity,
   Employees.EmpState, Employees.EmpZipCode
FROM Employees
UNION
SELECT Vendors.VendName, Vendors.VendStreetAddress,
   Vendors.VendCity, Vendors.VendState,
   Vendors.VendZipCode
FROM Vendors
```

Of course, if you want to filter the mailing list for a particular city, state, or range of zip codes, you can add a WHERE clause to any or all of the SELECT Statements. If, for example, you want to create a list for the customers, employees, and vendors only in a particular state, you must add a WHERE clause to *each* of the embedded SELECT Statements. You could also apply a filter to just one of the SELECT Statements—create a list for vendors in the state of Texas combined with all customers and all employees.

Sorting a UNION

What about sorting the result of a UNION? You'll find on many database systems that the Result Set appears as though it is sorted by the output columns from left to right. For example, in the UNION of three tables we just built in the previous section, the rows will appear in sequence first by name, then by street address, and so on.

To keep the postal service happy (and perhaps get a discount for a large mailing), sort your rows by zip code. You can add an ORDER BY clause to do this, but the trick is that this clause must appear at the very end after the last SELECT Statement. The ORDER BY applies to the result of the UNION, not the last SELECT Statement. Figure 10-10 shows you how to do this.

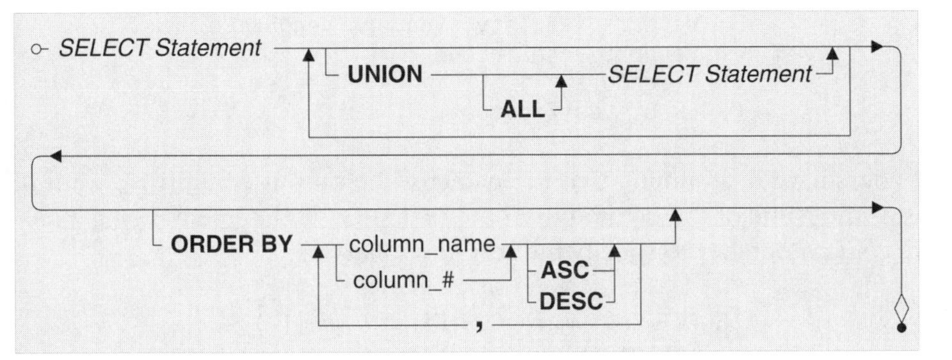

Figure 10-10 *Adding a sorting specification to a UNION query.*

As the diagram shows, you can loop through UNION–SELECT Statement as many times as you like to pick up all the Result Sets that you need to combine, but the ORDER BY clause must appear at the end. You might ask, "What do I use for column_name or column_# in the ORDER BY clause?" Remember that you're sorting the output of all the previous parts of the SELECT Expression. As discussed earlier, the output names of the columns are "implementation-dependent," but most database systems use the column names generated by the first SELECT Statement.

You can also specify the relative column number, starting with 1, as the first output column. In a query that outputs name, street address, city, state, and zip code, you need to specify a column_# of 5 (zip code is the fifth column) to sort by zip.

Let's sort the "mailing list" query using both techniques. Here's the correct syntax sorting by column name.

```
SQL       SELECT Customers.CustFirstName || ' ' ||
             Customers.CustLastName AS CustFullName,
             Customers.CustStreetAddress, Customers.CustCity,
             Customers.CustState, Customers.CustZipCode
          FROM Customers
```

(continued)

```
UNION
SELECT Employees.EmpFirstName || ' ' ||
   Employees.EmpLastName AS EmpFullName,
   Employees.EmpStreetAddress, Employees.EmpCity,
   Employees.EmpState, Employees.EmpZipCode
FROM Employees
UNION
SELECT Vendors.VendName, Vendors.VendStreetAddress,
   Vendors.VendCity, Vendors.VendState,
   Vendors.VendZipCode
FROM Vendors
ORDER BY CustZipCode
```

Of course, we're assuming that the name of the output column we want to sort is the name of the column from the first SELECT Statement. Using a relative column number to specify the sort looks like this.

SQL

```
SELECT Customers.CustFirstName || ' ' ||
   Customers.CustLastName AS CustFullName,
   Customers.CustStreetAddress, Customers.CustCity,
   Customers.CustState, Customers.CustZipCode
FROM Customers
UNION
SELECT Employees.EmpFirstName || ' ' ||
   Employees.EmpLastName AS EmpFullName,
   Employees.EmpStreetAddress, Employees.EmpCity,
   Employees.EmpState, Employees.EmpZipCode
FROM Employees
UNION
SELECT Vendors.VendName, Vendors.VendStreetAddress,
   Vendors.VendCity, Vendors.VendState,
   Vendors.VendZipCode
FROM Vendors
ORDER BY 5
```

Uses for UNION

You probably won't use UNION as much as INNER JOIN and OUTER JOIN. You most likely will use UNION to combine two or more similar Result Sets from different tables. Although you *can* UNION two Result Sets from the same table or set of tables, you usually can solve those sorts of problems with a simple SELECT Statement containing a more complex WHERE clause. We included a couple of examples in the following Sample Problems section and show you the more efficient way to solve the same problem with a WHERE clause instead of a UNION.

Here's just a small sample of the types of problems you can solve with UNION using the sample databases.

"Show me all the customer and employee names and addresses."

"List all the customers who ordered a bicycle combined with all the customers who ordered a helmet." (This is one of those problems that can also be solved with a single SELECT Statement and a complex WHERE clause.)

"Produce a mailing list for customers and vendors."

"List the customers who ordered a bicycle together with the vendors who provide bicycles."

"Create a list that combines agents and entertainers."

"Display a combined list of customers and entertainers."

"Produce a list of customers who like contemporary music together with a list of entertainers who play contemporary music."

"Create a mailing list for students and staff."

"Show me the students who have an average score of 85 or better in Art together with the faculty members who teach Art and have a proficiency rating of 9 or better."

"Find the bowlers who had a raw score of 155 or better at Thunderbird Lanes combined with bowlers who had a raw score of 140 or better at Bolero Lanes." (This is another problem that can also be solved with a single SELECT Statement and a complex WHERE clause.)

"List the tourney matches, team names, and team captains for the teams starting on the odd lane together with the tourney matches, team names, and team captains for the teams starting on the even lane."

"Create an index list of all the recipe titles and ingredients."

"Display a list of all ingredients and their default measurement amounts together with ingredients used in recipes and the measurement amount for each recipe."

Sample Statements

You now know the mechanics of constructing queries using UNION and have seen some of the types of requests you can answer with a UNION. Let's take a look at a fairly robust set of samples using UNION from each of the sample databases.

> ❖ **Note** Because many of these examples use complex joins, the optimizer for your database system may choose a different way to solve these queries. For this reason, the first few rows may not exactly match the result you obtain, but the total number of rows should be the same. To simplify the process, we have combined the Translation and Clean Up steps for all the following examples.

Sales Order Database

"Show me all the customer and employee names and addresses, including any duplicates, sorted by zip code."

Translation/ Clean Up
: Select customer first name, customer last name, customer street address, customer city, customer state, ~~and~~ customer zip code from ~~the~~ customers ~~table combined with~~ UNION all select employee first name, employee last name, employee street address, employee city, employee state, ~~and~~ employee zip code from ~~the~~ employees ~~table~~, order by zip code

SQL

```
SELECT Customers.CustFirstName,
   Customers.CustLastName,
   Customers.CustStreetAddress, Customers.CustCity,
   Customers.CustState, Customers.CustZipCode
FROM Customers
UNION ALL
SELECT Employees.EmpFirstName,
   Employees.EmpLastName,
   Employees.EmpStreetAddress, Employees.EmpCity,
   Employees.EmpState, Employees.EmpZipCode
FROM Employees
ORDER BY CustZipCode
```

Customers_UNION_ALL_Employees (37 rows)

CustFirstName	CustLastName	CustStreetAddress	CustCity	CustState	CustZipCode
Estella	Pundt	2500 Rosales Lane	Dallas	TX	75260
Michael	Davolio	672 Lamont Ave	Houston	TX	77201
Ryan	Ehrlich	455 West Palm Ave	San Antonio	TX	78284
Ryan	Ehrlich	455 West Palm Ave	San Antonio	TX	78284
Margaret	Peacock	667 Red River Road	Austin	TX	78710
Mark	Rosales	323 Advocate Lane	El Paso	TX	79915
Consuelo	Maynez	3445 Cheyenne Road	El Paso	TX	79915
Gregory	Piercy	4501 Wetland Road	Long Beach	CA	90809
<<more rows here>>					

(Notice that Ryan Ehrlich must be both a customer and an employee.)

"List all the customers who ordered a bicycle combined with all the customers who ordered a helmet."

Translation/ Clean Up: Select customer first name ~~and~~ customer last name from ~~the~~ customers ~~table~~ join~~ed with the~~ orders ~~table~~ on customer ID, ~~then~~ join~~ed with the~~ order details ~~table~~ on order number~~, and then~~ join~~ed with the~~ products ~~table~~ on product number where product name ~~contains~~ LIKE '%bike%,' ~~combined with~~ UNION Select ~~unique~~ DISTINCT customer first name ~~and~~ customer last name from ~~the~~ customers ~~table~~ join~~ed with the~~ orders ~~table~~ on customer ID, ~~then~~ join~~ed with the~~ order details ~~table~~ on order number~~, and then~~ join~~ed with the~~ products ~~table~~ on product number where product name ~~contains~~ LIKE '%helmet%'

```
SQL       SELECT Customers.CustFirstName,
             Customers.CustLastName, 'Bike' AS ProdType
          FROM ((Customers INNER JOIN Orders
          ON Customers.CustomerID = Orders.CustomerID)
          INNER JOIN Order_Details
          ON Orders.OrderNumber = Order_Details.OrderNumber)
          INNER JOIN Products
          ON Products.ProductNumber =
             Order_Details.ProductNumber
          WHERE Products.ProductName LIKE '%bike%'
          UNION
          SELECT Customers.CustFirstName,
             Customers.CustLastName, 'Helmet' AS ProdType
          FROM ((Customers INNER JOIN Orders
          ON Customers.CustomerID = Orders.CustomerID)
          INNER JOIN Order_Details
          ON Orders.OrderNumber = Order_Details.OrderNumber)
          INNER JOIN Products
          ON Products.ProductNumber =
             Order_Details.ProductNumber
          WHERE Products.ProductName LIKE '%helmet%'
```

Customer_Order_Bikes_UNION_Customer_Order_Helmets (54 rows)

CustFirstName	CustLastName	ProdType
Alaina	Hallmark	Bike
Alaina	Hallmark	Helmet
Allan	Davis	Bike
Allan	Davis	Helmet
Amelia	Buchanan	Bike
Amelia	Buchanan	Helmet
Andrea	Buchanan	Bike
Andrea	Buchanan	Helmet
<<more rows here >>		

Notice that this is one of those problems that can also be solved with a single SELECT Statement and a slightly more complex WHERE clause. The one advantage of using a UNION is that it's easy to add an artificial "set identifier" column (in this case, the ProdType column) to each Result Set so that you can see which customers came from which Result Set. However, most database systems solve a WHERE clause—even one with complex criteria—much faster than they solve a UNION. Following is the SQL to solve the same problem with a WHERE clause.

```
SQL        SELECT DISTINCT Customers.CustFirstName,
              Customers.CustLastName
           FROM
              ((Customers INNER JOIN Orders
           ON Customers.CustomerID = Orders.CustomerID)
           INNER JOIN Order_Details
           ON Orders.OrderNumber = Order_Details.OrderNumber)
           INNER JOIN Products
           ON Products.ProductNumber =
              Order_Details.ProductNumber
           WHERE Products.ProductName LIKE '%bike%'
           OR Products.ProductName LIKE '%helmet%'
```

Customers_Bikes_Or_Helmets
(27 rows)

CustFirstName	CustLastName
Alaina	Hallmark
Allan	Davis
Amelia	Buchanan
Andrea	Buchanan
Consuelo	Maynez
David	Callahan
David	Smith
Estella	Pundt
<<more rows here >>	

❖ **Note** You can see that you need a DISTINCT keyword to eliminate duplicates when you don't use UNION. Remember that UNION automatically eliminates duplicates unless you specify UNION ALL. You can specify DISTINCT in the UNION examples, but you're asking your database system to do more work than necessary.

Entertainment Database

"Create a list that combines agents and entertainers."

Translation/ Clean Up — Select agent full name from ~~the~~ agents ~~table combined with~~ UNION Select entertainer stage name from ~~the~~ entertainers ~~table~~.

SQL

```
SELECT Agents.AgtLastName || ', ' ||
   Agents.AgtFirstName AS Name, 'Agent' AS Type
FROM Agents
UNION
SELECT Entertainers.EntStageName,
   ‘Entertainer’ AS Type
FROM Entertainers
```

Agents_UNION_Entertainers (21 rows)

Name	Type
Albert Buchanan	Entertainer
Buchanan, Steven	Agent
Carol Peacock Trio	Entertainer
Caroline Coie Cuartet	Entertainer
Coldwater Cattle Company	Entertainer
Country Feeling	Entertainer
Fuller, Mary	Agent
Jazz Persuasion	Entertainer
<<more rows here >>	

School Scheduling Database

"Show me the students who have a grade of 85 or better in Art together with the faculty members who teach Art and have a proficiency rating of 9 or better."

Translation/Clean Up

Select student first name ~~aliased~~ as FirstName, student last name ~~aliased~~ as LastName, ~~and~~ grade ~~aliased~~ as Score from ~~the~~ students ~~table~~ join~~ed with the~~ student schedules ~~table~~ on student ID~~, then~~ join~~ed with the~~ student class status ~~table~~ on class status~~, then~~ join~~ed with the~~ classes ~~table~~ on class ID~~, and then~~ join~~ed with the~~ subjects ~~table~~ on subject ID where class status description ~~is~~ = 'completed' and grade ~~is greater than or equal to~~ >= 85 and category ID ~~is~~ = 'art' ~~combined with~~ UNION Select staff first name, staff last name, ~~and~~ proficiency rating ~~aliased~~ as Score from ~~the~~ staff ~~table~~ join~~ed with the~~ faculty subjects ~~table~~ on staff ID~~, and then~~ join~~ed with the~~ subjects ~~table~~ on subject ID where proficiency rating ~~is greater than~~ > 8 and category ID ~~is~~ = 'ART'

SQL

```
SELECT Students.StudFirstName AS FirstName,
   Students.StudLastName AS LastName,
   Student_Schedules.Grade AS Score,
   'Student' AS Type
FROM (((Students INNER JOIN Student_Schedules
ON Students.StudentID =
   Student_Schedules.StudentID)
INNER JOIN Student_Class_Status
ON Student_Class_Status.ClassStatus =
   Student_Schedules.ClassStatus)
INNER JOIN Classes
ON Classes.ClassID = Student_Schedules.ClassID)
INNER JOIN Subjects
ON Subjects.SubjectID = Classes.SubjectID
WHERE Student_Class_Status.ClassStatusDescription =
   'Completed'
AND Student_Schedules.Grade >= 85
AND Subjects.CategoryID= 'ART'
UNION
```

(continued)

```
SELECT Staff.StfFirstName, Staff.StfLastName,
   Faculty_Subjects.ProficiencyRating AS Score,
   'Faculty' AS Type
FROM (Staff INNER JOIN Faculty_Subjects
ON Staff.StaffID = Faculty_Subjects.StaffID)
INNER JOIN Subjects
ON Subjects.SubjectID = Faculty_Subjects.SubjectID
WHERE Faculty_Subjects.ProficiencyRating > 8
AND Subjects.CategoryID = 'ART
```

Good_Art_Students_And_Faculty (15 rows)

FirstName	LastName	Score	Type
Alaina	Hallmark	10	Faculty
Amelia	Buchanan	10	Faculty
David	Nathanson	87.05	Student
Elizabeth	Hallmark	93.27	Student
James	Leverling	9	Faculty
John	Leverling	9	Faculty
John	Leverling	10	Faculty
Kendra	Bonnicksen	88.27	Student
<<more rows here>>			

Bowling League Database

"List the tourney matches, team names, and team captains for the teams starting on the odd lane together with the tourney matches, team names, and team captains for the teams starting on the even lane."

Translation/Clean Up: Select tourney location, tourney date, match ID, team name, ~~and~~ captain name from ~~the~~ tournaments ~~table~~ join~~ed with the~~ tourney matches ~~table~~ on tourney ID~~, then~~ join~~ed with the~~ teams ~~table~~ on odd lane team ID ~~in the tourney matches table equals~~ = team ID ~~in the teams table, and then~~ join~~ed with the~~ bowlers ~~table~~ on captain ID ~~in the teams table equals~~ = bowler ID ~~in the bowlers table, combined with~~ UNION Select tourney location, tourney date, match ID, team name, ~~and~~

captain name from ~~the~~ tournaments ~~table~~ join~~ed with the~~ tourney matches ~~table~~ on tourney ID~~, then~~ join~~ed with the~~ teams ~~table~~ on even lane team ID ~~in the tourney matches table equals~~ = team ID ~~in the teams table, and then~~ join~~ed with the~~ bowlers ~~table~~ on captain ID ~~in the teams table equals~~ = bowler ID ~~in the bowlers table~~, order by tourney date and match ID

SQL

```
SELECT Tournaments.TourneyLocation,
   Tournaments.TourneyDate,
   Tourney_Matches.MatchID, Teams.TeamName,
   Bowlers.BowlerLastName || ' ' ||
   Bowlers.BowlerFirstName AS Captain,
   'Odd Lane' AS Lane
FROM ((Tournaments INNER JOIN Tourney_Matches
ON Tournaments.TourneyID =
   Tourney_Matches.TourneyID)
INNER JOIN Teams
ON Teams.TeamID =
   Tourney_Matches.OddLaneTeamID)
INNER JOIN Bowlers
ON Bowlers.BowlerID = Teams.CaptainID
UNION
SELECT Tournaments.TourneyLocation,
   Tournaments.TourneyDate,
   Tourney_Matches.MatchID, Teams.TeamName,
   Bowlers.BowlerLastName || ' ' ||
   Bowlers.BowlerFirstName AS Captain,
   'Even Lane' AS Lane
FROM ((Tournaments INNER JOIN Tourney_Matches
ON Tournaments.TourneyID =
   Tourney_Matches.TourneyID)
INNER JOIN Teams
ON Teams.TeamID =
   Tourney_Matches.EvenLaneTeamID)
INNER JOIN Bowlers
ON Bowlers.BowlerID = Teams.CaptainID
ORDER BY 2, 3
```

Notice that the two SELECT Statements are almost identical! The only difference is the first SELECT Statement links Tourney_Matches with Teams on OddLaneTeamID, and the second uses EvenLaneTeamID.

Bowling_Schedule (112 rows)

TourneyLocation	TourneyDate	MatchID	TeamName	Captain	Lane
Red Rooster Lanes	1999-06-05	1	Marlins	Fournier David	Odd Lane
Red Rooster Lanes	1999-06-05	1	Sharks	Patterson Ann	Even Lane
Red Rooster Lanes	1999-06-05	2	Barracudas	Sheskey Richard	Even Lane
Red Rooster Lanes	1999-06-05	2	Terrapins	Morgen-stern Iris	Odd Lane
Red Rooster Lanes	1999-06-05	3	Dolphins	Viescas Suzanne	Odd Lane
Red Rooster Lanes	1999-06-05	3	Orcas	Thomp-son Sarah	Even Lane
Red Rooster Lanes	1999-06-05	4	Manatees	Viescas Michael	Odd Lane
Red Rooster Lanes	1999-06-05	4	Swordfish	Rosales Joe	Even Lane
Thunderbird Lanes	1999-06-12	5	Marlins	Fournier David	Even Lane
Thunderbird Lanes	1999-06-12	5	Terrapins	Morgen-stern Iris	Odd Lane
<<more rows here >>					

Recipes Database

"Create an index list of all the recipe classes, recipe titles, and ingredients."

Translation/ Clean Up: Select recipe class description from ~~the~~ recipe classes ~~table combined with~~ UNION select recipe title from ~~the~~ recipes ~~table combined with~~ UNION select ingredient name from ~~the~~ ingredients ~~table~~.

SQL

```
SELECT Recipe_Classes.RecipeClassDescription
AS IndexName, 'Recipe Class' AS Type
FROM Recipe_Classes
UNION
SELECT Recipes.RecipeTitle, 'Recipe' AS Type
FROM Recipes
UNION
SELECT Ingredients.IngredientName,
   'Ingredient' AS Type
FROM Ingredients
```

Classes_Recipes_Ingredients (101 rows)

IndexName	Type
Asparagus	Ingredient
Asparagus	Recipe
Bacon	Ingredient
Balsamic vinaigrette dressing	Ingredient
Beef	Ingredient
Beef drippings	Ingredient
Bird's custard powder	Ingredient
Black olives	Ingredient
<<more rows here >>	

SUMMARY

We began the chapter by defining UNION and showing you the difference between linking two tables with a JOIN and combining two tables with a UNION.

We next explained how to construct a simple UNION using two SELECT Statements, each of which asked for columns from a single table. We then progressed to combining two complex SELECT Statements that each used a JOIN on multiple tables. Next we showed how to use UNION to combine more than two Result Sets. We wrapped up our discussion of UNION syntax by showing how to sort the result.

We explained how UNION is useful and listed a variety of requests that you can solve using UNION. The Sample Statements section shows you one or two examples of how to use UNION in each of the sample databases, including the logic behind constructing these requests.

The following section presents a number of requests that you can work out on your own.

Problems for You to Solve

Below, we show you the request statement and the name of the solution query in the sample databases. If you want some practice, you can work out the SQL you need for each request and then check your answer with the query we saved in the samples. Don't worry if your syntax doesn't exactly match the syntax of the queries we saved—as long as your Result Set is the same.

Sales Order Database

1. *"List the customers who ordered a helmet together with the vendors who provide helmets."*
   (Hint: This involves creating a UNION of two complex JOINs.)
   You can find the solution in Customer_Helmets_Vendor_Helmets (96 rows).

Entertainment Database

1. *"Display a combined list of customers and entertainers."*
   (Hint: Be careful to create an expression for one of the names so that you have the same number of columns in both SELECT Statements.)
   You can find the solution in Customers_UNION_Entertainers (28 rows).

2. *"Produce a list of customers who like contemporary music together with a list of entertainers who play contemporary music."*
   (Hint: You need to UNION two complex JOINs to solve this one.)
   You can find the solution in Customers_Entertainers_Contemporary (5 rows).

School Scheduling Database

1. *"Create a mailing list for students and staff, sorted by zip code."*
   (Hint: Try using a relative column number for the sort.)
   You can find the solution in Student_Staff_Mailing_List (45 rows).

Bowling League Database

1. *"Find the bowlers who had a raw score of 165 or better at Thunderbird Lanes combined with bowlers who had a raw score of 150 or better at Bolero Lanes."*
   (Hint: This is another of those problems that can also be solved with a single SELECT Statement and a complex WHERE clause.)
   You can find the solution using UNION in Good_Bowlers_TBird_Bolero_UNION (120 rows). You can find the solution using WHERE in Good_Bowlers_TBird_Bolero_WHERE (125 rows).
2. Can you explain why the row counts are different in the above solution queries? (Hint: Try using UNION ALL in the first query.)

Recipes Database

1. *"Display a list of all ingredients and their default measurement amounts together with ingredients used in recipes and the measurement amount for each recipe."*
   (Hint: You need one simple JOIN and one complex JOIN to solve this.)
   You can find the solution in Ingredient_Recipe_Measurements (144 rows).

11

Subqueries

"We can't solve problems by using the same kind of thinking we used when we created them."
—Albert Einstein

Topics Covered in This Chapter

In the previous three chapters, we showed you many ways to work with data from more than one table. All the techniques we've covered to this point have been focused on linking subsets of information—one or more columns and one or more rows from an entire table or a query embedded with the FROM clause or by using the UNION operator. In this chapter, we'll show you effective ways of fetching a single column from a table or query and using it either as a Value Expression in a SELECT clause or a WHERE clause.

There are two significant points you should learn in this chapter.

1. There's always more than one way to solve a particular problem in SQL. In fact, this chapter will show you new ways to solve problems already covered in previous chapters.
2. You can build complex filters that do not rely on the tables in your FROM clause. This is an important concept because using a Subquery in a WHERE

clause is the only way to get the correct number of rows in your answer when you want rows from one table based on the filtered contents from other related tables. We'll explain this in more detail later in the chapter.

> ❖ **Note** This chapter covers advanced concepts and assumes that you've read and thoroughly understood Chapter 7, Thinking in Sets; Chapter 8, INNER JOINs; and Chapter 9, OUTER JOINs.

What Is a Subquery?

Simply put, a *Subquery* is a SELECT Expression that you embed inside one of the clauses of a SELECT Statement to form your final query statement. In this chapter, we'll define more formally a Subquery and show how to use it other than in the FROM clause.

The SQL Standard defines three types of Subqueries:

1. **Row Subquery**—an embedded SELECT Expression that returns more than one column and no more than one row.
2. **Table Subquery**—an embedded SELECT Expression that returns one or more columns, and zero to many rows.
3. **Scalar Subquery**—an embedded SELECT Expression that returns only one column and no more than one row.

Row Subqueries

In Chapter 6, you learned how to filter the rows returned by a query. You did so by building a Comparison Predicate in a WHERE clause that compares the value in a column to a literal, an expression, or another column. To review, a simple query using a single Comparison Predicate might look like the following.

```
SQL       SELECT Customers.CustLastName
          FROM Customers
          WHERE Customers.CustAreaCode > 415
```

The SQL Standard defines a *row value constructor* for use as part of a Search Condition Predicate in a WHERE, HAVING, or ON clause. The bad news is that not many commercial database systems support this syntax. Here's an example of a WHERE clause that uses a row value constructor.

```
SQL         SELECT Customers.CustLastName
            FROM Customers
            WHERE
               (Customers.CustAreaCode, Customers.CustZipCode)
               > (415, '94110')
```

The preceding WHERE clause asks for rows where the combination of CustAreaCode and CustZipCode is greater than the combination of 415 and 94110. It's the same as requesting the following.

```
SQL         SELECT Customers.CustLastName
            FROM Customers
            WHERE (Customers.CustAreaCode > 415)
            OR ((Customers.CustAreaCode = 415)
            AND (Customers.CustZipCode > '94110'))
```

Here's where you could substitute a SELECT Statement that returns a single row of two columns—a Row Subquery—for the second part of the comparison. Most commercial databases support neither a row value constructor nor Row Subqueries. That's all we're going to say about them in this chapter.

Table Subqueries

Wait a minute! Didn't we already show you how to embed a SELECT Expression returning multiple rows and columns inside a FROM clause in the previous three chapters? The answer is Yes—we snuck it in on you! We've already liberally used Table Subqueries in the previous chapters to specify a complex result that we then embedded in the FROM clause of another query. In this chapter, we'll show you how to use a Table Subquery as the source for the list of comparison values for an IN Predicate—something about which you learned the basics in Chapter 6. We'll also teach you a few new Comparison Predicate keywords that are used only with Table Subqueries.

Scalar Subqueries

In this chapter we'll also show how to use a Scalar Subquery anywhere you might otherwise use a Value Expression. A Scalar Subquery lets you fetch a single column or calculated expression from another table that does not have to be in the FROM clause of the main query. You can use the single value fetched by a Scalar Subquery in the list of columns you request in a SELECT clause or as a comparison value in a WHERE clause.

Subqueries as Column Expressions

In Chapter 5, you learned a lot about using expressions to generate calculated columns to be output by your query. We didn't tell you then that you can also use a special type of SELECT Statement—a Subquery—to fetch data from another table, even if the table isn't in your FROM clause.

Syntax

Let's go back to the basics and take a look at a simple form of a SELECT Statement in Figure 11-1.

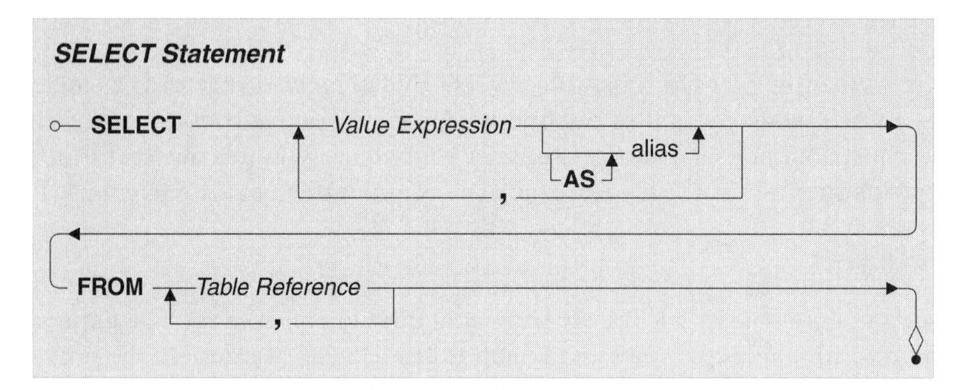

Figure 11-1 *A simple SELECT Statement.*

This looks simple, but it really isn't! In fact, *Value Expression* can be quite complex. Figure 11-2 shows all the options that can constitute a Value Expression.

In Chapter 5, we showed you how to create basic Value Expressions using Literal Values, Column References, and Functions. Notice that *SELECT Expression* now appears on the list. This means that you can embed a Scalar Subquery in the list of expressions immediately following the SELECT keyword. As noted earlier, a Scalar Subquery is a SELECT Expression that returns exactly one column and no more than one row. This makes sense because you're substituting the Subquery where you would normally enter a single column name or expression that results in a single column.

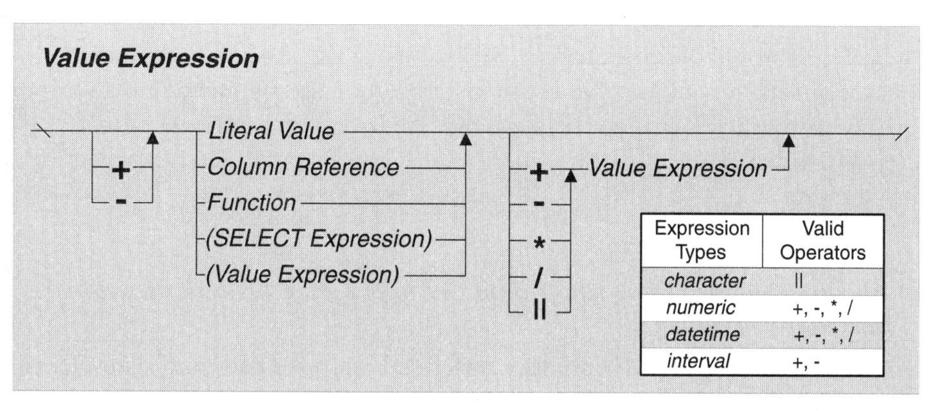

Figure 11-2 *The diagram for a Value Expression.*

You might be wondering at this point "Why is this useful?" A Subquery used in this way lets you "pluck" a single value from some other table or query to include in the output of your query. The table or query that is the source of the data in the FROM clause of the Subquery needn't be referenced at all in the FROM clause of the outer query. In most cases, you will need to add criteria in the WHERE clause of the Subquery to make sure it returns no more than one row. You can even have the criteria in the Subquery reference a value being returned by the outer query to pluck out the data related to the current row.

Let's take a look at some simple examples using just the Customers and Orders tables from the Sales Orders example database. Figure 11-3 shows the relationship between these two tables.

Now, let's build a query that lists all the orders for a particular date and that plucks the related customer last name from the Customers table using a Subquery.

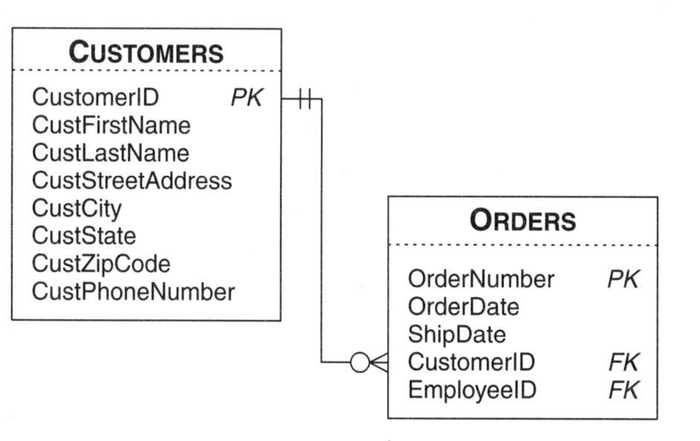

Figure 11-3 *Customers and Orders.*

> ❖ **Note** Throughout this chapter, we'll be using the "Request/Translation/Clean Up/SQL" technique that we introduced in Chapter 4. In addition, we'll include parentheses around the parts that are Subqueries in the Clean Up step and indent the Subqueries where possible to help you see how we are using them.

"Show me all the orders shipped on December 24, 1999 and the related customer last name."

Translation Select order number, order date, shipped date, and also select the related customer last name out of the customers table from the orders table where shipped date is December 24, 1999

Clean Up Select order number, order date, shipped date, ~~and also~~ (select ~~the related~~ customer last name ~~out of the~~ from customers ~~table~~ from ~~the~~ orders ~~table~~) where shipped date ~~is~~ = December 24, 1999

SQL
```
SELECT Orders.OrderNumber, Orders.OrderDate,
   Orders.ShippedDate,
   (SELECT Customers.CustLastName
   FROM Customers
   WHERE Customers.CustomerID =
      Orders.CustomerID)
FROM Orders
WHERE Orders.ShippedDate = '1999-12-24'
```

Notice that we had to restrict the value of the Customer ID in the Subquery to the value of the Customer ID in each row we're fetching from the Orders table; otherwise we'll get *all* the rows in Customers in the Subquery. Remember that this must be a Scalar Subquery, so we must do something to restrict what gets returned to no more than one row.

Those of you who really caught on to the concept of INNER JOIN in Chapter 8 are probably wondering why you would want to solve this problem as just described rather than JOIN Orders to Customers in the FROM clause of the outer query. Actually, right now we're focusing on the *concept* of using a Subquery to create an output column with a very simple example and, in truth, you probably should solve this particular problem with the following query using an INNER JOIN.

```
SQL       SELECT Orders.OrderNumber, Orders.OrderDate,
             Orders.ShippedDate, Customers.CustLastName
          FROM Customers INNER JOIN Orders
          ON Customers.CustomerID = Orders.OrderID
          WHERE Orders.ShippedDate = '1999-12-24'
```

An Introduction to Aggregate Functions—COUNT and MAX

Now that you understand the basic concept of using a Subquery to generate an output column, let's expand your horizons and see how this feature can be really useful. First, we need to give you an overview of a couple of aggregate functions. (We'll cover all the aggregate functions in detail in the next chapter.)

The SQL Standard defines many functions that calculate values in a query. One subclass of functions—aggregate functions—lets you calculate a single value for a group of rows in a Result Set. For example, you can use an aggregate function to count the rows, find the largest or smallest value within the set of rows, or calculate the average or total of some value or expression across the Result Set.

Let's take a look at a couple of these functions and then see how they can be most useful in a Subquery. Figure 11-4 shows the diagram for the COUNT and MAX functions that can generate an output column in a SELECT clause.

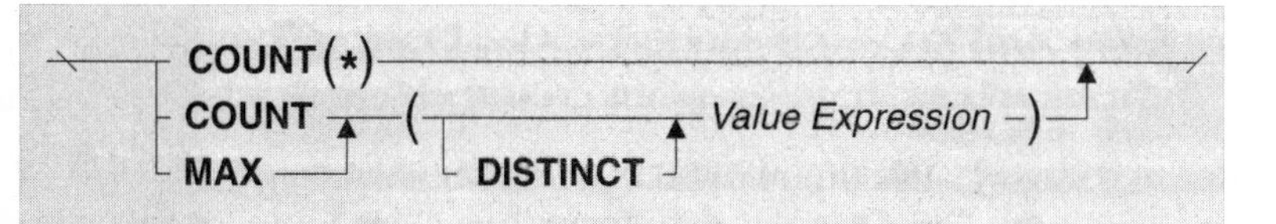

Figure 11-4 *Using the COUNT and MAX aggregate functions.*

You can use COUNT to determine the number of rows or non-Null values in a Result Set. Use COUNT(*) to find out how many rows are in the entire set. If you specify a particular column in the Result Set using COUNT (column_name), the database system counts the number of rows with non-Null values in that column. You can also ask to count only the unique values by adding the DISTINCT keyword.

Likewise, you can find the largest value in a column using MAX. If the Value Expression is numeric, you get the largest number value from the column or expression you specify. If the Value Expression returns a Character data type, the largest value will depend on the collating sequence of your database system.

Let's use these functions in a Subquery to solve a couple of interesting problems.

"List all the customer names and a count of the orders they placed."

Translation: Select customer first name, and customer last name, and also select the count of orders from the orders table for this customer from the customers table

Clean Up: Select customer first name, ~~and~~ customer last name, ~~and also~~ (select ~~the~~ count ~~of orders~~ (*) from ~~the~~ orders ~~table for this~~ where customerID = customerID) from ~~the~~ customers ~~table~~

SQL:

```
SELECT Customers.CustFirstName,
   Customers.CustLastName,
   (SELECT COUNT(*)
   FROM Orders
   WHERE Orders.CustomerID =
      Customers.CustomerID)
AS CountOfOrders
FROM Customers
```

Subqueries as output columns are starting to look interesting now! In the next three chapters, you'll learn more about creative ways to use aggregate functions. But if all you want is a count of related rows, a Subquery is a good way to do it. Let's look at an interesting problem that takes advantage of another aggregate function—MAX.

"Show me a list of customers and the last date on which they placed an order."

Translation: Select customer first name, and customer last name, and also select the highest order date from the orders table for this customer from the customers table

Clean Up: Select customer first name, ~~and~~ customer last name, ~~and also~~ (select ~~the highest~~ max(order date) from ~~the~~ orders ~~table for this~~ where customerID = customerID) from ~~the~~ customers ~~table~~

SQL:

```
SELECT Customers.CustFirstName,
   Customers.CustLastName,
   (SELECT MAX(OrderDate)
   FROM Orders
   WHERE Orders.CustomerID =
      Customers.CustomerID)
AS LastOrderDate
FROM Customers
```

As you can imagine, using MAX in this way works well for finding the highest or "latest" value from any related table. We'll show you a number of other ways to use these functions in the Sample Statements section later in this chapter.

Subqueries as Filters

In Chapter 6, you learned how to filter the information retrieved by adding a WHERE clause. You also learned how to use both simple and complex comparisons to get only the rows you want in your Result Set. Now we'll build on your skills and show you how to use a Subquery as one of the comparison arguments to do more sophisticated filtering.

Syntax

Let's revisit the previous SELECT Statement and look at the syntax for building a query with a simple Comparison Predicate in a WHERE clause. Figure 11-5 shows the simplified diagram.

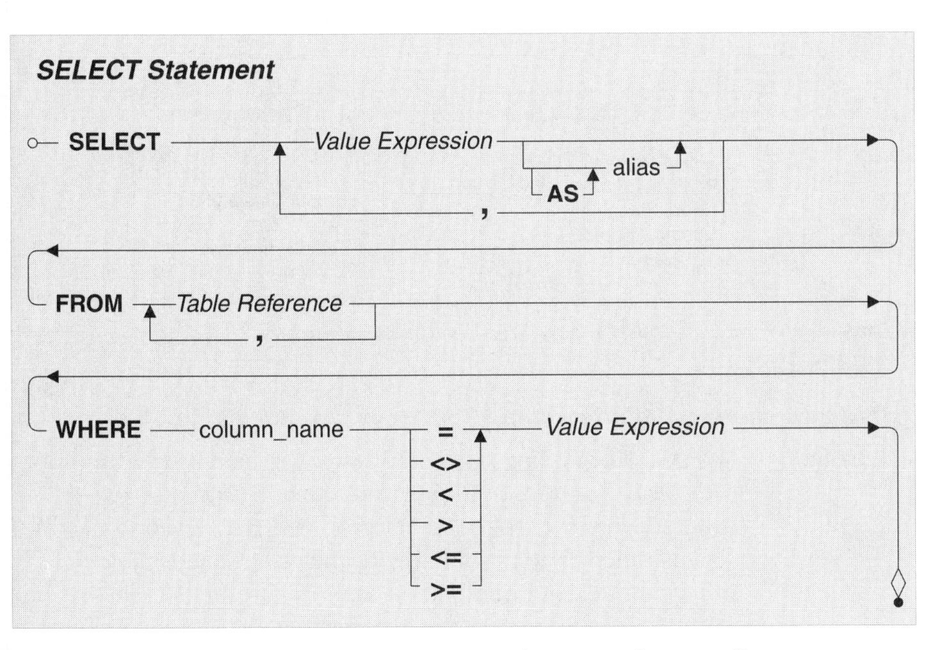

Figure 11-5 *Filtering a result using a simple comparison predicate.*

As you remember from Figure 11-2 on page 349, a Value Expression can be a Subquery. In the simple example in Figure 11-5 you're comparing the Value Expression to a single column. Thus, the Value Expression must be a single value—that is, a Scalar Subquery that returns exactly one column and no more than one row. Let's solve a simple problem requiring a comparison to a value returned from a Subquery. In this example, we are going to ask for all the details about customer orders, but we want only the *last* order for each customer. Figure 11-6 shows the tables needed.

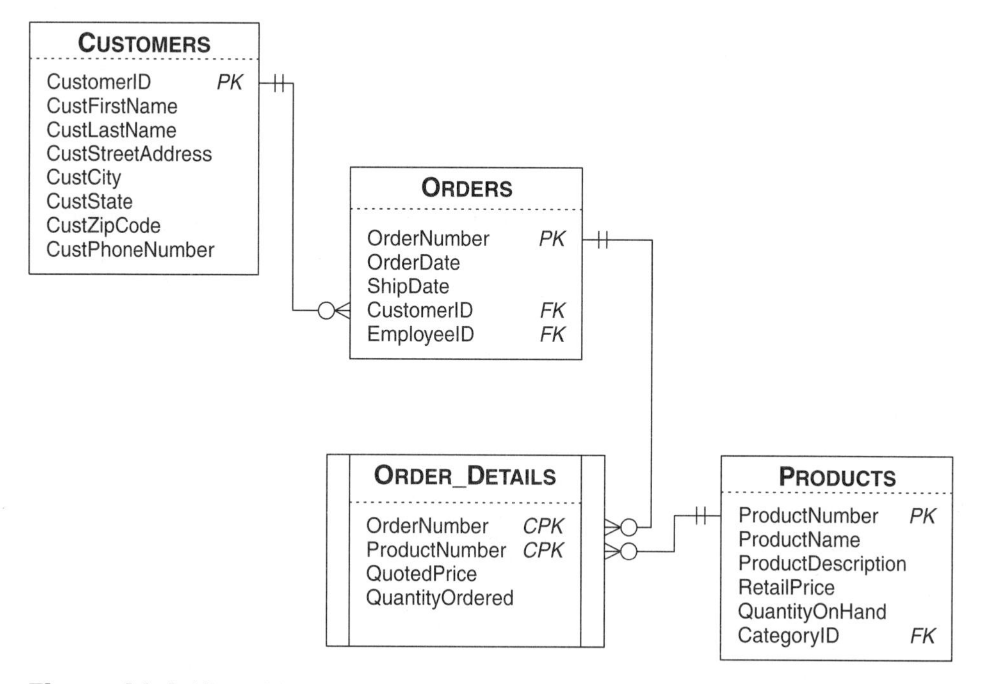

Figure 11-6 *The tables required to list all the details about an order.*

"List customers and all the details from their last order."

Translation Select customer first name, customer last name, order number, order date, product number, product name, and quantity ordered from the customers table joined with the orders table on customer ID, then joined with the order details table on order number, and then joined with the products table on product number where the order date equals the maximum order date from the orders table for this customer

Clean Up

Select customer first name, customer last name, order number, order date, product number, product name, ~~and~~ quantity ordered from ~~the~~ customers ~~table~~ join~~ed with the~~ orders ~~table~~ on customer ID~~, then~~ join~~ed with the~~ order details ~~table~~ on order number~~, and then~~ join~~ed with the~~ products ~~table~~ on product number where the order date ~~equals~~ = (Select ~~the~~ max~~imum~~ (order date) from ~~the~~ orders ~~table for this customer~~ where orders.customerID = customers.customerID)

SQL

```
SELECT Customers.CustFirstName,
   Customers.CustLastName, Orders.OrderNumber,
   Orders.OrderDate,
   Order_Details.ProductNumber,
   Products.ProductName,
   Order_Details.QuantityOrdered
FROM ((Customers
INNER JOIN Orders
ON Customers.CustomerID = Orders.CustomerID)
INNER JOIN Order_Details
ON Orders.OrderID = Order_Details.OrderID)
INNER JOIN Products
ON Products.ProductNumber =
   Order_Details.ProductNumber
WHERE Orders.OrderDate =
   (SELECT MAX(OrderDate)
   FROM Orders AS O2
   WHERE O2.CustomerID = Customers.CustomerID)
```

Did you notice that we gave an alias name to the second reference to the Orders table (that is, the Orders table in the Subquery)? Even if you leave out the alias name, many database systems will recognize that you mean the copy of the Orders table within the Subquery. In fact, the SQL Standard dictates that any unqualified reference should be resolved from the innermost query first. Still, we added the alias reference to make it crystal clear that the copy of the Orders table we're referencing in the WHERE clause of the Subquery is the one in the FROM clause of the Subquery. If you follow this practice, your request will be much easier to understand—either by you when you come back to it some months later or by someone else who has to figure out what your request meant.

Special Predicate Keywords for Subqueries

The SQL Standard defines a number of special Predicate keywords for use in a WHERE clause with a Subquery.

Set Membership—IN

You learned in Chapter 6 how to use the IN keyword in a WHERE clause to compare a column or expression to a list of values. You now know that each Value Expression in the IN list *could* be a Scalar Subquery. How about using a Subquery to generate the entire list? As Figure 11-7 shows, you can certainly do that!

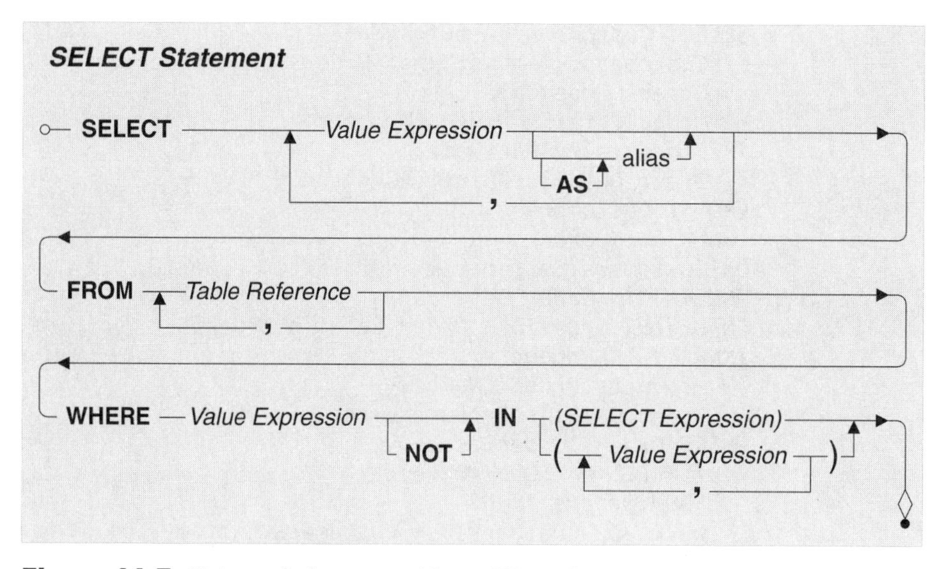

Figure 11-7 *Using a Subquery with an IN predicate.*

In this case, you can use a Table Subquery that returns one column and as many rows as necessary to build the list. Let's use the Recipes sample database for an example. Figure 11-8 shows the tables of interest.

Let's suppose you're having someone over for dinner who just adores seafood. Although you know you have a number of recipes containing seafood ingredients, you're not sure of all the ingredient names in your database. You do know that you have an IngredientClassDescription of Seafood, so you can join all the tables together and filter on IngredientClassDescription—or you can get creative and use Subqueries and the IN Predicate instead.

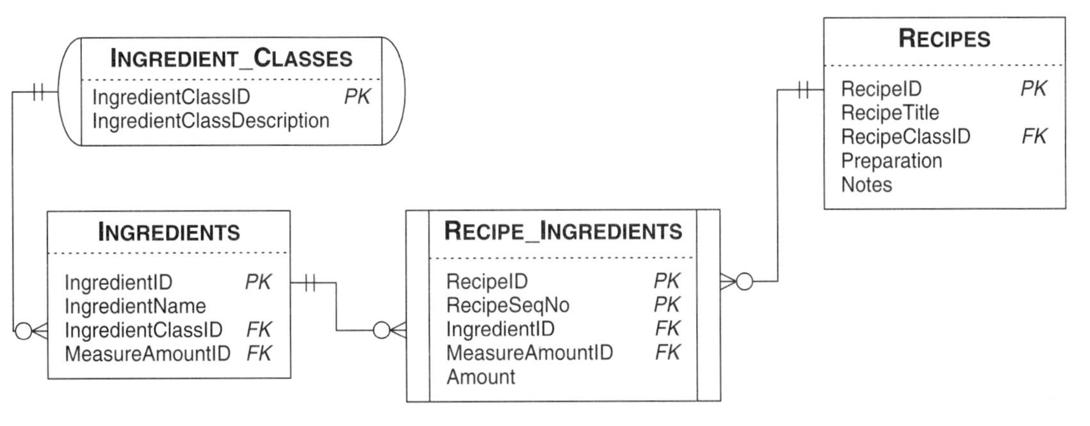

Figure 11-8 *Tables to list recipes and their ingredients.*

"List all my recipes that have a Seafood ingredient."

Translation: Select recipe title from the recipes table where the recipe ID is in the selection of recipe IDs from the recipe ingredients table where the ingredient ID is in the selection of ingredient IDs from the ingredients table joined with the ingredient classes table on ingredient class ID where ingredient class description is "seafood"

Clean Up: Select recipe title from ~~the~~ recipes ~~table~~ where ~~the~~ recipe ID ~~is~~ in ~~the~~ (select~~ion of~~ recipe ID~~s~~ from ~~the~~ recipe ingredients ~~table~~ where ~~the~~ ingredient ID ~~is~~ in ~~the~~ (select~~ion of~~ ingredient ID~~s~~ from ~~the~~ ingredients ~~table~~ join~~ed with~~ ~~the~~ ingredient classes table on ingredient class ID where ingredient class description ~~is~~ = "seafood"))

SQL:

```
SELECT RecipeTitle
FROM Recipes
WHERE Recipes.RecipeID IN
   (SELECT RecipeID
   FROM Recipe_Ingredients
   WHERE Recipe_Ingredients.IngredientID IN
      (SELECT IngredientID
      FROM Ingredients
      INNER JOIN Ingredient_Classes
      ON Ingredients.IngredientClassID =
         Ingredient_Classes.IngredientClassID
      WHERE
  Ingredient_Classes.IngredientClassDescription
      = 'Seafood'))
```

Did it occur to you that you could put a Subquery within a Subquery? We actually could have gone one level deeper by eliminating the INNER JOIN from the second Subquery. We could have stated the second Subquery using the following syntax.

```
SQL        . . (SELECT IngredientID
           FROM Ingredients
           WHERE Ingredients.IngredientClassID IN
              (SELECT IngredientClassID
              FROM Ingredient_Classes
              WHERE
             Ingredient_Classes.IngredientClassDescription
                 = 'Seafood'))
```

That would be overkill, however, because embedding IN clauses within IN clauses only serves to make the query harder to read. We did so in the previous example to show you that you *can* do it. It's worth restating, though, that just because you *can* do something doesn't mean you *should!* We think you'll agree that it's easier to see what's going on by using a single IN Predicate and a more complex JOIN in the Subquery. Here's another solution using this technique.

```
SQL        SELECT RecipeTitle
           FROM Recipes
           WHERE Recipes.RecipeID IN
              (SELECT RecipeID
              FROM (Recipe_Ingredients
              INNER JOIN Ingredients
              ON Recipe_Ingredients.IngredientID =
                 Ingredients.IngredientID)
              INNER JOIN Ingredient_Classes
              ON Ingredients.IngredientClassID =
                 Ingredient_Classes.IngredientClassID
              WHERE
             Ingredient_Classes.IngredientClassDescription
                 = 'Seafood')
```

You might be asking at this point, "Why go to all this trouble? Why not just do the complex join in the outer query and be done with it?" The reason is that you'll get the wrong answer! Actually, the rows returned will all be rows from the Recipes table for seafood recipes, but you may get some rows more than once. Let's try to solve this without the Subquery to see why you get duplicate rows.

```
SQL       SELECT RecipeTitle
          FROM ((Recipes
          INNER JOIN Recipe_Ingredients
          ON Recipes.RecipeID =
             Recipe_Ingredients.RecipeID)
          INNER JOIN Ingredients
          ON Recipe_Ingredients.IngredientID =
             Ingredients.IngredientID)
          INNER JOIN Ingredient_Classes
          ON Ingredients.IngredientClassID =
          Ingredient_Classes.IngredientClassID
          WHERE
          Ingredient_Classes.IngredientClassDescription
             = 'Seafood')
```

If you look back at Figure 11-8 on page 357, you can see that the Recipe_Ingredients table may have many rows for each row in the Recipes table. The Result Set defined by the FROM clause will contain at least as many rows as there are in Recipe_Ingredients, with the RecipeTitle column value repeated many times. Even when we add the filter to restrict the result to ingredients in class Seafood, we will still get more than one row per recipe in any recipe that has more than one seafood ingredient.

Using this Subquery technique also becomes really important when you want to list more than just the recipe title. For example, suppose you also want to list *all* the ingredients from *any* recipe that has a seafood ingredient. If you use a complex join in the outer query and filter for an ingredient class of Seafood as we just did above, all you will get is seafood ingredients—you won't get all the other ingredients for the recipes. Let's ask one additional and slightly more complex request.

"List all my recipes and all ingredients for recipes that have a Seafood ingredient."

Translation — Select recipe title and ingredient name from the recipes table joined with the recipe_ingredients table on recipe ID, and then joined with the ingredients table on ingredient ID where the recipe ID is in the selection of recipe IDs from the recipe_ingredients table joined with the ingredients table on ingredient ID, and then joined with the ingredient_classes table on ingredient class ID where ingredient class description is "seafood"

Clean Up: Select recipe title, ~~and~~ ingredient name from ~~the~~ recipes ~~table~~ join~~ed with the~~ recipe_ingredients ~~table~~ on recipe ID~~, and then~~ join~~ed with the~~ ingredients ~~table~~ on ingredient ID where ~~the~~ recipe ID ~~is~~ in ~~the~~ (select~~ion of~~ recipe ID~~s~~ from ~~the~~ recipe_ingredients ~~table~~ join~~ed with the~~ ingredients ~~table~~ on ingredient ID~~, and then~~ join~~ed with the~~ ingredient_classes ~~table~~ on ingredient class ID where ingredient class description ~~is~~ = "seafood")

SQL:

```
SELECT Recipes.RecipeTitle,
   Ingredients.IngredientName
FROM (Recipes
INNER JOIN Recipe_Ingredients
ON Recipes.RecipeID =
   Recipe_Ingredients.RecipeID)
INNER JOIN Ingredients
ON Ingredients.IngredientID =
   Recipe_Ingredients.IngredientID
WHERE Recipes.RecipeID IN
   (SELECT RecipeID
   FROM (Recipe_Ingredients
   INNER JOIN Ingredients
   ON Recipe_Ingredients.IngredientID =
      Ingredients.IngredientID)
   INNER JOIN Ingredient_Classes
   ON Ingredients.IngredientClassID =
      Ingredient_Classes.IngredientClassID
   WHERE
  Ingredient_Classes.IngredientClassDescription
      = 'Seafood')
```

The key here is that the complex outer join in the main part of the query retrieves *all* the ingredients for the recipes selected, and the complex Subquery returns a list of recipe IDs for just the seafood recipes. It seems like we're doing a complex join twice, but there's method in the madness!

Quantified—ALL/SOME/ANY

As you have just seen, the IN Predicate lets you compare a column or expression to a list to see if that column or expression is IN the list. In other words, the column or expression *equals* one of the members of the list. If you want to find out if the column or expression is greater than or less than any or all or some of the items in the list you can use a *Quantified* Predicate. Figure 11-9 shows the syntax.

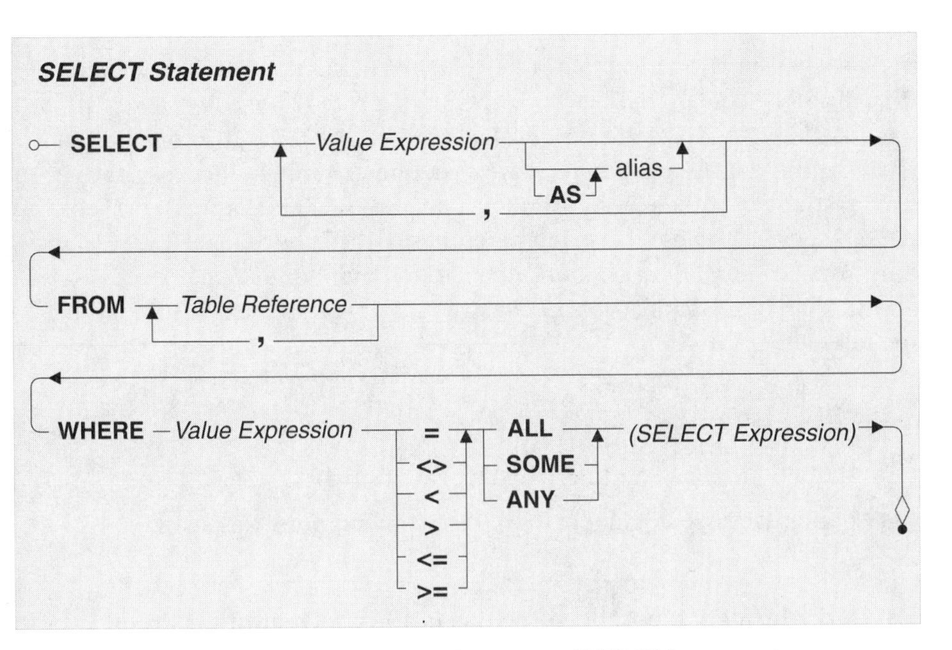

Figure 11-9 *Using a Quantified Predicate in a SELECT Statement.*

In this case, the SELECT Expression must be a Table Subquery that returns exactly one column and zero or more rows. When the Subquery returns more than one row, the values in the rows make up a list. As you can see, this Predicate combines a comparison operator with a keyword that tells your database system how to apply the operator to the members of the list. When you use the keyword ALL, the comparison must be true for all the values returned by the Subquery; when you use the keyword SOME or ANY, the comparison need be true for only one value in the list.

If you think about it, when the Subquery returns multiple rows, asking for = ALL will always be false unless all the values returned by the Subquery are the same and the Value Expression on the left of the comparison equals all of them. By the same logic, you might think that < > ANY will always be false if the Value Expression on the left *does* equal "any" of the values in the list. In truth, the SQL Standard treats SOME and ANY the same. So if you say < > SOME or < > ANY, then the Predicate is true if the Value Expression on the left does not equal at least one of the values in the list. Another confusing point is that if the Subquery returns no rows, then any Comparison Predicate with the ALL keyword is true, and any Comparison Predicate with the SOME or ANY keyword is false.

> ❖ **Note** As mentioned earlier in this chapter in the Row Subqueries section, the SQL Standard defines the concept of a *row value constructor*. If your database supports this part of the Standard, the SELECT Expression in a Quantified Predicate can return more than one column. In that case, the item on the left of the comparison must be a list of Value Expressions separated by commas and enclosed in parentheses. Also, the SELECT Expression must return a number of columns equal to the number of Value Expressions on the left. For example, you can construct an SQL statement that looks like the following.
>
> ```
> SELECT *
> FROM MyTable
> WHERE (MyTable.Column1, MyTable.Column2) > ALL
> (SELECT ColumnA, ColumnB FROM OtherTable)
> ```
>
> Check your database documentation to see if it supports this syntax.

Let's work through a couple of requests to see Quantified Predicates in action. First, let's do a problem in the Recipes database. Refer to Figure 11-8 on page 357 to see the tables we'll use.

"Show me the recipes that have beef or garlic."

Translation: Select recipe title from the recipes table where recipe ID is in the selection of recipe IDs from the recipe ingredients table where ingredient ID equals any of the selection of ingredient IDs from the ingredients table where ingredient name is "beef" or "garlic"

Clean Up: Select recipe title from ~~the~~ recipes ~~table~~ where recipe ID ~~is~~ in ~~the~~ (select~~ion of~~ recipe ID~~s~~ from ~~the~~ recipe ingredients ~~table~~ where ingredient ID ~~equals~~ = any ~~of the~~ (select~~ion of~~ ingredient ID~~s~~ from ~~the~~ ingredients ~~table~~ where ingredient name ~~is~~ in "beef" ~~or~~ "garlic"))

SQL
```
SELECT Recipes.RecipeTitle
FROM Recipes
WHERE Recipes.RecipeID IN
   (SELECT Recipe_Ingredients.RecipeID
   FROM Recipe_Ingredients
   WHERE Recipe_Ingredients.IngredientID = ANY
      (SELECT Ingredients.IngredientID
      FROM Ingredients
      WHERE Ingredients.IngredientName
      IN ('Beef', 'Garlic')))
```

Do you get the feeling we could have also used IN instead of = ANY? If so, you're right! We could have also created a JOIN between Recipe_Ingredients and Ingredients in the first Subquery to return the requisite list of RecipeIDs. As we stated at the beginning of the chapter, there's almost always more than one way to solve a particular problem in SQL. Sometimes, using a Quantified Predicate may make your request clearer.

Let's now solve a bit more complex problem to show you the real power of Quantified Predicates. This example uses the Sales Order sample database, and Figure 11-10 shows you the tables involved.

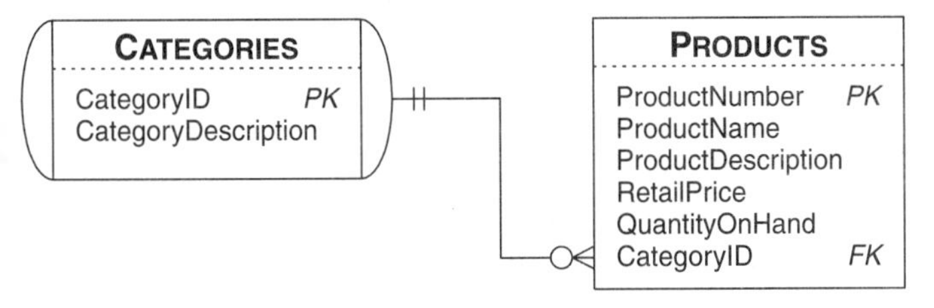

Figure 11-10 *Categories and their related Products.*

"Find all accessories that are priced greater than any clothing item."

Translation: Select product name and retail price from the products table joined with the categories table on category ID where category description is "accessories" and retail price is greater than all of the selection of retail price from the products table joined with the categories table on category ID where category name is "clothing"

Clean Up: Select product name ~~and~~ retail price from ~~the~~ products ~~table~~ join~~ed with the~~ categories ~~table~~ on category ID where category description ~~is~~ = "accessories" and retail price ~~is greater than~~ > all ~~of the~~ (select~~ion of~~ retail price from ~~the~~ products ~~table~~ join~~ed with the~~ categories ~~table~~ on category ID where category name ~~is~~ = "clothing")

SQL:

```
SELECT Products.ProductName,
   Products.RetailPrice
FROM Products
INNER JOIN Categories
ON Products.CategoryID = Categories.CategoryID
```

(continued)

```
WHERE Categories.CategoryDescription =
   'Accessories'
AND Products.RetailPrice > ALL
   (SELECT Products.RetailPrice
   FROM Products
   INNER JOIN Categories
   ON Products.CategoryID =
      Categories.CategoryID
   WHERE Categories.CategoryDescription =
      'Clothing')
```

What's happening here? The Subquery fetches all the prices for clothing items. The outer query then lists all accessories whose prices are greater than *all* the prices in the clothing items Subquery.

Existence—EXISTS

Both Set Membership (IN) and Quantified (SOME/ANY/ALL) Predicates perform a comparison with a Value Expression—usually a column from the source you specify in the FROM clause of your outer query. Sometimes it's useful to know simply that a related row EXISTS in the Result Set returned by a Subquery. In Chapter 8, we showed a technique for solving "AND" problems using complex INNER JOINs. You can also use EXISTS to solve those same sorts of problems. Let's take another look at a problem we solved in Chapter 8.

> *"Find all the customers who ordered a bicycle* and *who also ordered a helmet."*

Translation: Select customer ID, customer first name, and customer last name from the customers table where there exists some row from the orders table joined with the order details table on order ID, and then joined with the products table on product ID where product name contains "Bike" and the orders table customer ID equals the customers table customer ID, and there also exists some row from the orders table joined with the order details table on order ID, and then joined with the products table on product ID where product name contains "Helmet" and the orders table customer ID equals the customers table customer ID

Clean Up: Select customer ID, customer first name, ~~and~~ customer last name from ~~the~~ customers ~~table~~ where ~~there~~ exists ~~some row~~ (SELECT * from ~~the~~ orders ~~table~~ join~~ed with the~~ order details ~~table~~ on order ID~~, and then~~ join~~ed with the~~ products ~~table~~ on product ID where product name ~~contains~~ LIKE "Bike" and ~~the~~ orders ~~table~~ customer ID ~~equals~~ = ~~the~~ customers ~~table~~ customer ID)~~,~~ and ~~there also~~ exists ~~some row~~ (SELECT * from ~~the~~. orders ~~table~~ join~~ed with the~~ order details ~~table~~ on order ID~~, and then~~ join~~ed with the~~ products ~~table~~ on product ID where product name ~~contains~~ LIKE "Helmet" and ~~the~~ orders ~~table~~ customer ID ~~equals~~ = ~~the~~ customers ~~table~~ customer ID)

SQL

```
SELECT Customers.CustomerID,
   Customers.CustFirstName,
   Customers.CustLastName
FROM Customers
WHERE EXISTS
   (SELECT *
   FROM (Orders
   INNER JOIN Order_Details
   ON Orders.OrderNumber =
      Order_Details.OrderNumber)
   INNER JOIN Products
   ON Products.ProductNumber =
      Order_Details.ProductNumber
   WHERE Products.ProductName Like '%Helmet'
   AND Orders.CustomerID =
      Customers.CustomerID)
AND EXISTS
   (SELECT *
   FROM (Orders
   INNER JOIN Order_Details
   ON Orders.OrderNumber =
      Order_Details.OrderNumber)
   INNER JOIN Products
   ON Products.ProductNumber =
      Order_Details.ProductNumber
   WHERE Products.ProductName Like '%Bike'
   AND Orders.CustomerID =
      Customers.CustomerID)
```

Notice that you can use any column name from any of the tables in the FROM clause as the column to be fetched in the SELECT clause of the Subquery. We chose to use the shorthand "*" for all columns. Stated another way, this query is asking, "Give me the customers for which there exists some row in order details for a bike and for which there also exists some row in order details for a helmet." Because we didn't match on Order ID, we don't care if the customer ordered a bike in one order and a helmet in another one.

> ❖ **Note** Because this is such an interesting query, we saved this solution as "Cust_Bikes_And_Helmets_EXISTS" in the sample database. You can find the original INNER JOIN solution saved as "Cust_Bike_And_Helmets_JOIN."

Uses for Subqueries

At this point, you should have a pretty good understanding of the concept of using a Subquery either to generate an output column or to perform a complex comparison in a WHERE clause. The best way to give you an idea of the wide range of uses for Subqueries is to show you problems you can solve with Subqueries followed by a robust set of examples in the next section.

Column Expressions

As mentioned earlier in this chapter, using a Subquery to fetch a single value from a related table is probably more effectively done with a JOIN. When you consider aggregate functions, however, Subqueries to fetch the result of a function calculation make the idea much more interesting. We'll explore this use of aggregate functions further in the next chapter. In the meantime, here are some problems you can solve using a Subquery to generate an output column.

"List vendors and a count of the products they sell to us."

"Display products and the latest date the product was ordered."

"Show me entertainers and count of each entertainer's engagements."

"Display each customer and the date of the last booking they made."

"List all staff members and the count of classes each teaches."

"Display all subjects and the count of classes for each subject on Monday."

"Show me all the bowlers and a count of games each bowled."

"Display the bowlers and highest game each bowled."

"List all the meats and the count of recipes each appears in."

"Show me the types of recipes and the count of recipes in each type."

Filters

Now that you know about Subqueries, you can really expand your kit of tools for solving complex queries. In this chapter, we explored many interesting ways to use Subqueries as filters in a WHERE clause. In Chapter 14, we'll show you how to use Subqueries as filters for groups of information in a HAVING clause.

Here's a sample of problems you can solve using Subqueries as a filter for rows in a WHERE clause. Note that we solved many of these same problems in earlier chapters. Now, you get to think about solving them an alternate way using a Subquery!

❖ **Note** As a hint, we've included the keyword(s) you can use to solve the problem in parentheses after the problem statement.

"List customers who ordered bikes." (IN)

"Display customers who ordered clothing or accessories." (= SOME)

"Find all the customers who ever ordered a bicycle helmet." (IN)

"Find all customers who ordered a bicycle but who did not order a helmet." (NOT EXISTS)

"What products have never been ordered?" (NOT IN)

"List customers who have booked entertainers who play country or country rock." (IN)

"Find the entertainers who played engagements for customers Bonnicksen or Rosales." (= SOME)

"Display agents who haven't booked an entertainer." (NOT IN)

"List the entertainers who played engagements for customers Bonnicksen and *Rosales." (EXISTS)*

"Display students enrolled in a class on Tuesday." (IN)

"Show me the students who have an average score of 85 or better in Art and who also have an average score of 85 or better in Computer Science." (EXISTS)

"Display students who have never withdrawn from a class." (NOT IN)

"List the subjects taught on Wednesday." (IN)

"Display team captains with a current average higher than all other members on their team." (> ALL)

"Show me tournaments that haven't been played yet." (NOT IN)

"Find the bowlers who had a raw score of 170 or better at both Thunderbird Lanes and Bolero Lanes." (EXISTS)

"List all the bowlers who have a current average that's less than all the other bowlers on the same team." *(< ALL)*

"Show me the recipes that have beef and *garlic."* *(EXISTS)*

"Display all the ingredients for recipes that contain carrots." *(IN)*

"List the ingredients that are used in some recipe where the measurement amount in the recipe is not the default measurement amount." *(<> SOME)*

"List ingredients not used in any recipe yet." *(NOT IN)*

Sample Statements

You now know the mechanics of constructing queries using Subqueries and have seen some of the types of requests you can answer with a Subquery. Let's take a look at a fairly robust set of samples, all of which use one or more Subqueries. These examples come from each of the sample databases, and they illustrate the use of the Subqueries to either generate an output column or to act as a filter.

We've also included sample Result Sets that would be returned by these operations and placed them immediately after the SQL syntax line. The name that appears immediately above a Result Set is the name we gave each query in the sample data on the companion CD you'll find bound into the back of the book. We stored each query in the appropriate sample database (as indicated within the example) in the "Chapter11" subfolder on the CD. You can follow the instructions at the beginning of this book to load the samples onto your computer and try them out.

> ❖ **Note** Remember that all the column names and table names used in these examples are drawn from the sample database structures shown in Appendix B. Because many of these examples use complex joins, your database system may choose a different way to solve these queries. For this reason, the first few rows may not exactly match the result you obtain, but the total number of rows should be the same. To simplify the process, we have combined the Translation and Clean Up steps for all the following examples.

Subqueries in Expressions

Sales Order Database

"List vendors and a count of the products they sell to us."

Translation/ Clean Up: Select vendor name ~~and also~~ (select ~~the~~ count(*) ~~of products~~ from ~~the~~ product vendors ~~table for this vendor~~ WHERE vendors vendor ID = product vendors vendor ID) from ~~the~~ vendors ~~table~~

SQL:

```
SELECT VendName,
   (SELECT COUNT(*)
   FROM Product_Vendors
   WHERE Product_Vendors.VendorID =
      Vendors.VendorID)
AS VendProductCount
FROM Vendors
```

Vendors_Product_Count (10 rows)

VendName	VendProductCount
Shinoman, Incorporated	3
Viscount	6
Nikoma of America	5
ProFormance	3
Kona, Incorporated	1
Big Sky Mountain Bikes	22
Dog Ear	9
Sun Sports Suppliers	5
Lone Star Bike Supply	30
Armadillo Brand	6

Entertainment Database

"Display each customer and the date of the last booking they made."

Translation/ Clean Up: Select customer first name, customer last name, ~~and also~~ (select ~~the highest~~ MAX(start date) from engagements ~~for this customer~~ WHERE engagements customer ID = customers customer ID) from ~~the~~ customers ~~table~~.

SQL

```
SELECT Customers.CustFirstName,
   Customers.CustLastName,
   (Select Max(StartDate)
   FROM Engagements
   WHERE Engagements.CustomerID =
      Customers.CustomerID)
AS LastBooking
FROM Customers
```

Customers_Last_Booking (15 rows)

CustFirstName	CustLastName	LastBooking
Sally	Callahan	1999-12-23
Ann	Fuller	1999-12-17
James	Leverling	1999-12-26
Kenneth	Peacock	1999-12-24
Elizabeth	Hallmark	1999-12-19
Thomas	Fuller	1999-12-23
Amelia	Buchanan	1999-12-19
Samuel	Peacock	
Sarah	Thompson	1999-12-24
<<more rows here >>		

❖ **Note** The LastBooking column for some customers is blank (Null) because those customers have no bookings.

School Scheduling Database

"Display all subjects and count of classes for each subject on Monday."

Translation/ Clean Up: Select subject name ~~and also~~ (select ~~the~~ count(*) ~~of classes~~ from ~~the~~ classes ~~table~~ where Monday schedule ~~is~~ = true ~~for this subject~~ and classes subject ID = subjects subject ID) from ~~the~~ subjects ~~table~~

SQL

```
SELECT Subjects.SubjectName,
   (SELECT Count(*)
   FROM Classes
   WHERE MondaySchedule = -1
   AND Classes.SubjectID = Subjects.SubjectID)
AS MondayCount
FROM Subjects
```

❖ **Note** Be sure to use the test for "true" that your database system supports. Remember that some database systems require you to compare to a keyword "TRUE" or to the integer value 1.

Subjects_Monday_Count (56 rows)

SubjectName	MondayCount
Financial Accounting Fundamentals I	2
Financial Accounting Fundamentals II	1
Fundamentals of Managerial Accounting	1
Intermediate Accounting	1
Business Tax Accounting	1
Introduction to Business	0
Developing A Feasibility Plan	0
Introduction to Enterpreneurship	1
<<more rows here >>	

❖ **Note** Rather than return a Null value when there are no rows, the COUNT aggregate function returns a zero.

Bowling League Database

"Display the bowlers and highest game each bowled."

Translation/ Clean Up: Select bowler first name, bowler last name~~, and also~~ (select ~~the highest~~ MAX(raw score) from ~~the~~ bowler scores ~~table for this bowler~~ WHERE bowler scores bowler ID = bowlers bowler ID) from ~~the~~ bowlers ~~table~~

SQL

```
SELECT Bowlers.BowlerFirstName,
Bowlers.BowlerLastName,
   (SELECT MAX(RawScore)
   FROM Bowler_Scores
   WHERE Bowler_Scores.BowlerID =
   Bowlers.BowlerID)
AS HighScore
FROM Bowlers
```

Bowler_High_Score (32 rows)

BowlerFirstName	BowlerLastName	HighScore
Barbara	Fournier	164
David	Fournier	178
John	Kennedy	191
Sara	Kennedy	149
Ann	Patterson	165
Neil	Patterson	179
Carol	Viescas	195
David	Viescas	150
<<more rows here>>		

Recipes Database

"List all the meats and the count of recipes each appears in."

Translation/ Clean Up
: Select ingredient class description, ingredient name, ~~and also~~ (select ~~the~~ count(*) ~~of rows~~ from ~~the~~ recipe ingredients ~~table for this ingredient~~ where recipe ingredients ingredient ID = ingredients ingredient ID) from ~~the~~ ingredient classes ~~table~~ join~~ed with the~~ ingredients ~~table~~ on ingredient class ID where ingredient class description ~~is~~ = 'meat'

SQL

```
SELECT Ingredient_Classes.IngredientClassDescription,
   Ingredients.IngredientName,
   (SELECT COUNT(*)
   FROM Recipe_Ingredients
   WHERE Recipe_Ingredients.IngredientID =
      Ingredients.IngredientID)
AS RecipeCount
FROM Ingredient_Classes
INNER JOIN Ingredients
ON Ingredient_Classes.IngredientClassID =
   Ingredients.IngredientClassID
WHERE
  Ingredient_Classes.IngredientClassDescription
   ='Meat'
```

Meat_Ingredient_Recipe_Count (11 rows)

IngredientClassDescription	IngredientName	RecipeCount
Meat	Beef	2
Meat	Chicken, Fryer	0
Meat	Bacon	0
Meat	Chicken, Pre-cut	0
Meat	T-bone Steak	0
Meat	Chicken Breast	0
Meat	Chicken Leg	1
Meat	Chicken Wing	0
Meat	Chicken Thigh	1
Meat	New York Steak	0
Meat	Ground Pork	1

Subqueries in Filters

Sales Order Database

"Display customers who ordered Clothing or Accessories."

Translation/Clean Up

Select customer ID, customer first name, customer last name from ~~the~~ customers ~~table~~ where customer ID ~~is~~ in ~~the~~ (select~~ion of~~ customer ID from ~~the~~ orders ~~table~~ join~~ed with the~~ order details ~~table~~ on order number~~, then~~ join~~ed with the~~ products ~~table~~ on product number~~, and then~~ join~~ed with the~~ categories ~~table~~ on category ID where category description ~~is~~ = 'clothing' or category description ~~is~~ = 'accessories'

SQL

```
SELECT Customers.CustomerID,
   Customers.CustFirstName,
   Customers.CustLastName
FROM Customers
WHERE Customers.CustomerID = ANY
   (SELECT Orders.CustomerID
   FROM ((Orders
   INNER JOIN Order_Details
   ON Orders.OrderNumber =
      Order_Details.OrderNumber)
   INNER JOIN Products
   ON Products.ProductNumber =
      Order_Details.ProductNumber)
   INNER JOIN Categories
   ON Categories.CategoryID =
      Products.CategoryID
   WHERE Categories.CategoryDescription
      ='Clothing'
   OR Categories.CategoryDescription
      = 'Accessories')
```

Customers_Clothing_OR_Accessories (27 rows)

CustomerID	CustFirstName	CustLastName
1001	Suzanne	Viescas
1002	Will	Thompson
1003	Gary	Hallmark
1004	Michael	Davolio
1005	Kenneth	Peacock
1006	John	Viescas
1007	Laura	Callahan
1008	Neil	Patterson
<<*more rows here* >>		

Entertainment Database

"List the entertainers who played engagements for customers Bonnicksen and *Rosales."*

> ❖ **Note** We solved this problem in Chapter 8 with a JOIN of two complex Table Subqueries. This time, we'll use EXISTS.

Translation/ Clean Up

Select entertainer ID, ~~and~~ entertainer stage name from ~~the~~ entertainers ~~table~~ where ~~there~~ exists (SELECT * ~~some row~~ from ~~the~~ customers ~~table~~ join~~ed with the~~ engagements ~~table~~ on customerID where customer last name ~~is~~ = 'Rosales' and ~~the~~ entertainers ~~table~~ entertainer ID ~~equals~~ = ~~the~~ engagements ~~table~~ entertainer ID)~~,~~ and ~~there also~~ exists (SELECT * ~~some row~~ from ~~the~~ customers ~~table~~ join~~ed with the~~ engagements ~~table~~ on customerID where customer last name ~~is~~ = 'Bonnicksen' and ~~the~~ entertainers ~~table~~ entertainer ID ~~equals~~ = ~~the~~ engagements ~~table~~ entertainer ID)

SQL

```
SELECT Entertainers.EntertainerID,
   Entertainers.EntStageName
FROM Entertainers
WHERE EXISTS
   (SELECT *
   FROM Customers
   INNER JOIN Engagements
   ON Customers.CustomerID =
      Engagements.CustomerID
   WHERE Customers.CustLastName='Rosales'
   AND Engagements.EntertainerID =
      Entertainers.EntertainerID)
AND EXISTS
   (SELECT *
   FROM Customers
   INNER JOIN Engagements
   ON Customers.CustomerID =
      Engagements.CustomerID
   WHERE Customers.CustLastName='Bonnicksen'
   AND Engagements.EntertainerID =
      Entertainers.EntertainerID)
```

Entertainers_Bonnicksen_AND_Rosales_EXISTS (4 rows)

EntertainerID	EntStageName
1008	Country Feeling
1009	Katherine Ehrlich
1010	Saturday Revue
1011	Julia Schnebly

School Scheduling Database

"Display students who have never withdrawn from a class."

Translation/ Clean Up: Select student ID, student first name, ~~and~~ student last name from ~~the~~ students ~~table~~ where ~~the~~ student ID ~~is~~ not in ~~the~~ (select~~ion of~~ student ID from ~~the~~ student schedules ~~table~~ join~~ed with the~~ student class status ~~table~~ on class status where class status description ~~is~~ = 'withdrew'

```
SQL       SELECT Students.StudentID,
             Students.StudFirstName,
             Students.StudLastName
          FROM Students
          WHERE Students.StudentID NOT IN
             (SELECT Student_Schedules.StudentID
             FROM Student_Schedules
             INNER JOIN Student_Class_Status
             ON Student_Schedules.ClassStatus =
                Student_Class_Status.ClassStatus
             WHERE
             Student_Class_Status.ClassStatusDescription
                = 'Withdrew')
```

❖ **Note** This is a pretty simple query that finds all the students who ever withdrew from a class in the Subquery and then asks for all the students "NOT IN" this list. Can you think how you would solve this with an OUTER JOIN?

Students_Never_Withdrawn (15 rows)

StudentID	StudFirstName	StudLastName
1002	Andrew	Fuller
1003	Sarah	Leverling
1004	Carol	Peacock
1005	Sally	Callahan
1006	Steven	Buchanan
1007	Elizabeth	Hallmark
1008	Sara	Kennedy
1010	Mary	Fuller
<<more rows here>>		

Bowling League Database

"Display team captains with a current average higher than all other members on their team."

Translation/ Clean Up: Select team name, bowler ID, bowler first name, bowler last name, ~~and~~ current average from ~~the~~ bowlers ~~table~~ join~~ed with~~ ~~the~~ teams ~~table~~ on bowler ID matches = captain ID where ~~the~~ current average ~~is greater than~~ > all ~~of the~~ (select~~ion of~~ current average from bowlers where ~~the~~ bowler ID ~~is not equal~~ <> ~~the current~~ bowler ID and ~~the~~ team ID ~~is equal~~ = ~~to the~~ ~~current~~ team ID

SQL:

```
SELECT Teams.TeamName, Bowlers.BowlerID,
   Bowlers.BowlerFirstName,
   Bowlers.BowlerLastName,
   Bowlers.CurrentAverage
FROM Bowlers
INNER JOIN Teams
ON Bowlers.BowlerID = Teams.CaptainID
WHERE Bowlers.CurrentAverage > All
   (SELECT B2.CurrentAverage
   FROM Bowlers AS B2
   WHERE B2.BowlerID <> Bowlers.BowlerID
   AND B2.TeamID = Bowlers.TeamID)
```

❖ **Note** We explicitly gave the second copy of the Bowlers table in the Subquery an alias to make it crystal clear what's going on. We specifically do not want to compare against the average of the current bowler—that would cause the > ALL Predicate to fail. We also want to compare only with the other bowlers on the same team.

Team_Captains_High_Average (2 rows)

TeamName	BowlerID	BowlerFirstName	BowlerLastName	CurrentAverage
Sharks	5	Ann	Patterson	170.00
Barracudas	16	Richard	Sheskey	165.00

Recipes Database

"Display all the ingredients for recipes that contain carrots."

> ❖ **Note** We promised in Chapter 8 that we would show you how to solve this problem with a Subquery. We keep our promises!

Translation/ Clean Up

Select recipe title ~~and~~ ingredient name from ~~the~~ recipes ~~table~~ join~~ed with the~~ recipe ingredients ~~table~~ on recipe ID~~, and then~~ join~~ed with the~~ ingredients ~~table~~ on ingredient ID where recipe ID ~~is~~ in ~~the~~ (select~~ion of~~ recipe ID from ~~the~~ ingredients ~~table~~ join~~ed with the~~ recipe ingredients ~~table~~ on ingredient ID where ingredient name ~~is~~ = 'carrot'

SQL

```
SELECT Recipes.RecipeTitle,
   Ingredients.IngredientName
FROM (Recipes
INNER JOIN Recipe_Ingredients
ON Recipes.RecipeID =
   Recipe_Ingredients.RecipeID)
INNER JOIN Ingredients
ON Ingredients.IngredientID =
   Recipe_Ingredients.IngredientID
WHERE Recipes.RecipeID
IN
   (SELECT Recipe_Ingredients.RecipeID
   FROM Ingredients
   INNER JOIN Recipe_Ingredients
   ON Ingredients.IngredientID =
      Recipe_Ingredients.IngredientID
   WHERE Ingredients.IngredientName = 'carrot')
```

> ❖ **Note** If you place the filter for 'carrot' in the outer query, you will see only carrot ingredients in the output. In this problem, we want to see *all* the ingredients from any recipe that uses carrots, so the Subquery is a good way to solve it.

Recipes_Ingredients_With_Carrots (16 rows)

RecipeTitle	IngredientName
Irish Stew	Beef
Irish Stew	Onion
Irish Stew	Potato
Irish Stew	Carrot
Irish Stew	Water
Irish Stew	Guinness Beer
Salmon Filets in Parchment Paper	Salmon
Salmon Filets in Parchment Paper	Carrot
Salmon Filets in Parchment Paper	Leek
<<*more rows here* >>	

SUMMARY

We began the chapter with a definition of the three types of Subqueries defined by the SQL Standard—Scalar, Row, and Table—and recalled that we had already covered using Table Subqueries in a FROM clause. We also briefly described the use of a Row Subquery and explained that not many commercial implementations support this yet.

Next, we showed how to use a Subquery to generate a column expression in a SELECT clause. We discussed a simple example and then introduced two aggregate functions that are useful for fetching related summary information from another table. (We'll cover all the aggregate functions in detail in the next chapter.)

We then discussed using Subqueries to create complex filters in the WHERE clause. We first covered simple comparisons and then introduced special comparison keywords—IN, SOME, ANY, ALL, and EXISTS—that are useful for building Predicates with Subqueries.

We summarized why Subqueries are useful and provided a sample list of problems to solve using Subqueries. The rest of the chapter showed examples of how to use Subqueries. We broke these examples into two groups: using Subqueries for column expressions and using Subqueries to create filters.

The following section presents a number of requests that you can work out on your own.

Problems for You to Solve

Below, we show you the request statement and the name of the solution query in the sample databases. If you want some practice, you can work out the SQL you need for each request and then check your answer with the query we saved in the samples. Don't worry if your syntax doesn't exactly match the syntax of the queries we saved—as long as your Result Set is the same.

Sales Order Database

1. *"Display products and the latest date the product was ordered."*
   (Hint: Use the MAX aggregate function.)
   You can find the solution in Products_Last_Date (40 rows).
2. *"List customers who ordered bikes."*
   (Hint: Build a filter using IN.)
   You can find the solution in Customers_Order_Bikes (23 rows).
3. *"Find all customers who ordered a bicycle but who did not order a helmet."*
   (Hint: Start with the query above and add a filter using NOT EXISTS.)
   You can find the solution in Customer_Bikes_No_Helmets (2 rows).
4. *"What products have never been ordered?"*
   (Hint: Build a filter using NOT IN.)
   You can find the solution in Products_Not_Ordered (2 rows).

Entertainment Database

1. *"Show me entertainers and count of each entertainer's engagements."*
   (Hint: Use the COUNT aggregate function.)
   You can find the solution in Entertainers_Engagement_Count (13 rows).
2. *"List customers who have booked entertainers who play country or country rock."*
   (Hint: Build a filter using IN.)
   You can find the solution in Customers_Who_Like_Country (15 rows).
3. *"Find the entertainers who played engagements for customers Bonnicksen or Rosales."*
   (Hint: Build a filter using = SOME.)

You can find the solution in Entertainers_Bonnicksen_OR_Rosales_SOME (9 rows).

4. *"Display agents who haven't booked an entertainer."*
(Hint: Build a filter using NOT IN.)
You can find the solution in Bad_Agents (1 row).

School Scheduling Database

1. *"List all staff members and the count of classes each teaches."*
(Hint: Use the COUNT aggregate function.)
You can find the solution in Staff_Class_Count (27 rows).
2. *"Display students enrolled in a class on Tuesday."*
(Hint: Build a filter using IN.)
You can find the solution in Students_In_Class_Tuesdays (18 rows).
3. *"Show me the students who have an average score of 85 or better in Art and who also have an average score of 85 or better in Computer Science."*
(Hint: Build a filter using EXISTS.)
You can find the solution in Good_Art_CS_Students_EXISTS (1 row).
4. *"List the subjects taught on Wednesday."*
(Hint: Build a filter using IN.)
You can find the solution in Subjects_On_Wednesday (45 rows).

Bowling League Database

1. *"Show me all the bowlers and a count of games each bowled."*
(Hint: Use the COUNT aggregate function.)
You can find the solution in Bowlers_And_Count_Games (32 rows).
2. *"Show me tournaments that haven't been played yet."*
(Hint: Use a NOT IN filter.)
You can find the solution in Tourneys_Not_Played (6 rows).
3. *"Find the bowlers who had a raw score of 170 or better at both Thunderbird Lanes and Bolero Lanes."*
(Hint: Build a filter using EXISTS.)
You can find the solution in Good_Bowlers_TBird_And_Bolero_EXISTS (10 rows).
4. *"List all the bowlers who have a current average that's less than all of the other bowlers on the same team."*
(Hint: Build a filter using < ALL.)
You can find the solution in Bowlers_Low_Average (8 rows).

Recipes Database

1. *"Show me the types of recipes and the count of recipes in each type."*
   (Hint: Use the COUNT aggregate function.)
   You can find the solution in Count_Of_Recipe_Types (7 rows).
2. *"Show me the recipes that have beef* and *garlic."*
   (Hint: Build a filter using EXISTS.)
   You can find the solution in Recipes_Beef_And_Garlic (1 row).
3. *"List the ingredients that are used in some recipe where the measurement amount in the recipe is not the default measurement amount."*
   (Hint: Build a filter using <> SOME.)
   You can find the solution in Ingredients_Using_NonStandard_Measure (21 rows).
4. *"List ingredients not used in any recipe yet."*
   (Hint: Build a filter using NOT IN.)
   You can find the solution in Ingredients_No_Recipe (20 rows).

Part IV

Summarizing and Grouping Data

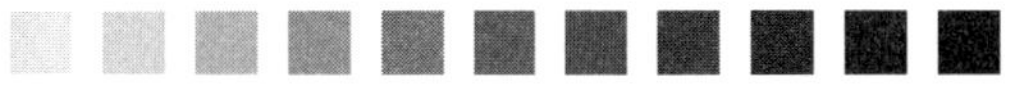

12

Simple Totals

"There are two kinds of statistics: the kind you look up and the kind you make up."
—Rex Stout
Death of a Doxy: A Nero Wolfe Novel

Topics Covered in This Chapter

You now know how to select the columns you need for a given request, define expressions that add extra levels of detail, join the appropriate tables that supply the columns you require, and define conditions to filter the data sent to the Result Set. We've shown you all these techniques so that you can learn how to retrieve detailed information from one or more tables in the database. In this and the next two chapters, we'll show you how to take a step back and look at the data from a much broader perspective, otherwise known as "Seeing the Big Picture."

In this chapter, you'll learn how to use aggregate functions to produce basic summary information. In Chapter 13, we'll show you how to organize data into groups with the GROUP BY clause of the SELECT Statement, and in Chapter 14 we'll show you various filtering techniques that you can apply to the data after it is grouped.

Aggregate Functions

The requests you've been working with so far have required answers involving individual column values from the rows returned by the FROM and WHERE clauses. However, you'll often encounter requests, such as those below, that require only calculated values across multiple rows for an answer.

"How many of our customers live in Seattle?"

"What is the smallest price and highest price we've assigned to any item in our inventory?"

"How many classes is Mike Hernandez teaching?"

"What time does our earliest class begin?"

"What is the average length of a class?"

"What is the total amount for order number 12?"

The SQL Standard provides a set of *aggregate functions* that allow you to calculate a single value from the rows in a Result Set or from the values returned by a Value Expression. You can apply a given function to all the rows or values, or you can use a WHERE clause to apply the function to a specific set of rows or values. For example, you can use an aggregate function to determine the largest or smallest value of a Value Expression, count the number of rows in a Result Set, or calculate a total using only distinct values from a Value Expression. Figure 12-1 shows the syntax for all the aggregate functions.

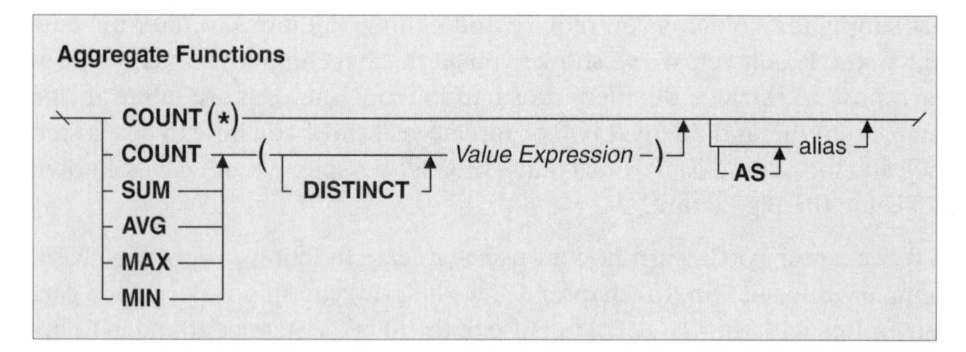

Figure 12-1 *Syntax diagram for aggregate functions.*

As you can see, aggregate functions have a very simple and straightforward syntax. In this chapter, we'll show you how to use these functions in the SELECT clause, and in Chapter 14 we'll explore using these functions in the HAVING clause.

In the previous chapter, we discussed using aggregate functions in a Subquery either to return a single calculated value in a SELECT clause or to fetch a calculated value that you can use in a Predicate in a WHERE clause. We'll show you a few more examples of this usage in this chapter.

Each aggregate function returns a single value, regardless of whether it is processing the rows in a Result Set or the values returned by a Value Expression. With the exception of COUNT(*), all aggregate functions automatically disregard Null values. You can use several aggregate functions in the SELECT clause at the same time, and you can even mix Value Expressions containing aggregate functions with Value Expressions containing *literal values*. However, you *cannot* mix Value Expressions containing aggregate functions with Value Expressions containing *Column References* unless those non-aggregate Value Expressions also appear in a grouping specification. You'll learn about grouping later in Chapter 13.

Let's look at each of these aggregate functions and how you might use them to answer a request.

Counting Rows and Values with COUNT

The SQL Standard defines two versions of the COUNT function. COUNT(*) processes rows in a Result Set, and COUNT (*Value Expression*) processes values returned by a Value Expression.

You use COUNT(*) to determine how many rows exist in a Result Set. The COUNT(*) function tallies *all* of the rows in a Result Set, including redundant rows and rows containing Null values. Here's a simple example of the type of question you can answer with this function.

> ❖ **Note** Throughout this chapter, we'll be using the "Request/Translation/Clean Up/SQL" technique that we introduced in Chapter 4. All examples assume you have thoroughly studied and understood the concepts covered in previous chapters, especially the chapters on JOIN and Subqueries.

"Show me the total number of employees we have in our company."

Translation Select the count of employees from the employees table

Clean Up Select ~~the~~ count ~~of employees~~ (*) from ~~the~~ employees ~~table~~

SQL
```
SELECT COUNT(*)
FROM Employees
```

Note that we use "(*)" in the clean up statement to indicate that we want to count all the rows in the Employees table. This is a good practice to follow when you work with this type of request because it helps ensure that you use the correct COUNT function. The SELECT Statement in this example generates a Result Set consisting of a single-column row containing a numeric value that represents the total number of rows in the Employees table.

There is no restriction on the number of rows the COUNT(*) function processes. You can indicate which rows COUNT(*) should tally by using a WHERE clause. For example, here's how you define a SELECT Statement that counts all the rows in the Employees table for those employees who live in Washington State.

SQL
```
SELECT COUNT(*)
FROM Employees
WHERE EmpState = 'WA'
```

As we work through this chapter, you'll see that you can use a WHERE clause to filter the rows or values processed by any aggregate function.

When you use an aggregate function in a SELECT Statement, you may or may not see a column name in the Result Set for the return value of the function. Some database systems provide a default column name, and others do not. But you can use the AS option of the function's syntax to provide a meaningful column name for the Result Set. Here's how you might apply this option to the previous example.

SQL
```
SELECT COUNT(*) AS TotalWashingtonEmployees
FROM Employees
WHERE EmpState = 'WA'
```

Now the Result Set consists of a column called TotalWashingtonEmployees that contains the return value of the COUNT(*) function. As the syntax diagram in Figure 12-1 on page 388 indicates, you can apply this technique to any aggregate function.

You use the COUNT(*Value Expression*) function to count the total number of *non-Null* values returned by a Value Expression. (This expression is more commonly known as COUNT, which is the name we'll use for the remainder of the book.) It tallies all values returned by a Value Expression, regardless of whether they are unique or duplicate, and automatically excludes any Null values from the final tally. You can use COUNT to answer this type of request.

> *"How many customers were able to indicate which county they live in?"*

Here you need to determine how many actual values exist in the county column. Remember that COUNT(*) *includes* Null values as well, so it won't provide you with the correct answer. Instead, you use the COUNT function and translate the request in this manner.

Translation	Select the count of non-null county values as NumberOfKnownCounties from the customers table
Clean Up	Select ~~the~~ count ~~of non-null~~ (county) ~~values~~ as NumberOfKnownCounties from ~~the~~ customers ~~table~~
SQL	`SELECT COUNT(CustCounty) AS NumberOfKnownCounties FROM Customers`

```
SELECT COUNT(CustCounty)
   AS NumberOfKnownCounties
FROM Customers
```

Note that the Translation and Clean Up statements explicitly ask for non-Null values. Although you already know that this function processes only non-Null values, it's a good idea to add this request to both statements so that you'll be sure to use the correct COUNT function. The SELECT Statement you've defined here will generate a Result Set that contains a numeric value representing the total number of county names found in the CustCounty column.

Remember that the COUNT function treats duplicate county names as though they were unique and includes every one of them in the final tally. You can, however, use the function's DISTINCT option to exclude duplicate values from the count. The next example shows how you might apply it to a given request.

> *"How many unique county names are there in the customers table?"*

Translation	Select the count of unique county names as NumberOfUniqueCounties from the customers table
Clean Up	Select ~~the~~ count ~~of unique~~ (distinct county) as NumberOfUniqueCounties ~~names~~ from ~~the~~ customers ~~table~~

SQL
```
SELECT COUNT(DISTINCT CustCounty)
   AS NumberOfUniqueCounties
FROM Customers
```

When you use the DISTINCT option, the database retrieves all the non-Null values from the county column, eliminates the duplicates, and *then* counts the values that remain. The database goes through much of this same process whenever you use DISTINCT with the SUM, AVG, MIN, or MAX functions.

In this next example, we use a slightly altered version of the previous request to show that you can apply a filter to the COUNT function.

"How many unique county names are there in the customers table for the state of Oregon?"

Translation Select the count of unique county names as NumberOfUniqueOregonCounties from the customers table where the state is 'OR'

Clean Up Select ~~the~~ count ~~of unique~~ (distinct county) as NumberOfUniqueOregonCounties ~~names~~ from ~~the~~ customers ~~table~~ where ~~the~~ state ~~is~~ = 'OR'

SQL
```
SELECT COUNT(DISTINCT CustCounty)
   AS NumberOfUniqueOregonCounties
FROM Customers
WHERE CustState = 'OR'
```

It's important to note that you *cannot* use DISTINCT with COUNT(*). This is a reasonable restriction because COUNT(*) tallies *all* rows in a table, regardless of whether any are redundant or contain Null values.

Computing a Total with SUM

You can calculate a total for a *numeric* Value Expression with the SUM function. It processes all the non-Null values of the Value Expression and returns a final total to the Result Set. Note that if the Value Expression in *all* the rows is Null or if the FROM and WHERE clauses together return an empty Result Set, then SUM returns a Null. Here's a sample request you can answer with SUM.

"What is the total amount we pay in salaries to our employees in California?"

Translation Select the sum of salary as TotalSalaryAmount from the employees table where the state is 'CA'

Clean Up Select ~~the~~ sum ~~of~~ (salary) as TotalSalaryAmount from ~~the~~ employee ~~table~~ where ~~the~~ state ~~is~~ = 'CA'

SQL
```
SELECT SUM(Salary) AS TotalSalaryAmount
FROM Employees
WHERE EmpState = 'CA'
```

The Value Expression we used here was a simple Column Reference. However, you can also use SUM on a Value Expression consisting of a numeric expression, as we demonstrate in the next example.

"How much is our current inventory worth?"

Translation Select the sum of wholesale price times quantity on hand as TotalInventoryValue from the products table

Clean Up Select ~~the~~ sum ~~of~~ (wholesale price ~~times~~ * quantity on hand) as TotalInventoryValue from ~~the~~ products ~~table~~

SQL
```
SELECT SUM(WholesalePrice * QuantityOnHand)
   AS TotalInventoryValue
FROM Products
```

As you know, a row must contain actual values in the WholesalePrice and QuantityOnHand columns in order for it to be processed by the SUM function. In this instance, the database processes the expression for all qualifying rows in the Products table, totals the results with the SUM function, and then sends the grand total to the Result Set.

Here's an example of how to use SUM to calculate a total for a unique set of numeric values.

"Calculate a total of all unique wholesale costs for the products we sell."

Translation Select the sum of unique wholesale costs as SumOfUniqueWholesaleCosts from the products table

Clean Up Select ~~the~~ sum ~~of unique~~ (distinct wholesale costs) as SumOfUniqueWholesaleCosts from ~~the~~ products ~~table~~

SQL
```
SELECT SUM(DISTINCT WholesaleCost)
   AS SumOfUniqueWholesaleCosts
FROM Products
```

Calculating a Mean Value with AVG

Another function you can use on *numeric* values is AVG, which calculates the arithmetic mean of all non-Null values returned by a Value Expression. You can use AVG to answer a request such as this.

> *"What is the average contract amount for vendor number 10014?"*

Translation — Select the average of contract price as AverageContractPrice from the vendor contracts table where the vendor ID is 10014

Clean Up — Select ~~the average of~~ avg (contract price) as AverageContractPrice from ~~the~~ vendor contracts ~~table~~ where the vendor ID ~~is~~ = 10014

SQL

```
SELECT AVG(ContractPrice)
   AS AverageContractPrice
FROM Vendor_Contracts
WHERE VendorID = 10014
```

As you work with your clean up statement, be sure to cross out the word "average" and replace it with "avg." This will keep you from accidentally using "Average" in the SELECT clause. Average is not a valid SQL keyword, so the SELECT Statement will fail if you try to use it.

You can also use AVG to process a numeric expression, just as you did with the SUM function. Remember that you cannot use AVG with a Value Expression that is not numeric. Most database systems will give you an error if you try to use these functions with character string or date/time data.

> *"What is the average item total for order 64?"*

Translation — Select the average of price times quantity ordered as AverageItemTotal from the order details table where order ID is 64

Clean Up — Select ~~the average of~~ avg (price ~~times~~ * quantity ordered) as AverageItemTotal from ~~the~~ order details ~~table~~ where order ID ~~is~~ = 64

SQL

```
SELECT AVG(Price * QuantityOrdered)
   AS AverageItemTotal
FROM Order_Details
WHERE OrderID = 64
```

Keep in mind that a row must contain actual values in the Price and QuantityOrdered columns in order for that row to be processed by the AVG function. Otherwise, the numeric expression evaluates to Null, and the AVG function disregards the row entirely. As with SUM, if the Value Expression in all rows is Null or if the FROM and WHERE clauses together return an empty Result Set, AVG returns a Null value.

In this next example, we use the DISTINCT option to average a unique set of numeric values.

"Calculate an average of all unique product prices."

Translation: Select the average of unique prices as UniqueProductPrices from the products table

Clean Up: Select ~~the average of unique~~ avg (distinct prices) as UniqueProductPrices from ~~the~~ products ~~table~~

SQL:

```
SELECT AVG(DISTINCT Price) AS UniqueProductPrices
FROM Products
```

Finding the Largest Value with MAX

You can determine the *largest* value returned by a Value Expression with the MAX function. The MAX function can process any type of data; the value it returns depends on the data it processes.

CHARACTER STRINGS	The value that MAX returns is based on the collating sequence used by your database system or computer. For example, if your database uses the ASCII character set and is case insensitive, it sorts company names in this manner: "...4th Dimension Productions...Al's Auto Shop...allegheny & associates...Zercon Productions...zorn credit services." In this instance, MAX will return "zorn credit services" as the MAX value.
NUMBERS	MAX returns the largest number.
DATES/TIMES	MAX evaluates dates and times in chronological order and returns the *most recent* (or latest) date or time.

Here are a couple of examples of how you might use MAX to answer a request.

"What is the largest amount we've paid on a contract?"

Translation: Select the maximum contract price as LargestContractPrice from the engagements table

Clean Up — Select ~~the~~ max~~imum~~ (contract price) as LargestContractPrice from ~~the~~ engagements ~~table~~

SQL

```
SELECT MAX(ContractPrice)
   AS LargestContractPrice
FROM Engagements
```

"What was the largest line item total for order 3314?"

Translation — Select the maximum price times quantity ordered as LargestItemTotal from the order details table where the order ID is 3314

Clean Up — Select ~~the~~ max~~imum~~ (price ~~times~~ * quantity ordered) as LargestItemTotal from ~~the~~ order details ~~table~~ where ~~the~~ order ID ~~is~~ = 3314

SQL

```
SELECT MAX(Price * QuantityOrdered)
   AS LargestItemTotal
FROM Order_Details
WHERE OrderID = 3314
```

In the next example, we use the DISTINCT option to return a unique instance of the most recent review date in a Staff table. In this case, two or more staff members may have been reviewed as recently as last Thursday, but we need to see only one occurrence of that date.

"What is the most recent date that we reviewed any of our staff?"

Translation — Select the maximum unique review date as MostRecentReviewDate from the staff table

Clean Up — Select ~~the~~ max~~imum unique~~ (distinct review date) as MostRecentReviewDate from ~~the~~ staff ~~table~~

SQL

```
SELECT MAX(DISTINCT ReviewDate)
   AS MostRecentReviewDate
FROM Staff
```

Although the SQL Standard specifies DISTINCT as an option for the MAX function, DISTINCT *has no effect* on the MAX function whatsoever. There can be only one maximum value, regardless of whether or not it is distinct. For example, both of the following expressions return the same value.

```
SELECT MAX(HireDate) FROM Agents
SELECT MAX(DISTINCT HireDate) FROM Agents
```

We present both versions of the function because they are part of the current SQL Standard, but we recommend that you just use the MAX function without the DISTINCT option.

Finding the Smallest Value with MIN

The MIN function allows you to determine the *smallest* value returned by a Value Expression. It works like the MAX function but returns the opposite value: first character string (based on the collating sequence), smallest number, and earliest date or time.

You can answer requests such as these with the MIN function.

"What is the lowest price we charge for a product?"

Translation Select the minimum price as LowestProductPrice from the products table

Clean Up Select ~~the~~ min~~imum~~ (contract price) as LowestProductPrice from ~~the~~ products ~~table~~

SQL

```
SELECT MIN(Price) AS LowestProductPrice
FROM Products
```

"What was the lowest line item total for order 3314?"

Translation Select the minimum price times quantity ordered as LowestItemTotal from the order details table where the order ID is 3314

Clean Up Select ~~the~~ min~~imum~~ (price ~~times~~ * quantity ordered) as LowestItemTotal from ~~the~~ order details ~~table~~ where ~~the~~ order ID ~~is~~ = 3314

SQL

```
SELECT MIN(Price * QuantityOrdered)
   AS LowestItemTotal
FROM Order_Details
WHERE OrderID = 3314
```

In the next example, we use the DISTINCT option to return a unique instance of the earliest hire date in an Employee table. In this case, two or more employees may have been hired on May 16, 1977, but we need to see only one occurrence of that date.

"When did we hire our first employees?"

Translation: Select the minimum unique hire date as EarliestHireDate from the employees table

Clean Up: Select ~~the~~ min~~imum unique~~ (distinct hire date) as EarliestHireDate from ~~the~~ employees ~~table~~

SQL:
```
SELECT MIN(DISTINCT HireDate)
   AS EarliestHireDate
FROM Employees
```

It's important to note that the DISTINCT option *has no effect* whatsoever on the MIN function. (As you know, this was the case with the MAX function as well.) There can be only one minimum value, regardless of whether or not it is distinct. For example, both of the following expressions return the same value.

```
SELECT MIN(ReviewDate) FROM Agents
SELECT MIN(DISTINCT ReviewDate) FROM Agents
```

We present both versions of the function because they are part of the current SQL Standard, but we recommend that you just use the MIN function without the DISTINCT option.

Using More Than One Function

As we mentioned at the beginning of this section, you can use several aggregate functions at the same time. This gives you the ability to show contrasting information using a single SELECT Statement. For example, you can use the MIN and MAX functions to show the earliest and most recent order dates for a specific customer, or the MAX, MIN, and AVG functions to show the highest, lowest, and average grades for a given student. Here are other examples of how you might use two or more aggregate functions.

"Show me the earliest and most recent review dates for the employees in the advertising department."

Translation: Select the minimum review date as EarliestReviewDate and the maximum review date as RecentReviewDate from the employees table where the department is "Advertising"

Clean Up: Select ~~the~~ min~~imum~~ review date as EarliestReviewDate ~~and the~~ max~~imum~~ review date as RecentReviewDate from ~~the~~ employees ~~table~~ where ~~the~~ department ~~is~~ = "Advertising"

SQL

```
SELECT MIN(ReviewDate) AS EarliestReviewDate,
   MAX(ReviewDate) AS RecentReviewDate
FROM Employees
WHERE Department = "Advertising"
```

"How many different products were ordered on order number 553 and what was the total cost of that order?"

Translation — Select the count of product ID as TotalProductsPurchased and the sum of price times quantity ordered as OrderAmount from the order details table where the order number is 553

Clean Up — Select ~~the~~ count ~~of~~ (product ID) as TotalProductsPurchased ~~and~~ ~~the~~ sum ~~of~~ (price ~~times~~ * quantity ordered) as OrderAmount from ~~the~~ order details ~~table~~ where ~~the~~ order number ~~is~~ = 553

SQL

```
SELECT COUNT(ProductID) AS
   TotalProductsPurchased, SUM(Price *
   QuantityOrdered) AS OrderAmount
FROM Order_Details
WHERE OrderNumber = 553
```

There are a couple of restrictions you must keep in mind when you work with two or more aggregate functions. The first is that you cannot embed one aggregate function within another. This restriction makes the following expression illegal.

```
SUM(AVG(LineItemTotal))
```

The second is that you cannot use a Subquery as the Value Expression of an aggregate function. For example, the following expression is illegal under this restriction.

```
AVG((SELECT Price FROM Products WHERE Category = 'Bikes'))
```

Despite these restrictions, you've learned how easily you can use aggregate functions in a SELECT clause to retrieve relatively complex statistical information. Let's now look at how you might use aggregate functions to filter the information in a Result Set.

Using Aggregate Functions in Filters

Because an aggregate function returns a single value, you can use it as part of a Comparison Predicate in a Search Condition. You have to place the aggregate function within a Subquery, however, and then use the Subquery as part of the Comparison Predicate. If you're thinking that this sounds familiar, you're right. In Chapter 11, you learned how to use a Subquery as part of a Search Condition in a WHERE clause and an aggregate function within a Subquery. So you already know, in a general sense, how to use an aggregate function to filter the data sent to a Result Set. Now let's expand on that knowledge.

Using an aggregate function as part of a Comparison Predicate allows you to test the value of a Value Expression against a single statistical value. Although you could use a Literal Value for the task, a Subquery gives you more flexibility and provides a more dynamic aspect to the condition. For example, suppose you're posing the following request to the database.

> *"List the engagement numbers that have a contract price greater than or equal to the overall average contract price."*

One method you can use to answer this request is to calculate the overall average contract price manually and then use that value in a Comparison Predicate.

Translation — Select the engagement number from the engagements table where the contract price is greater than or equal to $24,887.00

Clean Up — Select ~~the~~ engagement number from ~~the~~ engagements ~~table~~ where ~~the~~ contract price ~~is greater than or equal to~~ >= ~~$~~24,887.00

SQL

```
SELECT EngagementNumber
FROM Engagements
WHERE ContractPrice >= 24,887.00
```

Another way to handle this is to use an aggregate function in a Subquery and let the database system do the work for you.

Translation — Select the engagement number from the engagements table where the contract price is greater than or equal to the overall average contract price in the engagements table

Clean Up — Select ~~the~~ engagement number from ~~the~~ engagements ~~table~~ where ~~the~~ contract price ~~is greater than or equal to the~~ >= ~~overall average~~ (select avg contract price ~~in the~~ from engagements ~~table~~)

SQL

```
SELECT EngagementNumber
FROM Engagements
WHERE ContractPrice >=
   (SELECT AVG(ContractPrice)
   FROM Engagements)
```

It should be obvious that using a Subquery with an aggregate function is your best course of action. If you use a Literal Value, you must be certain that you always recalculate the average contract price before executing the SELECT Statement, just in case you've modified any existing contract prices. You then have to make sure that you enter the value correctly in the Comparison Predicate. But you won't have to worry about any of this if you use a Subquery instead. The AVG function is always evaluated whenever you execute the SELECT Statement, and it always returns the correct value regardless of whether you've modified any of the contract prices. (This is true for any aggregate function you use in a Subquery.)

You can limit the rows that an aggregate function evaluates by using a WHERE clause in the Subquery. This allows you to narrow the scope of the statistical value returned by the aggregate function. You already learned how to apply a WHERE clause to a Subquery back in Chapter 11, so let's look at an example of how you might apply this technique.

"List the engagement number and contract price of all engagements that have a contract price larger than the total amount of all contract prices for the entire month of May in 1999."

Translation — Select engagement number and contract price from the engagements table where the contract price is greater than the sum of all contract prices of engagements dated between May 1, 1999 and May 31, 1999

Clean Up — Select engagement number, ~~and~~ contract price from ~~the~~ engagements ~~table~~ where ~~the~~ contract price ~~is greater than~~ > ~~the~~ (select sum ~~of all~~ (contract price~~s~~) ~~of~~ from engagements where ~~dated~~ start date between ~~May 1, 1999~~ '1999-05-01' and '1999-05-31') ~~May 31, 1999~~

SQL

```
SELECT EngagementNumber, ContractPrice
FROM Engagements
WHERE ContractPrice >
   (SELECT SUM(ContractPrice) FROM Engagements
      WHERE  StartDate BETWEEN '1999-05-01'
      AND '1999-05-31')
```

You may find that you rarely have a need to use aggregate functions in filters, but they certainly come in handy when you have to answer those occasional "off the wall" requests.

Sample Statements

In this chapter, you've learned how to use aggregate functions in a SELECT clause and within a Subquery being used as part of a Comparison Predicate. Now let's look at some examples of working with aggregate functions using the tables from each of the sample databases.

> ❖ **Note** Remember that all the column names and table names used in these examples are drawn from the sample database structures shown in Appendix B. To simplify the process, we have combined the Translation and Clean Up steps for all the following examples.

Sales Order Database

"How many customers do we have in the state of California?"

Translation/ Clean Up: Select ~~the~~ count(*) ~~of all customers~~ from ~~the~~ customers ~~table~~ where ~~the~~ state ~~is~~ = 'CA'

SQL

```
SELECT COUNT(*) AS NumberOfCACustomers
FROM Customers
WHERE CustState = 'CA'
```

Number_Of_California_Customers (1 Row)

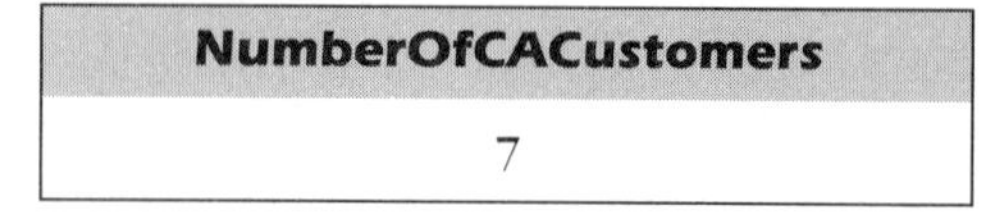

NumberOfCACustomers
7

"List the product names and numbers that have a quoted price greater than or equal to the overall average retail price in the products table."

Translation/ Clean Up: Select ~~the~~ product name, ~~and~~ ~~the~~ product number from ~~the~~ products ~~table~~ join~~ed with the~~ order_details ~~table~~ on product number where ~~the~~ quoted price >= ~~is greater than or equal to the average~~ (select avg(retail price) from ~~in the~~ products ~~table)~~

SQL

```
SELECT DISTINCT Products.ProductName,
   Order_Details.ProductNumber
FROM Products
INNER JOIN Order_Details
ON Products.ProductNumber =
   Order_Details.ProductNumber
WHERE Order_Details.QuotedPrice >=
   (SELECT AVG(RetailPrice)
   FROM Products)
```

❖ **Note** We chose to ask for DISTINCT products because (we hope) a particular product may have been ordered more than once. We need to see each product name and number only once.

Quoted_Price_vs_Average_Retail_Price (4 Rows)

ProductName	ProductNumber
Eagle FS-3 Mountain Bike	2
GT RTS-2 Mountain Bike	11
Trek 9000 Mountain Bike	1
Viscount Mountain Bike	6

Entertainment Database

"List the engagement number and contract price of our earliest contracts."

Translation/ Clean Up: Select engagement number, ~~and~~ contract price from ~~the~~ engagements ~~table~~ where ~~the~~ start date = ~~is equal to the earliest~~ (select min(start date) ~~in the~~ from engagements ~~table)~~

SQL

```
SELECT EngagementNumber, ContractPrice
FROM Engagements
WHERE StartDate =
   (SELECT MIN(StartDate) FROM Engagements)
```

Earliest_Contracts (2 Rows)

EngagementNumber	ContractPrice
2	$200.00
8	$1,850.00

"What was the total value of all engagements booked in August of 1999?"

Translation/ Clean Up: Select ~~the~~ sum ~~of~~ (contract price) as TotalBookedValue from ~~the~~ engagements ~~table~~ where ~~the~~ start date ~~is~~ between '1999-08-01' and '1999-08-31' ~~August 1, 1999 and August 31, 1999~~

SQL

```
SELECT SUM(ContractPrice) AS TotalBookedValue
FROM Engagements
WHERE StartDate
   BETWEEN '1999-08-01' AND '1999-08-31'
```

Total_Booked_Value_For_August_1999 (1 Row)

TotalBookedValue
$ 30,005.00

School Scheduling Database

"What is the largest salary we pay to any staff member?"

Translation/ Clean Up: Select ~~the~~ max~~imum~~ (salary) as LargestStaffSalary from ~~the~~ staff ~~table~~

SQL:

```
SELECT Max(Salary) AS LargestStaffSalary
FROM Staff
```

Largest_Staff_Salary (1 Row)

LargestStaffSalary
$ 60,000.00

"What is the total salary amount paid to our staff in California?"

Translation/ Clean Up: Select ~~the~~ sum ~~of~~ (salary) as TotalSalaryAmount from ~~the~~ staff ~~table for all our California staff~~ where state = 'CA'

SQL:

```
SELECT SUM(Salary) AS TotalSalaryAmount
FROM Staff
WHERE StfState = 'CA'
```

Total_Salary_Paid_To_California_Staff (1 Row)

TotalAmountPaid
$209,000.00

Bowling Database

"How many tournaments have been played at Red Rooster Lanes?"

Translation/ Clean Up: Select ~~the~~ count ~~of~~ (tourney location)~~s~~ as NumberOfTournaments from ~~the~~ tournaments ~~table~~ where ~~the~~ tourney location ~~is~~ = 'Red Rooster Lanes'

SQL

```
SELECT COUNT(TourneyLocation)
   AS NumberOfTournaments
FROM Tournaments
WHERE TourneyLocation = 'Red Rooster Lanes'
```

Number_Of_Tournaments_At_Red_Rooster_Lanes (1 Row)

NumberOfTournaments
2

"List the last name and first name, in alphabetical order, of every bowler whose personal average score is greater than or equal to the overall current average score."

Translation/ Clean Up: Select ~~the~~ last name, ~~and~~ first name from ~~the~~ bowlers ~~table~~ where ~~the~~ current average >= ~~is greater than or equal to the overall~~ (select avg(current average) ~~score in the~~ from bowlers) ~~table~~

SQL

```
SELECT BowlerLastName, BowlerFirstName
FROM Bowlers
WHERE CurrentAverage >=
   (SELECT AVG(CurrentAverage)FROM Bowlers)
ORDER BY BowlerLastName, BowlerFirstName
```

Better_Than_Overall_Average (16 Rows)

BowlerLastName	BowlerFirstName
Cunningham	David
Fournier	David
Hallmark	Alaina
Hallmark	Gary
Hernandez	Michael
Kennedy	John
McLain	Susan
Patterson	Kathryn
Patterson	Neil
Patterson	Rachel
Piercy	Greg
Pundt	Steve
Thompson	Mary
Thompson	Will
Viescas	Carol
Viescas	John

Recipes Database

"How many recipes contain a beef ingredient?"

Translation/ Clean Up	Select ~~the~~ count (*) ~~of recipes~~ as NumberOfRecipes from ~~the~~ recipes ~~table~~ where ~~the~~ recipe ID ~~is~~ in ~~the~~ (select~~ion~~ ~~of~~ recipe ID~~s in the~~ from recipe ingredients ~~table joined with the~~ inner join ingredients ~~table~~ on ingredient ID where ~~the~~ ingredient name ~~is~~ like 'Beef')

SQL

```
SELECT COUNT(*) AS NumberOfRecipes
FROM Recipes
WHERE Recipes.RecipeID IN
   (SELECT RecipeID
    FROM Recipe_Ingredients
    INNER JOIN Ingredients ON
       Recipe_Ingredients.IngredientID =
       Ingredients.IngredientID
    WHERE  Ingredients.IngredientName
       LIKE 'Beef%')
```

Recipes_With_Beef_Ingredient (1 Row)

NumberOfRecipes
3

"How many ingredients are measured by the cup?"

Translation/ Clean Up	Select ~~the~~ count (*) ~~of ingredients~~ as NumberOfIngredients from ~~the~~ ingredients ~~table joined with the~~ inner join measurements ~~table~~ on measureamount ID where ~~the~~ measurement description ~~is~~ = 'Cup'

SQL

```
SELECT COUNT(*) AS NumberOfIngredients
FROM Ingredients
INNER JOIN Measurements ON
   Ingredients.MeasureAmountID =
   Measurements.MeasureAmountID
WHERE MeasurementDescription = 'Cup'
```

Number_of_Ingredients_Measured_by_the_Cup (1 Row)

NumberOfIngredients
12

SUMMARY

We began this chapter by introducing you to aggregate functions. You learned that there are six different functions and that you can use them in the SELECT and WHERE clauses of a SELECT Statement. You also learned that each aggregate function—except COUNT(*)—disregards all Null values as it performs its operation.

Next we showed how to use each aggregate function. You learned how to perform tallies with the COUNT functions, how to find the largest and smallest values with the MAX and MIN functions, how to calculate a mean average with the AVG function, and how to total a set of values with the SUM function. We also showed how to use the DISTINCT option with each function and explained that DISTINCT has no effect on the MAX and MIN functions.

We closed the chapter by showing you how to use aggregate functions in filters. You now know that you must use the aggregate function within a Subquery and then use the Subquery as part of the filter. You also learned that you can apply a filter to the Subquery as well so that the aggregate function bases its value on a specific set of data.

We've only just begun to show you what you can do with aggregate functions. In the final two chapters, we'll show you how to provide more sophisticated statistical information by using aggregate functions on *grouped* data.

Problems for You to Solve

Below, we show you the request statement and the name of the solution query in the sample databases. If you want some practice, you can work out the SQL you need for each request and then check your answer with the query we saved in the samples. Don't worry if your syntax doesn't exactly match the syntax of the queries we saved—as long as your Result Set is the same.

Sales Order Database

1. *"What is the average retail price of a mountain bike?"*
   You can find the solution in Average_Price_Of_A_Mountain_Bike (1 row).
2. *"What was the date of our most recent order?"*
   You can find the solution in Most_Recent_Order_Date (1 row).

3. *"What was the total amount for order number 8?"*
   You can find the solution in Total_Amount_For_Order_Number_8 (1 row).

Entertainment Database

1. *"What is the average salary of a booking agent?"*
   You can find the solution in Average_Agent_Salary (1 row).
2. *"Show me the engagement numbers for all engagements that have a contract price greater than or equal to the overall average contract price."*
   (Hint: You'll have to use a Subquery to answer this request.)
   You can find the solution in Contract_Price_>=_Average_Contract_Price (52 rows).
3. *"Which vendors do we work with that don't have a Web site."*
   You can find the solution in Number_Of_Bellevue_Entertainers (1 row).

School Scheduling Database

1. *"What is the current average class duration?"*
   You can find the solution in Average_Class_Duration (1 row).
2. *"List the last name and first name of each staff member who has been with us the longest amount of time."*
   (Hint: You'll have to use a Subquery containing an aggregate function that evaluates the DateHired column.)
   You can find the solution in Most_Senior_Staff_Members (3 rows).
3. *"How many classes are held in room 3346?"*
   You can find the solution in Number_Of_Classes_Held_In_Room_3346 (1 row).

Bowling Database

1. *"What is the largest handicap held by any bowler at the current time?"*
   You can find the solution in Current_Highest_Handicap (1 row).
2. *"Which locations hosted the very first tournaments?"*
   (Hint: You'll have to determine the earliest tournament date.)
   You can find the solution in Tourney_Locations_For_Earliest_Dates (2 rows).
3. *"What is the most recent tournament date we have in our schedule?"*
   You can find the solution in Most_Recent_Tourney_Date (1 row).

Recipes Database

1. *"Which recipe requires the most cloves of garlic?"*
   (Hint: You'll need to use INNER JOINs and a Subquery to answer this request.)
   You can find the solution in Recipe_With_Most_Cloves_of_Garlic (1 row).
2. *"Count the number of main course recipes."*
   (Hint: This requires a JOIN between Recipe_Classes and Recipes.)
   You can find the solution in Number_Of_Main_Course_Recipes (1 row).
3. *Calculate the total number of teaspoons of salt in all recipes."*
   You can find the solution in Total_Salt_Used (1 row).

13

Grouping Data

"Don't drown yourself with details.
Look at the whole."
— Marshal Ferdinand Foch
Commander-in-Chief,
Allied armies in France

Topics Covered in This Chapter

Chapter 12 explained how to use the aggregate functions (COUNT, MIN, MAX, AVG, and SUM) to ask SQL to calculate a value across all the rows in the table defined in your FROM and WHERE clauses. We pointed out, however, that once you include any Value Expression that contains an aggregate function in your SELECT clause, *all* your Value Expressions must either be a literal constant or contain an aggregate function. This characteristic is useful if you want to see only one row of totals across a Result Set, but what if you want to see some subtotals? In this chapter, we'll show you how to ask for subtotals by grouping your data.

Why Group Data?

When you're working in the Sales Order database, finding out the number of orders (COUNT), the total sales (SUM), the average of sales (AVG), the smallest order (MIN), or the largest order (MAX) is useful, indeed. And if you want to calculate any of these values by customer, order date, or product, you can add a filter (WHERE) to fetch the rows for one particular customer or product. But what if you want to see subtotals for *all* customers, displaying the customer name along with the subtotals? To do that, you need to ask your database system to *group* the rows.

Likewise in the Entertainment Agency database, it's easy to find out the number of contracts, the total contract price, the smallest contract price, or the largest contract price for all contracts. You can even filter the rows so that you see these calculations for one particular entertainer, one particular customer, or across a specific range of dates. Again, if you want to see one total row for each customer or entertainer, you must group the rows.

Are you starting to get the idea? When you ask your database system to group rows on column values or expressions, it forms subsets of rows based on matching values. You can then ask your database to calculate aggregate values *on each group*. Let's look at a simple example from the Entertainment Agency database. First, we need to build a query that fetches the columns of interest—entertainer name and contract price. Here's the SQL.

```
SQL       SELECT Entertainers.EntStageName,
             Engagements.ContractPrice
          FROM Entertainers
          INNER JOIN Engagements
          ON Entertainers.EntertainerID =
             Engagements.EntertainerID
          ORDER BY EntStageName
```

The result looks like the following table. (In the sample database, we saved this request as Entertainers_And_ContractPrices.)

EntStageName	ContractPrice
Albert Buchanan	$200.00
Albert Buchanan	$500.00
Albert Buchanan	$185.00
Albert Buchanan	$200.00
Albert Buchanan	$110.00
Albert Buchanan	$770.00
Albert Buchanan	$230.00
Albert Buchanan	$365.00
Albert Buchanan	$470.00
Carol Peacock Trio	$1,670.00
Carol Peacock Trio	$1,670.00
Carol Peacock Trio	$1,670.00
Carol Peacock Trio	$320.00
Carol Peacock Trio	$1,400.00
Carol Peacock Trio	$410.00
Carol Peacock Trio	$140.00
Carol Peacock Trio	$410.00
Carol Peacock Trio	$1,940.00
Carol Peacock Trio	$770.00
Carol Peacock Trio	$680.00
Caroline Coie Cuartet	$650.00
<<*more rows here* >>	

You already know that you can count all the rows, or find the smallest, largest, sum, or average of the ContractPrice column—as long as you eliminate the entertainer stage name column. You can keep this column as long as you ask your database to group on it. If you ask to group on entertainer stage name, your database will form one group containing the first nine rows ("Albert Buchanan"), a second group containing the next eleven rows ("Carol Peacock Trio"), and so on through the entire table. You can now ask for the COUNT of the rows or the SUM, MIN, MAX, or AVG of the contract price column, and you will get one aggregate row per entertainment group. The result looks like the following table.

EntStageName	NumContracts	TotPrice	MinPrice	MaxPrice	AvgPrice
Albert Buchanan	9	$3,030.00	$110.00	$770.00	$336.67
Carol Peacock Trio	11	$11,080.00	$140.00	$1,940.00	$1,007.27
Caroline Coie Cuartet	11	$15,070.00	$290.00	$2,450.00	$1,370.00
Coldwater Cattle Company	10	$19,100.00	$350.00	$3,800.00	$1,910.00
Country Feeling	16	$36,230.00	$275.00	$14,105.00	$2,264.38
Jazz Persuasion	8	$7,780.00	$500.00	$2,300.00	$972.50
Julia Schnebly	9	$4,665.00	$275.00	$875.00	$518.33
JV & the Deep Six	11	$18,820.00	$950.00	$3,650.00	$1,710.91
<<more rows here >>					

Looks interesting, doesn't it? We bet you'd like to know how we did that! We'll show you all the details in the following sections.

The GROUP BY Clause

As you discovered in Chapter 12, you can find out all sorts of interesting information using aggregate functions. However, you may have noticed that all the examples we gave you applied the aggregate functions across *all* the rows returned by the FROM and WHERE clauses. You could filter the Result Set down to one group using the WHERE clause, but there was really no way to look at the results from multiple groups in one request. To accomplish this summarizing by group in a single request, we need to add one more major clause to your SQL vocabulary—GROUP BY.

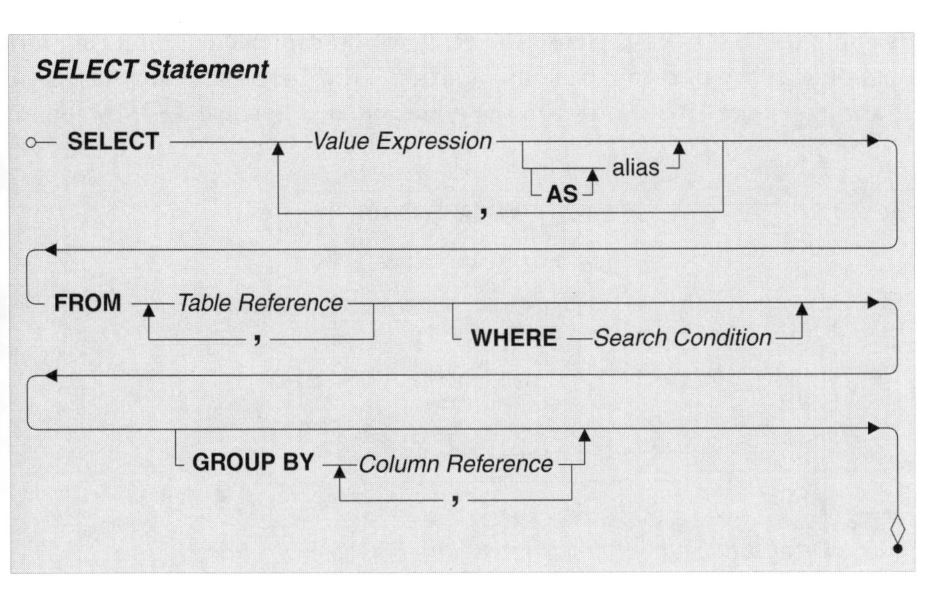

Figure 13-1 *The SELECT Statement with a GROUP BY clause.*

Syntax

Let's take a close look at the GROUP BY clause. Figure 13-1 shows the basic diagram for a SELECT Statement with GROUP BY added.

As you recall from earlier chapters, you define the tables that are the source of your data in the FROM clause. Your FROM clause can be as simple as a single table name or as complex as a JOIN of multiple tables. As discussed in Chapter 8, you can even embed an entire Table Subquery (a SELECT Statement) as a Table Reference. Next, you can optionally provide a WHERE clause to include or exclude certain rows supplied by the FROM clause. We covered the WHERE clause in detail in Chapter 6.

When you add a GROUP BY clause, you specify the columns in the logical table formed by the FROM and WHERE clauses that you want your database system to use as the definition for groups of rows. Rows that have the same values in the list of columns you specify will be gathered together into a group. You can use the columns that you list in the GROUP BY clause in Value Expressions in your SELECT clause, and you can use any of the aggregate functions we discussed in the previous chapter to perform calculations across each group.

Let's apply the GROUP BY clause to see how you can calculate information about contract prices by entertainment group—the sample we tantalized you with earlier. Figure 13-2 shows you the tables needed to solve this problem.

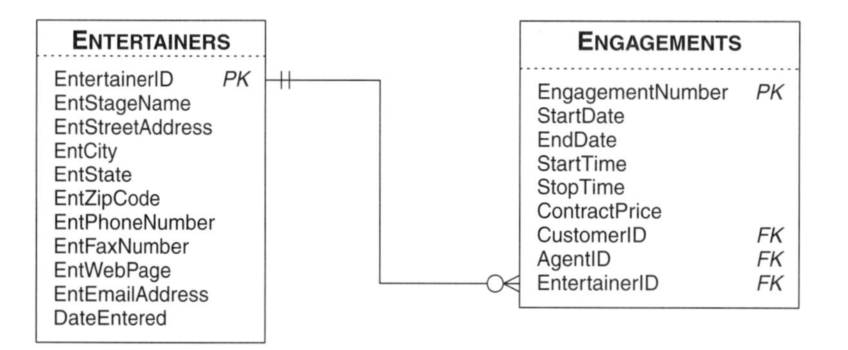

Figure 13-2 *The relationship between Entertainers and Engagements tables.*

> ❖ **Note** Throughout this chapter, we'll be using the "Request/Translation/Clean Up/SQL" technique that we introduced in Chapter 4.

"Show me for each entertainment group the group name, the count of contracts for the group, the total price of all the contracts, the lowest contract price, the highest contract price, and the average price of all the contracts."

(Hint: When you see a request that wants the count, total, smallest, largest, or average of values at a detail level (contracts) *for each* value at a higher level (entertainers), you are going to need to use aggregate functions and grouping in your request. Remember that for each entertainer there are most likely many contracts.)

Translation Select entertainer name, the count of contracts, the sum of the contract price, the lowest contract price, the highest contract price, and the average contract price from the entertainers table joined with the engagements table on entertainer ID, grouped by entertainer name

Clean Up Select entertainer name, ~~the~~ count ~~of~~ (*) ~~contracts~~, ~~the~~ sum ~~of the~~ (contract price), ~~the lowest~~ min(contract price), ~~the highest~~ max(contract price), ~~and the~~ ~~average~~ avg(contract price) from ~~the~~ entertainers ~~table~~ join~~ed with the~~ engagements ~~table~~ on entertainer ID, group~~ed~~ by entertainer name

SQL

```
SELECT Entertainers.EntStageName,
   COUNT(*) AS NumContracts,
   SUM(Engagements.ContractPrice) AS TotPrice,
   MIN(Engagements.ContractPrice) AS MinPrice,
   MAX(Engagements.ContractPrice) AS MaxPrice,
   AVG(Engagements.ContractPrice) AS AvgPrice
FROM Entertainers
INNER JOIN Engagements
ON Entertainers.EntertainerID =
   Engagements.EntertainerID
GROUP BY Entertainers.EntStageName
```

Note that we substituted MIN for lower, MAX for higher, and AVG for average as we showed you in the previous chapter. We also asked for COUNT(*) since we want to count all the engagement (contract) rows regardless of any Null values. Adding the GROUP BY clause is what gets us the aggregate calculations *per entertainment group*. It also allows us to include the entertainer name in the SELECT clause. (We saved this request as Aggregate_Contract_Info_By_Entertainer in the sample database.)

What if you want (or need) to group on more than one value? Let's look at this same problem, but from the perspective of customers rather than entertainers, and let's assume you want to display in your Result Set both the Customer's Last Name and First Name. Figure 13-3 shows the necessary tables.

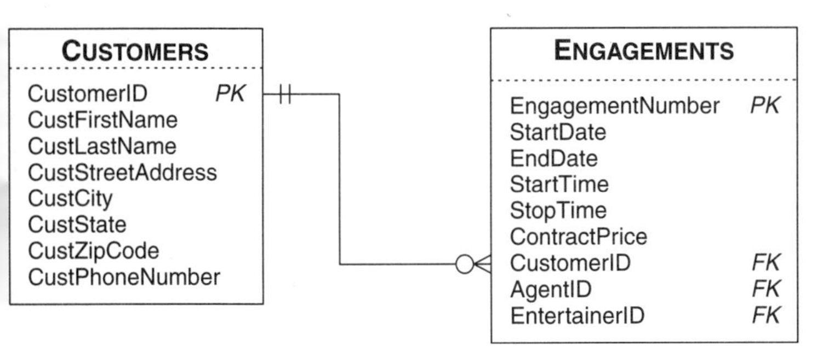

Figure 13-3 *The relationship between Customers and Engagements tables.*

"Show me for each customer the customer first and last name, the count of contracts for the customer, the total price of all the contracts, the lowest contract price, the highest contract price, and the average price of all the contracts."

Translation: Select customer last name, customer first name, the count of contracts, the sum of the contract price, the lowest contract price, the highest contract price, and the average contract price from the customers table joined with the engagements table on customer ID, grouped by customer last name and customer first name

Clean Up: Select customer last name, customer first name, ~~the~~ count ~~of~~ (*) ~~contracts~~, ~~the~~ sum ~~of the~~ (contract price), ~~the lowest~~ min(contract price), ~~the highest~~ max(contract price), ~~and the average~~ avg(contract price) from ~~the~~ customers ~~table~~ join~~ed with the~~ engagements ~~table~~ on customer ID, group~~ed~~ by customer last name, ~~and~~ customer first name

SQL

```
SELECT Customers.CustLastName,
   Customers.CustFirstName,
   COUNT(*) AS NumContracts,
   SUM(Engagements.ContractPrice) AS TotPrice,
   MIN(Engagements.ContractPrice) AS MinPrice,
   MAX(Engagements.ContractPrice) AS MaxPrice,
   AVG(Engagements.ContractPrice) AS AvgPrice
FROM Customers
INNER JOIN Engagements
ON Customers.CustomerID =
   Engagements.CustomerID
GROUP BY Customers.CustLastName,
   Customers.CustFirstName
```

The result looks like the following table. (In the sample database, we saved this request as Aggregate_Contract_Info_By_Customer.)

CustLastName	CustFirstName	NumContracts	TotPrice	MinPrice	MaxPrice	AvgPrice
Bonnicksen	Joyce	8	$7,000.00	$320.00	$2,150.00	$875.00
Buchanan	Amelia	7	$4,685.00	$200.00	$1,490.00	$669.29
Callahan	Sally	9	$11,520.00	$140.00	$2,750.00	$1,280.00
Ehrlich	Mel	8	$7,015.00	$110.00	$2,930.00	$876.88
Ehrlich	Zachary	13	$12,455.00	$230.00	$1,550.00	$958.08
Fuller	Ann	10	$12,320.00	$350.00	$2,450.00	$1,232.00
Fuller	Thomas	10	$13,745.00	$200.00	$2,675.00	$1,374.50
Hallmark	Elizabeth	8	$25,585.00	$410.00	$14,105.00	$3,198.13
<<more rows here>>						

Because it takes two columns to display the customer name, we had to include them *both* in the GROUP BY clause. Remember that if you want to include a column in the output that is not the result of an aggregate calculation, you must also include it in the GROUP BY clause. We did not include ContractPrice in the GROUP BY clause because that's the column we're using in many of the aggregate function expressions. If we had included ContractPrice, we would have gotten unique groups of customers and prices. MIN, MAX, and AVG will all return that grouped price. COUNT will be greater than one only if more than one contract with the same price exists for a given customer. If you think about it, though, grouping by customer and price and asking for a COUNT would be a good way to find customers who have multiple contracts at the same price.

Mixing Columns and Expressions

Suppose you want to list the customer name as one output column, the full customer address as another output column, the last engagement date, and the sum of engagement contract prices? The customer name is in two columns: CustFirstName and CustLastName. The columns you need for a full address are CustStreetAddress, CustState, CustCity, and CustZipCode. Let's see how you should construct the SQL for this request. (We saved this request as Customers_Last_Booking in the sample database.)

"Show me for each customer the customer full name, the customer full address, the latest contract date for the customer, and the total price of all the contracts."

Translation Select customer last name and customer first name as customer full name; street address, city, state, and zipcode as customer full address; the latest contract start date; and the sum of the contract price from the customers table joined with the engagements table on customer ID, grouped by customer last name, customer first name, customer street address, customer city, customer state, and customer zip code

Clean Up Select customer last name ~~and~~ || ',' || customer first name as customer full name~~;~~, street address~~,~~ || ',' || city~~,~~ || ',' || state~~,~~ ~~and~~ || ' ' || zipcode as customer full address~~;~~, ~~the latest~~ MAX(~~contract~~ start date) as latest date~~;~~, ~~and~~ ~~the~~ sum ~~of the~~ (contract price) as total contract price from ~~the~~ customers ~~table~~ join~~ed with the~~ engagements ~~table~~ on customer ID, group~~ed~~ by customer last name, customer first name, customer street address, customer city, customer state, ~~and~~ customer zip code

SQL

```
SELECT Customers.CustLastName || ', ' ||
   Customers.CustFirstName AS CustomerFullName,
   Customers.CustStreetAddress || ', ' ||
   Customers.CustCity || ', ' ||
   Customers.CustState || ' ' ||
   Customers.CustZipCode AS CustomerFullAddress
   MAX(Engagements.StartDate) AS LatestDate,
   SUM(Engagements.ContractPrice),
   AS TotalContractPrice
FROM Customers
INNER JOIN Engagements
ON Customers.CustomerID =
   Engagements.CustomerID
GROUP BY Customers.CustLastName,
   Customers.CustFirstName,
   Customers.CustStreetAddress,
   Customers.CustCity, Customers.CustState,
   Customers.CustZipCode
```

Notice that we had to list each and every one of the columns we used in an output expression that did not include an aggregate function. We used StartDate and ContractPrice in aggregate expressions, so we don't need to list them in the GROUP BY clause. In fact, it doesn't make sense to group on either StartDate or ContractPrice because we want to use these in an aggregate calculation across multiple customers. If, for example, we grouped on StartDate, MAX(StartDate) would return the grouping value, and SUM(ContractPrice) would return only the sum of contract prices for a customer on any given date. You wouldn't get the sum of more than one contract unless a customer had more than one contract for a given date—not likely.

Using GROUP BY in a Subquery in a WHERE Clause

In Chapter 11, we introduced the COUNT and MAX aggregate functions to show how to filter rows using an aggregate value fetched with a Subquery. In Chapter 12, we showed how to use MIN, AVG, and SUM in a Subquery filter as well. Let's look at a request that requires both a Subquery with an aggregate function and a GROUP BY clause in the Subquery.

"Display the engagement contract whose price is greater than the sum of all contracts for any other customer."

Translation: Select customer first name, customer last name, engagement start date, and engagement contract price from the customers table joined with the engagements table on customer ID where the contract price is greater than the sum of all contract prices for customers other than the current customer, grouped by customer ID

Clean Up: Select customer first name, customer last name, engagement start date, ~~and~~ engagement contract price from ~~the~~ customers ~~table~~ join~~ed with the~~ engagements ~~table~~ on customer ID where ~~the~~ contract price ~~is greater than~~ > ALL (SELECT ~~the~~ sum ~~of all~~ contract prices ~~for~~ customer~~s~~ ID <> ~~other than the current~~ customer ID~~,~~ group~~ed~~ by customer ID)

SQL

```
SELECT Customers.CustFirstName,
   Customers.CustLastName,
   Engagements.StartDate,
   Engagements.ContractPrice
FROM Customers
INNER JOIN Engagements
ON Customers.CustomerID =
   Engagements.CustomerID
WHERE Engagements.ContractPrice > ALL
   (Select SUM(ContractPrice)
   FROM Engagements AS E2
   WHERE E2.CustomerID <> Customers.CustomerID
   GROUP BY E2.CustomerID)
```

Let's analyze what the Subquery is doing. For each engagement that the query looks at in the JOIN of customers and engagements, the Subquery calculates the SUM of all contract prices for all *other* customers and groups them by customer ID. Because there are multiple customers in the database, the Subquery will return multiple SUM values—one for each of the other customers. For this reason, we cannot ask for a simple greater than (>) comparison. We can, however, use the quantified greater than all (> ALL) comparison to check a set of values as you learned in Chapter 11. If you run this query in the sample Entertainment Agency database for this chapter (we saved it as "Biggest_Big_Contract"), you'll find that one contract fits the bill as shown below.

CustFirstName	CustLastName	StartDate	ContractPrice
Elizabeth	Hallmark	1999-11-21	$14,105.00

Simulating a SELECT DISTINCT Statement

Did it occur to you that you can use a GROUP BY clause and not include any aggregate functions in your SELECT clause? Sure you can! When you do this, you get the same effect as using the DISTINCT keyword covered in Chapter 4. (See the Eliminating Duplicate Rows section in that chapter.)

Let's look at a simple request that requires unique values and solve it using both techniques.

"Show me the unique city names from the customers table."

Translation 1 Select the distinct city names from the customers table

Clean Up Select ~~the~~ distinct city name~~s~~ from ~~the~~ customers ~~table~~

SQL

```
SELECT DISTINCT Customers.CustCityName
FROM Customers
```

Translation 2 Select city name from the customers table, grouped by city name

Clean Up Select city name from ~~the~~ customers ~~table,~~ group~~ed~~ by city name

SQL

```
SELECT Customers.CustCityName
FROM Customers
GROUP BY Customers.CustCityName
```

Remember that GROUP BY groups all the rows on the grouping column(s) you specify and returns one row per group. This is a slightly different way to get to the same result that you obtain with the DISTINCT keyword. Which one is better? We think that DISTINCT may be a clearer statement of what you want, but you may find that your database system solves the problem faster when you use GROUP BY.

"Some Restrictions Apply"

We already mentioned that adding a GROUP BY clause places certain restrictions on constructing your request. Let's review those restrictions to make sure you don't fall into common traps.

Column Restrictions

When you add a GROUP BY clause, you're asking your database system to form unique groups of rows from those returned by the tables defined in your FROM clause and filtered by your WHERE clause. You can use as many aggregate expressions as you like in your SELECT clause, and these expressions can use any of the columns in the table defined by the FROM and WHERE clauses. As we pointed out in an earlier example, it probably does not make sense to reference a column in an aggregate expression and also include that column in your grouping specification.

If you choose to also include expressions that reference columns but do not include an aggregate function, you must list *all* columns you use this way in the GROUP BY clause. One of the most common mistakes is to assume that you can reference columns in non-aggregate expressions as long as the columns come from unique rows. For example, let's take a look at an incorrect request that includes a Primary Key value—something that we know by definition is unique.

"Display the customer ID, customer full name, and the total of all engagement contract prices."

Translation Select customer ID, customer first name, and customer last name as customer full name, and the sum of contract prices from the customers table joined with the engagements table on customer ID, grouped by customer ID

Clean Up Select customer ID, customer first name ~~and~~ || ' ' || customer last name as customer full name,~~and the~~ sum ~~of~~ (contract price)~~s~~ from ~~the~~ customers ~~table~~ join~~ed with the~~ engagements ~~table~~ on customer ID, group~~ed~~ by customer ID

SQL
```
SELECT Customers.CustomerID,
   Customers.CustFirstName || ' ' ||
   Customers.CustLastName AS CustFullName,
   SUM(Engagements.ContractPrice) AS TotalPrice
FROM Customers
INNER JOIN Engagements
ON Customers.CustomerID =
   Engagements.CustomerID
GROUP BY Customers.CustomerID
```

We *know* that CustomerID is unique per customer. Grouping on CustomerID alone should be sufficient to fetch unique customer first and last name information within the groups formed by CustomerID. However, SQL is a language based on syntax, not semantics. In other words, SQL does not take into account any knowledge that could be implied by the design of your database tables—including which columns are a Primary Key. SQL demands that your request be syntactically "pure" and translatable without any knowledge of the underlying table design. So, the above SQL statement will fail on a database system that is fully compliant with the SQL Standard because we've included columns in the SELECT clause that are not in an aggregate function and are also not in the GROUP BY clause (CustFirstName and CustLastName). The correct SQL request is as follows.

SQL
```
SELECT Customers.CustomerID,
   Customers.CustFirstName || ' ' ||
   Customers.CustLastName AS CustFullName,
   SUM(Engagements.ContractPrice) AS TotalPrice
FROM Customers
INNER JOIN Engagements
ON Customers.CustomerID =
   Engagements.CustomerID
GROUP BY Customers.CustomerID,
   Customers.CustFirstName,
   Customers.CustLastName
```

This may seem like overkill, but it's the correct way to do it!

❖ **Note** In some database systems, you must exactly duplicate the *expressions* you use in the SELECT clause in the GROUP BY clause. Oracle and Microsoft Access are examples of systems that require this. In the above example, you would have to

```
GROUP BY Customers.CustomerID,
   Customers.CustFirstName || ' ' ||
   Customers.CustLastName
```

instead of listing the separate columns. This isn't compliant with the SQL Standard, but you may find that this is the only way you can get your request to work on your system.

Grouping on Expressions

We showed you earlier some correct examples of creating expressions that do not include aggregate functions. One of the most common mistakes is to attempt to group on the expression you create in the SELECT clause rather than on the individual columns. Remember that the GROUP BY clause must refer to columns created by the FROM and WHERE clauses. It cannot use an expression you create in your SELECT clause.

Let's take another look at an example we solved earlier to show you what we mean, but this time, let's make the mistake. (We're skipping the Translation and Clean Up steps here because we covered them earlier.)

"Show me for each customer in the state of Washington the customer full name, the customer full address, the latest contract date for the customer, and the total price of all the contracts."

```
SQL        SELECT Customers.CustLastName || ', ' ||
              Customers.CustFirstName AS CustomerFullName,
              Customers.CustStreetAddress || ', ' ||
              Customers.CustCity || ', ' ||
              Customers.CustState || ' ' ||
              Customers.CustZip AS CustomerFullAddress
              MAX(Engagements.StartDate) AS LatestDate,
              SUM(Engagements.ContractPrice)
              AS TotalContractPrice
           FROM Customers
           INNER JOIN Engagements
           ON Customers.CustomerID =
              Engagements.CustomerID
```

(continued)

```
WHERE Customers.CustState ='WA'
GROUP BY CustomerFullName,
   CustomerFullAddress
```

Some database systems will let you get away with this, but it's not correct. The CustomerFullName and CustomerFullAddress columns don't exist until *after* your database system has evaluated the FROM, WHERE, and GROUP BY clauses. The GROUP BY clause won't find these columns in the result created in the FROM and WHERE clauses, so on a database system that strictly adheres to the SQL Standard you'll get a syntax error.

We showed you earlier one correct way to solve this: You must list all the columns you use in both the CustomerFullName and CustomerFullAddress expressions. Another way is to make the FROM clause generate the calculated columns by embedding a Table Subquery. Here's what it looks like.

```
SQL       SELECT CE.CustomerFullName,
             CE.CustomerFullAddress,
             MAX(CE.StartDate) AS LatestDate,
             SUM(CE.ContractPrice)
             AS TotalContractPrice
          FROM
            (SELECT Customers.CustLastName || ', ' ||
             Customers.CustFirstName AS CustomerFullName,
               Customers.CustStreetAddress || ', ' ||
               Customers.CustCity || ', ' ||
               Customers.CustState || ' ' ||
               Customers.CustZip AS CustomerFullAddress,
               Engagements.StartDate,
               Engagements.ContractPrice
             FROM Customers
             INNER JOIN Engagements
             ON Customers.CustomerID =
               Engagements.CustomerID
             WHERE Customers.CustState ='WA')
          AS CE
          GROUP BY CE.CustomerFullName,
             CE.CustomerFullAddress
```

This works now because we've generated the CustomerFullName and CustomerFullAddress columns as output in the FROM clause. You have to admit, though, that this makes the query very complex. In truth, it's better to just list all the individual columns you plan to use in non-aggregate expressions rather than try to generate the expressions as columns inside the FROM clause.

Uses for GROUP BY

At this point, you should have a pretty good understanding of how to ask for subtotals across groups using aggregate functions and the GROUP BY clause. The best way to give you an idea of the wide range of uses for GROUP BY is to show you problems you can solve with this new clause followed by a robust set of examples in the next section.

> *"Show me each vendor and the average by vendor of the number of days to deliver products."*
>
> *"Display for each product the product name and the total sales."*
>
> *"List for each customer and order date the customer full name and the total cost of items ordered on each date."*
>
> *"Display each entertainment group ID, entertainment group member, and the amount of pay for each member based on the total contract price divided by the number of members in the group."*
>
> *"Show each agent name, the sum of the contract price for the engagements booked, and the agent's total commission."*
>
> *"For completed classes, list by category and student the category name, the student name, and the student's average grade of all classes taken in that category."*
>
> *"Display by category the category name and the count of classes offered."*
>
> *"List each staff member and the count of classes each is scheduled to teach."*
>
> *"Show me for each tournament and match the tournament ID, the tournament location, the match number, the name of each team, and the total of the handicap score for each team."*
>
> *"Display for each bowler the bowler name and the average of their raw game scores."*
>
> *"Show me how many recipes exist for each class of ingredient."*
>
> *"If I want to cook all the recipes in my cookbook, how much of each ingredient must I have on hand?"*

Sample Statements

You now know the mechanics of constructing queries using a GROUP BY clause and have seen some of the types of requests you can answer. Let's take a look at a set of samples, all of which request that the information be grouped. These examples come from each of the sample databases.

We've also included sample Result Sets that would be returned by these operations and placed them immediately after the SQL syntax line. The name that appears immediately above a Result Set is the name we gave each query in the sample data on the companion CD you'll find bound into the back of the book. We stored each query in the appropriate sample database (as indicated within the example) in the "Chapter13" subfolder on the CD. You can follow the instructions at the beginning of this book to load the samples onto your computer and try them out.

> ❖ **Note** Remember that all the column names and table names used in these examples are drawn from the sample database structures shown in Appendix B. To simplify the process, we have combined the Translation and Clean Up steps for all the examples.
>
> These samples assume you have thoroughly studied and understood the concepts covered in previous chapters, especially the chapters on JOIN and Subqueries.

Sales Order Database

"List for each customer and order date the customer full name and the total cost of items ordered on each date."

Translation/Clean Up: Select customer first name ~~and~~ || ' ' || customer last name as customer full name, order date, ~~and the~~ sum ~~of~~ (quoted price ~~times~~ * quantity ordered) as total cost from ~~the~~ customers ~~table~~ join~~ed with the~~ orders ~~table~~ on customer ID~~, and then~~ join~~ed with the~~ order details ~~table~~ on order number, group~~ed~~ by customer first name, customer last name, ~~and~~ order date

SQL

```
SELECT Customers.CustFirstName || ' ' ||
   Customers.CustLastName AS CustFullName,
   Orders.OrderDate,
   SUM(Order_Details.QuotedPrice *
   Order_Details.QuantityOrdered) AS TotalCost
FROM (Customers
INNER JOIN Orders
ON Customers.CustomerID = Orders.CustomerID)
INNER JOIN Order_Details
```

```
ON Orders.OrderNumber =
   Order_Details.OrderNumber
GROUP BY Customers.CustFirstName,
   Customers.CustLastName, Orders.OrderDate
```

Order_Totals_By_Customer_And_Date (847 rows)

CustFullName	OrderDate	TotalCost
Alaina Hallmark	1999-07-02	$4,699.98
Alaina Hallmark	1999-07-14	$4,433.95
Alaina Hallmark	1999-07-18	$353.25
Alaina Hallmark	1999-07-21	$3,951.90
Alaina Hallmark	1999-07-22	$10,388.68
Alaina Hallmark	1999-07-30	$3,088.00
Alaina Hallmark	1999-08-11	$6,775.06
Alaina Hallmark	1999-08-21	$15,781.10
<<more rows here>>		

Entertainment Agency Database

"Display each entertainment group ID, entertainment group member, and the amount of pay for each member based on the total contract price divided by the number of members in the group."

❖ **Note** This one is really tricky because each member may belong to more than one entertainer group. You must sum the contract prices for each entertainer and then divide by the count of members in that group (assuming each member gets equal pay). Fetching the count requires a Subquery filtered on the current entertainer ID (the ID of the group, not the ID of the member), which means you also must group on entertainer ID. Oh yes, and don't forget to exclude members who are not active (Status = 3).

Translation/ Clean Up

Select entertainer ID, member first name, member last name, ~~and the~~ sum ~~of~~ (contract price)~~s~~ ~~divided by~~ / ~~the~~ (SELECT count(*) ~~of active members~~ FROM entertainer_members AS EM2 ~~in the current entertainer group~~ WHERE ~~the~~ EM2 entertainer ID = ~~the~~ entertainer members entertainer ID) from ~~the~~ members ~~table~~ join~~ed with the~~ entertainer members ~~table~~ on member ID~~, then~~ join~~ed with the~~ entertainers ~~table~~ on entertainer ID~~, and finally~~ join~~ed with the~~ engagements ~~table~~ on entertainer ID~~,~~ where member status ~~is not equal~~ ~~to~~ <> 3~~,~~ group~~ed~~ by entertainer ID, member first name, ~~and~~ member last name, ~~sorted~~ ORDER by member last name

SQL

```
SELECT Entertainers.EntertainerID,
   Members.MbrFirstName, Members.MbrLastName,
   SUM(Engagements.ContractPrice)/
      (SELECT COUNT(*)
       FROM Entertainer_Members AS EM2
       WHERE EM2.Status <> 3
       AND EM2.EntertainerID =
       Entertainers.EntertainerID)
     AS MemberPay
FROM ((Members
INNER JOIN Entertainer_Members
ON Members.MemberID =
   Entertainer_Members.MemberID)
INNER JOIN Entertainers
ON Entertainers.EntertainerID =
   Entertainer_Members.EntertainerID)
INNER JOIN Engagements
ON Entertainers.EntertainerID =
   Engagements.EntertainerID
WHERE Entertainer_Members.Status<>3
GROUP BY Entertainers.EntertainerID,
   Members.MbrFirstName, Members.MbrLastName
ORDER BY Members.MbrLastName
```

Member_Pay (40 rows)

EntertainerID	MbrFirstName	MbrLastName	MemberPay
1010	Kendra	Bonnicksen	$3,675.00
1013	Kendra	Bonnicksen	$3,767.50
1004	Albert	Buchanan	$3,030.00
1007	Andrea	Buchanan	$3,820.00
1001	Laura	Callahan	$3,693.33
1008	George	Chavez	$7,246.00
1013	George	Chavez	$3,767.50
1010	Caroline	Coie	$3,675.00
<<more rows here >>			

Bowling League Database

"Show me for each tournament and match the tournament ID, the tournament location, the match number, the name of each team, and the total of the handicap score for each team."

Translation/ Clean Up: Select tourney ID, tourney location, match ID, team name, ~~and the~~ sum ~~of~~ (handicap score) as TotHandicapScore from ~~the~~ tournaments ~~table~~ join~~ed with the~~ tourney matches ~~table~~ on tournament ID~~, then~~ join~~ed with the~~ match games ~~table~~ on match ID~~, then~~ join~~ed with the~~ bowler scores ~~table~~ on match ID and game number~~, then~~ join~~ed with the~~ bowlers ~~table~~ on bowler ID~~, and finally~~ join~~ed with the~~ teams ~~table~~ on team ID~~,~~ group~~ed~~ by tourney ID, tourney location, match ID, ~~and~~ team name

SQL

```
SELECT Tournaments.TourneyID,
   Tournaments.TourneyLocation,
   Tourney_Matches.MatchID, Teams.TeamName,
   Sum(Bowler_Scores.HandiCapScore)
   AS TotHandiCapScore
FROM ((((Tournaments
INNER JOIN Tourney_Matches
ON Tournaments.TourneyID =
   Tourney_Matches.TourneyID)
INNER JOIN Match_Games
ON Tourney_Matches.MatchID =
   Match_Games.MatchID)
INNER JOIN Bowler_Scores
ON (Match_Games.MatchID =
   Bowler_Scores.MatchID) AND
   (Match_Games.GameNumber =
   Bowler_Scores.GameNumber))
INNER JOIN Bowlers
ON Bowlers.BowlerID = Bowler_Scores.BowlerID)
INNER JOIN Teams
ON Teams.TeamID = Bowlers.TeamID
GROUP BY Tournaments.TourneyID,
   Tournaments.TourneyLocation,
   Tourney_Matches.MatchID, Teams.TeamName
```

As you can see, the difficult part of this request is assembling the complex JOIN clauses to link all the tables in the correct manner.

Tournament_Match_Team_Results (112 rows)

TourneyID	TourneyLocation	MatchID	TeamName	TotHandiCapScore
1	Red Rooster Lanes	1	Marlins	2351
1	Red Rooster Lanes	1	Sharks	2348
1	Red Rooster Lanes	2	Barracudas	2289
1	Red Rooster Lanes	2	Terrapins	2391
1	Red Rooster Lanes	3	Dolphins	2389
1	Red Rooster Lanes	3	Orcas	2395
1	Red Rooster Lanes	4	Manatees	2292
1	Red Rooster Lanes	4	Swordfish	2353
2	Thunderbird Lanes	5	Marlins	2297
2	Thunderbird Lanes	5	Terrapins	2279
<<more rows here >>				

School Scheduling Database

"For completed classes, list by category and student the category name, the student name, and the student's average grade of all classes taken in that category."

Translation/ Clean Up

Select category description, student first name, student last name, ~~and the~~ ~~average~~ AVG(~~of~~ grade) as AvgOfGrade from ~~the~~ categories ~~table~~ join~~ed with the~~ subjects ~~table~~ on category ID~~, then~~ join~~ed with the~~ classes ~~table~~ on subject ID~~, then~~ join~~ed with the~~ student schedules ~~table~~ on class ID~~, then~~ join~~ed with the~~ student class status ~~table~~ on class status~~, and finally~~ join~~ed with the~~ students ~~table~~ on student ID where class status description ~~is~~ = 'Completed,' group~~ed~~ by category description, student first name, ~~and~~ student last name

SQL

```
SELECT Categories.CategoryDescription,
   Students.StudFirstName,
   Students.StudLastName,
   Avg(Student_Schedules.Grade) AS AvgOfGrade
FROM ((((Categories
INNER JOIN Subjects
ON Categories.CategoryID = Subjects.CategoryID)
INNER JOIN Classes
ON Subjects.SubjectID = Classes.SubjectID)
INNER JOIN Student_Schedules
ON Classes.ClassID = Student_Schedules.ClassID)
INNER JOIN Student_Class_Status
ON Student_Class_Status.ClassStatus =
   Student_Schedules.ClassStatus)
INNER JOIN Students
ON Students.StudentID =
   Student_Schedules.StudentID
WHERE Student_Class_Status.ClassStatusDescription =
   'Completed'
GROUP BY Categories.CategoryDescription,
   Students.StudFirstName,
   Students.StudLastName
```

Student_GradeAverage_By_Category (45 rows)

CategoryDescription	StudFirstName	StudLastName	AvgOfGrade
Accounting	Andrew	Fuller	79.43
Accounting	Elizabeth	Hallmark	90.24
Accounting	John	Kennedy	71.45
Accounting	Michael	Viescas	90.01
Accounting	Sara	Kennedy	89.92
Accounting	Sarah	Leverling	90.67
Accounting	Steven	Buchanan	87.82
Accounting	Steven	Pundt	84.37
Art	Carol	Peacock	80.78
<<*more rows here* >>			

Recipes Database

"Show me how many recipes exist for each class of ingredient."

> ❖ **Note** The challenge here is you don't want to count a particular recipe class more than once per recipe. For example, if a recipe contains multiple herbs or dairy ingredients, that recipe should be counted only once per class. Sounds like it's time to use COUNT(DISTINCT *Value Expression*), doesn't it?

Translation/ Clean Up	Select ingredient class description, ~~and the unique~~ count ~~of~~ (DISTINCT recipe ID) from ~~the~~ ingredient classes ~~table~~ join~~ed with the~~ ingredients ~~table~~ on ingredient class ID~~, and then~~ join~~ed with the~~ recipe ingredients ~~table~~ on ingredient ID~~,~~ group~~ed~~ by ingredient class description

SQL
```
SELECT
   Ingredient_Classes.IngredientClassDescription,
   Count(DISTINCT RecipeID) AS CountOfRecipeID
FROM (Ingredient_Classes
INNER JOIN Ingredients
ON Ingredient_Classes.IngredientClassID =
   Ingredients.IngredientClassID)
INNER JOIN Recipe_Ingredients
ON Ingredients.IngredientID =
   Recipe_Ingredients.IngredientID
GROUP BY
   Ingredient_Classes.IngredientClassDescription
```

IngredientClass_Distinct_Recipe_Count (18 rows)

IngredientClassDescription	CountOfRecipeID
Butter	3
Cheese	2
Chips	1
Condiment	3
Dairy	2
Fruit	1
Grain	2
Herb	1
<<more rows here>>	

❖ **Note** Because Microsoft Access 2000 does not support COUNT DISTINCT, you'll find that the query in the Access sample database first selects the DISTINCT values of Recipe ID using a Table Subquery in the FROM clause and then counts the resulting rows.

SUMMARY

We began the chapter by explaining to you why you might want to group data to get multiple subtotals from a Result Set. After tantalizing you with an example, we proceeded to show how to use the GROUP BY clause to solve the example problem and several others. We also showed how to mix column expressions with aggregate functions.

We next explored an interesting example of using GROUP BY in a Subquery that acts as a filter in a WHERE clause. We subsequently pointed out that constructing a query using GROUP BY and no aggregate functions is the same as using DISTINCT in your SELECT clause. Then we warned you to carefully construct your GROUP BY clause to include the columns and not the expressions.

We wrapped up our discussion of the GROUP BY clause by explaining some common pitfalls. We showed that SQL does not consider any knowledge of Primary Keys. We also explained common mistakes you might make when using column expressions in your SELECT clause.

We summarized why the GROUP BY clause is useful and gave you a sample list of problems you can solve using GROUP BY. The rest of the chapter gives examples of how to build requests that require the GROUP BY clause. The following section presents a number of requests that you can work out on your own.

Problems for You to Solve

Below, we show you the request statement and the name of the solution query in the sample databases. If you want some practice, you can work out the SQL you need for each request and then check your answer with the query we saved in the samples. Don't worry if your syntax doesn't exactly match the syntax of the queries we saved—as long as your Result Set is the same.

Sales Order Database

1. *"Show me each vendor and the average by vendor of the number of days to deliver products."*
   (Hint: Use the AVG aggregate function and group on vendor.)
   You can find the solution in Vendor_Avg_Delivery (10 rows).
2. *"Display for each product the product name and the total sales."*
   (Hint: Use SUM with a calculation of quantity times price and group on product name.)
   You can find the solution in Sales_By_Product (38 rows).

Entertainment Agency Database

1. *"Show each agent's name, the sum of the contract price for the engagements booked, and the agent's total commission."*
   (Hint: You must multiply the sum of the contract prices times the agent's commission. Be sure to group on the commission rate as well!)
   You can find the solution in Agent_Sales_And_Commissions (8 rows).

Bowling League Database

1. *"Display for each bowler the bowler name and the average of their raw game scores."*
   (Hint: Use the AVG aggregate function and group on bowler name.)
   You can find the solution in Bowler_Averages (32 rows).

School Scheduling Database

1. *"Display by category the category name and the count of classes offered."*
   (Hint: Use COUNT and group on category name.)
   You can find the solution in Category_Class_Count (16 rows).
2. *"List each staff member and the count of classes each is scheduled to teach."*
   (Hint: Use COUNT and group on staff name.)
   You can find the solution in Staff_Class_Count (23 rows).

Recipes Database

1. *"If I want to cook all the recipes in my cookbook, how much of each ingredient must I have on hand?"*
   (Hint: Use SUM and group on ingredient name and measurement description.)
   You can find the solution in Total_Ingredients_Needed (65 rows).

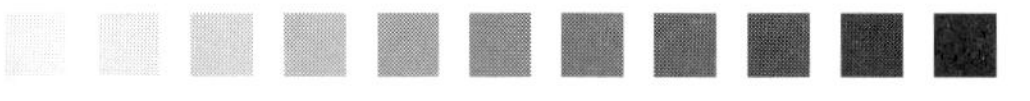

14

Filtering Grouped Data

Let schoolmasters puzzle their brain;
With grammar, and nonsense, and learning;
Good liquor, I stoutly maintain;
Gives genius a better discerning.
—Oliver Goldsmith

Topics Covered in This Chapter

In Chapter 12, we gave you the details about all the aggregate functions defined in the SQL Standard. We followed that up in Chapter 13 with a discussion of how to ask your database system to group sets of rows together and then calculate aggregate values on each group. One of the advantages to grouping is that you can also display Value Expressions based on the grouping columns to identify each group.

In this chapter, we'll put the final piece of the puzzle into place. Once you group rows and calculate aggregate values, it's often useful to filter further the final result using a Predicate on an aggregate calculation. As you'll soon see, you need the final piece of the puzzle—the HAVING clause—to do that.

A New Meaning of "Focus Groups"

You now know that once you've gathered your information into groups of rows, you can request the MIN, MAX, AVG, SUM, or COUNT of all the values in each group. Suppose you want to refine further the final Result Set—"focus" the groups—by testing one of the aggregate values. Let's take a look at a simple request.

> *"Show me the entertainer groups who play in a jazz style and who have more than three members."*

Doesn't sound too difficult, does it? Figure 14-1 shows the tables needed to solve this request.

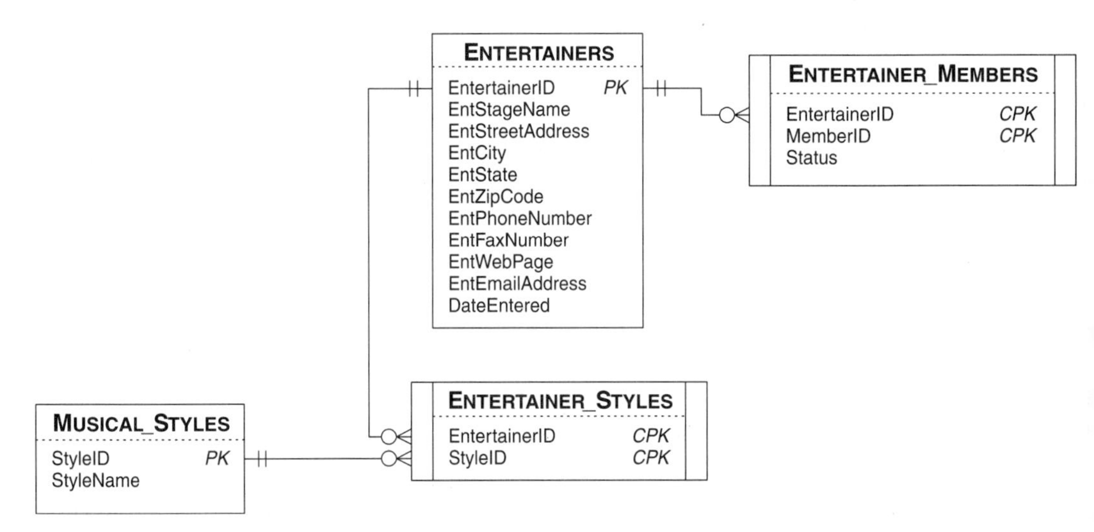

Figure 14-1 *The tables needed to figure out which entertainers play jazz and also have more than three members.*

> ❖ **Note** We'll again be using the "Request/Translation/Clean Up/SQL" technique that we first introduced in Chapter 4. We're also going to be using JOIN techniques you learned in Chapters 8 and 9 and Subqueries that we explained in Chapter 11.

Without knowing about the HAVING clause, you're probably tempted to solve it in the following *incorrect* manner.

Translation: Select the entertainer stage name and the count of members from the entertainers table joined with the entertainer members table on entertainer ID where the entertainer ID is in the selection of entertainer IDs from the entertainer styles table joined with the musical styles table on style ID where the style name is "Jazz" and where the count of the members is greater than 3, grouped by entertainer stage name

Clean Up: Select ~~the~~ entertainer stage name ~~and the~~ count(*) ~~of members~~ as Count of Members from ~~the~~ entertainers ~~table~~ join~~ed with the~~ entertainer members table on entertainer ID where ~~the~~ entertainer ID ~~is~~ in ~~the~~ (select~~ion of~~ entertainer ID~~s~~ from ~~the~~ entertainer styles ~~table~~ join~~ed with the~~ musical styles ~~table~~ on style ID where ~~the~~ style name ~~is~~ = "Jazz") and ~~where the~~ count(*) ~~of the members is greater than~~ > 3, group~~ed~~ by entertainer stage name

SQL:

```
SELECT Entertainers.EntStageName,
   COUNT(*) AS CountOfMembers
FROM Entertainers
INNER JOIN Entertainer_Members
ON Entertainers.EntertainerID =
   Entertainer_Members.EntertainerID
WHERE Entertainers.EntertainerID
IN
  (SELECT Entertainer_Styles.EntertainerID
   FROM Entertainer_Styles
   INNER JOIN Musical_Styles
   ON Entertainer_Styles.StyleID =
      Musical_Styles.StyleID
   WHERE Musical_Styles.StyleName = 'Jazz')
AND COUNT(*) > 3
GROUP BY Entertainers.EntStageName
```

What's wrong with this picture? The key is that any column you reference in a WHERE clause (remember Chapter 6?) *must* be a column in one of the tables defined in the FROM clause. Is COUNT(*) a column generated from the FROM clause? We don't think so! In fact, you can calculate COUNT for each group only after the rows are grouped.

Looks like we need a new clause after GROUP BY. Figure 14-2 shows you the entire syntax for a SELECT Statement, including the new HAVING clause.

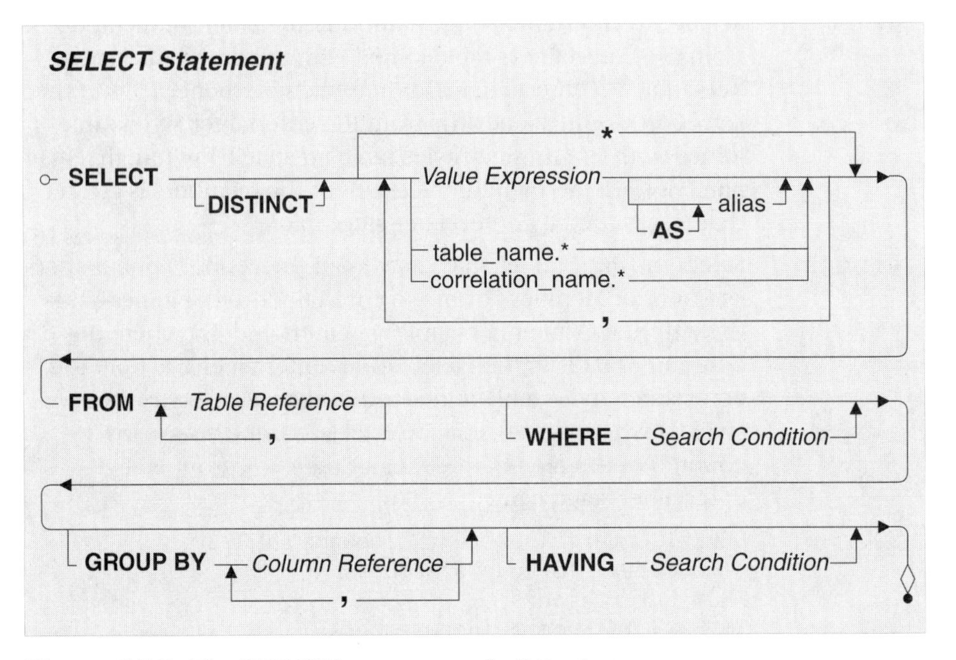

Figure 14-2 *The SELECT Statement and all its clauses.*

Because the HAVING clause acts on rows *after* they have been grouped, the SQL Standard defines some restrictions on the columns you reference in any Predicate in the Search Condition. Note that when you do not have a GROUP BY clause, the HAVING clause operates on all rows returned by the FROM and WHERE clauses as though they are a single group.

The restrictions are the same as those for columns referenced in the SELECT clause of a grouped query. Any reference to a column in a Predicate within the Search Condition of a HAVING clause either must name a column listed in the GROUP BY clause or must be enclosed within an aggregate function. This makes sense because any column comparisons must use something generated from the grouped rows—either a grouping value or an aggregate calculation across rows in each group.

Now that you know a bit about HAVING, let's solve the above problem the correct way.

"Show me the entertainer groups who play in a jazz style and who have more than three members."

Translation: Select the entertainer stage name and the count of members from the entertainers table joined with the entertainer members table on entertainer ID where the entertainer ID is in the selection of entertainer IDs from the entertainer styles table joined with the musical styles table on style ID where the style name is "Jazz," grouped by entertainer stage name, and having the count of the members greater than 3

Clean Up: Select ~~the~~ entertainer stage name ~~and the~~ count(*) ~~of members~~ as CountOfMembers from ~~the~~ entertainers ~~table~~ join~~ed with the~~ entertainer members ~~table~~ on entertainer ID where ~~the~~ entertainer ID ~~is~~ in ~~the~~ (select~~ion of~~ entertainer ID~~s~~ from ~~the~~ entertainer styles ~~table~~ join~~ed with the~~ musical styles ~~table~~ on style ID where ~~the~~ style name ~~is~~ = "Jazz"), group~~ed~~ by entertainer stage name, and ~~having the~~ count(*) ~~of the members greater than~~ > 3

SQL:

```
SELECT Entertainers.EntStageName,
   COUNT(*) AS CountOfMembers
FROM Entertainers
INNER JOIN Entertainer_Members
ON Entertainers.EntertainerID =
   Entertainer_Members.EntertainerID
WHERE Entertainers.EntertainerID
IN
  (SELECT Entertainer_Styles.EntertainerID
   FROM Entertainer_Styles
   INNER JOIN Musical_Styles
   ON Entertainer_Styles.StyleID =
      Musical_Styles.StyleID
   WHERE Musical_Styles.StyleName = 'Jazz')
GROUP BY Entertainers.EntStageName
HAVING COUNT(*) > 3
```

Although we also included the count in the final output of the request, we didn't need to do that in order to ask for COUNT(*) in the HAVING clause. As long as any calculated value or Column Reference we use in HAVING can be derived from the grouped rows, we're OK. We saved the above query in the Entertainment Agency sample database as Jazz_Entertainers_More_Than_3.

When You Filter Makes a Difference

You now know two ways to filter your final Result Set: WHERE and HAVING. You also know that there are certain limitations on the Predicates you can use within a Search Condition in a HAVING clause. In some cases, however, you have the choice of placing a Predicate in either clause. Let's take a look at the reasons for putting your filter in the WHERE clause instead of the HAVING clause.

Should You Filter in WHERE or in HAVING?

You learned in Chapter 6 about five major types of Predicates you can build to filter the rows returned by the FROM clause of your request. These are Comparison (=, <>, >=, <=), Range (BETWEEN), Set Membership (IN), Pattern Match (LIKE), and Null (IS NULL). In Chapter 11, we expanded your horizons by showing you how to use a Subquery as one of the arguments in Comparison and Set Membership Predicates, and we introduced you to two additional classes of Predicates—Quantified (ANY, SOME, ALL) and Existence (EXISTS)—that require a Subquery as one of the arguments.

Keep in mind that the Search Condition in a WHERE clause filters rows *before* your database system groups them. In general, when you want to ultimately group just a subset of rows, it's better to eliminate unwanted rows first in the WHERE clause. For example, let's assume you want to solve the following problem.

> *"Show me the states on the west coast of the U.S. where the total of the orders is greater than $1 million."*

Figure 14-3 shows the tables needed to solve this problem.

You could legitimately state the request in the following manner, placing the Predicate on customer state into the HAVING clause.

```
SQL       SELECT Customers.CustState,
             SUM(Order_Details.QuantityOrdered *
             Order_Details.QuotedPrice) AS SumOfOrders
          FROM (Customers
             INNER JOIN Orders
             ON Customers.CustomerID = Orders.CustomerID)
          INNER JOIN Order_Details
          ON Orders.OrderNumber =
             Order_Details.OrderNumber
```

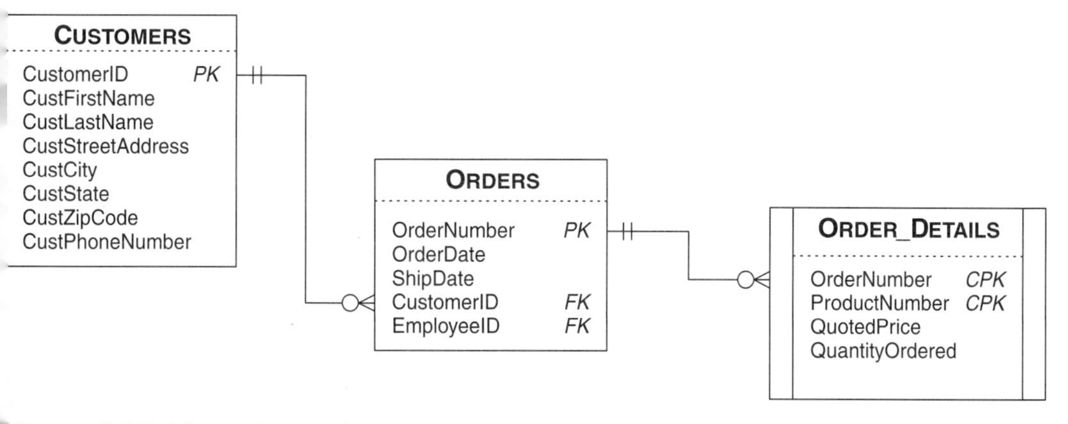

Figure 14-3 *The tables needed to sum all orders by state.*

```
 GROUP BY Customers.CustState
HAVING SUM(Order_Details.QuantityOrdered *
   Order_Details.QuotedPrice) > 1000000
AND CustState IN ('WA', 'OR', 'CA')
```

Because you are grouping on the state column, you *can* construct a Predicate on that column in the HAVING clause, but you may be asking your database system to do more work than necessary. As it turns out, the total of all orders for customers in the state of Texas also exceeds $1 million. If you place the filter on customer state in the HAVING clause as in the above example, your database will calculate the total for all the rows in Texas as well, evaluate the first Predicate in the HAVING clause and keep the result, and then finally throw it out when the Texas group isn't one you want.

If you want to calculate a result based on grouping by customer state but want only customers in Washington, Oregon, and California, it makes more sense to filter down to the rows in those three states using a WHERE clause before you ask to GROUP BY state. If you don't do so, the FROM clause returns rows for all customers in all states and must do extra work to group rows you're not even going to need. Here's the better way to solve the problem.

Translation Select customer state and the sum of quantity ordered times quoted price as SumOfOrders from the customers table joined with the orders table on customer ID, and then joined with the order details table on order number where customer state is in the list: "WA","OR","CA", grouped by customer state, and having the sum of the orders greater than $1 million

Clean Up

Select customer state ~~and~~ ~~the~~ sum ~~of~~ (quantity ordered ~~times~~ * quoted price) as SumOfOrders from ~~the~~ customers ~~table~~ join~~ed with the~~ orders ~~table~~ on customer ID~~, and then~~ join~~ed with the~~ order details ~~table~~ on order number where customer state ~~is~~ in ~~the list:~~ ("WA","OR","CA"), group~~ed~~ by customer state, ~~and~~ having ~~the~~ sum of the orders ~~greater than~~ > ~~$1 million~~ 1000000

SQL

```
SELECT Customers.CustState,
   SUM(Order_Details.QuantityOrdered *
   Order_Details.QuotedPrice) AS SumOfOrders
FROM (Customers
   INNER JOIN Orders
   ON Customers.CustomerID = Orders.CustomerID)
INNER JOIN Order_Details
ON Orders.OrderNumber =
   Order_Details.OrderNumber
WHERE Customers.CustState IN ('WA', 'OR', 'CA')
GROUP BY Customers.CustState
HAVING SUM(Order_Details.QuantityOrdered *
   Order_Details.QuotedPrice) > 1000000
```

We saved this query in the sample database as West_Coast_Big_Order_States.

Avoiding the HAVING COUNT Trap

Many times you may want to know which categories of items have fewer than a certain number of members. For example, you might want to know which entertainment groups have two or fewer members, which recipes have two or fewer dairy ingredients, or which subjects have three or fewer full-time professors teaching. The trick here is you *also* want to know which categories have *zero* members.

Let's look at a request that illustrates the trap you can fall into.

> *"Show me the subject categories that have three or fewer full professors teaching that subject."*

Figure 14-4 shows the tables needed to solve this problem.

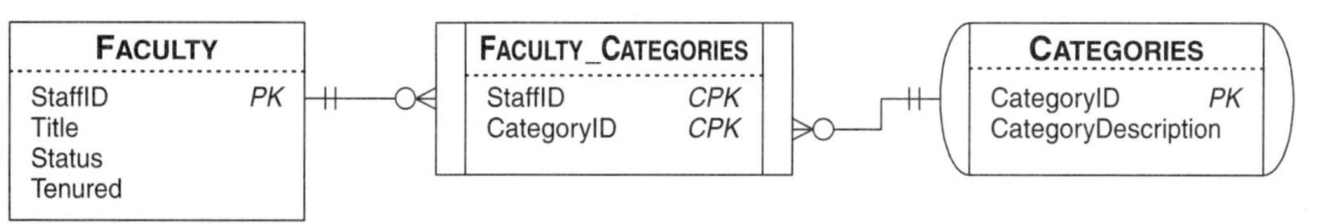

Figure 14-4 *Subject categories and the faculty teaching in that category.*

Translation: Select category description and the count of staff ID as ProfCount from the categories table joined with the faculty categories table on category ID, and then joined with the faculty table on staff ID where title is 'Professor,' grouped by category description, and having the count of staff ID less than 3

Clean Up: Select category description ~~and the~~ count ~~of~~ (staff ID) as ProfCount from ~~the~~ categories ~~table~~ join~~ed with the~~ faculty categories ~~table~~ on category ID~~, and then~~ join~~ed with the~~ faculty ~~table~~ on staff ID where title ~~is~~ = 'Professor,' group~~ed~~ by category description, ~~and~~ having ~~the~~ count ~~of~~ (staff ID) ~~less than~~ < 3

SQL:

```
SELECT Categories.CategoryDescription,
   COUNT(Faculty_Categories.StaffID) AS
   ProfCount
FROM (Categories
INNER JOIN Faculty_Categories
ON Categories.CategoryID =
   Faculty_Categories.CategoryID)
INNER JOIN Faculty
ON Faculty.StaffID = Faculty_Categories.StaffID
WHERE Faculty.Title='Professor'
GROUP BY Categories.CategoryDescription
HAVING COUNT(Faculty_Categories.StaffID) < 3
```

Looks good, doesn't it? Below is the Result Set returned from this query.

Subjects_Fewer_3_Professors_WRONG

CategoryDescription	ProfCount
Accounting	1
Business	2
Computer Information Systems	1
Economics	1
Geography	1
History	1
Journalism	1
Math	1
Political Science	1

Do you notice that the Result Set lists *no* subject categories with zero professors? This happened because the COUNT function is counting only the rows that are left in the Faculty_Categories table after filtering for full professors. We threw away any potential zero rows with the WHERE clause!

Just to confirm our suspicions that some categories exist with no full professors, let's construct a query that will test our theory. Remember that the COUNT aggregate function will return a zero if we ask it to count an empty set, and we can get an empty set if we force the request to consider how many rows exist for a specific subject category. We do this by forcing the query to look at the subject categories one at a time. We'll be counting category rows, not faculty subject rows. Consider the following Select Statement.

```
SQL         SELECT COUNT(Faculty.StaffID)
            AS BiologyProfessors
            FROM (Faculty
            INNER JOIN Faculty_Categories
            ON Faculty.StaffID =
               Faculty_Categories.StaffID)
            INNER JOIN Categories
            ON Categories.CategoryID =
               Faculty_Categories.CategoryID
```

```
WHERE Categories.CategoryDescription =
   'Biology'
AND Faculty.Title = 'Professor'
```

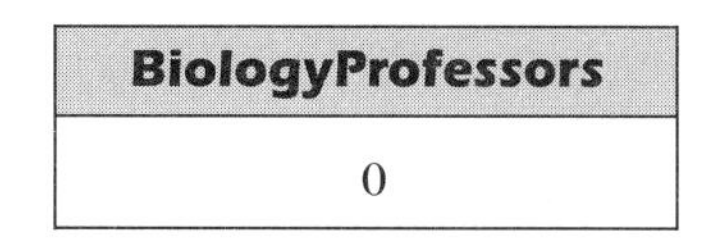

BiologyProfessors
0

We saved this query as Count_Of_Biology_Professors in the sample database. As you can see, there really are no full professors in the School Scheduling sample database who teach biology. We asked the query to consider just one subject category. Because there are no rows that are both Professor and Biology, we get a legitimate empty set. The COUNT function, therefore, returns a zero.

Now that we know this, we can embed this request as a Subquery in a WHERE clause that extracts a match on category ID from the outer query. This forces the request to consider the categories one at a time as it fetches the category descriptions one row at a time from the Categories table in the outer request. The SQL is as follows.

```
SQL        SELECT Categories.CategoryDescription,
              (SELECT COUNT(Faculty.StaffID)
              FROM (Faculty
              INNER JOIN Faculty_Categories
              ON Faculty.StaffID =
                 Faculty_Categories.StaffID)
              INNER JOIN Categories AS C2
              ON C2.CategoryID =
                 Faculty_Categories.CategoryID
              WHERE C2.CategoryID = Categories.CategoryID
              AND Faculty.Title = 'Professor')
              AS ProfCount
           FROM Categories
           WHERE
              (SELECT COUNT(Faculty.StaffID)
              FROM (Faculty
              INNER JOIN Faculty_Categories
              ON Faculty.StaffID =
                 Faculty_Categories.StaffID)
              INNER JOIN Categories AS C3
              ON C3.CategoryID =
                 Faculty_Categories.CategoryID
              WHERE C3.CategoryID = Categories.CategoryID
              AND Faculty.Title = 'Professor') < 3
```

We saved this query as Subjects_Fewer_3_Professors_RIGHT in the sample database. Notice that we also included a copy of the Subquery in the SELECT clause so that we can see the actual counts per category. This now works correctly because the Subquery in the WHERE clause legitimately returns zero for a category that has no full professors. The correct result is below.

Subjects_Fewer_3_Professors_RIGHT

CategoryDescription	ProfCount
Accounting	1
Biology	0
Business	2
Chemistry	0
Computer Information Systems	1
Computer Science	0
Economics	1
Geography	1
History	1
Journalism	1
Math	1
Physics	0
Political Science	1
Psychology	0
French	0
German	0

As you can see, many subject categories actually have *no* full professors assigned to teach the subject. Although this final solution does not use HAVING at all, we include it to make you aware that HAVING isn't always the clear solution for this type of problem. Keep in mind that you can still use HAVING for many "...having fewer than..." problems. For example, if you want to see all customers who spent less than $500 last month but you don't care about customers who bought nothing at all, then the HAVING solution works just fine (and will most likely execute faster). However, if you also need to see customers who bought nothing, you will have to use the non-HAVING technique that we just showed you.

Uses for HAVING

At this point, you should have a pretty good understanding of how to ask for subtotals across groups using aggregate functions and the GROUP BY clause and how to filter the grouped data using HAVING. The best way to give you an idea of the wide range of uses for HAVING is to show you problems you can solve with this new clause followed by a robust set of examples in the next section.

"Show me each vendor and the average by vendor of the number of days to deliver products that is greater than the average delivery days for all vendors."

"Display for each product the product name and the total sales that is greater than the average of sales for all products in that category."

"List for each customer and order date the customer full name and the total cost of items ordered that is greater than $1,000."

"How many orders are for only one product?"

"Which agents booked more than $3000 worth of business in December 1999?"

"Show me the entertainers who have more than two overlapped bookings."

"Show each agent name, the sum of the contract price for the engagements booked, and the agent's total commission for agents whose total commission is more than $1000."

"Do any team captains have a raw score that is higher than any other member on the team?"

"Display for each bowler the bowler name and the average of their raw game scores for bowlers whose average is greater than 155."

"List the bowlers whose highest raw score is at least 20 pins higher than their current average."

"For completed classes, list by category and student the category name, the student name, and the student's average grade of all classes taken in that category for those students who have an average of 90 or better."

"Display by category the category name and the count of classes offered for those categories that have three or more classes."

"List each staff member and the count of classes each is scheduled to teach for those staff members who teach at least one but fewer than three classes."

"List the recipes that contain both beef and garlic."

"Sum the amount of salt by recipe class and display those recipe classes that require more than three teaspoons."

"For what type of recipe do I have two or more recipes?"

Sample Statements

You now know the mechanics of constructing queries using a HAVING clause and have seen some of the types of requests you can answer. Let's take a look at a set of samples, all of which request that the information be grouped and then filtered on an aggregate value from the group. These examples come from each of the sample databases.

We've also included sample Result Sets that would be returned by these operations and placed them immediately after the SQL syntax line. The name that appears immediately above a Result Set is the name we gave each query in the sample data on the companion CD you'll find bound into the back of the book. We stored each query in the appropriate sample database (as indicated within the example) in the "Chapter14" subfolder on the CD. You can follow the instructions at the beginning of this book to load the samples onto your computer and try them out.

❖ **Note** Remember that all the column names and table names used in these examples are drawn from the sample database structures shown in Appendix B. To simplify the process, we have combined the Translation and Clean Up steps for all the examples. These samples assume you have thoroughly studied and understood the concepts covered in previous chapters, especially the chapters on JOIN and Subqueries.

Sales Order Database

"List for each customer and order date the customer full name and the total cost of items ordered that is greater than $1,000."

Translation/ Clean Up

Select customer first name ~~and~~ || ' ' || customer last name as CustomerFullName, order date, ~~and the~~ sum ~~of~~ (quoted price ~~times~~ * quantity ordered) as TotalCost from ~~the~~ customers ~~table~~ join~~ed with the~~ orders ~~table~~ on customer ID~~, and then~~ join~~ed with the~~ order details ~~table~~ on order number, group~~ed~~ by customer first name, customer last name, ~~and~~ order date, having ~~the~~ sum ~~of~~ (quoted price ~~times~~ * quantity ordered) ~~greater than~~ > 1000

SQL

```
SELECT Customers.CustFirstName || ' ' ||
   Customers.CustLastName AS CustFullName,
   Orders.OrderDate,
   SUM(Order_Details.QuotedPrice *
   Order_Details.QuantityOrdered) AS TotalCost
FROM (Customers
INNER JOIN Orders
ON Customers.CustomerID = Orders.CustomerID)
INNER JOIN Order_Details
ON Orders.OrderNumber =
   Order_Details.OrderNumber
GROUP BY Customers.CustFirstName,
   Customers.CustLastName, Orders.OrderDate
HAVING SUM(Order_Details.QuotedPrice *
   Order_Details.QuantityOrdered) > 1000
```

Order_Totals_By_Customer_And_Date_GT1000 (649 rows)

CustFullName	OrderDate	TotalCost
Alaina Hallmark	1999-07-02	$4,699.98
Alaina Hallmark	1999-07-14	$4,433.95
Alaina Hallmark	1999-07-21	$3,951.90
Alaina Hallmark	1999-07-22	$10,388.68
Alaina Hallmark	1999-07-30	$3,088.00
Alaina Hallmark	1999-08-11	$6,775.06
Alaina Hallmark	1999-08-21	$15,781.10
Alaina Hallmark	1999-08-29	$15,969.50
<<more rows here >>		

Entertainment Agency Database

"Which agents booked more than $3000 worth of business in December 1999?"

Translation/Clean Up: Select ~~the~~ agent first name, agent last name, ~~and the~~ sum ~~of~~ (contract price) as TotalBooked from ~~the~~ agents ~~table~~ join~~ed with the~~ engagements ~~table~~ on agent ID where ~~the~~ engagement start date ~~is~~ between ~~December 1, 1999,~~ '1999-12-01' and ~~December 31, 1999,~~ '1999-12-31' having ~~the~~ sum ~~of~~ (contract price) ~~greater than~~ > $3000

SQL

```
SELECT Agents.AgtFirstName, Agents.AgtLastName,
   SUM(Engagements.ContractPrice)
   AS TotalBooked
FROM Agents
INNER JOIN Engagements
ON Agents.AgentID = Engagements.AgentID
WHERE Engagements.StartDate
BETWEEN '1999-12-01' And '1999-12-31'
GROUP BY Agents.AgtFirstName, Agents.AgtLastName
HAVING SUM(Engagements.ContractPrice)>3000
```

Agents_Book_Over_3000_12_99 (4 rows)

AgtFirstName	AgtLastName	TotalBooked
Gregory	Piercy	$4,785.00
Margaret	Peacock	$4,350.00
Mary	Fuller	$7,120.00
Will	Thompson	$6,555.00

Bowling League Database

"List the bowlers whose highest raw score is at least 20 pins higher than their current average."

Translation/Clean Up: Select bowler first name, bowler last name, current average, ~~and the~~ max~~imum~~ (raw score) as HighGame from ~~the~~ bowlers ~~table~~ join~~ed with the~~ bowler scores ~~table~~ on bowler ID, group~~ed~~ by bowler first name, bowler last name, ~~and~~ bowler current average, having ~~the~~ max~~imum~~ (raw score) ~~greater than the~~ > current average ~~plus~~ + 20

```
SQL         SELECT Bowlers.BowlerFirstName,
               Bowlers.BowlerLastName,
               Bowlers.CurrentAverage,
               Max(Bowler_Scores.RawScore) AS HighGame
            FROM Bowlers
            INNER JOIN Bowler_Scores
            ON Bowlers.BowlerID = Bowler_Scores.BowlerID
            GROUP BY Bowlers.BowlerFirstName,
               Bowlers.BowlerLastName,
               Bowlers.CurrentAverage
            HAVING Max(Bowler_Scores.RawScore) >
               (Bowlers.CurrentAverage+20)
```

❖ **Note** We took advantage of the fact that the Bowlers table has a CurrentAverage column in it. For this table design to work, the application using this table has to recalculate and update this column every time new games are entered for the bowler—but that was designed this way on purpose to avoid recalculating the average over possibly hundreds of games every time we need the number. We could have also calculated the absolute current average using a Subquery on the Bowler_Scores table, but that would have been slower. For details about when to "break the rules" in database design, see *Database Design for Mere Mortals* (Reading, MA: Addison-Wesley, 1997).

Bowlers_Big_High_Score (15 rows)

BowlerFirstName	BowlerLastName	CurrentAverage	HighGame
Alaina	Hallmark	158.00	180
Carol	Viescas	168.00	195
David	Fournier	157.00	178
Gary	Hallmark	157.00	179
Greg	Piercy	164.00	193
John	Kennedy	166.00	191
John	Viescas	168.00	193
Kathryn	Patterson	162.00	191
<<more rows here >>			

School Scheduling Database

"For completed classes, list by category and student the category name, the student name, and the student's average grade of all classes taken in that category for those students who have an average of 90 or better."

Translation/ Clean Up

Select category description, student first name, student last name, ~~and the~~ ~~average~~ avg(~~of~~ grade) as AvgOfGrade from ~~the~~ categories ~~table~~ join~~ed with the~~ subjects ~~table~~ on category ID~~, then~~ join~~ed with the~~ classes ~~table~~ on subject ID~~, then~~ join~~ed with the~~ student schedules ~~table~~ on class ID~~, then~~ join~~ed with the~~ student class status ~~table~~ on class status~~, and finally~~ join~~ed with the~~ students ~~table~~ on student ID where class status description ~~is~~ = 'Completed,' group~~ed~~ by category description, student first name, ~~and~~ student last name, ~~and~~ having ~~the~~ ~~average~~ avg(~~of~~ grade) ~~greater than~~ > 90

SQL

```
SELECT Categories.CategoryDescription,
   Students.StudFirstName,
   Students.StudLastName,
   AVG(Student_Schedules.Grade) AS AvgOfGrade
FROM ((((Categories
INNER JOIN Subjects
ON Categories.CategoryID = Subjects.CategoryID)
INNER JOIN Classes
ON Subjects.SubjectID = Classes.SubjectID)
INNER JOIN Student_Schedules
ON Classes.ClassID = Student_Schedules.ClassID)
INNER JOIN Student_Class_Status
ON Student_Class_Status.ClassStatus =
   Student_Schedules.ClassStatus)
INNER JOIN Students
ON Students.StudentID =
   Student_Schedules.StudentID
WHERE Student_Class_Status.ClassStatusDescription =
   'Completed'
GROUP BY Categories.CategoryDescription,
   Students.StudFirstName,
   Students.StudLastName
HAVING AVG(Student_Schedules.Grade) > 90
```

A_Students (13 rows)

CategoryDescription	StudFirstName	StudLastName	AvgOfGrade
Accounting	Elizabeth	Hallmark	90.24
Accounting	Michael	Viescas	90.01
Accounting	Sarah	Leverling	90.67
Art	Kendra	Bonnicksen	90.63
Art	Sarah	Leverling	91.72
English	Elizabeth	Hallmark	92.90
English	John	Kennedy	93.70
English	Mel	Ehrlich	93.86
English	Sarah	Thompson	97.39
Music	Karen	Smith	92.08
Music	Mary	Fuller	98.26
Music	Mel	Ehrlich	93.26
Music	Nancy	Davolio	93.28

"List each staff member and the count of classes each is scheduled to teach for those staff members who teach at least one but fewer than three classes."

> ❖ **Note** We avoided the HAVING COUNT zero problem by specifically stating that we want staff members who teach at least one class.

Translation/Clean Up: Select staff first name, staff last name, ~~and the~~ count ~~of classes~~ (*) as ClassCount from ~~the~~ staff ~~table~~ join~~ed with the~~ faculty classes ~~table~~ on staff ID, group~~ed~~ by staff first name ~~and~~ staff last name, ~~and~~ having ~~the~~ count ~~of classes~~ (*) ~~less than~~ < 3

SQL

```
SELECT Staff.StfFirstName, Staff.StfLastName,
   Count(*) AS ClassCount
FROM Staff
INNER JOIN Faculty_Classes
ON Staff.StaffID = Faculty_Classes.StaffID
GROUP BY Staff.StfFirstName, Staff.StfLastName
HAVING COUNT(*) < 3
```

Staff_Class_Count_1_To_3 (8 rows)

StfFirstName	StfLastName	ClassCount
Allan	Davis	1
David	Callahan	2
James	Leverling	2
Joyce	Bonnicksen	2
Katherine	Ehrlich	2
Laura	Callahan	2
Ryan	Ehrlich	2
Suzanne	Viescas	2

Recipes Database

"List the recipes that contain both beef and garlic."

Translation/ Clean Up: Select recipe title from ~~the~~ recipes ~~table~~ where ~~the~~ recipe ID ~~is~~ in ~~the~~ (select~~ion of~~ recipe ID from ~~the~~ ingredients ~~table~~ join~~ed with the~~ recipe ingredients ~~table~~ on ingredient ID where ~~the~~ ingredient name ~~is~~ = 'Beef' or ~~the~~ ingredient name ~~is~~ = 'Garlic,' group~~ed~~ by recipe ID ~~and~~ having ~~the~~ count (*) ~~of rows equal to~~ = 2

SQL

```
SELECT Recipes.RecipeTitle
FROM Recipes
WHERE Recipes.RecipeID
IN (SELECT Recipe_Ingredients.RecipeID
   FROM Ingredients
   INNER JOIN Recipe_Ingredients
   ON Ingredients.IngredientID =
      Recipe_Ingredients.IngredientID
   WHERE Ingredients.IngredientName = 'Beef'
   OR Ingredients.IngredientName = 'Garlic'
   GROUP BY Recipe_Ingredients.RecipeID
   HAVING COUNT(Recipe_Ingredients.RecipeID) = 2)
```

❖ **Note** This illustrates a creative use of GROUP BY and HAVING in a Subquery to find recipes that have *both* ingredients. When a recipe has neither of the ingredients, the COUNT will be zero. Only when a recipe has both will the COUNT be 2. Be careful, though. If a particular recipe calls for both minced and whole garlic but no beef, this technique won't work! You will get a count of 2 for the two garlic entries, so the recipe will be selected even though it has no beef. If you wonder why we used an OR operator when we want both beef and garlic, be sure to review the Using OR topic in the Using Multiple Conditions section in Chapter 6. We showed you an alternative way to solve this problem in Chapter 8.

Recipes_Beef_And_Garlic (1 row)

RecipeTitle
Roast Beef

SUMMARY

We started the chapter with a discussion about "focusing" the groups you form by using the HAVING clause to filter out groups based on aggregate calculations. We introduced the syntax of this final clause for a SELECT Statement and explained a simple example.

Next we showed an example of when to use the WHERE clause rather than the HAVING clause to filter rows. We explained that when you have a choice, you're better off placing your filter in the WHERE clause. Before you got too comfortable with HAVING, we showed you a common trap to avoid when counting groups that may contain a zero result. We also showed you an alternative way to solve this type of problem.

Finally, we summarized why the HAVING clause is useful and gave you a sample list of problems you can solve using HAVING. The rest of the chapter provides examples of how to build requests that require the HAVING clause. The following section presents a number of requests that you can work out on your own.

Problems for You to Solve

Below, we show you the request statement and the name of the solution query in the sample databases. If you want some practice, you can work out the SQL you need for each request and then check your answer with the query we saved in the samples. Don't worry if your syntax doesn't exactly match the syntax of the queries we saved—as long as your Result Set is the same.

Sales Order Database

1. *"Show me each vendor and the average by vendor of the number of days to deliver products that is greater than the average delivery days for all vendors."*
   (Hint: You need a Subquery to fetch the average delivery time for all vendors.)
   You can find the solution in Vendor_Avg_Delivery_GT_Overall_Avg (5 rows).
2. *"Display for each product the product name and the total sales that is greater than the average of sales for all products in that category."*
   (Hint: To calculate the comparison value, you must first SUM the sales for each product within a category and then AVG those sums by category.)
   You can find the solution in Sales_By_Product_GT_Category_Avg (13 rows).

3. *"How many orders are for only one product?"*
(Hint: You need an inner query that lists the order numbers for orders having only one row and then COUNT those rows.)
You can find the solution in Single_Item_Order_Count (1 row).

Entertainment Agency Database

1. *"Show me the entertainers who have more than two overlapped bookings."*
(Hint: Use a Subquery to find those entertainers with overlapped booking HAVING a COUNT greater than 2.)
You can find the solution in Entertainers_MoreThan_2_Overlap (1 row).
2. *"Show each agent's name, the sum of the contract price for the engagements booked, and the agent's total commission for agents whose total commission is more than $1000."*
(Hint: Use the similar problem from the previous chapter and add a HAVING clause.)
You can find the solution in Agent_Sales_Big_Commissions (4 rows).

Bowling League Database

1. *"Do any team captains have a raw score that is higher than any other member on the team?"*
(Hint: You find out the top raw score for captains by JOINing teams to bowlers on captain ID and then to bowler scores. Use a HAVING clause to compare the MAX value for all other members from a Subquery.)
You can find the solution in Captains_Who_Are_Hotshots (0 rows). (There are no captains who bowl better than their teammates!)
2. *"Display for each bowler the bowler name and the average of their raw game scores for bowlers whose average is greater than 155."*
(Hint: You need a simple HAVING clause comparing the AVG to a numeric literal.)
You can find the solution in Good_Bowlers (16 rows).

School Scheduling Database

1. *"Display by category the category name and the count of classes offered for those categories that have three or more classes."*
(Hint: JOIN categories to subjects, and then to Classes. COUNT the rows and add a HAVING clause to get the final result.)
You can find the solution in Category_Class_Count_3_Or_More (11 rows).
2. *"List each staff member and the count of classes each is scheduled to teach for those staff members who teach fewer than three classes."*
(Hint: This is a HAVING COUNT zero trap! Use Subqueries instead.)
You can find the solution in Staff_Teaching_LessThan_3 (12 rows).

Recipes Database

1. *"Sum the amount of salt by recipe class and display those recipe classes that require more than 3 teaspoons."*
   (Hint: This requires a complex JOIN of five tables to filter out salt and teaspoon, SUM the result, and then eliminate recipe classes that use more than 3 teaspoons.)
   You can find the solution in Recipe_Classes_Lots_Of_Salt (1 row).
2. *"For what class of recipe do I have two or more recipes?"*
   (Hint: JOIN recipe classes with recipes, count the result, and keep the ones with two or more with a HAVING clause.)
   You can find the solution in Recipe_Classes_Two_Or_More (4 rows).

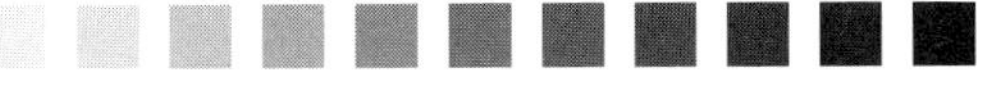

In Closing

"That is what learning is.
You suddenly understand something
you've understood all your life, but in a new way."
—Doris Lessing

You now have all the tools you need to query a database successfully. You've learned how to create both simple and complex SELECT Statements and how to work with various types of data. You've also learned how to filter data with Search Conditions, work with multiple tables using JOINs, and produce statistical information by grouping data.

As with any new endeavor, there's always more to learn. Your next task is to take the techniques you've learned in this book and apply them within your database system. Be sure to refer to your database system's documentation to determine whether there are any differences between standard SQL syntax and the SQL syntax your database uses. If your database allows you to create queries using a graphical interface, you'll probably find that the interface now makes more sense and is much easier to use.

Also remember that we focused only on the data manipulation portion of SQL—there are still many parts to SQL that you can delve into, should you be so inspired. For example, you could learn how to create data structures, incorporate several tables into a single *View*, or embed SQL statements within an application program. If you want to learn more about SQL, we suggest you start with any of the books we've listed in Appendix C.

We hope you've enjoyed reading this book as much as we've enjoyed writing it. We know that books on this subject tend to be rather dry, so we decided to have a little fun and inject some humor wherever we could. There's absolutely no reason why learning should be boring and tedious. On the contrary, you should look forward to learning something new each day.

Writing a book is always a humbling experience. It makes you realize just how much more there is to learn about the subject at hand. And as you work through the writing process, it is inevitable that you'll see things from a fresh perspective and in a different light. We found out just how much Doris Lessing's statement rings true.

We hope you will, too.

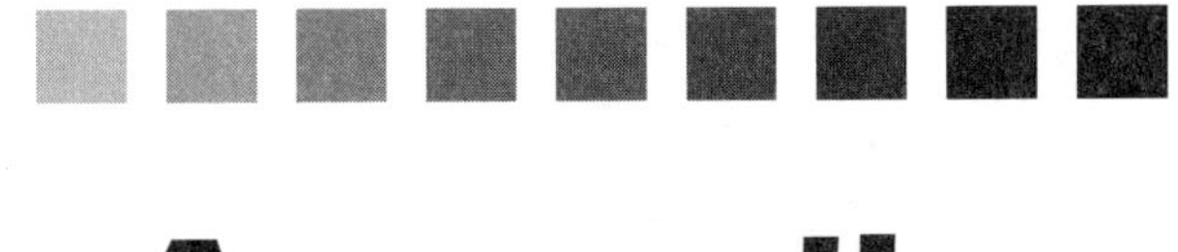

Appendices

SQL Standard Diagrams

Here are the complete diagrams for all the SQL grammar and syntax we've covered throughout the book.

SELECT Query

SELECT Expression
ORDER BY
column_name
column_#
ASC
DESC
,

SELECT Expression

SELECT Statement
UNION
INTERSECT
EXCEPT
ALL
SELECT Statement

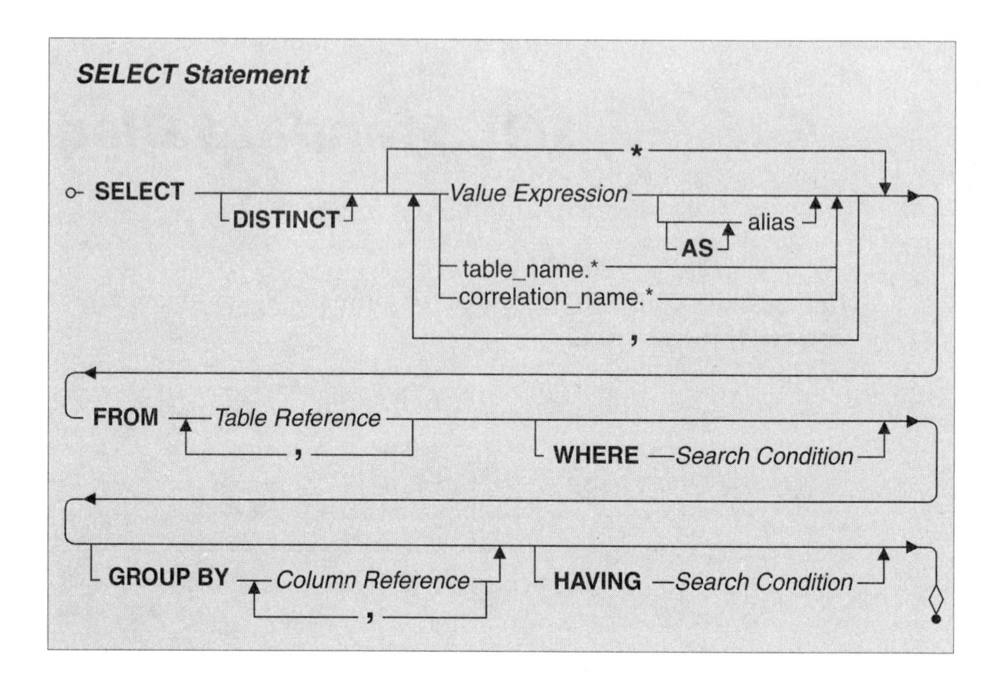

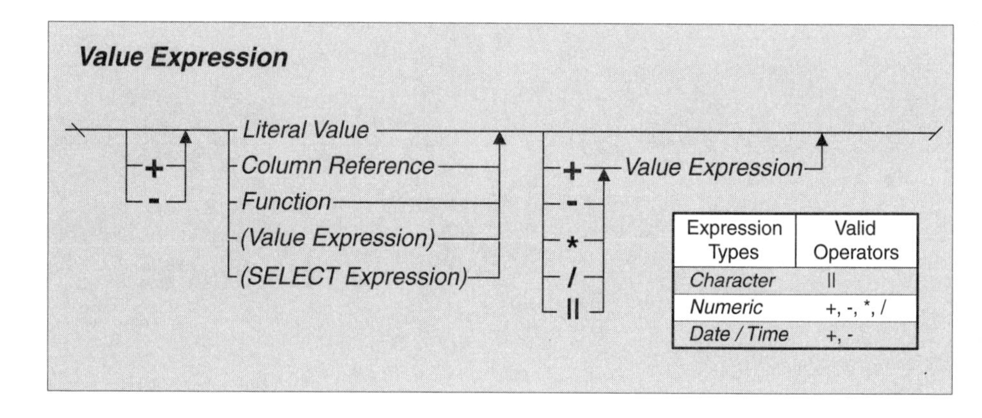

Expression Types	Valid Operators
Character	||
Numeric	+, -, *, /
Date / Time	+, -

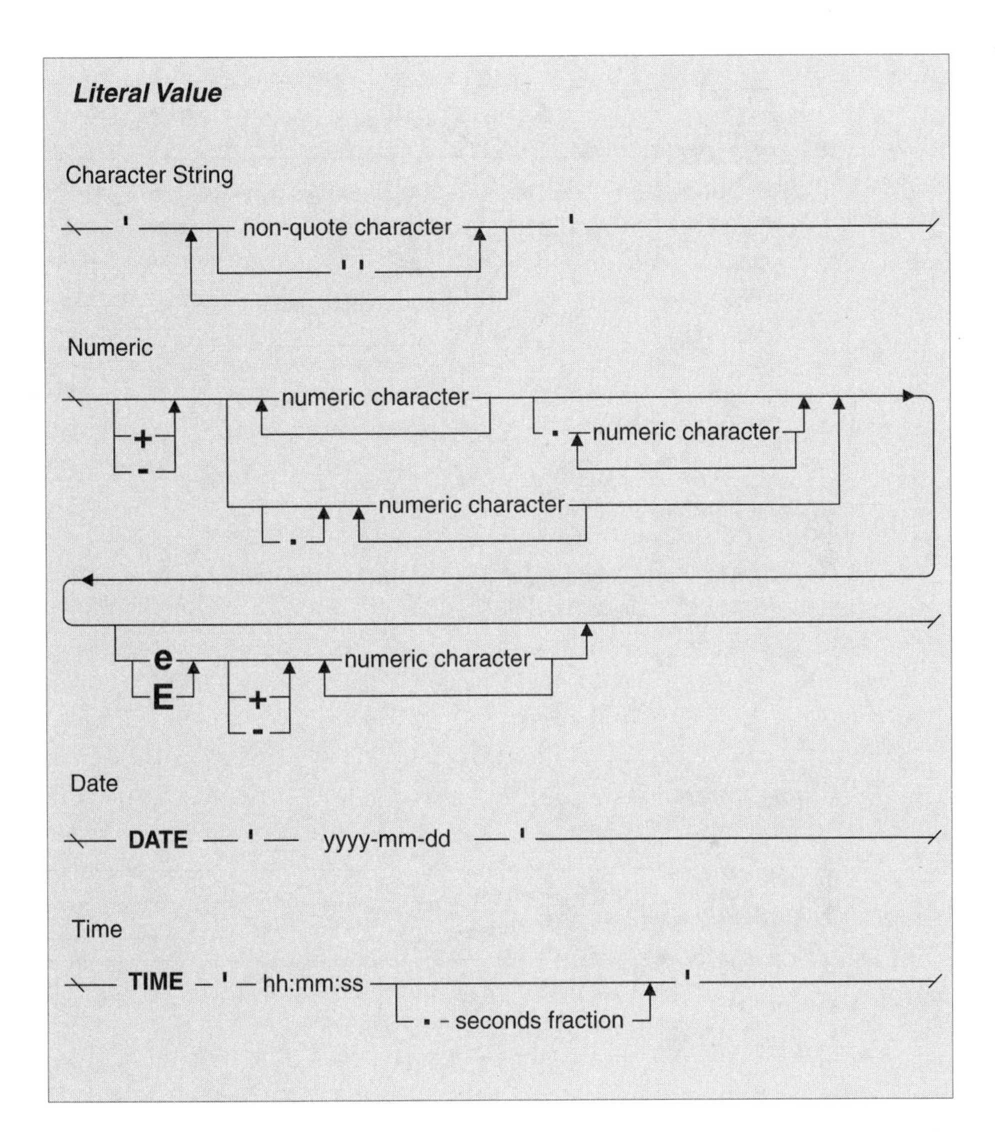
Literal Value
Character String
'
non-quote character
''
'
Numeric
+
-
numeric character
.
numeric character
.
numeric character
e
E
+
-
numeric character
Date
DATE
'
yyyy-mm-dd
'
Time
TIME
'
hh:mm:ss
.
seconds fraction
'

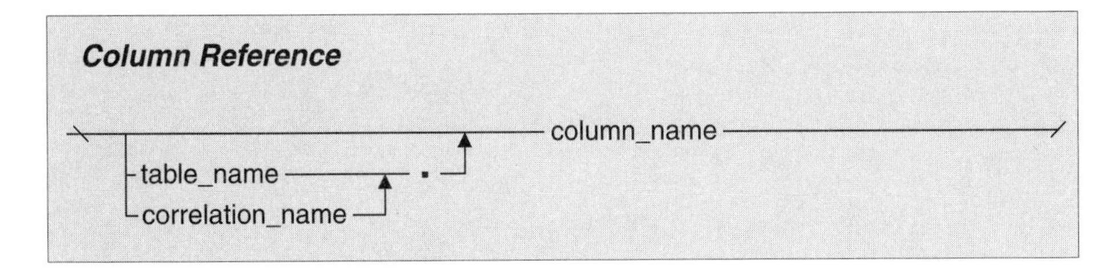
Column Reference
column_name
table_name
correlation_name
.

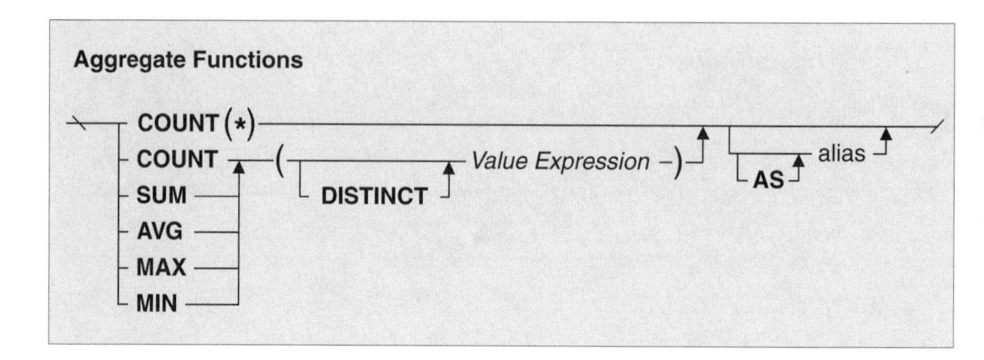
Aggregate Functions
COUNT (*)
COUNT
SUM
AVG
MAX
MIN
(
DISTINCT
Value Expression
)
AS
alias

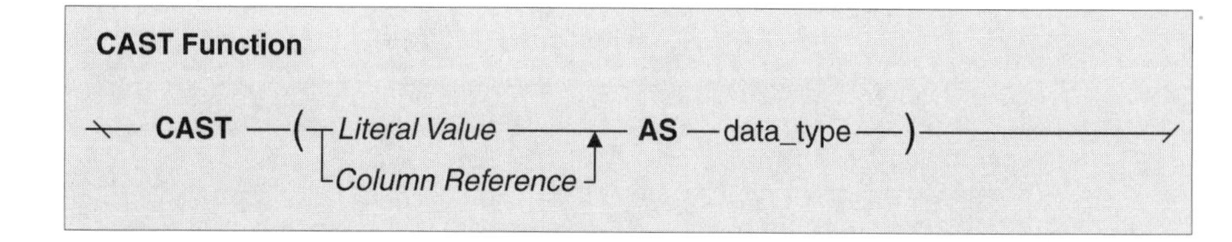
CAST Function
CAST
(
Literal Value
Column Reference
AS
data_type
)

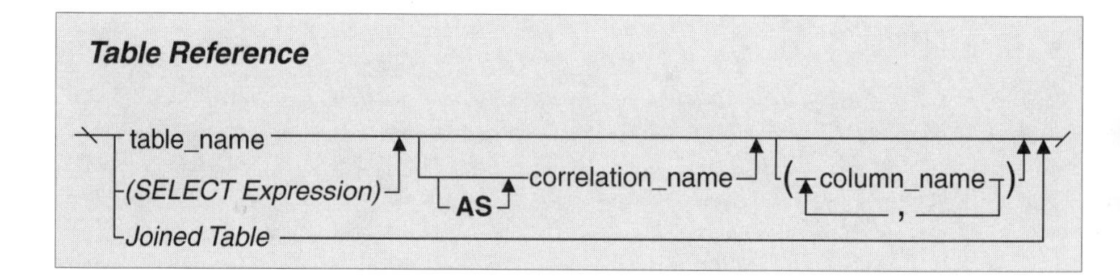
Table Reference
table_name
(SELECT Expression)
Joined Table
AS
correlation_name
(
column_name
,
)

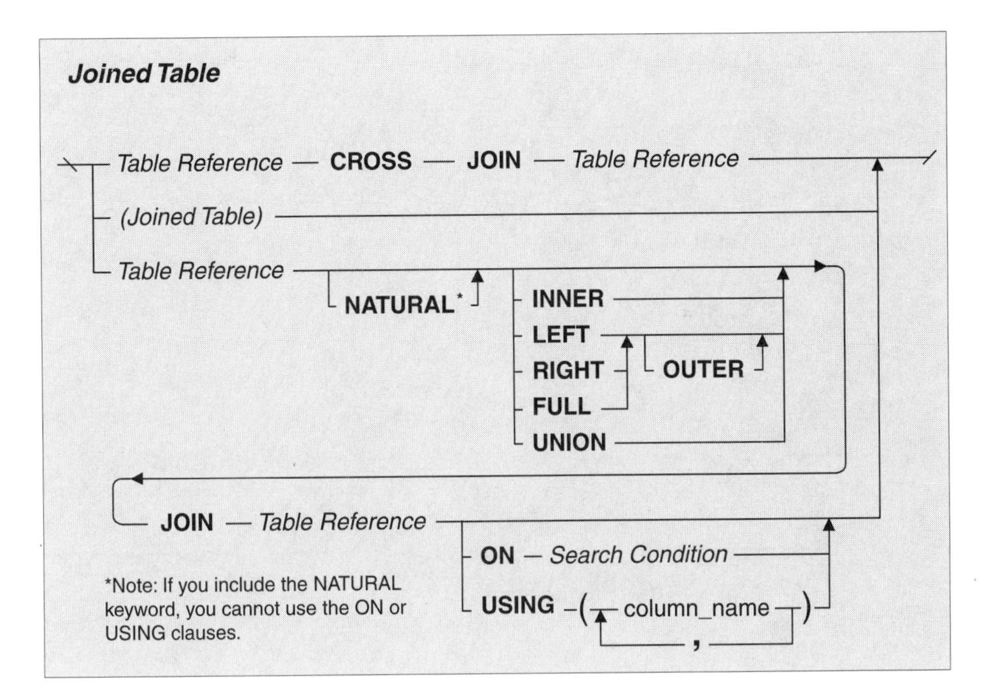
Joined Table
Table Reference — CROSS — JOIN — Table Reference
(Joined Table)
Table Reference
NATURAL*
INNER
LEFT
RIGHT
FULL
UNION
OUTER
JOIN — Table Reference
ON — Search Condition
USING –(column_name)
,
*Note: If you include the NATURAL keyword, you cannot use the ON or USING clauses.

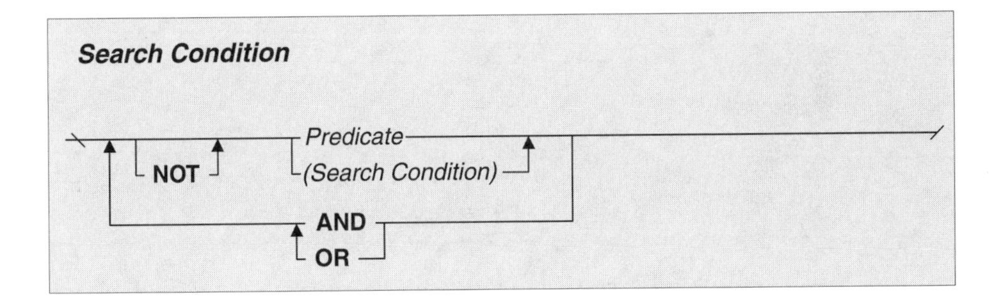
Search Condition
NOT
Predicate
(Search Condition)
AND
OR

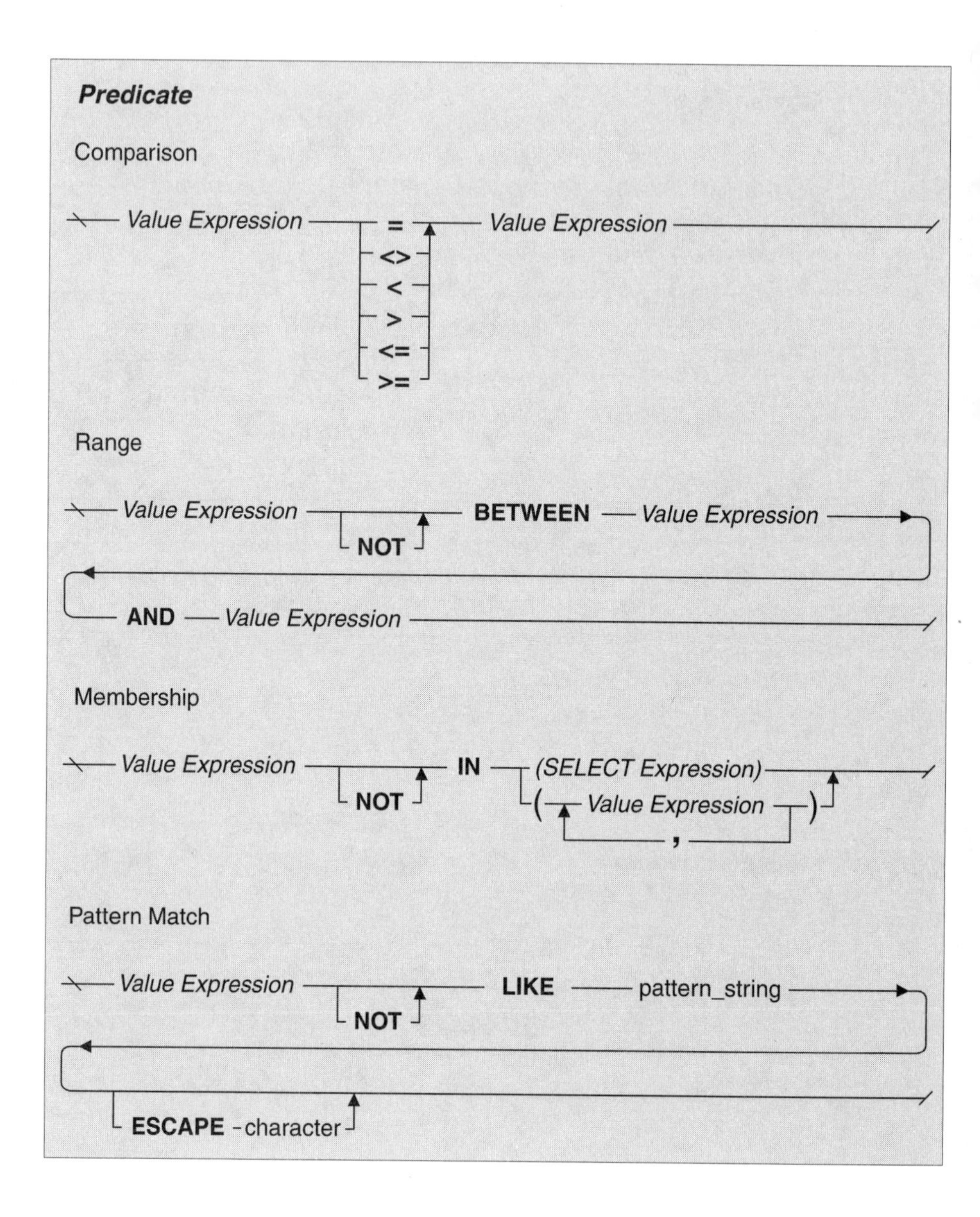
Predicate
Comparison
Value Expression
=
<>
<
>
<=
>=
Value Expression
Range
Value Expression
NOT
BETWEEN
Value Expression
AND
Value Expression
Membership
Value Expression
NOT
IN
(SELECT Expression)
(
Value Expression
)
,
Pattern Match
Value Expression
NOT
LIKE
pattern_string
ESCAPE
-character

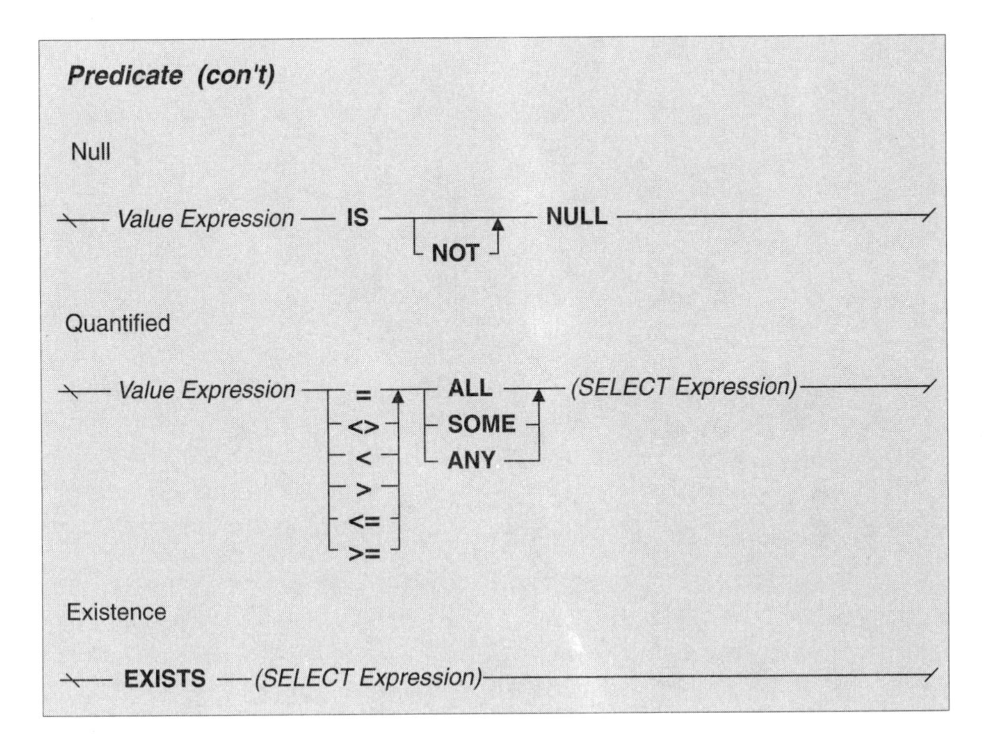
Predicate (con't)
Null
Value Expression — IS — NOT — NULL
Quantified
Value Expression — = <> < > <= >= — ALL SOME ANY — (SELECT Expression)
Existence
EXISTS — (SELECT Expression)

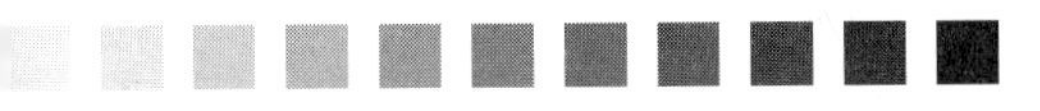

Schema for the Sample Databases

Sales Order Database

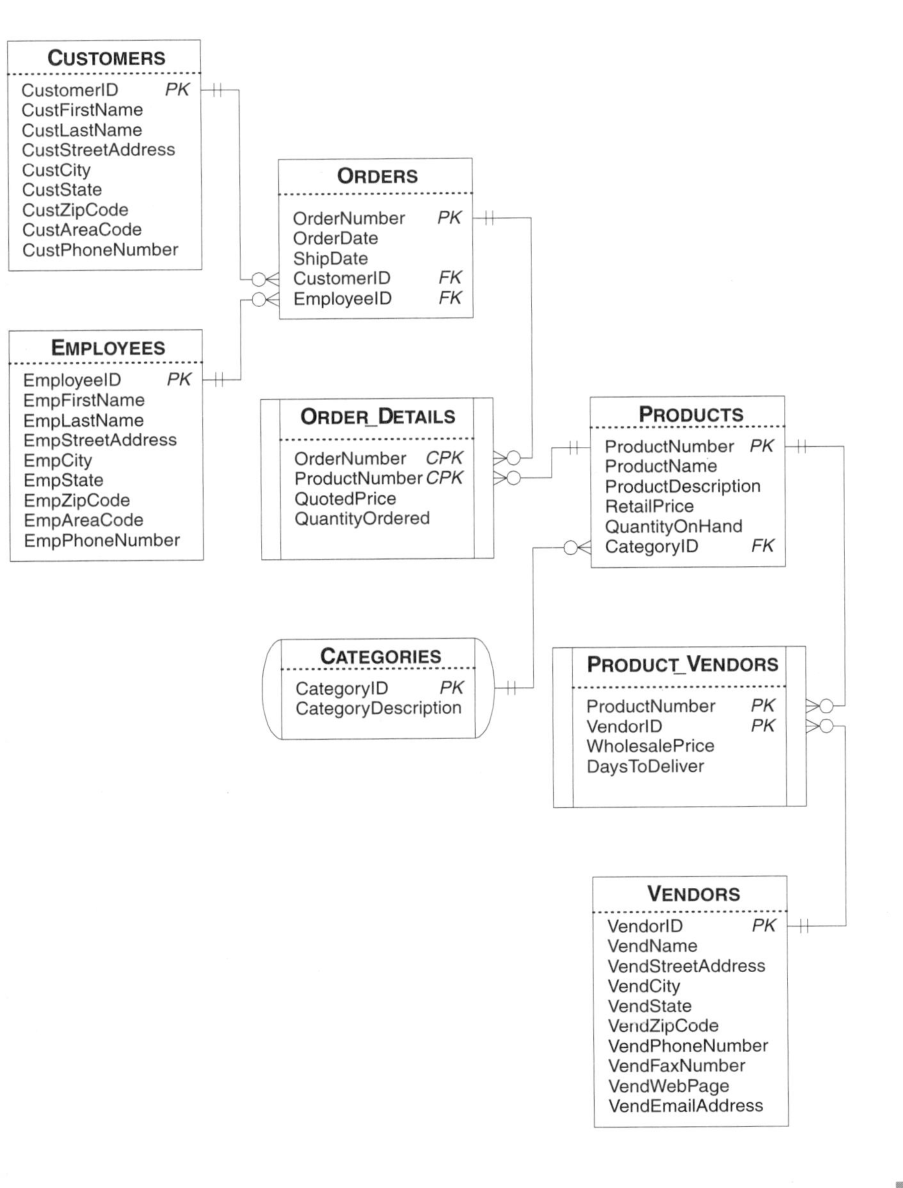

Entertainment Agency Database

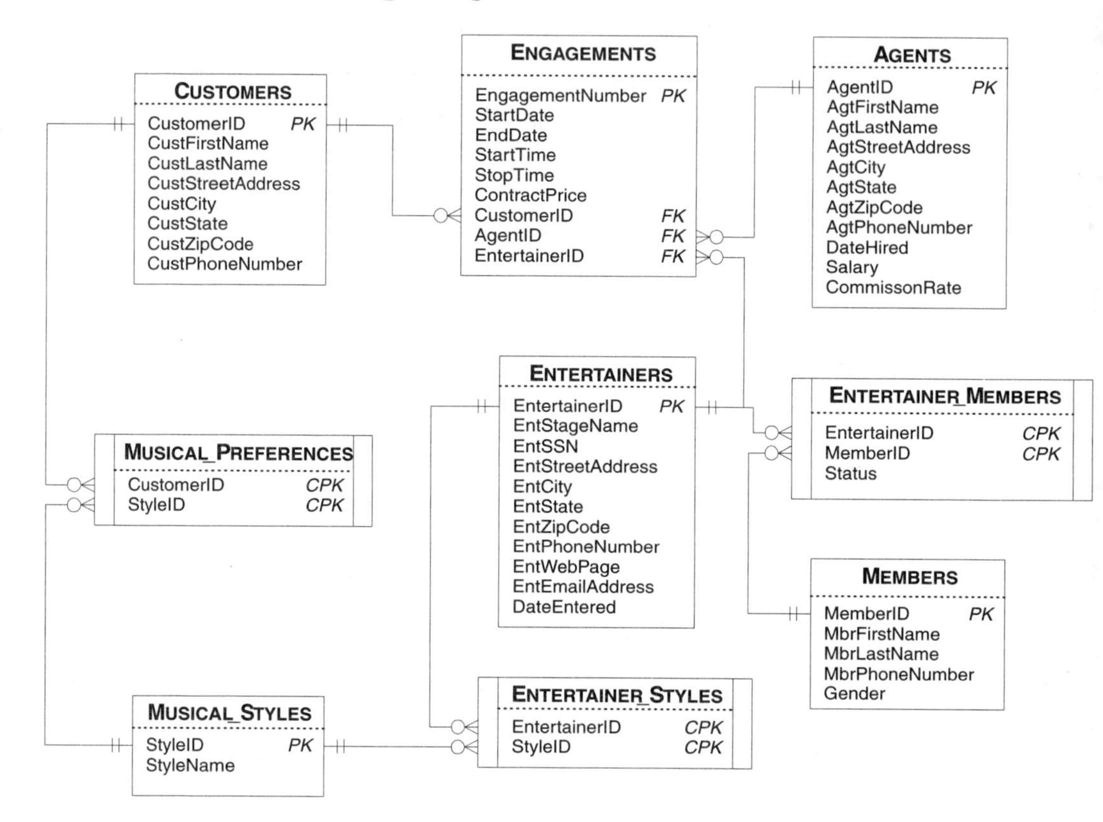

School Scheduling Database

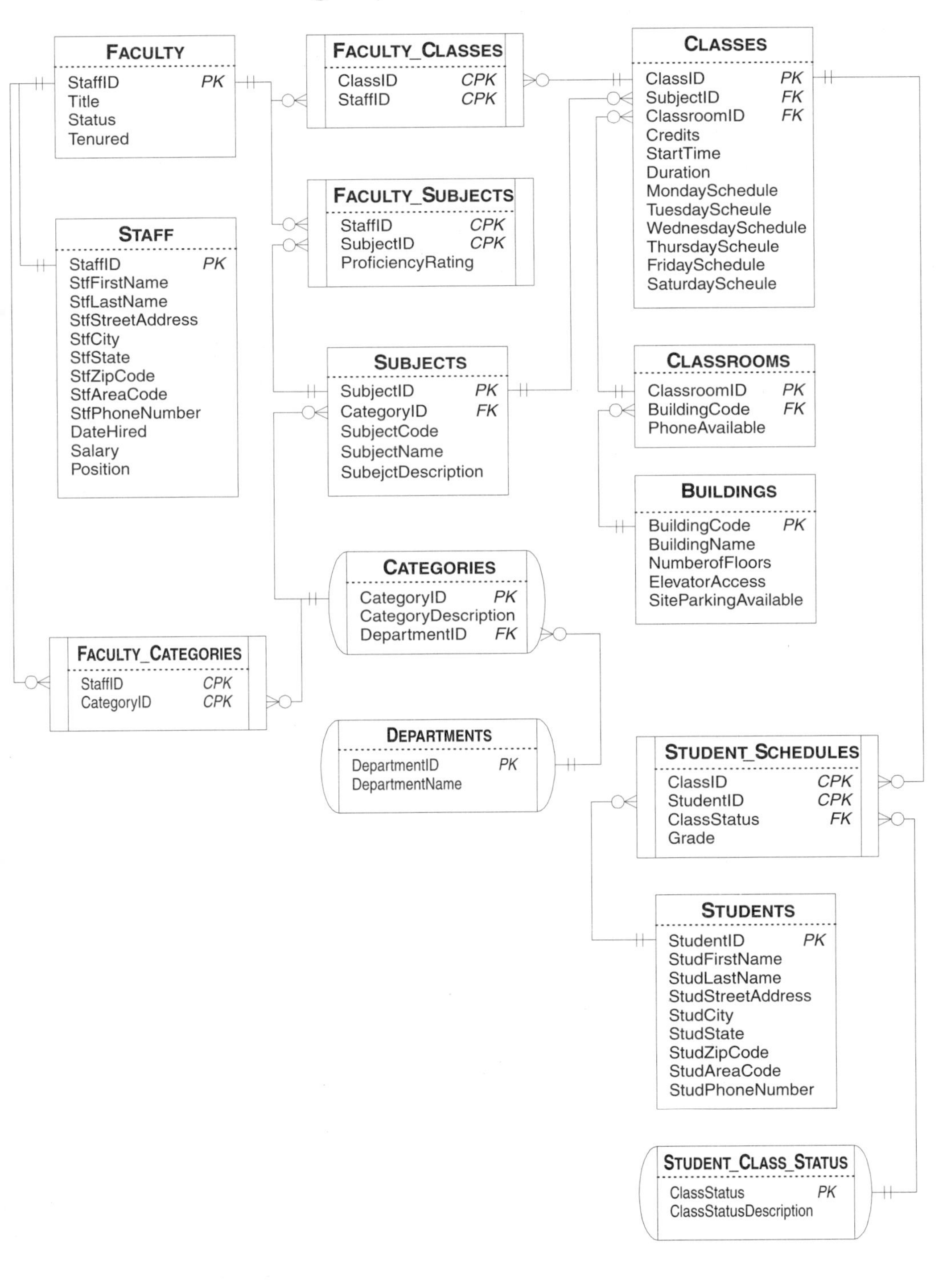

Bowling League Database

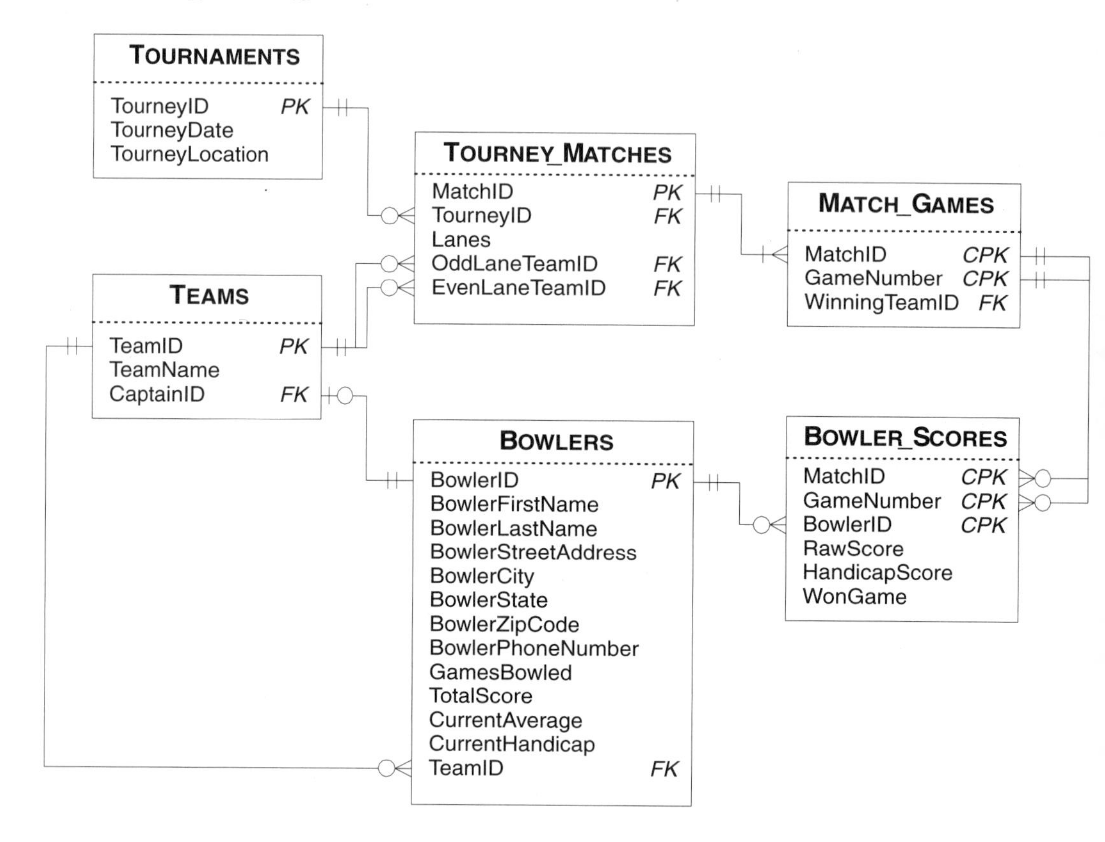

Recipes Database

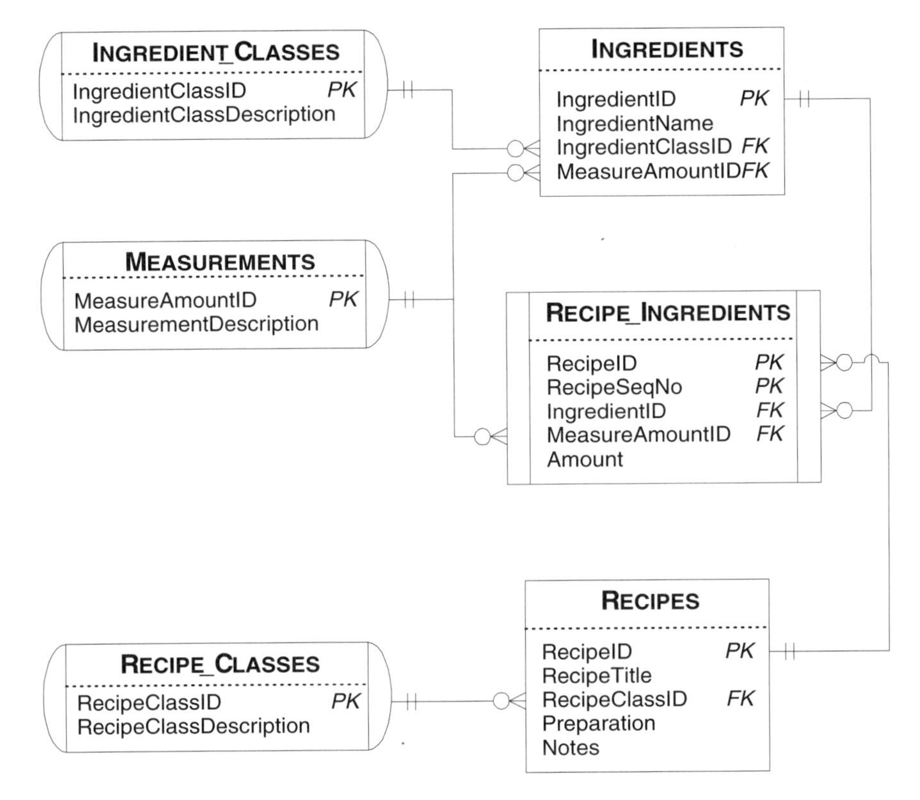

C

Recommended Reading References

These are the books we recommend you read if you want to learn more about database design or expand your knowledge of SQL. Keep in mind that some of these books will be challenging because they are more technical in nature. Also, some authors assume that you have a fairly significant background in computers, databases, and programming.

Database Books

Date, C. J. *An Introduction to Database Systems (7th Edition)*. Reading, MA: Addison-Wesley, 1999.

Connolly, Thomas, Carolyn Begg, and Anne Strachan. *Database Systems—A Practical Approach to Design, Implementation, and Management*. Essex, England: Addison-Wesley, 1995.

Hernandez, Michael J. *Database Design for Mere Mortals*. Reading, MA: Addison-Wesley, 1997.

Books on SQL

Bowman, Judith S., Sandra L. Emerson, and Marcy Darnovsky. *The Practical SQL Handbook (3rd Edition)*. Reading, MA: Addison-Wesley, 1996.

Celko, Joe. *Instant SQL Programming*. Chicago, IL: Wrox Press Ltd., 1995.

Celko, Joe. *Joe Celko's SQL for Smarties: Advanced SQL Programming (Second Edition)*. San Francisco, CA: Morgan Kaufmann Publishers, 1999.

Date, C. J., and Hugh Darwen. *A Guide to the SQL Standard (4th Edition)*. Reading, MA: Addison-Wesley, 1997.

Groff, James R., and Paul N. Weinberg. *LAN Times Guide to SQL*. Berkeley, CA: Osborne McGraw-Hill, 1994.

Gruber, Martin. *SQL Instant Reference*. Alameda, CA: Sybex Inc., 1993.

Melton, Jim, and Alan R. Simon. *Understanding the New SQL: A Complete Guide*. San Francisco, CA: Morgan Kaufmann Publishers, 1993.

Index

Database Design for Mere Mortals

A Hands-On Guide to Relational Database Design

Michael J. Hernandez

Sound design can save you hours of development time before you write a single line of code. Based on the author's years of experience teaching this material, *Database Design for Mere Mortals* is a straightforward, platform-independent tutorial on the basic principles of relational database design. Database design expert Michael J. Hernandez introduces the core concepts of design theory and method without the technical jargon. *Database Design for Mere Mortals* will provide any developer with a commonsense design methodology for developing databases that work.

0-201-69471-9 • Paperback • 480 pages • ©1997

The Practical SQL Handbook, Third Edition

Using Structured Query Language

Judith S. Bowman, Sandra L. Emerson, and Marcy Darnovsky

The Practical SQL Handbook is the best-selling guide to learning SQL—the standard language for accessing information in relational databases. This book not only teaches SQL as it has been established by the ANSI standards committee but also as the language is used to solve real business problems. Step-by-step you'll learn the basic vocabulary and functions of the language and the processes and issues involved in developing robust applications. This book provides a thorough grounding in the basics of database design, security, and integrity. You will learn SQL pragmatically, by creating a sample database and then working through dozens of examples with it.

0-201-44787-8 • Paperback • 496 pages • ©1996

The Guru's Guide to Transact-SQL

Ken Henderson

Since its introduction more than a decade ago, the Microsoft SQL Server query language, Transact-SQL, has become increasingly popular and more powerful. The current version sports advanced features such as OLE Automation support, cross-platform querying facilities, and full-text search management. This book is the consummate guide to Microsoft Transact-SQL. From data type nuances to complex statistical computations to the bevy of undocumented features in the language, *The Guru's Guide to Transact-SQL* imparts the knowledge you need to become a virtuoso of the language as quickly as possible. This book contains the information, explanations, and advice needed to master Transact-SQL and develop the best possible Transact-SQL code. Some 600 code examples not only illustrate important concepts and best practices, but also provide working Transact-SQL code that can be incorporated into your own real-world DBMS applications.

0-201-61576-2 • Paperback • 592 pages • ©2000

Introduction to SQL, Third Edition

Mastering the Relational Database Language

Rick van der Lans

According to Ian Cargill of Soliton Software, Rick van der Lans has written "a first class book. A thorough and well-written introduction to a complex subjec I wish this book had been available when I was learning SQL." SQL was, is, and always will be the database language for relational database systems such as Oracle, DB2, Sybase, Informix, and Microsoft SQL Server. *Introduction to SQL* describes, in depth, the full capacity of SQL as it is implemented by the commercial databases, without neglecting the most recent changes to the standard, bringing the book up to date and fully compliant with SQL3. Uniqu in the extent of its coverage, this book takes you from the beginning to the en of SQL, the concepts to the practice, the apprentice to the master.

0-201-59618-0 • Paperback • 720 pages • ©2000

A Guide to the SQL Standard, Fourth Edition

C.J. Date with Hugh Darwen

The SQL language has established itself as the lingua franca for database management; it provides the basis for systems interoperability, application portability, client/server operation, distributed databases, and more. SQL is supported by just about every DBMS on the market today. SQL2—or, to give its official name, the International Standard Database Language SQL (1992)— represents a major set of extensions to the earlier SQL standard. For a start, th new specification is well over 600 pages, compared with less than 100 for th original version. No database professional can afford to ignore it. This Fourth Edition of *A Guide to the SQL Standard* covers extensive integrity support, powerful new operators, and national and international character data support—all features of SQL2; comprehensive date and time support and a clear explanation of the complexities of Dynamic SQL—features of SQL. This book provides a tutorial treatment of SQL2.

0-201-96426-0 • Paperback • 544 pages • ©1997

Practical Issues in Database Management

A Reference for the Thinking Practitioner

Fabian Pascal

Three decades ago relational technology put the database field on a sound, scientific foundation for the first time. But the database industry—vendors, users, experts, and the trade press—has essentially flouted its principles, focusing instead on a "cookbook," product-specific approach, devoid of conceptual understanding. The consequences have been costly: DBMS products, databases, development tools, and applications don't always perform up to expectation or potential, and they can encourage the wrong questions and provide the wrong answers. *Practical Issues in Database Management* is an attempt to remedy this intractable and costly situation. Written for database designers, programmers, managers, and users, it addresses the core, commonly recurring issues and problems that practitioners—even the most experienced database professionals— seem to systematically misunderstand.

0-201-48555-9 • Paperback • 288 pages • ©2000

CD-ROM Warranty

Addison-Wesley warrants the enclosed disc to be free of defects in materials and faulty workmanship under normal use for a period of ninety days after purchase. If a defect is discovered in the disc during this warranty period, a replacement disc can be obtained at no charge by sending the defective disc, postage prepaid, with proof of purchase to:

Editorial Department
Addison-Wesley Professional
75 Arlington Street, Suite 300
Boston, Massachusetts 02116
Email: AWPro@awl.com

Addison-Wesley and Michael J. Hernandez and John L. Viescas make no warranty or representation, either express or implied, with respect to this software, its quality, performance, merchantability, or fitness for a particular purpose. In no event will Michael J. Hernandez and John L. Viescas or Addison-Wesley, its distributors, or dealers be liable for direct, indirect, special, incidental, or consequential damages arising out of the use of or inability to use the software. The exclusion of implied warranties is not permitted in some states. Therefore, the above exclusion may not apply to you. This warranty provides you with specific legal rights. There may be other rights that you may have that vary from state to state. The contents of this CD-ROM are intended for noncommercial use only.

More information and updates are available at
http://www.awl.com/cseng/titles/0-201-43336-2

Microsoft SQL Server 7.0—120-day Evaluation Edition This program was reproduced by Addison-Wesley under a special arrangement with Microsoft Corporation. For this reason, Addison-Wesley is responsible for the product warranty and for support. If your diskette is defective, please return it to Addison-Wesley, which will arrange for its replacement. PLEASE DO NOT RETURN IT TO MICROSOFT CORPORATION. Any product support will be provided, if at all, by Addison-Wesley. PLEASE DO NOT CONTACT MICROSOFT CORPORATION FOR PRODUCT SUPPORT. End users of this Microsoft program shall not be considered "registered owners" of a Microsoft product and therefore shall not be eligible for upgrades, promotions, or other benefits available to "registered owners" of Microsoft products.